ON THE VIRTUES

Capreolus as "Prince of Thomist Theologians" facing Dominic of Flanders, "Prince of Thomist Philosophers" (From Dominic of Flanders, *In XII librorum Metaphysicsa Aristotelis,* Cologne, 1621).

John Capreolus

ON THE VIRTUES

Translated by Kevin White and

Romanus Cessario, O.P.

with a Foreword by Servais Pinckaers, O.P.

The Catholic University of America Press

Washington, D.C.

Printed in the United States of America

The paper used in this publication meets the minimum requirements of American National Standards for Information Science—Permanence of Paper for Printed Library materials, ANSI Z39.48-1984.
∞

LIBRARY OF CONGRESS CATALOGING-IN-PUBLICATION DATA

Capreolus, Jean, ca. 1380–1444.
[Defensiones theologiae Divi Thomae Aquinatis. Book 3. English]
On the virtues / John Capreolus ; translated and edited by Kevin White and Romanus Cessario ; with a foreword by Servais Pinckaers.
p. cm.
Includes bibliographical references and indexes.
ISBN 978-0-8132-3155-6 (alk. paper)
1. Virtues. 2. Thomas, Aquinas, Saint, 1225?–1274. Scriptum super IV libros Sententiarum. Liber 3. 3. Peter Lombard, Bishop of Paris, ca. 1100–1160. Sententiarum libri IV. Liber 3. I. White, Kevin, 1952– II. Cessario, Romanus. III. Title.
BV4630 .C36 2001
241′.4—dc21
00-047357

For

Guy-Thomas Bedouelle

qui et amat

"antiquam sancti Thomae veritatem"

(III, dd.31–32, ad finem)

Contents

Foreword: Capreolus's Defense of St. Thomas's Teaching on the Virtues

When I agreed to write the Foreword for this English translation of these texts of John Capreolus, I was a bit apprehensive. I thought that to venture into his writings would get me into a scholastic maze. But happily, from the beginning I realized that Capreolus is no long-winded hair-splitter and that his work is no mere rehearsal of outmoded debates.

One might almost think, without exaggeration, that Capreolus's teaching on the virtues speaks directly to our time, from a distance of over five hundred years. Capreolus undertook to defend St. Thomas's moral theology, which is based on the doctrine of the virtues and gifts, against a trend which he called "new" and which, beginning with the consideration of particular acts, called into question and strongly reduced the role of the virtues. Today we can surely observe a renewal and strengthening of virtue-based morality. For example, we find modest but real evidence of such morality in the *Catechism of the Catholic Church* and in the encyclical *Veritatis Splendor,* although it co-exists with the morality of casuistry and of commandments which has prevailed since the end of the Middle Ages—Capreolus's period. The continuity of the moral problematic of Capreolus down to our own times is real. This is not surprising, for the movement of ideas at the level of thought-categories is as slow as the shifting of geological substrata, which can take centuries. Capreolus can help our reflection and can throw light on the moral problems we face today, revealing the deep foundations on which they rest.

Capreolus can also teach us how to think in a straightforward manner and reason in a firm and disciplined way. He belongs to the scholastic tradition formed in the universities during the thirteenth century. In him we still find this tradition in its vigor, before it was discredited by a proliferation of argumentation and logical excesses. Today's students would certainly profit from reading him and would learn how to listen attentively to opposing opinions, assess arguments accurately, and make nuanced and precise responses. Capreolus is a master at these intellectual manoeuvres. He knows how to dialogue, and at the same time to sustain firmly the truth he is defending. In this work of theological combat he is never overcome by the ardors of the joust. Careful as he is to expound objections and responses thoroughly, he never becomes prolix. His thinking remains concise and sticks to the essentials.

Hence Capreolus knows how to reason. He does so with strength and precision. Yet he is not a "creative" theologian. He is a commentator on St. Thomas, or rather a defender, as the title of his work indicates: *Defense of the Theology of Saint Thomas Aquinas.* He is not commenting on the Angelic Doctor as a teacher would for students in a class. His object is to defend the doctrine of the Master against the attacks of adversaries: Duns Scotus, Peter Aureolus, Durandus of Saint-Pourçain, and others, whose names he does not always mention. In order to answer them, he has St. Thomas speak for himself, in texts so well chosen that one would think St. Thomas had prepared them in advance in order to reply to objections formulated after his time.

The *Defense* follows the *Sentences of Peter Lombard,* which was still the basic text for teaching in the universities of Capreolus's day. He regularly divides his exposition into three parts, called articles. The first article gives the "conclusions," that is to say the principal points of St. Thomas's teaching on the subject under discussion, which a later period will refer to as "theses." The second article proposes the objections of adversaries to these various "conclusions," with their more or less numerous arguments. The third article contains responses, point by point, to these objections and arguments. The responses are composed largely of texts of St. Thomas taken from the *Summa Theologiae, Disputed Questions,* and the *Commentary on the Sentences.* Thus Capreolus ensures the defense of the Angelic Doctor by having him speak for himself in the manner that best fits the objections of his adversaries. Capreolus adds very little of his own devising, and intervenes only when he feels the need to connect quotations or to harmonize texts that seem contradictory. Thus he effaces himself in the presence of his Master, but his work shows a penetrating understanding of theology, sure and faithful. He is a good representative of the Thomist school at war.

1. *The Teaching on the Virtues*

I shall now take up the subject that this volume presents, Capreolus's teaching on the virtues. Virtue is treated in Distinctions 23–36 of Book III of Peter Lombard's *Sentences.* It is in his commentary on these distinctions that one finds St. Thomas's first elaboration of a treatise on the virtues, which demonstrates the fact that the moral theology of the Angelic Doctor was indeed, from his earliest works, a morality based on virtues and not commandments, as some have maintained.[1] Capreolus follows the plan of St. Thomas, while limiting his exposition and discussion to the chief controversial theses.

Let me comment briefly on the significance of the following questions addressed by Capreolus:

1. Whether habitual virtues <*virtutes habituales,* an expression not found in St. Thomas> are necessary to man (Distinction 23);
2. Whether virtuous *habitus* are acquired by human acts, and whether they exist in the sensible appetite, concupiscible and irascible, as their subject (Distinction 33);
3. Whether the gifts of the Holy Spirit are *habitus* distinct from the virtues (Distinctions 34–35);
4. Whether the cardinal virtues are interconnected in such a way that he who possesses one possesses all (Distinction 36; note, however, Capreolus includes the remaining distinctions of Book III [Distinctions 37–40], which concern the Ten Commandments, under this question).

The following discussion is accordingly limited to four topics: the necessity of virtuous *habitus,* either acquired by repeated actions or infused; their location in the sensible appetite; the distinction between the virtues and the gifts; and the interconnection between the virtues.

The Necessity of Virtuous Habitus

At first glance we would seem to be dealing with hoary scholastic discussions. However, if we know a bit about the problematics involved, we will see on closer inspection that Capreolus is witness to a vastly important episode in the history of Western moral theology: the cleavage, initiated at the beginning of the fourteenth century and widening thereafter, between a morality based on virtue, which was that of the Fathers and which received from St. Thomas its classic form, and a morality based on individual acts, which was to take over in the modern era, particularly in the form of casuistry. On one hand, a morality concerned with interior qualities and awareness of the perdurance and continuity of actions in an overall personal development; on the other hand, a morality concerned with individual actions in their particularity.

1. See Giuseppe Abbà, *Lex et virtus* (Rome: Las, 1983).

The latter stems from a freedom which is always variable and is confronted with a law which limits it from without by obligations and prohibitions.

The whole debate centers on the question of *habitus*. What are *habitus,* if not precisely those acquired capacities, those dispositions to action which ensure the quality and continuity of our actions and enable us to act better and better? *Habitus* are like forces that link actions together, forming and coordinating them from within so as to improve them.

The rejection of the doctrine of *habitus* was tragic, for it led to the loss of the word itself, so much so that we no longer use it in our modern languages to express the human experience signified by *habitus*. What shall we call the skill acquired by an artisan or an artist, which makes them masters of their art? The ordinary term "habit" is inadequate and misleading, because it designates a psychic mechanism which tends to diminish the human engagement that such work demands. It cannot signify an advance in perfection or in the power to create a work. Can we explain the masterly composition or performance of a musician by saying that he has a habit of playing the piano or the violin? But this is precisely what a *habitus* is, the capacity of acting to perfection, of creating a new and excellent work.

Virtuous *habitus* are thus defined as powers of acquiring and exercising our human "works" in accord with truth and goodness, producing excellence in action and progress in living. The problem is a vast one therefore: to maintain the necessity of *habitus* means to establish morality on the foundation of good *habitus* and to organize it around the theological and cardinal virtues, perfected by the gifts. The *habitus* thus gains priority over action as the interior principle of the latter's production and quality, and as the prolongation of the natural inclination to the good. The teaching on *habitus* is a necessary element in a morality which tends to ensure excellence of action ordered to an ultimate end, in which human perfection and happiness are completed.

To refuse the necessity of *habitus* and to reduce them to simple habits, more or less useful in performing acts, leads to another conception and organization of morality resting on the primacy accorded to individual actions. These are seen as the emanations of a freedom endowed with the power to choose at each instant between contraries, regardless of all inclination or predetermination, natural or acquired. This is called freedom of indifference. On the other hand, a morality based on *habitus* and virtues presupposes a freedom which is naturally ordered to quality and excellence—freedom for the good.

Let us note in passing that with this problem we approach the basic question dealt with in the encyclical *Veritatis Splendor* in its critique of freedom considered as an absolute, and its stance in favor of freedom for the good and for truth. It is necessary to mention these matters so as to show what is at stake in Capreolus's debate. How does he proceed? He recalls what is essential in St. Thomas's teaching in the *Summa* (I–II, qq.49 and 55) and in his *Commentary on the Sentences* (III d.23, q.1, a.1) (see pp. 1–6 below). A *habitus* is necessary when three conditions are present:

1. when something which requires a disposition is ordered to something other than itself in a relationship of potency to act, as happens with our faculties;
2. when it may be determined in more than one way;
3. when several elements concur in an action and may be combined in several ways, good or evil.

These conditions are fulfilled especially in our spiritual faculties, intellect and will, whose sphere of action is the broadest, opening out onto the universality of the true and the good. Grafted on the potentiality of these faculties, the *habitus* is necessary to them as a stable disposition, a determination in view of the perfection of their action.

Capreolus limits himself strictly to St. Thomas's texts, which he selects, moreover, judiciously. He does not prolong the consideration by showing the larger systematization involved.

The Objections of Durandus of Saint-Pourçain

Let us now look at the arguments advanced by the adversaries of the teaching on *habitus*. We shall try to discern the differences in viewpoint which reveal another way of considering action.

The chief adversary in this matter is Durandus of Saint Pourçain. A Dominican, and a dissident in the area of theology, he was called in his day *Doctor modernus* and *Doctor resolutissimus,* because of his cleverness in resolving theological problems. Durandus belonged to the second generation following St. Thomas. Born between 1275 and 1280, he was a contemporary of the English Franciscan William of Ockham and was with him at Avignon in the papal court of John XXII. He was to be a member of the commission which would censure fifty-one propositions taken from the works of Ockham, whom he knew well. His commentary on the *Sentences* ran into several editions, the last of which was dated between 1317 and 1327.

We shall accept Durandus's teaching as Capreolus presents it to us. We will not go into all the details of the debate, but will simply try to bring out some characteristic features of this rather subtle and technical confrontation.

Durandus attacks the doctrine of the necessity of *habitus* on three points: the determination to good and evil by *habitus;* the facility of action provided by *habitus;* and the greater intensity of action caused by *habitus.*

Regarding the first point, which is the most important, Durandus introduces a preliminary distinction between the act in its natural being *(quantum ad esse naturae)* and the act in its moral being *(quantum ad esse morale)*. He begins with the universal concept that we can perform an action, independently of all determination as to its kind, this or that, and its moral quality, good or evil, and therefore in this sense the act is an indifferent one. If I understand it rightly, he is considering the act as an expenditure of energy. This universal concept does not really differ from an individual action, which is, in itself, determined, since the distinction is made only at the conceptual level. The real determination of the individual act is inherent to it and does not come to it by means of any other agent.

From the point of view of the *esse naturae* we have to say, on the one hand, that the *habitus,* when it exists in a faculty, determines it to some qualification which excludes the contrary qualification; but that, on the other hand, if we consider the determination of the faculty to its action as caused by the *habitus,* we have to say that the good or evil *habitus* does not determine the natural being of the act, for the latter is a general effect calling for a cause common to all acts, whether they precede or follow the *habitus.*

We also have to say that no *habitus* determines or inclines any faculty whatsoever to produce an act in its individuality according to its natural being, for this is a case of an effect common to all actions, whatever they may be.

As to its moral character, the act receives it not from the sole singularity of its real existence, but from its conformity or lack of conformity to right reason alone. From this point of view, as to the determination to good or evil, we have to say that the *habitus* does not cause such conformity or non-conformity by itself, but accidentally, through the mediation of the foundation, the natural being, of the act. In effect, acts which precede the *habitus* and form it are already determined to good or evil, which determination cannot therefore be produced by the *habitus.*

Let us pause for a moment. Durandus clearly places in the foreground of his study, no longer the *habitus* in its dynamism, but the act taken in its singularity, able, as such, to precede or follow the *habitus,* and included under the general concept "undifferentiated act" that we can determine for ourselves. The point is no longer to show the role of the *habitus* in the formation of acts, but to discover whether there is still a need for it in the determination of individual acts.

The preliminary distinction between the *esse naturae* and the *esse moris* is characteristic. It can doubtless be related to the distinction between the natural goodness of acts, caused by God, and moral goodness, a distinction that was common enough among Lombard's commentators to account for human sin in the tradition of the Augustinian problematic of evil. We find it in St. Albert and St. Bonaventure. But St. Thomas shifted the perspective and gave priority to the *esse moris* in the voluntary act, following upon its ordering to the end.[2] In Durandus the distinction becomes conceptual and is more clear-cut.

This consideration of the act as starting with its physical being, which then becomes moral by its relation to reason and law, is encountered once more in casuistry and, in our own day, in a more pronounced manner, in consequentialism, which bases the evaluation of acts on their consequences at the pre-moral, physical, or ontic level, as distinguished from the moral level which is constituted by the intervention of the will following the rational judgment.

When the question is put this way, from the point of view of acts each separate in their singularity, *habitus* can only play a secondary and limited role, for *habitus* implies a continuity between acts owing to an interior finality we can call "long-range," because it links acts in an ordered whole in view of a distant or ultimate end, God as the end of life, in contrast to a "short-term" finality that subsists in individual acts in relation to the immediate intention of the subject, such as for example the act of stealing by someone who wishes to buy drugs. *Habitus,* virtues, finality, everything that assures continuity between acts, is relegated to the background in this view of the human act; only traces of them remain, the minimum.

This kind of analysis is diametrically opposed to that of St. Thomas, who gives priority to the moral dimension of the human act, determined in the

2. For further discussion, see my *Le Renouveau de la Morale* II, ch. III "Le rôle de la fin dans l'action morale", pp. 114–124, Paris, 1979.

first place by its end, the direct object of the will, and the principle of its dynamism through the succession of acts.[3]

Capreolus's Answer

How does Capreolus answer Durandus? If we compare his questions to an article of St. Thomas, we perceive that for him the objections/responses are primary, while the "body" of the article is practically limited to selected texts from St. Thomas, and does not provide the original overview of the totality of all the data—that masterly determination which gives to the responses of the Angelic Doctor their forcefulness. We are dealing rather with a "defense," which has the drawback of accepting to some degree the position of the problems posed by the adversary, such as, here, the distinction between the *esse naturae* and the *esse moris,* which St. Thomas would surely have critiqued.

Nonetheless Capreolus's responses are pertinent. He observes rightly that, at the level of their nature as of their morality, acts are not determined formally by themselves but by their principle, the acting subject, and by their term distinct from the subject, such as the object, circumstances, and end, particularly at the level of the interior act. Also, according to him, the *habitus* determines the faculty to produce its act or to receive it *in esse naturae* as well as *in esse moris.*

Even so, we perceive a weakness in Capreolus's argument. Though he firmly establishes the necessity of *habitus* to determine faculties to their acts, he does not seem to see that *habitus* are rooted in the natural inclinations to goodness and truth which are components of our spiritual faculties and which assure their development. He writes in conclusion:

> . . . a habitless power [*potentia non habituata,* a term not found in St. Thomas and which seems to indicate a tendency to habitude] is not more inclined to an act that is morally good than to one that is morally evil; nor is it inclined to acting pleasurably or easily or readily; rather it remains in an indistinct potentiality to this and that object, and similarly to a good and an evil act, and similarly again to a certain way of operating and its opposite—or rather, it is of itself indisposed to one of the two, but through habit is inclined towards one object and away from its opposite (and the same is true of the act and the manner of operating). This is clear in the case of the habit of temperance, which inclines the concupis-

3. For further discussion see my *The Sources of Christian Ethics,* trans. Sr. Mary Thomas Noble, O.P. (Washington: The Catholic University of America Press, 1995), Part One.

> cible power to certain objects and to certain acts and modes of operating. (*D.23, a.3 [I. To the Arguments of Durandus]; p. 21)*

It seems therefore that for Capreolus the entire determination of acts comes from *habitus,* which increases their necessity in a morality based on virtues, but takes away their natural root. On this point one might wonder whether Capreolus is influenced by the theory of freedom of indifference that holds for the radical indetermination of the will in its action, notably in regard to natural inclinations, onto which, in St. Thomas's account, the *habitus* are grafted.

Other Objections: Durandus and Peter Aureolus

The other arguments are similar to those we have just considered. Durandus again attacks *habitus* from the angle of the facility attributed to them. According to him, this facility comes not from the *habitus* but from the acting subject. It can perfectly well happen, therefore, that an act preceding a *habitus* should be exactly like an act following it and have the same intensity. It should be added that for him, if the *habitus* by itself rendered the act easier, it would diminish its merit and would thus be more harmful than helpful to the act. Here we see the idea that virtue is connected with difficulty and valued in accordance with it, like merit.

With the help of St. Thomas's texts Capreolus responds that the act which precedes a *habitus* is never quite like one which follows it and is elicited by it; the latter is normally more perfect. As to the question of ease, Capreolus shows that merit depends more on the perfection of the act, assured by the *habitus,* than on the difficulty entailed, which could result from the weakness of the subject. He sums up his reply thus: the *habitus* does not render the act either easy or difficult in itself, but lets us perform it either easily and promptly, or with difficulty.

Finally, Durandus tries to show that the *habitus* does not contribute to the intensity of the act. For example, the act of knowing is no more intense after than before the acquisition of an intellectual *habitus;* the *habitus* only renders the subject's adherence to the known truth firmer.

Furthermore, if the *habitus* were a force capable of increasing the intensity of the act, it should eventually be able to produce the act alone, which is not the case, since the faculty's contribution is always required.

Capreolus rules out the separation made by Durandus between the contribution of the faculty and that of the *habitus* to the intensity of the act, as if it were a case of two separable forces. Faculty and *habitus* are coordinated as that which acts *(quod agit)* and that by means of which it acts *(quo agit)*. He opportunely recalls the difference between a purely intellectual *habitus*, which Durandus cites in his example, and moral *habitus;* these last not only confer the power to act easily *(facultas bene operandi)*, but also determine effective action *(ad usum)*. This is the special case of prudence, which is not limited to judging what ought to be done but determines that it shall be done through *praeceptum* or command. Finally, contrary to Durandus's assertion, the faculty endowed with a *habitus* can act more intensely than before, that is, in the order of knowledge, for the intellectual *habitus* throws a greater intensity of light, coming from the *habitus* of first principles, on the acting intellect.

We should note that in his objections Durandus tends to remove *habitus* from the realm of knowledge in order to introduce them into the appetitive order. Here they would no longer be able to contribute directly to the formation of a moral judgment, to the development of moral knowledge or of prudence, or to the formation of conscience. We are heading for moral voluntarism.

Let us set aside this lengthy discussion with Durandus and listen briefly to the objections of the Franciscan Peter of Auriol, traditionally called *Doctor facundus*, and of the others whose names are not cited. Peter was born at Gourdon in le Quercy in 1280 and died at Avignon in 1322. He was thus a contemporary of Durandus and Ockham.

Peter's objections as set forth by Capreolus tend to reduce the importance of *habitus* by affirming that virtue is not an absolute form but an accidental being, a pure relation of fittingness or non-fittingness, which can eventually change as a person's state changes. Thus what is a virtue in one man can be a vice in another; for example, taciturnity is a virtue in the young, but in the old a vice.

To illustrate the subtlety of the argumentation, I quote from among ten responses of Capreolus to Peter of Auriol and unnamed adversaries, in a veritable battle of logic over the definition of a snub nose, the conclusion of which is that *simitas* ("snubness") occurs principally and directly in the concavity, but as a terminus and obliquely in the nose (ad 8) (!).

Capreolus's answer can be summed up as follows: In the thought of St.

Thomas, virtue is not a pure relation, but it includes a certain relationship in a secondary and oblique order, notably to the subject, the nature, and the operation which is its end.

We get the impression that here Capreolus accepts too easily the problematic of his adversaries and concedes too much. As they see it, virtue must have a nature of its own in order to be considered. Neither do they see its dynamic nature to be necessary for the realization of a finality which carries man toward divine beatitude. And, like virtue, morality itself becomes a simple relation of congruence, the fitness of acts with regard to reason and law. The powerful system worked out by St. Thomas falls to the ground in the view of his adversaries, because in their account the cement linking the virtues has disintegrated.

2. *The Moral Virtues in the Sense Appetites*

A second thesis defended by Capreolus has to do with the positing of virtues in the sense appetites. St. Thomas, contrary to the Franciscan doctors, situated certain moral virtues, such as temperance and courage, in the concupiscible and irascible appetites, and not only in the will.

The question is still of interest today. It is a matter of determining the part sensibility plays in the moral life. Does the latter unfold entirely at the level of will and reason, as was held by Descartes and Kant as well as by the casuists—in which case the movements of the sense appetites will be regarded with suspicion and reduced to a psychic mechanism—or can sensibility indeed be actively associated with the moral life, that is, at the theological level, as St. Thomas thought? St. Thomas actually took the trouble to compose a vast treatise on the passions as a preparation for the study of the virtues: a study of desire, for example, in view of hope, and a study of love in view of charity. Once more we note that we are dealing with two different moral systems and even two anthropologies, the one separating the component parts of man, the other tending to harmonize them.

To be brief, let me simply mention the opposing positions. Duns Scotus is foremost here. For him, the virtues are located in our higher faculties, particularly in the will, which, being indeterminate in regard to contraries, needs an inclination to determine it to act rightly. This is virtue. Scotus invokes the opinion of Aristotle for this proposition, then St. Augustine, who defines the moral virtues as forms of charity, which is a virtue of the will. Peter of Auriol, for his part, adopts a compromise and situates the virtues equally in the sensible and rational appetites.

The position of St. Thomas is very different. The will, which tends naturally toward the good, needs virtue only in view of a good that surpasses man, whether as an individual (the virtue of justice) or in his nature (the virtue of charity). According to Capreolus, Aristotle never denied the existence of virtue in the sensible appetite, and the affirmation of St. Augustine that every virtue is a form of love does not oblige us to situate the virtues exclusively in the will.

The discussion moves on to the acquisition of virtues by means of the repetition of acts, which Durandus criticizes, maintaining that this repetition is not an active but a passive principle of the formation of acts, like a disposition to receive similar acts, as soft wax is disposed to receive different forms.

Then comes the attack on St. Thomas's teaching on the infused moral virtues, led by Durandus: the theological virtues and the grace given by baptism suffice for salvation; the infused moral virtues are in no way necessary or useful. The consideration of the effects of baptism at the moral level, the comparison between the state of a sinner before and after conversion, or of a pagan trained in virtue, do not indicate the influence of the infused virtues, which would be evidenced by more perfect conduct.

Behind St. Thomas's teaching on the infused moral virtues there is at stake the practical influence of the grace of the Holy Spirit upon the action of the Christian which raises him to a higher level according to spiritual experience. This teaching goes hand in hand with that on the gifts and the Gospel beatitudes.

Capreolus takes up a final point regarding the permanence of the moral virtues after this life: they do not perdure in regard to their material object, which is in the sensible order, but they do in regard to their formal object, the *ordo rationis*, the submission of acts and passions to reason.

3. The Distinction between the Virtues and the Gifts of the Holy Spirit

The discussion of the virtues extends to the gifts of the Holy Spirit: Are they distinct from the virtues, and are they necessary, as St. Thomas holds?

The teaching of the Angelic Doctor on the virtues and gifts finds its place in the spiritual tradition represented by St. Gregory the Great, which thirteenth-century theologians tried to develop. Elaborated in an original reflection on the text of Isaiah, chapter 11, which furnishes the list of the gifts in the Augustinian tradition, this doctrine seems to be truly the fruit of St. Thomas's personal experience. The gifts are properly speaking inspirations: "We are obviously given to understand that these seven which are enumerated [in the text of Isaiah] are in us by divine inspiration" (Ia IIae q. 68, a. 1). Moral theology based on the virtues should thus culminate in the doctrine of the gifts of the Holy Spirit, so as to take Christian experience into account and to clarify the mode of collaboration between the virtues and the movements of the Spirit. Virtue represents the active aspect of the spiritual life, while the gifts, seen as dispositions to receive spiritual impulses with docility, represent the passive aspect. In *Summa Theologiae* Ia IIae, St. Thomas is careful to relate each principal virtue with the corresponding gift. St. Thomas's moral theology is therefore profoundly spiritual.

We note that this richness of moral teaching was soon to be lost after Capreolus. Following the line of nominalism, post-Tridentine moralists were to separate morality, focused on obligations, from asceticism and mysticism. They would place the virtues, joined with personal effort, under asceticism, and the gifts of the Holy Spirit would fall under a mysticism reserved for those enjoying extraordinary graces.

But we have not yet arrived at this point. The principal adversary here is Duns Scotus, who takes issue with the distinction of the gifts in the name of the adequacy of the virtues. His argument is to become classic. We come across it, for example, in Dom Lottin, that excellent historian of the thirteenth century, when he expresses his personal opinion.

In the thought of Duns Scotus, there is no need to consider the gifts, any more than the beatitudes or the fruits of the Holy Spirit, as *habitus* distinct from the virtues. It is reasonable to retain only the necessary *habitus*, taught by the Church. These are, for us wayfarers, the theological virtues relating to God, and prudence and the other moral virtues relating to creatures. These suffice, if brought to perfection. It is not necessary to add other *habitus*.

Scotus also rejects the distinction between the human mode of action of the virtues and the supra-human mode of the gifts. The virtues, especially charity (says Scotus), dispose man to act with the greatest perfection as well as with the least.

Here we see a separation from the spiritual sap of moral theology, or at least a different orientation. According to St. Thomas, the sap rises through the virtues as in a tree in springtime. The more branches, the more clearly the power of life is manifested. Hence the spreading of the tree of virtues, to which are added the gifts, beatitudes, and fruits of the Spirit. For Scotus everything leads to charity, since virtue is centered in the will. In his eyes, the necessity of joining *habitus* to the virtues has yet to be proved. At this point we are no longer dealing with a moral theology organized around virtue. The Franciscan tradition is already oriented toward a morality based on commandments, which is what the morality of nominalism will be.

Capreolus replies by using the argumentation of his Master to set up the distinction between virtues and gifts, and by responding in detail to the objections formulated by Duns Scotus. He likewise answers the objections of Durandus of Saint Pourçain against the permanence of the gifts *in patria:* the gifts will not perdure in regard to their material objects, it is true, but they will in regard to their formal object, which is conformity to the rule of the Holy Spirit.

4. *The Interconnection of the Virtues*

The discussion with Duns Scotus subsequently takes up St. Thomas's teaching on the interconnection of the virtues through the work of prudence and charity. The establishment of the precise way in which the virtues form an organism of action is the centerpiece of virtue-based morality. In his exposition of moral theology, in which analysis dominates, St. Thomas studied the multiplicity of virtues in detail; it is essential for him to show how they yet constitute a dynamic unity, an organism comparable to the human body with its various members acting together. This unity is assured by prudence at the level of the moral virtues and by charity for the totality of the virtues. The sense of unity in the life of virtue is predominant in St. Augustine, for example, for whom the four principal virtues became forms of charity. It was equally the case with the Stoics, who presented virtue as basically one.

The discussion will bear essentially on prudence. For St. Thomas, prudence cannot exist without the moral virtues, nor the moral virtues without prudence. This means that in the concrete all the virtues coexist and act together. This argument presupposes a close, natural collaboration between our spiritual faculties, intellect and will, to form moral action, especially in choosing, which is the proper act of freedom. The entire Thomistic analysis of freedom and choice rests on this connection between the sense of truth and the aspiration to the good.[4]

In Scotus's objections we can see that this link between the spiritual faculties and the virtues is in the process of being dissolved. The Subtle Doctor wants to show that prudence can perfectly well exist without the moral virtues: a right prudential judgment could perfectly well be accompanied by a voluntary, bad choice. It is also possible to acquire perfection in the realm of one virtue, while remaining imperfect in regard to others, he holds.

Capreolus rightly replies that a capital point in this matter is to understand that prudence is not limited to judging and counseling well, but finds its completion in the "command" or *imperium* which forms the choice; we could call this the decision to act joined to the impetus to act. We should note that, in the analysis of the prudential act, the command is not external to but interior to the acting subject, and proceeds from his "willing reason." In order to form this command to act, and to act in this particular way, prudence has need of the appetite's rectitude, which is produced by temperance, courage, and justice.

Capreolus also observes that the *habitus* of prudence is not acquired by a single act, but requires much experience and also hindsight, which contribute to its connection with the moral virtues. A morality of individual acts could not account for all that prudence presupposes. He might have added that, in a morality based on virtues, prudence presupposes not only a succession of acts which form a *habitus* but also deep-seated intentions and a long-range view, which order action to its ultimate end and procure for prudence higher criteria of judgment. This is the way that prudence is linked to charity.

Conclusion

I have tried to disentangle the principal threads of Capreolus's problematic of virtue while indicating their historical connections, as they go back to St. Thomas and forward to ourselves. This introduction has not gone into all the details of Capreolus's treatment of virtue, nor does it presume to have untangled all the threads. Many points still remain to be clarified, and I trust that the contemporary reader will find the present volume a great help in this task.

The interesting thing about Capreolus's work is that it represents a stage in the vast debate on Christian morality which has gone on for several cen-

4. See *The Sources. . . ,* Part Three.

turies in scholastic theology. It can be summed up in the confrontation of two principal orientations. On the one hand there is a morality based on the organic structure of the virtues and gifts, with the teaching on *habitus* as its capstone. St. Thomas provided the most systematic model for this morality, and so handed on the heritage of the Fathers and of ancient philosophy. On the other hand, very soon after the Angelic Doctor died, the system of virtues was attacked: by a reduction to charity and the moral virtues; by a separation among these virtues; and by a change of perspective which favored the consideration of the individual act to the detriment of those elements which assure continuity in acting, namely, the *habitus* and finality. These developments opened up the road to the casuistry that was to flourish from the seventeenth century on.

Capreolus was not an innovator but a defender. In the fifteenth century—when nominalism was largely taking over in Western universities, and imposed, in the name of the divine law and reason, a morality regulated by obligations—Capreolus was a courageous and skillful defender of a stronghold: the teaching of St. Thomas on the virtues and gifts. It is somewhat surprising that he does not quote contemporary authors, and that all his adversaries come from the preceding century. Doubtless time passed more slowly in the Middle Ages, especially for speculative minds not much concerned about the historical dimension of doctrines.

What is important to remember is that Capreolus took up his defense when the earliest controversies regarding St. Thomas were formulating their major objections. He replied point by point, always solid and faithful to the Master. He could not know the later development of the teaching of moral theology in the Church, which helps us to see his value more clearly.

I shall close by mentioning an impression I have had throughout my study of Capreolus. On rereading the texts of St. Thomas which he quotes, I felt as if I were present at the flow of a powerful intellectual and spiritual torrent, all the more vigorous for having been well channeled by Capreolus. In the end, then, I had the impression of a creative energy unleashed. We should be grateful to Capreolus for having vigorously defended the doctrine of the virtues and gifts at a time when it was "out of season," and for having contributed from afar to the current renewal of virtue-based morality.

Servais Pinckaers, O.P. (Université de Fribourg)
Translated by Sr. Mary Thomas Noble, O.P.

Translators' Introduction

At the start of the third millenium, it may be difficult for the student of theology or philosophy to fathom the depth of the influence connoted by the notion of a "school." This is particularly true in regard to the Thomist school, whose contributions to the understanding and development of theological and philosophical issues are far-reaching. Arguably even those developments most antithetical to this tradition could scarcely have achieved self-consciousness, much less any balanced theoretic elaboration, without contradistinction from it. Nor is this tradition a mere historical artifact: rather, as the encyclical letter *Fides et ratio* confirms, it participates fully in the theological and philosophical issues of the present period, and indeed constitutes one of the central, normative *loci* of the Catholic intellectual tradition.

In light of current interest—both Catholic and non-Catholic—in the thought of Aquinas, rediscovery of the work and influence of John Capreolus (1380–1444) is particularly important. Known as *Princeps Thomistarum*—"Prince of Thomists"—he established a mode of Thomistic theological and philosophical engagement that has set the pattern for Thomistic thinkers after him. Yet despite the scope of his contribution and example, his influence has not always received the prominence it deserves. Twentieth-century scholarship on Capreolus has tended to focus exclusively on questions concerning metaphysics, the person, and the beatific vision. The purpose of the present translation of his questions on the virtues is to bring to the fore another aspect of his thought, his theological ethics. The foregoing discussion by Servais Pinckaers demonstrates the richness and contemporaneity of Capreolus's reflections on the virtues and the moral life, which the present volume is intended to make accessible to a wide audience.

The period of Capreolus's life, in the aftermath of the Black Death (which has been called "the single most important natural phenomenon in European history"), brings to mind a wide range of historically significant events—for instance, political troubles (not excluding Jean le Petit's controversial defense of tyrannicide) at the University of Paris, where from 1395 Jean Gerson was chancellor; the flourishing of Rhineland mysticism and the consequent suspicion on the part of ecclesiastical authorities it elicited; the birth of Italian humanism, with which Capreolus's follower and epitomist Prieiras would later contend; the Great Schism (1378–1409) at the end of the Avignon papacy, with its different "obediences" that divided religious life in Western Europe; and the swirl of theological debate culminating in the Council of Constance (1414–18)—which Capreolus may well have attended—and the Church's attempt to deal with conciliar theory. In contrast to these much-studied events that form its backdrop, Capreolus's life is remarkable for its relative obscurity, although a colloquium devoted to him at his native city of Rodez in 1994 did turn up a few new biographical facts. What is known of his life can be briefly related.

The relevant documents refer to Capreolus more frequently as *Tholosanus* ("of Toulouse") than as *Ruthensis* ("of Rodez"). This is explained by the fact that the Dominican house in Rodez—where Capreolus joined the order—belonged to the Dominican province of Toulouse, and also by the fact that Capreolus was for a time regent of studies at the house in Toulouse. It is in any case certain that Capreolus was born either in the village of Rodez or in the surrounding region, known as "the Rouergue." The name "Capreolus"—meaning "little goat"—seems to be a local Latinizing coinage, one also found in the Rouergue in the forms "Cabrole" and "Cabrolier." It is unknown whether "John" is his baptismal name or a religious name adopted on his entry into the Dominican order.

On May 15, 1407, the Dominican general chapter at Poitiers ordered Capreolus to proceed to the University of Paris to comment on Peter Lombard's *Book of Sentences.* In 1409 he completed the first book of his life's work, *Defensiones Theologiae Divi Thomae Aquinatis* (a title that might be translated as *Arguments in Defense of the Theology of Saint Thomas Aquinas*), a work that may be regarded as a highly innovative contribution to the Parisian tradition of commentaries on the *Book of Sentences.* In 1411 and 1412 he took examinations for the Licentiate in Theology, passing with a standing of twelfth place, but first among mendicants, in his class of twenty-five.

After these examinations Capreolus may have stayed on in Paris, or he may have gone back to Rodez, to which he certainly had returned permanently by 1426. Recent research has uncovered the fact that Capreolus preached in the Rodez cathedral during the Lenten season of 1415. It was at some point during the period 1412–1426 that he served as regent of studies in Toulouse.

While in Rodez, Capreolus concentrated his efforts on completing his great work. The second book was completed on Saturday, September 14, 1426; the third "after lunch, at 2:00 p.m." on November 7, 1428; and the fourth and last on February 18, 1432. After completing all four books of the *Defense of the Theology of Saint Thomas Aquinas*—his only work to have come down to us—Capreolus lived for another twelve years, remaining at Rodez, and dying on April 6, 1444.

Capreolus's great work, his *Defensiones,* constitutes a significant juncture in the history of Western theology; as such, it looks to both past and future. In one respect one may say that it is an exercise in the traditional genre of question-commentaries on Lombard's *Book of Sentences,* a work composed during the 1150s that since 1225 had been the prime official text for theology at Paris. The typical question-commentary on the *Sentences* considers the various aspects of questions related to the units or "distinctions" in each of its four books. The first book of this work concerns God, the second creation, the third Christ and the virtues, and the fourth the sacraments and "the last things." The *Sentences* thus provided a sequence of topics drawn from ancient tradition, serving as pretext and occasion for the introduction of questions of current interest in theological circles, ones perhaps only indirectly related to Lombard's presentation.

In Capreolus's hands, however, the format of the traditional *Sentences* commentary itself becomes a pretext for accomplishing a purpose more original and focused than that of any preceding commentator on Lombard's work. Capreolus states his intention at the very beginning of his work:

> Before proceeding to the conclusions, I make one prefatory remark that I would like to be regarded as a given throughout the whole of this commentary, and that is this: that my intention is to introduce nothing of my own, but only to relate opinions that seem to me to have been those of Saint Thomas, and to introduce no proofs for the conclusions other than his own words, except rarely. Furthermore, I plan to introduce, in the proper place, objections of Aureolus, Scotus, Durandus, John of Ripa, Henry, Guido of Carmello, Garo, Adam, and others who attack Saint Thomas, and to solve these objections by means of what Saint Thomas said.

This statement of intention simultaneously presents both the polemical attitude and the literary structure adopted by Capreolus. The polemical stance adopted in the passage—the defense of opinions of St. Thomas against his well-known opponents from the period 1275–1350—is what gives the work its historical importance and bestows upon Capreolus his status as "first of

Thomists." The later great Thomists, including Cajetan, Ferrariensis, Soto, John of St. Thomas—all of whom refer to Capreolus—are indebted to the "first" of their number for instituting the strategy of the "defense" of Thomistic doctrine against its adversaries.

The foregoing quotation also sets forth the literary pattern of Capreolus's questions, a pattern which is both different from and more complex than the style of question used by St. Thomas. Capreolus follows Lombard's division into four books. Within each book, he raises questions, each of which is related to one or several of Lombard's distinctions.

1. Capreolus introduces the discussion of each question with a statement of the question; a brief argument on the side of the question ("yes" or "no") which he will oppose; and a still briefer argument on the other side of the question.

2. Then follow the three "articles" which constitute the main part of the question.

a. The first article consists of a number of "conclusions," each of which is supported by one or more extensive quotations from the writings of St. Thomas, often from the *Summa Theologiae* and/or Thomas's own *Sentences* commentary, and a brief summarizing argument by Capreolus himself.

b. The second article consists of one or more sets of "objections," drawn from anti-Thomistic authors, to each of the conclusions.

c. The third article consists of responses to or "solutions" of each objection in each set of objections to each conclusion. In each case, Capreolus again quotes St. Thomas, although as a rule he also makes his own voice heard here somewhat more than it is in the first article. It is important to note that each question presents all of its conclusions, then all of the objections, and finally all of the solutions. The various threads of debate within a question are thus interwoven, so that a conclusion, an objection to it and the solution to the objection are widely separated from one another in the text.

3. Finally, a brief closing section responds to the argument presented on the other side of the question, again, usually by way of quotation from St. Thomas.

4. Each question concludes with "Blessed be God. Amen."

There are 182 distinctions in Lombard's work, and 190 questions, comprising 755 conclusions, in Capreolus's commentary. Capreolus's three-article structure of conclusions-objections-solutions can seem rather unwieldy, with each conclusion giving rise to a proliferation of objections and responses to objections, yet he never loses track of the different units of his text.

Approximately one third of each question is given over to direct quotations from the writings of Aquinas. Thus Capreolus's work may be read as an anthology of Thomistic passages, passages chosen with a view to the points on which the opinions of Thomas were put into question during the three-quarters of a century following his death. It is clear that Capreolus was not only a champion, but also a connoisseur, of Thomas's writings. It would be interesting to know something about his method of work. Did he dictate or write by hand? Both in Paris and in Rodez, he must have had access to a large collection of Thomas's writings. Did the Dominican house in each place possess a sort of *Opera omnia* of Thomas's works? Had Capreolus committed large sections of Thomas's work to memory?

In any case, the polemical and literary traits of Capreolus's work make it a useful hermeneutic tool for understanding the doctrine of St. Thomas. This is so because of a canon of all textual interpretation: One cannot interpret a work save by taking into account the kind of work that it is and is meant to be. In the case of Thomas Aquinas's immense contributions to theology, we are in the presence of systematic theological and philosophic exposition that is by nature both speculative and dialogic. With respect to dialogue, Aquinas's genius embraces not only Christian but also non-Christian thought about the world inasmuch as our judgments about creation can deeply affect our account of God.

In harvesting the writing of Thomas for the resources with which to respond to criticisms of his doctrine, Capreolus inaugurates a speculative and dialogic tactic for interpreting the Common Doctor. While necessarily more complicated than the structure of Thomas's own writing, Capreolus's engagement both with Lombard's *Sentences* and with the criticisms of Thomistic doctrine places it in a threefold dialogue with the traditions of commentary on Lombard's *Sentences,* the teaching itself of Thomas, and the critics of the latter. Capreolus's strategy for positioning Thomistic doctrine in a later age showcases the perennial relevance and fecundity of the Angelic Doctor's principles, arguments, and conclusions. Capreolus's achievement in this regard—

confirmed through acknowledgment of the *Defensiones* and its method by later Thomistic commentators—is particularly notable when we see his work in the context of the late fourteenth and early fifteenth centuries, a period largely dominated by nominalist and Scotistic anti-nominalist teaching. In contrast with the attention devoted to doctrines of Scotus and Ockham in these years, the work of Thomas appears to have been either expressly rejected or relegated to the periphery of discourse. In sustaining the intelligibility of Thomas's metaphysics and theology amidst a sea of nominalist doctrine and over against the very different challenges presented by Scotus, Capreolus is the father of a successful strategy for the perpetuation and faithful development of Thomas's teaching.

A word now regarding the *fortuna* of Capreolus's work. Capreolus died on the eve of the invention of the printing press. Still, two extant manuscript witnesses to his work were copied after this invention: a copy of the first book made in 1477, now in the Lorenzo de' Medici Library in Florence, and a copy of the third book made in 1480, now in the Vatican Library. In 1483 the first printed edition was produced by Octavius Scotus in Venice, with a preface by the editor, Thomas of St.-Germain. At Cremona in 1497 the epitomist Sylvester Prierias published a compendium of the *Defensiones.* The second edition of the *Defensiones* was published in Venice in 1514, and the third in 1519. In 1522 the first edition of a compendium of Capreolus begun by Paul Barbus Soncinas (d. 1523) and completed by his student Isidore of Isolanus (d. 1523) was published at Pavia. In 1528 the second edition of the Soncinas-Isolanus compendium was published at Lyons. In 1580 two editions of the Soncinas-Isolanus compendium were published, one at Lyons and one at Salamanca. In 1589 the fourth edition of Capreolus's work was published in Venice.

The period of little over a century between 1483 and 1589 was the time of Capreolus's great publishing success. Between the four editions of his work and the several compendia published, this was a period of wide diffusion of his thought—and thereby, indirectly, that of Thomas—in Italy, France, and Spain. There then follows a period of three centuries during which Capreolus seems to have been more or less neglected. (An edition of the *Defensiones* planned in 1686 never saw the light of day.) Interest in Capreolus picks up again in the last quarter of the nineteenth century as a result of the 1879 encyclical letter *Aeterni Patris,* which re-established Catholic interest in the works of Aquinas and his commentators.

On December 21, 1881, the Bishop of Rodez, in a letter to his clergy, echoed the encyclical's call by recommending the study of Capreolus in his diocese. In 1895 the Oblate Father Bonnet initiated a new edition of the *Defensiones,* an edition announced in the *Revue Thomiste* in 1897. During 1900–1908, this fifth printed edition of Capreolus's work was produced by two Dominicans of Toulouse, Ceslas Paban and Thomas Pègues, published by Alfred Cattier in Tours; a photographic reimpression of this edition was done by Minerva at Frankfurt-am-Main in 1967.

During September 2–4, 1994, thirty-five scholars gathered from several nations in Rodez to commemorate the 550th anniversary of Capreolus's death with an international conference. The papers delivered at this conference, together with additional contributions, were published in 1997 under the title *Jean Capreolus en son temps (1380–1444)* by Éditions du Cerf in Paris.

One of the interesting phenomena of this history is the lack of any English version of Capreolus's work. Of course, the former proficiency in Latin among students in ecclesiastical faculties would go far toward explaining this fact. Still, since not only the teaching of St. Thomas but the interpretative character of Capreolus's work engages issues of decisive doctrinal and methodological importance, one might have anticipated an earlier translation of all or part of the *Defensiones.* The present volume, which translates the section of the *Defensiones* dealing with the theological and moral virtues, is offered partly in the hope that it will contribute to furthering the recovery and appreciation of the commentatorial tradition.

The following translation of Capreolus's nine questions on the virtues is based on the Paban-Pègues edition (Volume V, pp. 287–445); for ease of reference, the edition's pagination has been entered into the translation in curly brackets. At all times, the aim has been to render Capreolus's Latin into as faithful an English as is compatible with readability. Because Capreolus quotes St. Thomas so often and at such length, a large part of the work of translation involves translation of Thomistic passages. Some of these passages, such as Capreolus's selections from the *Summa Theologiae,* have previously been translated into English, in some cases more than once; others, such as the selections from Thomas's *Sentences* commentary, have never appeared in English before, and therefore may prove useful to students without access to the originals. Both kinds of texts have been translated from the Paban-Pègues edition for the present translation.

The questions translated here concern Distinctions 23–40 in Book Three of Lombard's *Sentences.* Capreolus presents 9 questions on the virtues, which contain 31 conclusions, 41 sets of objections to the conclusions (comprising 139 individual objections), and a reply to each objection. These 9 questions, as their titles show, articulate and defend central theses of St. Thomas Aquinas concerning the moral life:

Whether habitual virtues are necessary to man

Whether faith is a virtue infused by God

Whether faith is of things seen

Whether hope is a theological virtue really distinct from faith and charity

Whether a man ought, out of charity, to love God more than himself

Whether faith remains in heaven

Whether by human acts habits of virtue are acquired which exist in the sensitive appetite, that is, in the concupiscible or irascible powers, as their subject

Whether the gifts of the Holy Spirit are habits distinct from the virtues

Whether the cardinal virtues are interconnected in such a way that he who possesses one possesses all

Capreolus's defense of the Thomistic positions on these questions at the very summit of the influence of contrary schools of thought—nominalism and Scotism—offers theological students of the twenty-first century not only a fine exposition but an important illustration of the character of St. Thomas's achievement. The words of his sixteenth-century epitomist, Prieirias, who called Capreolus "the father of all theologians of our time, the one from whom all Thomists of the present day have received whatever good they may possess" *(Conflatum,* f.286*v)*—point to Capreolus's lasting place in the history of Thomism.

Acknowledgments

We wish to thank the following for their encouragement, assistance, and support in our preparation of this volume: Jude P. Dougherty, Dean Emeritus of the School of Philosophy at The Catholic University of America; the Dominican Fathers at the Albertinum in Fribourg, Switzerland; the Reverend Librarian and his staff at Saint John's Seminary in Brighton, Massachusetts. For their assistance in proofreading and indexing, we extend thanks to the

Dominican Nuns at the Monastery of Our Lady of the Rosary, Buffalo, New York; Dr. John Janaro; Reverend Daniel Scheidt; Mr. Michael Storck; and Mr. Aaron Price. Special thanks to Dr. Timothy B. Noone, who provided information for the notes on John Duns Scotus, Peter Aureolus, and Henry of Ghent. Special thanks also to Susan Needham and to Elizabeth Benevides, both of The Catholic University of America Press, for their kind and professional help in preparing the volume for publication.

Romanus Cessario, O.P., and Kevin White
Brighton, Massachusetts

Whether Habitual Virtues Are Necessary to Man

In relation to the twenty-third distinction of the third book of *The Sentences,* the question is raised: Whether habitual virtues are necessary to man.

It is argued that they are not, as follows. No habit is necessary; but virtues are habits; therefore, they are not necessary. The minor premise is evident. The major premise is argued for as follows. "Habit" implies directedness to an act; but "power" sufficiently implies a principle of act, for even natural powers, which are without habits, are principles of acts; therefore, it is not necessary that there be habits.

Argument is made for the opposite conclusion as follows. Habits and virtues are certain perfections; but a perfection, since it has the nature of an end, is most necessary to a thing; therefore, it is necessary that there be habits and virtues.

In this question there will be three articles: in the first the conclusions will be presented, in the second the objections, and in the third the solutions.

Article I: Conclusions

First Conclusion: Habits Are Necessary to Man

SAINT THOMAS presents this conclusion in *ST* I–II, q.49, a.4, where he speaks as follows:

> "Habit" signifies a disposition directed to a thing's nature and to its operation or end, a disposition according to which the thing is well or badly disposed in relation to

> something else. But in order for a thing to need to be disposed toward something else, three conditions are required.
>
> The first is that what is disposed be other than that toward which it is disposed and be related to it as potentiality to actuality. Hence, if there be something whose nature is not composed of potentiality and actuality, whose substance is its operation, and which exists for its own sake, then habit or disposition has no place in it; and this is evidently true in the case of God.
>
> Second, it is required that what is in potentiality to something else be able to be determined in several ways and to several things. Hence, if something is in potentiality to only one thing, then disposition or habit has no place in it, because such a subject has the required relation to such an actuality by its nature. Hence, assuming that a heavenly body is composed of matter and form, then, since that matter is not in potentiality to any other form, there is no place in it for a disposition or habit directed to a form—nor one directed to an operation, because the nature of a heavenly body is in potentiality to only one determinate motion.
>
> Third, it is required that several things that can be proportioned to one another in various ways concur in disposing the subject to one of the things to which it is in potentiality, so that it may be well or badly disposed in relation to form or operations. Hence the simple qualities of the elements, each of which corresponds to the nature of the elements in one determinate way, are not called "dispositions" or "habits," but rather "simple qualities." But we do call "dispositions" or "habits" health, beauty, and other such things which imply a certain proportioning of several things that can be proportioned to one another in various ways. For this reason THE PHILOSOPHER says in *Metaphysics* 5 that "habit is a disposition, and disposition is an ordering of what has parts, whether with respect to potentiality, or with respect to place, or with respect to species." Because, therefore, there are many beings whose natures and operations require the coming-together of several things that can be proportioned to one another in various ways, it is necessary that there be habits.

Thus SAINT THOMAS. Again, in *In 3 Sent.*, d.23, q.1, a.1, he speaks as follows:

> In the case of all things that have a rule and measure, their goodness and rightness consists in conformity to the rule or measure, and their badness in disagreement with it. But the first measure and rule of all things is the divine wisdom. Hence, the goodness and rightness, or the truth, of anything whatsoever consists in its reaching that to which it is directed by the divine wisdom, as ANSELM says. Similarly, in the case of other, secondary rules, the

goodness and rightness of what is ruled also consists in conformity with the rules.

Now some powers are limited to predetermined actions or affections *(passiones)*, and conform to their rule inasmuch as they accomplish these actions or affections, because they are directed to them by the divine wisdom. And because the inclination of nature is always to one thing, such powers are sufficiently able to have rightness and goodness from their very nature as powers, and badness is present in them due to their failure as powers. But higher and more universal powers, such as the rational powers, are not limited to some one object or way of operating, because they can have rightness in relation to different things and in different ways; hence, they cannot be determined to what is right and good for them by their very nature as powers, but rather must {288} be made right by receiving rightness from their rule. Now this can occur in two ways. In one way, such that rightness is received as an affection, that is, by the very fact that the power being ruled is moved by what rules it. But because, as is clear from *Ethics* 3, the definition of "violence" consists in a thing's being affected and contributing nothing to an act, and because violence, as is said in *Metaphysics* 5, involves difficulty and adversity, the above-mentioned reception of rightness does not suffice to make the power that is ruled perfectly right. It must, therefore, be the case that the rightness is received in another manner, namely as an inherent quality, that is, in such a way that the rightness of the rule becomes a form of the ruled power, for thus what is right will be done easily and pleasantly, as something befitting the form. Now this quality or form, while it is still imperfect, is called a "disposition." But when it has been perfected, and converted, as it were, into a nature, it is called "habit," which, as may be gathered from *Ethics* 2 and *Metaphysics* 5, is that according to which we stand well or badly in relation to something. Hence it is that, in the *Categories*, disposition is said to be "easily removed" and habit "not easily removed," because what is natural is not easily changed. Hence it is, too, that habit, like nature, inclines to one thing, as is said in *Ethics* 5. For this reason, also, a sign of a developed habit is pleasure taken in a deed, as is said in *Ethics* 2, for what is appropriate to a nature is pleasurable and easy. Again for this reason habit is defined by THE COMMENTATOR in *De anima* 3 as that by which someone acts when he would, having the deed to be done ready to hand, as it were. And hence habit is compared to possession in *Ethics* 1, since things possessed are had on command, while operation is compared to application.

It is clear, then, that natural powers, because they are of themselves de-

> termined to one thing, do not require habits. Similarly, neither do powers of sensitive apprehension, because they have a determined way of operating from which they do not fail except through a defect of the power. Similarly, neither does the human will, inasmuch as it is naturally determined to the ultimate end and to the good insofar as it is its object. Similarly, neither does the agent intellect, which has a determined action, namely to bring objects capable of being understood into actuality, just as light brings objects capable of being seen into actuality. And similarly neither is there any habit in God Himself, for He is the first rule, unruled by any other; hence He is good essentially, and not through participation in rightness from another; and evil cannot occur in Him.
>
> But the possible intellect, which of itself is, like prime matter, undetermined, does require habit, by which it may participate in the rightness of its rule: a natural habit with respect to those things, namely first principles, that are immediately determined by the very light of the agent intellect that is its rule; an acquired habit with respect to the things that can be brought forth from those principles; and an infused light or habit by which it participates in the rightness of the first rule in those things that go beyond the agent intellect. Similarly, we require habits in the will, with respect to that to which it is not determined by nature, as well as in the irascible and concupiscible powers, according as all these powers participate in the rightness of reason that is their rule, or—in what is beyond human nature and in the case of infused habits—in the rightness of the first measure. And similarly in the animated body there is the habit of health, inasmuch as the body participates from the soul in the disposition by which it is able to accomplish its operation rightly; for the eye is called healthy that is able to accomplish the operation of an eye rightly, as is said in *De animalibus* 10. Hence it is clear that such qualities, which we call "habits," are found in animate things, and especially in those that have choice, as is said in *Metaphysics* 5.

Thus SAINT THOMAS. From these texts argument can be made for the conclusion as follows. That is necessary to man in his deeds without which he cannot make the acts of his powers perfectly right; but habits are this kind of thing; therefore, etc.

Second Conclusion: Human Virtues Are Habits

SAINT THOMAS presents this conclusion in *In 3 Sent.*, d.23, q.1, a.3, qla.1, where he speaks as follows:

> The noun "virtue," according to its primary application, seems to suggest a certain violence; hence, in *De caelo* 3 it is said that accidental, that is, "violent" motion is that which comes from "virtue," that is, "violence," rather than by the help of nature. But because one thing is able to inflict violence on something else only by means of a perfected power according to which it acts and is not acted upon, the noun "virtue" has been used to signify every perfected power, whether that by which a thing is able to subsist in itself or that by which it is able to operate. Thus it is said in *De caelo* 1 that virtue is the "extremity" *(ultimum)* of a power, because the perfection of a power is measured by the limit and the maximum of which anyone is capable. And because evil in an act arises from a deficiency in the power of the agent, the perfection of a power requires that it operate well within its genus. For this reason it is said in *Ethics* 2 that virtue is that which makes the one who has it good **{289}** and renders his operation good; and in *Physics* 7 it is said that virtue is the disposition of what has been perfected for the best, that is, for the best of those things to which a power extends. And because we are speaking of human virtue, human virtue will accordingly be that which will perfect a human power for the good and the best act. But since man is man by the fact that he possesses reason and intellect, those powers are human that are in some way rational, whether essentially, as are those in the intellective part, or by participation, as are those in the sensitive part that are obedient to reason. Now these powers cannot be determined to good acts by their nature as powers, nor can they be determined to perfection except by habits. Hence the human virtues of which we are speaking are not powers, but habits.

Thus SAINT THOMAS. Again, in *ST* I–II, q.55, a.1, he speaks as follows:

> "Virtue" names a certain perfection of a power. But the perfection of anything is considered especially in relation to the thing's being directed to its end. But the end of a power is an act. Therefore a power is said to be perfected according as it is determined to its own act. Now there are some powers, such as natural active powers, which are of themselves determined to their acts, and such natural active powers are accordingly themselves called "virtues." But rational powers, which are the powers proper to man, are not determined to one thing, but related indeterminately to many, and determined to acts through habits; therefore human virtues are habits.

Thus SAINT THOMAS. From these texts argument can be made for the conclusion as follows. That which perfectly determines the rational power to its perfection and to its good act is a habit; but human virtue is such; therefore, it is a habit.

Here the first article terminates.

Article II: Objections

§1. Against the First Conclusion

I. Arguments of Durandus In the second article argument is to be made against the conclusions.

Against the first conclusion, DURANDUS (*In 3 Sent.*, d.23, q.3) argues that the function, effect or activity of a habit is not to determine an act or to determine a power to an act. He argues that a habit is not necessary for determining an act, as follows:

> "Determination of an act" occurs merely according to reason, which is both universal, and particular or singular. For in the nature of things, no act is found that is not determined to a natural existence *(esse naturae)* with respect to its singularity, or, if it is a deliberate act, to a moral existence *(esse moris)* with respect to good and evil. But according to our concept, we are able to understand an act as a universal that, as such, is indifferently related to this or that act and to good or evil. And just as a universal does not really differ from the singular in which it is present, so an indeterminate and a determinate act differ not really, but only according to concept: because what is conceived indeterminately exists determinately, such that its real existence in the nature of things is its real determination, which, formally, comes from itself and not through something joined to it. All this is with respect to natural existence. But the determination of an act to the good with respect to moral existence comes not from the mere singularity of its real existence, for an evil act exists as a singular just as does a good one; rather, an act is formally good from its conformity to right reason and evil from its nonconformity to right reason.
>
> This having been said, it is clear, first that a power is itself formally determined by a habit; and second that we must consider whether it is determined by the habit to a determinate act.
>
> The first point is clear of itself: for every subject that is in potency to receiving many things incompatible with one another, in receiving one of them, is determined by it in such a way that, while it is present, the subject cannot receive another; but the rational powers are in potency to receiving good and bad habits, which are incompatible with one another; therefore, a

power that receives one of them is determined by it in such a way that, while it is present, the power is not indifferent to the receiving of the other.

But because a habit includes directedness to an act, we must see whether it determines a power to producing or receiving a determinate act.

Now it must be said that a good or evil habit contributes nothing to the determination of an act in its natural existence. The reason for this is as follows: a common effect requires a common cause; but the determination of an act in natural existence, since it is its own real singularity, is an effect common to every act existing in the nature of things, whether it be before or after the acquisition of a habit, and whether it be good or evil; therefore the cause of such a determination is common to all acts without any exception. But a habit, even if taken in a general way, is not common in this sense, since prior to every habit there will be acts determined in the above-mentioned way; and much less will a habit taken with reference to the particular case be common. Therefore, etc.

This argument proves not only that habit is not of itself the cause of such a determination, but also that it in no way determines or inclines the power to the act thus determined: for nothing is determined or can be determined **{290}** to what is common to all, since determination occurs in relation to something special; but singularity is common to all acts existing in the nature of things; therefore, no power is "determined" to producing a singular act.

Again, there is no need of anything determining to that to which a power of its own nature is determined in such a way that it cannot be determined to the opposite; but any power is of its nature determined to producing or receiving a singular act in such a way that it can in no way be determined to the opposite; therefore, no power can be determined to producing or receiving an act determined with a determination of singularity according to natural existence.

But concerning the determination of an act to good or evil with respect to moral existence the explanation must be different. For although habit of itself contributes nothing to this determination, it does, nevertheless, accidentally do so. That habit of itself contributes nothing to such a determination is evident as follows: the good or evil of a moral act consists in its conformity or non-conformity to right reason; but conformity and non-conformity are relations in respect of which an action does not exist of itself and immediately, but only through the mediation of a foundation, as is evident from *Physics* 5; therefore, nothing can of itself be the cause of such conformity or non-conformity except that which is of itself the cause of the entity that is the act according to its natural existence, this natural existence being the ground of such relations. But the following establishes that habit is not of itself the cause of the entity that is the act according to its natural existence: no effect can be posited without its per se cause; but the acts that precede a habit belong to a determinate entity on which conformity or nonconformity to right reason is founded, for acts by which a good habit is generated are determinately good, and those by which bad habits are generated are determinately bad; therefore habit is not of itself the cause of such a determination.

II. Other Arguments of Durandus Further, DURANDUS (d.23, q.4) argues that a habit does not render an act easy or difficult in itself. *First,* as follows:

> When two acts are completely similar with respect to all that is in them, if one of them is easy and the other difficult, or one is easier than the other, this must be entirely from the point of view of the agent, and not from the point of view of the act, the point of view in which the act is posited as completely the same in both cases. But an act that precedes acquisition of a habit and one that follows it are sometimes completely similar with respect to all that is in them. Therefore, since the act that follows is said to be easier than the act that precedes, it must be that this is entirely from the point of view of the agent.
>
> The major premise is clear enough. But against the minor premise someone might say that it is false, because the act that follows acquisition of a habit is always more intense than that which precedes.—But this objection is invalid, because it is not universally true that an act that follows acquisition of a habit is more intense than one that precedes. And even granted that it were so, the conclusion would be all the more strongly established: for, among acts specifically the same, a more intense act is of itself more difficult; if, then, an act that follows acquisition of a habit is necessarily and always more intense than an act that precedes, it follows that, of itself at any rate, it will be more difficult; if, therefore, it is easier to the one doing it, it must be that all of the ease comes from the side of the doer.

Second, the same point is made clear as follows:

> Ease on the side of the thing done diminishes merit. If, then, ease were a feature belonging to an act through a habit, it would follow that habit would take away from the merit of an act, which is false.

Third, he argues as follows:

> A virtuous habit concerns what is good and difficult. But if the goodness of an act were removed by habit, then a virtuous habit would not help but hinder. Similarly, therefore, if difficulty were removed by habit, a good habit would hinder more than help.

III. Other Arguments of Durandus Further, he argues (d.23, q.2) that habit of itself contributes nothing to the intensiveness of an act. *First* as follows:

> What pertains of itself to an acquired habit pertains of itself to every such habit; but it does not pertain to every acquired habit to intensify an act.
>
> The major premise is clear, because what pertains of itself to anything pertains of itself to everything included under it.
>
> The minor premise is proved as follows. Every acquired habit is either intellectual or moral, as is said at the end of *Ethics* 1; but these habits do not of themselves contribute to the intensification of an act, as will be made clear; therefore, etc.
>
> The minor premise of this argument is clear if one first makes an induction in the case of intellectual habits, for example, science, opinion, and acquired faith. For if there is someone who first knows a certain conclusion merely on the authority of one who says it—for example believes in a future eclipse on the authority of an astrologer who predicts it—and does not yet have the habit, but later the habit of this belief is established in him, although he holds such a conclusion on authority alone; then, although he believes more firmly on account of the truth of the sayings of the astrologer—a truth that he has, perhaps, experienced—nevertheless he does not know the truth of what was said any more clearly than he did before: although he may perhaps adhere to it more firmly, this firmness comes not primarily or solely from the authority, nor from the habit caused by the authority, but from experience of the fulfillment of the things said by the astrologer. And even if the firmness did come from the authority or the habit, we are now investigating not the firmness but the clarity of knowledge, for the latter alone pertains to the intensiveness of an act of knowing: for firmness of adhesion contributes nothing to clarity of knowing, since one who opines may adhere as firmly to his opined conclusion as one who demonstrates does **{291}** to his demonstrated conclusion, as is said in *Ethics* 7. Similarly, if someone has a dialectical or a demonstrative argument for a certain conclusion, and a habit of opinion or science is caused in him by his repetition of the argument, then, after the habit has been caused, if he knows the same conclusion by the same means by which he knew it before, it is not evident that for this reason he knows it more clearly—although he is now more ready to enter into the

act of knowing, since he has a habit that he can use when he wants. However, we are investigating not readiness, but rather clarity of knowing, for the latter alone pertains to the intensiveness of the act. That this is so is argued as follows.

Intensiveness in an act of knowing seems to be something that can occur not per se, but only from the point of view of the light under which a thing is known, or of the object represented, or of the power of knowing, or of the disposition of the power that is per se required for reception of the act: for all other things seem to be accidentally related to the act and its intensiveness. But an intellectual habit is none of these. Therefore, etc.

The major premise is clear. For we see intensiveness in an act vary from the point of view of the light of the sun, inasmuch as what is seen by the light of the sun is, other things being equal, seen more clearly than what is seen by the light of the moon. Again, from the point of view of the presentation of the object itself, the same visible object presented in the same light seems clearer or more obscure by reason of its nearness or distance. Similarly, from the point of view of the power, the same visible object in the same light at the same distance seems clearer to a young man than to an old one, because the power of vision, since it is bodily, is weaker or stronger according to bodily condition. Again, from the point of view of the disposition that is per se required, the same visible object, equally near and in the same light, seems more or less intense to the same power that is of itself equally intense, if the transparency of the eye, which is of itself required for reception of the species or vision, varies. Now apart from these it is not clear what source there could be of variation of intension and remission in an act. And thus the major premise is clear.

The minor premise is similarly clear. For an acquired habit is not a light under which something is known; moreover, it is supposed that the same object is presented through the same presenting medium, and thus equally well, both before and after the acquisition of the habit; but the intellective power does not admit of more and less; again, the acquired habit is not a disposition that is necessary to receiving the act, since the act precedes the habit. Therefore, etc.

Second, the same point is made clear as follows:

If power and habit of themselves contributed to the intensiveness of an act, this would be either because a habit intensifies a power, which, having been intensified, issues in a more intensified act; or because, as some say, power and habit are two imperfect agents taking the place of one perfect agent in relation to the intensified act, inasmuch as neither of these agents is of itself sufficient for producing it. Now the first alternative is impossible, because the intellective power admits of neither intension nor remission. Nor is the second alternative possible. For principles that are immediately related to a given act and operate under their own strength have the nature of "power" univocally in relation to that act. If, then, habit and power were related as two imperfect agents taking the place of one perfect agent, then, since it follows from this that each of them is related to the act both immediately and by its own force (otherwise there would not be two imperfect agents taking the place of one perfect agent in the manner posited), it also follows that the nature of "power" belongs univocally to, say, the intellective power and to a habit. But this is not so: for although habits are called "powers," this is not with respect to that nature according to which a so-called active or passive power is called a "power" simply speaking, but according to another, different manner of speaking, as is clear from *Metaphysics* 5.

Again, the principles that are of themselves required for any perfect act of a certain kind seem to be necessarily required for any act of the same kind. But a habit is not required for every act that is the same in kind as the act that follows from the habit, because the acts which precede the habit do not come from the habit, although they are the same in kind as the acts which follow from it. Therefore, etc. The minor premise is already clear. The major premise is proved as follows.

First, from the examples given: for just as hardness and sharpness are required in an axe for cutting intensely or quickly, so they are required for any cutting.

Second, because the principles of effects that are the same in species and differ only according to intension and remission are themselves the same in species, differing only according to intension and remission.

Thus the major premise is clear, and consequently the whole of the argument.

Third, he argues as follows:

That which naturally of itself intensifies an act can of itself cause a similar act unless there is a prevailing resistance on the part of the receiver. But a habit of itself, apart from anything else, is not able to cause any act. Therefore it does not of itself contribute to the intensification of the act. The minor premise is clear of itself. The major premise is proved as follows.

Since the intensification of an act is understood with reference to the very essence of the act, that which is of itself capable of intensifying an act is

> of itself capable of producing the essence of the act, setting aside any prevailing impediment. I say "setting aside any impediment" because if the agent that intensifies the act has a strength {292} weaker than that of the resistance to being affected, it would of itself cause nothing; for example, when a weak man comes to the aid of a strong man who is pulling a ship, and the weak man causes a more intense movement, it is not necessarily the case that of himself he could cause the movement of that ship, the weight of which is perhaps greater than the strength of the weak man who is pulling it, although if there were no resistance, he would move it however weak his forces. Since, then, the powers of the soul have no resistance to their own acts, but are rather of themselves most highly disposed to them, it follows that what of itself intensifies their acts is able of itself alone, however weak it may be, to cause an act of a particular kind. And this is the major premise.

Thus DURANDUS argues in form.

§2. Against the Second Conclusion

I. Arguments of Aureolus Against the second conclusion AUREOLUS (*Quodlibet* II, a.I) argues that virtue is not an absolute form, but rather includes a relation, indirectly and in the manner of something connoted. *First,* as follows:

> In order for a form to be a virtue, someone must be well or badly disposed according to it; but goodness and evil consist in agreement or disagreement.

Second, he argues as follows:

> If the relation alone is altered, the virtue is altered; or rather, the same form that was a virtue becomes a vice on account of the alteration of the relation. For example, taciturnity in a young man is a virtue, but if he becomes a teacher and takes on the authority of speaking, then the same quality becomes a vice. This is also evident in the case of bodily habit: for what is beauty in the face would be ugliness in another part, or conversely, ugliness in the nose would be beauty in the pupil or some other part; and what is health in one person would be sickness in another. All of these vary according to agreement. Therefore, virtue indirectly includes a relation.

II. Arguments of Others Others, whose remarks SCOTUS relates, argue that virtue is not an absolute form, but a mere relation. *First,* as follows:

> It is said in *Physics* 7 that just because justice and virtue are "directed toward something" *(ad aliquid),* it does not follow that there is motion in them.

> Now, either ARISTOTLE understands that they are "directed toward something" only in their foundation, and then the argument of THE PHILOSOPHER is invalid, for whiteness is "directed toward something" in its foundation, and yet there can be a movement toward whiteness in the thing; or he understands that justice and virtue are formally "directed toward something," and thus our point is made.

Second, they argue as follows:

> Habit and virtue are required not for the substance of an act, but for its mode, that is, for acting easily and readily. Therefore, it is not necessary that a habit or virtue be an absolute form: rather, it is enough that it be a mode of a thing and custom that is for the sake of the mode of an act.

Third, they argue as follows:

> The habits in question are acquired through acts of intellect and will, which are immanent acts.

Fourth, they argue as follows:

> Things such as habits are destroyed by the cessation of acts, without anything positive to corrupt them, and this would not happen if they were absolute forms.

Fifth, they argue as follows:

> More is not required for acting in the case of a rational power such as intellect or will than in the case of an irrational power. But in the case of an irrational power no absolute quality is required for acting well and easily, as is clear in the case of the brutes: for a horse is disposed to plowing, drawing, or any such thing, through a mode of custom, not by some absolute quality. Therefore, etc.

Sixth, they argue as follows:

> All definitions of virtue include a relation of agreement. No one ever has defined or could define virtue without this relation. Hence AUGUSTINE says that "virtue is a good quality of mind." And THE PHILOSOPHER says in *Ethics* 2 that virtue is "that which perfects the one who has it," and in the same place, that it "consists in the mean with respect to us"; and in *Physics* 7 he says that it is "the disposition of what has been perfected to what is best." All these remarks speak of relation to a nature and of agreement.

Seventh, they argue as follows:

> No act is or is understood to be virtuous unless the understanding establishes a basis for fittingness according to circumstances, as is clear from *Ethics* 2: for circumstances are always considered according as the "how much," the "when," the "where," and the "for whose sake" are fitting and are necessary.

III. Arguments of Others Further, others argue, according to AUREOLUS (*Quodlibet* II, a.I) that virtue is neither a pure quality nor a pure relation, but a composite of both and an accidental being. *First,* as follows:

> Everything that includes things belonging to two categories, however it includes them, is an accidental being; and it is no less so if it includes one directly and the other indirectly, than if it includes both directly, because in the former case it recedes even more from unity. This is clear from *Metaphysics* 7, where THE PHILOSOPHER says that things composed from substance and the other categories do not make up something of itself one; and the same judgment applies to anything composed of any two categories. But virtue principally and directly includes something absolute, and indirectly includes a relation, the former being in the category of quality and the latter in the category of relation. Therefore, virtue is an accidental being.

Second, they argue as follows:

> The essence of virtue either consists entirely and precisively in something pure and absolute; or it does not entirely and precisively consist in this, but rather a relation is included as a part. But {293} the first alternative is impossible: for according to it, the third and the first kinds of quality, being the same with respect to the "something absolute," will not differ essentially. Similarly, virtue and vice will be essentially the same, because an absolute that is specifically the same has the nature of virtue in one case and of vice in another. Similarly, there will be no qualities that are essentially specifically opposed. All these conclusions involve inconsistency. Therefore it remains that the second alternative holds, namely that a relation of fittingness enters as part into the essence of virtue. But every essence which has both an absolute part and a part that is a relation is an accidental being, as is clear in the case of a father and other similar cases. Therefore, the essence of virtue will be an accidental being, even granted that the relation is a part of it indirectly.

Third, they argue as follows:

> "An absolute under a relation, actually founding the relation" is as such something beyond the absolute, namely what is meant by this expression:

"what can be present or absent while the absolute remains the same." But everything that includes, beyond what is absolute, something that can be present or absent to it, is an accidental being: for it includes two things, one of which is accidental to the other, and thus it is an accidental being, as is clear from *Metaphysics* 5 and from the definition of "accident." Therefore virtue, if it signifies an absolute not precisely, but under a certain relation, is necessarily an accidental being.

This is confirmed as follows: the "founding in actuality" is neither the something absolute, since this is separable from its being a foundation, nor the relation founded, as is evident; therefore it will be an intermediate relation, whether real or of reason.

It is also confirmed as follows. To be able to be a foundation involves relation to a potency, a relation intermediate between the foundation and the relation. Therefore, actually to be a foundation does so as well.

Fourth, they argue as follows:

The relation of fittingness is itself related to the virtue either as a property *(propria passio)* of the virtue or as part of the virtue's essence. But the first alternative cannot be maintained. First, because a property is related to its subject in the second mode of per se, and consequently God would be able to cause a virtue without the relation, the opposite of which is usually said. Again, because a subject can be understood without its property, although the converse is not true; accordingly, the relation and the virtue will not be mutually understood in one another. Again, because a virtue is acquired, and varies specifically, by variation caused in the relation alone; thus the relation seems to be an intrinsic difference that places the virtue in a species, and not a property. Again, because nothing that is acquired merely by way of variation includes a relation as part of itself unless it is itself a pure relation; but when merely the status of a person is changed, what was before a virtue becomes a vice, as is clear in the case of taciturnity, which is a virtue in a young man and a vice in an old; or in the case of whiteness, which is a virtue and a beauty in the skin, and a "vice" in the pupil.

Therefore, the relation of fittingness cannot be a property of virtue, but in some way belongs to its essence. But it is established that everything that includes both a relation and something absolute is an accidental being. Therefore, the same conclusion follows as before.

Fifth, they argue as follows:

"White thing" *(album)* is an accidental being, and hence, because it signifies two things, is not in a category. But "white thing," as is said in the *Cate-*

> *gories,* signifies the quality alone, but connotes the subject; and THE COMMENTATOR, in opposition to AVICENNA, says the same thing in *Metaphysics* 5, namely that "it signifies the accident primarily and the subject secondarily." Therefore a name that connotes something beyond what is signified is the name of an accidental being. But "virtue" is such a name. Therefore, etc.

Sixth, they argue as follows:

> What is relative according to being *(esse)* is an accidental being *(ens per accidens),* as is clear in the case of the similar or the equal. But virtue is something relative according to being—at least some virtues, such as justice and friendship, are: for the definition of what is relative according to being, which says that "whatever is 'directed to something' *(ad aliquid),* the thing's 'what it is' belongs to another," fits them, since neither friendship nor justice is a virtue directed toward oneself, but both are "directed toward another." Therefore, at least some virtues are accidental beings.

Seventh, they argue as follows:

> An absolute under a relation, as such, either is something more than the pure absolute; or it is several things; or it is nothing. But it cannot be said that it is nothing, because then the essence of virtue would be nothing: for the essence of virtue of itself [reading *per se* for *per te*] is not an absolute taken precisively, but an absolute under a relation; but as such, it is nothing. Therefore, either virtue must be several things, in the manner of a heap, and so virtue will be essentially a heap, and consequently an accidental being; or it must be something, and consequently a being and a unity, although, since it includes both a relative and an absolute, it is not something one of itself, and therefore it is something accidentally one.

Eighth, they argue as follows:

> THE PHILOSOPHER says in *On Sophistical Refutations* 1 that if a name and an expression signify the same thing, for example the term "twice" and the expression "twice half of twice," something superfluous is involved; hence the term "twice" indicates the "half" in a different way than does the expression "twice half of twice." One may ask, therefore, whether "virtue" signifies an absolute precisively, that is, in such a way that relation does not enter into what is signified, as "half" does not enter into the significance of "twice"; or whether "virtue" signifies both together, signifying the absolute directly and the relation indirectly, in the way that the expression "twice half of twice" signifies "twice" directly and "half" indirectly. If the first alternative

> is granted, then we have our conclusion, namely that "virtue" signifies an absolute precisively, {294} and does not signify relation at all, either indirectly or directly; and consequently that it can be understood without relation. But if the second alternative is granted, it follows that, just as the expression "twice half of twice" signifies an accidental being, so does the term "virtue": for that which signifies two things in such a way that both enter into what is signified by it expresses a being per accidens.

Ninth, they argue as follows:

> What is absolute in virtue, taken precisively *(terminative)*, does not provide a foundation for a relation of fittingness, any more than what is absolute in whiteness founds a relation of similarity: for it is a property of qualities that "similar" and "dissimilar" are said of them, as "equal" and "unequal" are said of quantities. But no name is given to signify whiteness, or any other quality, as standing in a relation of similarity, or as founding this relation. Therefore, neither should a special name be given to signify a quality as founding a relation of fittingness.

Tenth, they argue as follows:

> The whole nature of virtue is complete outside the intellect. But the relation of agreement is not complete outside the intellect, at least according to those who hold that the completion of a relation comes from the soul. Therefore, the nature of virtue does not consist in an absolute as actually founding inasmuch as the latter actually underlies a relation of fittingness.
>
> This is confirmed as follows. At least in God, the attribute of justice, or that of virtue or of knowledge, cannot signify divinity as underlying a real relation, because such a relation is not present in God; neither can it signify divinity as underlying a relation of reason, because then the whole essence of justice, science, or virtue would not be present in God, apart from his act of understanding it.

Here ends the second article.

Article III: Solutions

§1. To the Arguments against the First Conclusion

I. To the Arguments of Durandus In the third article response will be made to the foregoing objections.

In response to the *first* arguments of DURANDUS brought against the first conclusion [p. 6], we say *first* that every human act that actually exists in reality, outside the power that elicits it, is formally determined to its specific natural being not by itself alone, but by its principle or terminus, according to what SAINT THOMAS says excellently in *ST* I–II, q.1, a.3.

Second, we say that any such act is formally determined to its individual natural being not by itself alone, but by its subject, just as any other accident also receives its individuation from its subject, as SAINT THOMAS says in many places, most notably in *In 4 Sent.,* d.12, q.1, a.1, qla.3, ad 3.

Third, we say that any such act is formally determined to its specific moral being *(esse moris)* not by itself alone, but by something else. For, according to what SAINT THOMAS determines in *ST* I–II, q.18, human action taken in general gets its goodness or evil from its object, circumstances, and end. Now the goodness of an interior act of will depends on the object, the end, conformity to right reason, and the eternal law, as SAINT THOMAS proves at length in q.19. But the goodness or evil of an exterior act depends in one respect on the interior will and in another respect on the object or material and on the circumstances, as SAINT THOMAS shows in I–II, q.20.

Fourth, we say that just as any such act is formally determined to its individuality in natural being by its subject, so it is likewise determined in its moral being.

Fifth, we say that the acts that follow upon a habit and are elicited by it receive both specific determinations—namely, in its natural being and in its moral being—from the power and the habit from which they are elicited, as from efficient causes.

Sixth, we say that a habit does not formally determine a power merely with respect to the power itself; rather, it formally determines the power for the production or receiving of a special act, with respect to both the natural being and the moral being or genus of the act.

In response to the argument against this last point we say that the common cause, or common inclining force, of the determination of acts, or of powers to their acts, is what is related, through a mode of form and first act, to the receptive or eliciting power. And because some powers are first placed in actuality through habit while others are not, some are determined and inclined to the production of their acts through habit while others are not, as was said in the first conclusion.

When the opponent says that the acts preceding the habit have been determined in the above-mentioned way, we agree that this is true, because the principle of such acts is not habit, but rather the power together with its object. But the case is different concerning acts elicited from and following upon a habit. Therefore, more things concur for the determination of acts that follow upon than of those that precede a habit.

When the opponent says that nothing can be determined to what is common to all acts etc., we say that, although an act posited in existence has been specifically and individually determined in natural existence, nevertheless the power, before the production of its act, has not at some point been determined to the production of acts of a certain species, and neither, consequently, to the production of a certain indicated individual act. In the same way, the possible intellect, before it is in act through intelligible species, **{295}** is not determined to producing knowledge of "ass" or of "man"; rather, it is determined to this or that through an intelligible species, which can be called a "habit," as SAINT THOMAS says in I–II, q.50, a.6, and in many other places.

When the opponent further says that any power has been determined of its own nature, etc., we say *first* that that is simply false, because there are many powers that of their nature are unable to produce any act without an actuality being first added to them, as is clear in the case of every sensitive and intellective power, at least every human or created one.

Second, we say that, although a certain power might be determined to producing or receiving an individual act in the sense that it cannot produce or receive a universal or non-individual act, nevertheless it is not determined to producing or receiving this or that individual act, nor an act of this or that species, and therefore it needs some determinant. Hence this argument and the foregoing one err through the fallacy of equivocation, because they make equivocal what I am calling "a determined act": for this can have a supposition that is simple or one that is personal; in other words, it can have a supposition that is confused or one that is determinate. But the opponent's arguments proceed according to the first meaning, and our conclusion according to the second. For we concede that no power needs to be determined by a habit to producing a determinate act if the supposition is simple or confused; but if the supposition is personal and determinate, we say the opposite, because there are many powers that are indifferent to acts of diverse species, such as sense, intellect, and will. Therefore the opponent has labored in vain to prove what anyone would have freely granted him: for no-one, except a madman, has ever dreamt that any power could produce a universal act, one with no determination to genus, species, and individual.

Further, when the opponent says that habit of itself contributes nothing to the determining of a power or act in its moral being, we say that habit contributes to both of these not merely accidentally, but of itself. For that it determines an act to its moral being is clear, because, according to THE PHILOSOPHER in *Ethics* 7, the moral virtues make men well disposed concerning the proximate end of virtue, while prudence makes men well disposed concerning those things that are directed to the end. Concerning this point SAINT THOMAS speaks in many places, most notably in I–II, q.58, aa.4–5 and in II–II, q.47, a.6, but also in many other places.

Now in response to the argument against this solution we say *first* that the goodness or evil of human acts does not consist precisively or principally in this kind of relation of conformity or non-conformity, but rather in the foundation of this relation, according to what has been seen in *Sent.* 2.

Second, we say that the activity of a habit does not immediately touch these relations, but rather their foundations, namely the substance of the act. To the argument against this point we say that, although the acts preceding the habit are determinately good or evil, and get neither this kind of determination nor their entity from the habit, nevertheless it is not inconsistent with this that the acts that follow upon the habit do get their entity and determination from the habit as from the co-principle, or co-cause, or nature of the power's action, and that this is so not accidentally, but per se. For there is something which is the per se cause of a given individual that is not the cause of all of the individuals of the same species; this is most evident where such individuals can be produced by causes of different species, as is clear in the case of fire, which can be produced by other fire, by the sun, and by many other per se causes that cause its production. Hence, just as it does not follow that "This fire of itself produces fire; therefore, fire cannot be produced without fire," so, in the question at issue, with respect to act and habit. There is in the opponent's argument the fallacy of the consequent, or of equivocation, arguing from the perseity of the cause to the perseity of the proposed effect, and from the perseity of the inconvertible to something convertible and reciprocal.

Third, we say that this argument, like the preceding ones, does not go directly against the conclusion or the meaning of the conclusion. For when it is said that a habit is necessary for determining a power to its act in moral being, it is not the meaning of the conclusion that a bare power, without a habit, elicits an act in moral existence that is indifferent; or that without a habit it is unable to produce or receive an act which is determinately good or evil, but can do so only through a habit. Yet all of DURANDUS's arguments proceed according to this meaning. The meaning of the conclusion is rather that a habitless power is not more inclined to an act that is morally good than to one that is morally evil; nor is it inclined to acting pleasurably or easily or readily; rather it remains in an indistinct potentiality to this and that object, and similarly to a good and to an evil act, and similarly again to a certain way of operating and to its opposite—or rather, of itself it is not disposed to one of the two, but through habit it becomes inclined toward one object and away from its opposite (and the same is true of the act and the mode of operating). This is clear in the case of the habit of temperance, which inclines the concupiscible power to certain objects and to certain acts and modes of operating. Hence, all of the opposing arguments are sophistical.

II. To the Other Arguments of Durandus In response to the second group of arguments brought against the first conclusion [p. 8], we answer as follows. **{296}**

In response to the *first* argument—that is, to the response in it proving negation of the minor premise—we say that the act that precedes acquisition of a habit is never at all points similar or equal to the act following upon and elicited by the habit. Concerning this point BLESSED THOMAS speaks as follows in *ST* II–II, q.23, a.2:

> No act is perfectly produced by any active power unless the act is made connatural with the power by some form that is a principle of action. Hence God, Who moves all things to their due ends, has inserted into individual things forms by which they are inclined to ends pre-established for them by God; accordingly, "He has disposed all things sweetly," as is said in *Wisdom* 8. But it is clear that the act of charity exceeds the nature of the will's power. Therefore, unless there were superadded to the natural power some form by which it would be inclined to the act of charity, that act would accordingly be less perfect than natural acts and than the acts of the other virtues, and it would not be easy and pleasurable.

Thus SAINT THOMAS, who speaks similarly in *In 1 Sent.*, d.17, q.1, a.1, and in many other places.

But when the opponent, in order to prove the minor premise, introduces the example concerning the intensification of the act, we say that the argument does not hold, because we do not say that every act that follows upon a habit is more intensified than any act that precedes the habit. Thus BLESSED THOMAS, in *ST* I–II, q.52, a.3, speaks as follows:

> Because the use of habits resides in the will of man, so, just as it can happen that someone who has a habit does not use it, or even performs an act contrary to it, it can also happen that one makes use of a habit in an act that does not proportionally correspond to the intensity of the habit.

And he says something similar in II–II, q.24, a.6.

But we do say that any act elicited from a habit, especially one proportioned to the habit, is more perfect than the acts preceding acquisition of the habit, even if it is not more perfect in intensity.

Again, even assuming we would say that an act following upon acquisition of a habit is always more intense, it cannot be argued from this that it would be more difficult than one preceding the habit, because more principles concur in producing the act following upon acquisition of the habit, as is self-evident. Or again, granting that it would be more difficult in itself, nevertheless, as will be said below, it would not be so to the agent to which the power belongs.

SAINT THOMAS responds in form to the second argument in *In 3 Sent.*, d.23, q.1, a.1, obj.4, where he presents the following argument:

> Difficulty contributes to merit. But habit removes difficulty. Therefore, habits should not be given to us for those acts by which we obtain merit.

Thus the argument; the response is as follows:

> We must say, he says, that, as is said in *Metaphysics* 2, difficulty, as well as ease, can come either from us or from things. Therefore the ease that comes from the nature of acts that are not of themselves a great burden diminishes the nature of merit; but the ease that comes from readiness of the one operating does not diminish, but rather increases, the relation of the essential reward to the act; because inasmuch as one acts with greater charity, one tolerates things more easily and obtains more merit. And similarly, inasmuch as one operates more pleasurably on account of the habit of virtue, the act is more pleasurable and more meritorious.

Thus SAINT THOMAS. From this text it is clear that not every ease of operation diminishes merit (rather sometimes such ease increases merit), but only that ease in a meritorious deed arising from the lightness that it has because it is in itself not very burdensome. And if it be said that from this the conclusion of the opponent follows, namely that such ease is not a condition of the deed in itself, but only of the one doing it, we say that the argument concludes only that there is a cause of ease on the part of the one acting, not that ease is not formally present in the act: for the easy and the difficult are spoken of relatively, as are the great and the small, and therefore something can formally be easy in relation to one thing and difficult in relation to another.

In response to the *third* argument we say that the case of the goodness of the act and that of its difficulty are not similar, because the former necessarily belongs to the virtuous act but the latter does not.

Again, a virtue or habit does not wholly remove the difficulty of an act, because an act that is difficult is difficult either in itself or in relation to the habituated power.

Again, granted that habit removes the difficulty of an act, it nevertheless makes the act better. Concerning this point SAINT THOMAS, in II–II, q.27, a.8, ad 3, speaks as follows:

> The good contributes more to the nature of merit and of virtue than does the difficult. Hence, not everything that is more difficult need be more meritorious, but only that which is more difficult in such a way that it is also better.

Again, in I–II, q.114, a.4, ad 2, he speaks as follows:

> A deed can be more laborious and difficult in two ways. In one way, from the magnitude of the deed, and thus magnitude of labor does pertain to increase of merit; in this way charity does not diminish labor, but rather causes one to take on the greatest deeds: "for it does great things if it is present," as Gregory says in some homily. In a second way, from a deficiency in the doer, for what someone does not do with a ready will is laborious and difficult to him; such labor diminishes merit and is removed by charity.

Thus SAINT THOMAS. And what he says of charity can be said of the other virtuous habits, namely that they remove the difficulty that hinders merit but not the difficulty that increases it.

In response to all the foregoing objections, however, we might speak more briefly—and shake off the difficulty in question more easily—**{297}** by saying that a habit does not make an act in itself easy or difficult, but makes it be done with ease or with difficulty. Now for a deed or act to be done easily is for it to be done readily, without the necessity of preceding inquiry or deliberation. Of this SAINT THOMAS, in *Questions on the Virtues,* "On the Virtues in General," q.1, a.1, speaks as follows:

> We need the habits of the virtues for three reasons. First, in order that there be firmness in their right operation: because a power that depends on another principle for its right operation is easily changed if it is not stabilized by

> some habitual inclination. Secondly, in order that perfect operation may be held in readiness: for unless the rational power is in some way inclined through habit to one object, an inquiry concerning the deed will always have to precede whenever it is necessary to act, as is clear in the case of one who wishes to contemplate but does not yet have the habit of science, or the case of one who wishes to act according to virtue but lacks the habit of virtue; hence THE PHILOSOPHER says in *Ethics* 3 that sudden acts proceed from habit. Thirdly, in order that the perfect operation be accomplished pleasurably: this occurs by means of habit, which, since it inclines in the way a nature does, renders its proper operation connatural, as it were, and consequently pleasurable, since agreement is a cause of pleasure. Hence THE PHILOSOPHER, in *Ethics* 1, posits pleasure in the deed as a sign of a generated habit.

Thus SAINT THOMAS. From this text, what was said before is clear, namely that habit causes one to act readily and with ease. Nevertheless, we must say that, apart from the kind of ease just discussed, the deeds themselves are also rendered easy by means of habit: for they would be difficult for one doing them without the habit, as is clear in the case of the temperate man, for whom it is easy to moderate his passions, which is difficult for the incontinent man; and similarly, for one who has great charity it is easy to conquer every temptation, which is difficult or impossible for one who has little charity, or one who lacks charity and grace. SAINT THOMAS discusses this point extensively in *In 3 Sent.*, d.31, q.1, a.3, where he speaks as follows:

> "To resist temptation" is said in two ways: in one way such that one is not conquered by the temptation; in another way such that one conquers the temptation.
>
> Someone is said to be conquered by temptation when he is drawn by temptation away from a proposed good to a consenting to sin. This is the case with an incontinent man, who possesses right reason but is led away; for one who does not have a proposed good, such as an intemperate or lustful man, is not "conquered," since he freely does what he does.
>
> But someone conquers who not only is not conquered by a temptation that comes over him, and is not led away to an act of sin, but who also, from the greatness of his virtue, despises the temptation as nothing.
>
> But one who experiences difficulty in temptation but is not led away indeed resists the temptation in the mode of form and first act, since he does not consent to it, but he does not properly speaking conquer it.
>
> Accordingly, if we speak of "resistance to sin" in the first sense, charity

> is able to resist sin on account of the free choice that has been liberated from sin, even if it experiences difficulty on account of the force of the temptation. But if we speak of temptation in the second sense, the charity that is small at the beginning of temptation is able to resist temptation, because it becomes great at the end of the temptation, since God always administers aid to one who struggles. But if it is assumed that the charity remains small, it would not be able to resist temptation in the way mentioned.

Thus SAINT THOMAS. Again, in *Quodlibetal Questions,* q.4, a.19, he speaks as follows:

> In the acts of the virtues two things are to be noted, namely what is done and the manner of doing it. The same thing done as a result of a perfect virtue can also be done not only by one who has little virtue, but even by one who does not have virtue at all, as, for instance, someone who does not have the virtue of justice can perform a just deed. But if we pay attention to the manner of doing it, one who does not have virtue cannot act like one who does have it. Nor can one who has little virtue act like one who has great virtue, and who acts with ease, and readily and pleasurably—which one who lacks virtue, or has little virtue, cannot do. Thus we must say that the deed of offering oneself to martyrdom, or even of suffering martyrdom, can be performed not only with perfect charity, but also with imperfect charity, and, what is more, even by one who lacks charity, as THE APOSTLE says in *1 Corinth.* 13: "If I give my body to be burned, but have not charity. . . ." But perfect charity performs it readily and pleasurably, as is clear in the case of Laurence and Vincent, who showed cheerfulness in their torments; but imperfect charity, or one who lacks charity, cannot do this.

Thus SAINT THOMAS.

III. To the Other Arguments of Durandus We must now respond to the third group of arguments brought against the first conclusion [p. 9].

In response to the *first* argument we say that the major premise can be denied with proof. For an acquired habit can have the property of intensifying an act not merely because of the nature of its genus, that is, not just because it is a habit, but also because of the nature of its proper species; or again, because of the nature of its proximate genus, for instance, because it is a habit of the appetitive part. Now I say this because an intellectual habit is differently related to its act than is a moral one, as SAINT THOMAS shows in *ST* I–II, q.56, a.3, where he speaks as follows:

> Virtue is a habit which one uses for good. But a habit is directed to a good act in two ways. In one way inasmuch as by means of the habit a man acquires a facility for the good act. For example, by means of the habit {298} of grammar, a man possesses a facility for speaking rightly, although the grammtical habit does not make him speak rightly always, for a grammatical man can commit a barbarism or solecism; and the argument is the same in the case of the other sciences and arts. In a second way, the habit not only causes facility of acting, but also brings it about that one will use that facility rightly; as justice not only brings it about that a man has a ready will for doing just things, but also that he act justly, etc.

Thus SAINT THOMAS. Again, in q.57, a.1, he speaks as follows:

> A habit is called a "virtue" for two reasons: one is because it causes a facility for acting well, and the other is because, together with the facility, it causes good use. The latter point concerns only those habits that pertain to the appetitive power, because the soul's appetitive power is the one that causes the soul to make use of powers and habits. Accordingly, since the speculative intellectual habits do not perfect or in any way concern the appetitive part, but only the intellective part, they can indeed be called "virtues" to the extent that they cause facility for a good operation, namely consideration of truth, for this is the good operation of the intellect; however, they are not called "virtues" in the second respect, as if they caused one to make good use of a power or habit. For the fact that someone has within himself a habit of speculative knowledge does not incline him to make use of it, but makes him capable of considering what is true in those matters of which he possesses knowledge; it is rather by a movement of the will that he makes use of the knowledge he possesses. Hence a virtue that perfects the will, such as charity or justice, also causes one to use the speculative habits well.

Thus SAINT THOMAS. From these texts it is evident that habits of the intellective part and habits of the appetitive part are related in different ways to the acts of the powers they inform. Therefore it does not follow that if the latter habits intensify the act, or of themselves contribute to the intensity of the act, that the former habits do so as well.

Second, we say that, if the major premise must in some sense be conceded, the minor premise must be denied. For every habituated power can elicit a more intense act than can a non-habituated power, if, by a command of the will, it uses its habit for intensifying the act. However, it does not follow that the habituated power can intensify all of its acts through the habit: rather, it can intensify only the act to which the habit is directed. Hence it is clear that the proofs of the minor premise, if they are understood to concern all acts of a habituated power, do not hold. For when the opponent says that a habit of belief does not cause evidence or clarity of knowledge, etc., it is clear that he errs by the fallacy of the consequent, arguing from negation of the lower to negation of the higher; because although the habit in question does not intensify knowledge, it does, nevertheless, intensify assent, which is an act of the intellect.

Nor does his remark that here we are asking only about intensity and clarity of cognition, etc., hold. For this is not true: rather, we are inquiring in general whether habits contribute of themselves to the intensity of any act.

Similarly it is clear that what he says about a habit caused by a dialectical or demonstrative argument does not hold: for, although such a habit does not cause greater clarity or evidence than do the acts by which the habit is caused, nevertheless it does cause a more intense assent; but assent is an act of the intellect, and we are inquiring about this act as much as any other.

Similarly, the response to the opponent's argument for this conclusion is clear. For the argument shows, if anything, only that the acquired habit does not cause new clarity or evidence, and does not intensify either clarity or evidence; but it does not show that the habit would not be able to contribute to the intensity of other acts of the intellect to which the habit is immediately directed, such as assent, judgment, and other such acts.

Nevertheless, the argument does not even show the former point sufficiently. For, as has been said, an intelligible species is a habit, and yet it is according to greater or less perfection of the intelligible species in distinctly representing the intelligible object that there is greater or less clarity and evidence, and more or less intense cognition in the intellect.

And when the opponent says that the habit is not a light by which anything is known, etc., this is not a difficulty for us: for the habit of which we are speaking *is* a light with respect to cognition, and is a necessary disposition of the power in order that it may know.

Again, as was said before, the opponent's argument concerns only habits of the intellective part, not those of the appetitive part.

Now SAINT THOMAS shows the way that an intelligible species illuminated by the light of the agent intellect may be called a "habit" in *In 3 Sent.*, d.14, q.1, a.1, qla.2, where he speaks as follows:

No passive power can go into act unless it has been completed by the form of its active object, a form by which it is made to be in actuality; for nothing acts except according as it is in actuality. Now the impressions of active things can be present in passive powers in two ways: in one way, as an "affection," as happens when the passive power is being altered; in another way, as a quality and form, as happens when the impression of what is active has already been made connatural with the passive power. This is how THE PHILOSOPHER, in the *Categories,* distinguishes between an "affection" *(passio)* and an "affective quality" *(passibilis qualitas).*

Now sense is a passive power, because it cannot exist with the actuality of all the objects to which, by its nature as a power, its operation extends: for sense cannot be something which in actuality has all colors. Hence sight must be cognitive of all colors inasmuch as it is, in a way, potentially all colors, so that when it is affected by colors, it becomes them in actuality, is assimilated to them, and knows them. Similarly, the intellect is cognitive of all beings, because "a being" and "a true <thing>"—the latter of which is the proper object of the intellect—are convertible with one another. Now a creature, {299} because it is a finite being, cannot exist with the actuality of the whole of being, for this belongs to God alone, who is the source of all beings and in a way pre-contains all things within Himself, as DIONYSIUS says. Therefore no creature can understand without the intellect that is a passive, that is, a receptive power. Hence, neither the sense-power nor the possible intellect can act unless they are perfected or moved by their active objects. But because the sense-power senses only in the presence of the sensible object, the impression of its active object merely as an affection suffices for the power's perfect operation. In the intellect, however, perfection of operation requires that the impression of its active object be present in the power not merely as an affection, but also as a quality and form that has become connatural; and we call this form "a habit." And because what is connatural remains firmly, is there in readiness for a man when he uses his natural power, and is pleasurable to him because it agrees with his nature, a habit such as scientific knowledge is not easily removed, and the man can use it when he wishes, and it makes the operation pleasurable. Now in the case of the sense of sight, there are two things active: one is the prime agent and mover, namely light; the other is a moved mover, namely the color made visible in actuality by light. So, too, in the case of the intellect, there is both the light of the agent intellect as the first agent, and the species made intelligible in actuality by the agent intellect as a moved mover. Hence the habit of the intellective part is made up of, on the one hand, a light, and, on the other, the intelligible species of the things known by means of the species.

Thus SAINT THOMAS. From this text it follows that there is a habit that contributes to the substance and the intensity of the act; and that there is another habit, which is both the light necessary for understanding and the disposition necessary to the power for acting.

In response to the *second* argument we say that a power and a habit concur in producing or intensifying the same act: not in the first way, so that the habit intensifies the power even while it perfects it; nor in the second way, so that, because the habit is not a "that which" *(quod),* but a "that whereby" *(quo),* the power and the habit are two partial agents taking the place of one perfect agent; but rather in the third way, so that the power is "that which" acts, if we may so speak, and the habit is that "whereby" it acts, or the nature of the power's acting, or the power's perfection for acting.

Now if someone should wish to attack this view by means of the opponent's argument that principles immediately related, etc.,—we say that this is true in the case where several principles, each of which is a "that which," act, but it is not necessarily true where one is the "that which" and another the "whereby," as is clear in the case of the sense-power and the species by which it is informed.

In response to the *second* argument we say that the major premise is clearly false, because more things are required for a perfect than for an imperfect act.

We should not even respond to the *first* argument for the major premise of this argument, because the example used is given not by SAINT THOMAS, but by HERVAEUS or some others, so that they can respond if they want to. We can, however, say that sharpness is not required for all cutting, but only for cutting perfectly.

In response to the *second* argument for the major premise, which is more relevant, we say *first* that, if we are speaking of a habit concerning what is incomplex *(de habitu incomplexorum),* for example the intelligible species, then this habit is required for every act of the intellect, whether intense or remiss. But if we are speaking of a habit concerning complexities *(de habitu respectu complexorum),* for example principles or conclusions, then we say that acts elicited from the habituated power in proportion to the habit vary not only with respect to intensity and remission, but also in other ways: for, as has often been said, an habituated power elicits an act pleasurably, firmly, and readily, as an unhabituated power does not.

Again, it is clearly false to say that acts that are specifically the same, and differ only according to intensity and remission, necessarily have principles that are themselves specifically the same, and differ only according to intensity and remission. This is clearly false where the same specific effect can be produced by diverse causes that differ specifically and are equivocal with their effects. This is evident in the case of fire, which can be produced by other fire, by the sun, by the striking of flint, and by many other causes. For it is evident that the effects of such specifically different causes are specifically the same, and differ only in their intensity and remission. Similarly, in the present argument, one must say that intense and remiss acts that are specifically the same can proceed from specifically different principles, especially when such principles are partial and not total, as is the case when a habit concurs with a power in the production of an act.

In response to the *third* argument we deny the major premise. We are speaking of what of itself intensifies an act not as the principle "which," but as the principle "whereby," a principle that is not the agent, but the perfection of the agent and the nature of the acting. Such a principle is one that, in union with the power, is of itself able to contribute to the intensity of the act, but by itself is insufficient of itself to cause the act. This is clear in the case of a species in the sense-power or intellect; in union with the cognitive power the species concurs in causing and intensifying the act, but yet, by itself, does not suffice to produce the act.

In response to the proof of the major premise we say that what of itself contributes to the intensifying of the act, of itself contributes to the production of the act's essence. But both in intensifying and in producing it concurs as a partial cause—or rather, not as a "that which" but as a "whereby"; and it does not concur as an agent properly speaking, but as the perfection of an agent. Hence, just as alone it does not of itself suffice to intensify the act, neither does it alone suffice {300} to produce it; but it can of itself concur in either in the way stated.

This suffices against the arguments of DURANDUS.

However, it should be known that SAINT THOMAS sometimes seems to say, in *In 4 Sent.*, d.49, q.1, a.2, qla.2, ad 2, that habit does *not* contribute to the substance of an act; for he speaks there as follows:

> Two things must be considered in an act: the substance of the act; and its form, from which it gets its perfection. Thus, the principle of an act with respect to its substance is a natural power; but its principle with respect to its form is a habit, etc.

But from his remarks both in this text and elsewhere, it is clear that his view was not that habit in no way contributes to the substance of an act; rather, he meant that it does not directly so contribute, and that it is not required for the substance of the act as necessarily as it is for the act's fulness and perfection, which proceed from the side of the object or that of the manner of acting. For a habit determines a power to a determinate object and manner of acting, as SAINT THOMAS himself shows in *Questions on Truth,* q.20, a.2, where he speaks as follows:

> We must know what a habit is and what we need habits for. As appears at once, "habit" seems to signify something added to a power by which the latter is perfected for its operation. Now a power needs something added to it for two reasons: because of the condition of the nature, and because of the essence *(ratio)* of the power itself. This is not inappropriate, for the action that proceeds from the power also depends on the nature that is the source of the power.
>
> From the point of view of the nature, a power needs something added to it in order to operate when the operation is such as to exceed the ability and condition of the nature; for example, it exceeds the condition of human nature to be affected by a comradely love toward God, as if one were a sharer in His inheritance, so that for this operation our affective power needs a habit of charity.
>
> From the point of view of the power, something additional is needed when the power is directed to universal objects. For example, sight is directed to knowing all colors; but it was not possible for all colors to be present in actuality in the organ of sight; and so things were otherwise disposed, namely in such a way that a likeness of any color could be added to the power of sight, so that the latter would proceed to the act of sight.
>
> Now it must be known that what is added to a power is received in it sometimes as a habit and sometimes as an affection. It is received as an affection when what is received does not remain in the receiver, and is not made a quality of the receiver, but rather is a momentary alteration caused by, as it were, contact with an agent, an alteration that passes. For example, THE PHILOSOPHER says in the *Categories* that blushing is an affection, and not a passible quality, when someone, because of shame, momentarily undergoes the change to redness. But what is added is retained as a habit when what is received is made connatural, as it were, with the receiver. Hence it is that habit is called by THE PHILOSOPHER "a quality difficult to change." Hence it is, too, that operations that proceed from a habit are

> pleasurable, prompt, and carried out with ease, because they are, as it were, connatural effects.
>
> What is added to the sensitive powers, therefore, is added not as a habit, but as an affection; but what is added in the intellective powers of the soul is added as a habit: for the sensitive part of the soul is "put into act" by an instinct of nature more than it "acts"; but the intellective part is the mistress of her act, and therefore it is proper to her to possess a readiness for the act in order to be able to act whenever she pleases.

Thus SAINT THOMAS.

§2. To the Arguments against the Second Conclusion

I. To the Arguments of Aureolus In responding to the *first* group of arguments brought against the second conclusion [p. 12], certain preliminaries must be presented.

The first point is that it is not the view of SAINT THOMAS that virtue, with which the question is concerned, is a pure relation *(relatio aut respectus)*. The second point is that it was his view that virtue does include a relation to something. On both of these points he speaks as follows in *In 7 Phys.*, where he is explaining ARISTOTLE's remark that ". . . nor in the case of habits, for both virtues and vices are habits, but every virtue and vice is directed to something, etc.":

> Habits, which are in the first species of quality, are virtues and vices; even bodily habits are virtues and vices. For, universally speaking, the virtue of any thing is that which makes what possesses it good and renders its operation good. Hence there is said to be a virtue of the body by which the body is in a good state and operates well, for example health; and there is a contrary vice, namely sickness. Now every virtue and vice are spoken of as directed to something. ARISTOTLE illustrates this point by means of examples. Health, which is a virtue of the body, is a balancing of the hot and the cold. Now I say that this balancing is brought about by the proper proportioning of what is within the body, that is, a proportioning of the "humors" of which the body is composed, a proportioning of them both in relation to one another and in relation to the body itself. For the mixture of humors that is health in a lion would not be health, but rather death, in a man, because human nature could not endure it. Similarly, beauty and leanness are spoken of "as directed to something" ("leanness" here refers to the disposition by which someone is ready for movement and action); for these are dispositions of what is perfected in its nature, in relation to what is best, that is, to the end,

> which is its operation, because it is from this that such dispositions {301} are called "virtues," because they make the one who possesses them good and render his operation good; thus they are spoken of in relation to good operation, which is the best thing belonging to anything. And lest anyone should take "what is perfected" to mean what has already attained the end, ARISTOTLE says that "what is perfected" is here taken to mean what has been made whole, and has been disposed according to its nature. But it is not to be understood that the "directed to something" is what these habits and dispositions are, because thus they would be not in the genus of quality, but in that of relation; however, their nature does depend on a relation. Because, then, these habits are "directed to something," and because "in relation to something," as has been proved in *Physics* 5, is not a movement, a generation, or an alteration, it is clear that in these habits there is no alteration primarily and per se; rather, change in them follows upon some prior change in the hot or the cold, or other such things, just as relations, too, begin to be as a result of certain motions.

Thus SAINT THOMAS. Again, in *In 4 Sent.*, d.1, q.1, a.4, qla.2, he speaks as follows:

> Some say that the supernatural virtue which is present in the sacraments is nothing but an ordering "to something." But this is meaningless, because "virtue" always names the principle of some action, but the being "directed to something," or relation, cannot be a principle of action, or a terminus, as is proved in *Physics* 5. Therefore the ordering in question can have neither the name nor the nature of virtue.

Thus SAINT THOMAS. Again, in *In 3 Sent.*, d.23, q.1, a.3, qla.3, he speaks as follows:

> Virtue, properly speaking, includes a relation to something of which it is the principle, such as running, being, etc.

Again, in *Questions on Truth*, q.21, a.6, he speaks as follows:

> A name can imply a relation in two ways. In one way such that the name is given to signify a relation, as are the names "father," "son," or "paternity" itself. But some names are said to imply a relation because they signify a thing in some category that is accompanied by a relation, although the name itself is not given to signify that relation; for instance, the name "science" is given to signify a quality from which a relation follows, not to signify the relation itself. In the same way, the nature of a good thing implies a relation, not because the name "good thing" signifies the relation alone, but because it sig-

> nifies both that from which the relation follows and the relation itself. The relation implied in the name "good thing" is a relation belonging to what causes perfection inasmuch as a thing is able to cause perfection, and does so not only with respect to the nature of a species, but also with respect to the being which the good thing has in other things.

Thus SAINT THOMAS. And what he says of the name "good thing" can also, in his view, be said of the names "virtue" or "vice." From these texts it is clear that "virtue" names neither a pure relation nor something purely absolute, but something absolute accompanied by a relation; that it signifies both, but principally signifies what is absolute and secondarily and indirectly signifies the relation; and that it expresses "a habit that causes good operation."

Having set forth these preliminaries, in response to the *first* argument of AUREOLUS we say that it rightly concludes that virtue includes a relation secondarily and indirectly, but not principally and directly; and that, willingly or not, it does not disagree with SAINT THOMAS, but rather asserts what he says.

In response to the *second* argument of the same objector we say *first* that, with respect to the virtues that exist in the powers of the soul, which are the subject of the present discussion, it must be conceded that, in some cases, the same form and quality that is a virtue can also not be a virtue, and can, while remaining itself, both be and not be a virtue, for example, if it loses the form or perfection that it receives from a higher virtue. On this point SAINT THOMAS, in *ST* II–II, q.4, a.5, speaks as follows:

> Informed faith is a virtue. But unformed faith is not a virtue, because, even if it had the perfection owed to the act of unformed faith on the part of the intellect, it still would lack the required perfection on the part of the will. Similarly, if there were temperance in the concupiscible part and no prudence in the rational part, the temperance would not be a virtue, because the act of temperance requires both an act of reason and an act of the concupiscible part, just as the act of faith requires both an act of the will and an act of the intellect.

Thus SAINT THOMAS. And in the preceding article, the fourth one, he shows that the same habit is sometimes faith that is informed, and then later is unformed. He says something similar in *In 3 Sent.*, d.23, q.3, a.1, namely that the same habit and quality that was formerly a virtue can cease to be a virtue.

Second, we say that a habit of mind that was formerly a virtue does not cease to be a virtue in the way the opponent says, namely through variation in age or personal fortune, such that a habit that was a virtue in a young or a rich man ceases to be a virtue in the same man become old or poor. Nor do the arguments concerning taciturnity and loquaciousness, or generosity and lack of it with respect to money, hold. For neither virtue itself nor what is meant by "virtue" consists in such acts. Rather, it consists in an inner choice and a preparation of the soul for eliciting such acts according to right reason. On this point, SAINT THOMAS, in *ST* II–II, q.134, a.1, obj.1, presents the following argument: **{302}**

> He who has one virtue has all. But one can have other virtues without magnificence: for THE PHILOSOPHER says in *Ethics* 4, "Not every generous man is magnificent." Therefore, magnificence is not a virtue.

Thus the argument; the response is as follows:

> It must be said that not every generous man is magnificent in actuality, because a generous man may lack what is needed for a magnificent act; nevertheless, every generous man has the habit of magnificence either in actuality or in a disposition of readiness.

Thus SAINT THOMAS. Again, in q.152, a.3, ad 2, he speaks as follows:

> The interconnection of the virtues is understood with respect to what is formal in them, namely charity or prudence, and not with respect to what is material in them. For nothing prevents a virtuous man from being sufficient in the material of one virtue but not that of another; for example, a poor man possesses the material of temperance but not the material of magnificence. Thus someone who has the other virtues may lack the material of virginity, namely the above-mentioned integrity of the flesh; but she can still possess what is formal in virginity by holding in readiness in her mind the intention to preserve the above-mentioned integrity, as if such preservation were appropriate to her. Similarly, a poor man may hold in readiness the intention to make magnificent expenditures; and similarly, one who enjoys prosperity may hold in readiness in his soul the intention to endure adversities with equanimity. And without this readiness of soul no-one can be virtuous.

Thus SAINT THOMAS. Again, in q.144, a.4, he speaks as follows:

> The old and the virtuous lack a sense of shame. They are, however, so disposed that, if there were anything unseemly in them, they would be ashamed of it. Hence THE PHILOSOPHER says in *Ethics* 4 that "the virtue of shame is based on the presupposition that one is good."

Thus SAINT THOMAS. Again, in the first article of the same question, in response to the fifth objection, he speaks as follows:

> By the experience of frequently being ashamed there is caused the habit of an acquired virtue by which one avoids the unseemly things that are the object of shame. But the purpose of this habit is not to make one ashamed again in the future; rather, the habit disposes one to be more ashamed *if* the material of shame is present.

Thus SAINT THOMAS. From these texts, if they are considered carefully, it is clear that a habit which at first was a moral virtue does not cease to be a moral virtue, and that it does not change into a vice through a variation in age, or fortune, or status, while it remains itself. It follows only that a habit that, in relation to some time, place, or personal condition, once caused an inclination to some act ceases to cause an inclination to it when these circumstances change, and now causes an inclination to the opposite of that act: for example, the habit of magnificence inclines a rich man to an act to which it does not incline the same man when he becomes poor; similarly, the virtue of modesty inclines a young man to different acts than it does an old man; and the same is true of the habit of shame, although the habits of shame and taciturnity are not perfect virtues according to what BLESSED THOMAS says.

Third, we say that bodily habits, such as beauty and health, can lose the nature of virtue and take on the nature of vice or evil merely by a variation in their proportion to the subject or nature to which they are applied. On this point the opponent speaks in conformity with SAINT THOMAS, *In 7 Phys.,* as was stated before. It does not, however, follow from this that virtue is a relation, but only that a relation to the nature or subject in which it is present, or to the act to which it is directed, belongs to the essence *(ratio)* of virtue. On this point SAINT THOMAS, in *ST* I–II, q.49, a.3, speaks as follows:

> A habit's possession of directedness to an act can be both with respect to the nature of habit and with respect to the nature of the subject in which the habit is present.
>
> With respect to the essence of habit, every habit of every kind possesses directedness to an act. For it is of the essence of habit that it implies a relation and a directedness to the nature of a thing, inasmuch as the habit is or is not suitable to it. But because the nature of the thing, which is the end of generation, is further directed to another end, namely operation, or something that one reaches through operation, habit implies a directedness not only to the very nature of the thing, but also, subsequently, to operation,

> inasmuch as the latter is or leads to the end of the nature. Hence, in *Metaphysics* 5 it is said in the definition of habit that "it is a disposition according to which what is disposed is well or badly disposed, whether of itself"—that is, according to its nature—"or in relation to another"—that is, in its directedness to the end.
>
> But there are some habits that, even from the point of view of the subject in which they are present, primarily and principally imply directedness to an act. For habit primarily and of itself implies a relation to the nature of a thing. If, then, the nature of the thing in which the habit is present consists in the very directedness to act, it will follow that habit principally implies directedness to an act. Now it is clear that the nature and essence of a power is such as to be the principle of an act. Hence every habit which belongs to a power as its subject primarily implies directedness to an act.

Thus SAINT THOMAS. Again, in q.50, a.1, ad 3, he speaks as follows:

> A balancing of passible qualities in agreement with a nature possesses the nature of a disposition. Hence, when an alteration occurs in the passible qualities hot, cold, moist and dry, there does occur, as a result, an alteration with respect to sickness and health. But alteration does not, primarily {303} and of itself, occur with respect to these habits and dispositions.

Thus SAINT THOMAS. From these texts it is clear that bodily habits, which cause a disposition in relation to first actuality, do possess the nature of a good or bad habit according as they agree or disagree with their subject; and that the same quality, through its intension or remission, can be now in agreement with its subject and later in disagreement with it, so that the quality that was at first a virtue can cease to be a virtue and begin to be a vice. Nevertheless, such bodily habits do not properly possess the nature of habit, and consequently do not properly possess the essence of virtue. SAINT THOMAS shows that they do not properly possess the essence of habit in the same text, q.50, a.1, where he speaks as follows:

> If we speak of the disposition of a subject in relation to a form, a habitual disposition can be present in a body, which is related to the soul as is a subject to a form, and thus health, beauty, and the like are called habitual dispositions. They do not, however, possess the nature of habits perfectly, because their causes are by nature easily altered.

Thus SAINT THOMAS. Again, in q.55, a.2, he speaks as follows:

> Human virtue, of which we are speaking, cannot pertain to a body, but only to what belongs to the soul. Hence human virtue implies directedness not to being, but rather to acting.

Thus SAINT THOMAS.

II. To the Arguments of Others [*p. 12*] In response to the *first* argument we say that the division that it provides is insufficient. For ARISTOTLE proves that "neither justice nor virtue is moved" not by the fact that virtue is formally "directed to something" and is a relative form; nor by the fact that virtue provides the basis for a relation; but rather by saying that virtue, in its nature, is principally something absolute and secondarily a relation (as we earlier mentioned SAINT THOMAS says in *In 7 Phys.*), and also by the fact that alteration in such habits presupposes some prior alteration. Hence SAINT THOMAS, in I–II, q.52, a.1, ad 3, speaks as follows:

> Alteration is first present in qualities of the third kind. But there can be alteration subsequently in qualities of the first kind: for when an alteration with respect to hot and cold has occurred, it follows that the animal is altered with respect to health and sickness; similarly, when an alteration with respect to the passions of the sensitive appetite, or with respect to the sensitive powers, has occurred, there follows an alteration with respect to the sciences and the virtues, as is said in *Physics* 7.

Thus SAINT THOMAS. And he makes the same point more explicitly in q.53, a.3.

In response to the *second* argument we say that some habits are directly and in a principal way required for the substance of an act, as has often been said concerning the intelligible species without which the possible intellect cannot produce any act. Some habits, however, although they are not directly and in a principal way required for the substance of the act, but only for the manner of the act, nevertheless do contribute to causing the very substance of the act, and also intensify the act, as was said before in response to the arguments of DURANDUS. But a pure relation, which cannot be either a principle or a terminus of motion, can cause no such thing.

In response to the *third* argument we say that although some habits are caused by immanent acts of intellect and will, nevertheless the first active principle of such acts differs from the passive principle, as SAINT THOMAS shows in I–II, q.51, a.2, where he speaks as follows:

> Sometimes there is present in the agent only the active principle of its act, as there is present in fire only the active principle of heating. A habit cannot be caused in such an agent by the agent's own act, and hence natural things cannot become accustomed or unaccustomed to anything, as is said in *Ethics* 2. But there is a kind of agent in which both the active and the passive principles of its act are present, as is clear in the case of human acts: for acts of the appetitive power proceed from the appetitive power according as it is moved by the apprehensive power, which represents an object; moreover, the intellective power, inasmuch as it reasons about conclusions, has as an active principle a proposition known per se. Hence, some habits can be caused in some agents by acts of this kind, not with respect to the first active principle, but with respect to the act's principle that is a moved mover. For everything which is affected and moved by another is disposed by the act of the agent. Hence, by repeated acts there is generated in the moved power a quality called a habit. For example, the habits of the moral virtues are caused in the appetitive powers according as the latter are moved by reason; and the habits of the sciences are caused in the intellect according as the latter is moved by first principles.

Thus SAINT THOMAS. From this text it is clear that absolute forms, and not merely relations, can be caused by acts of intellect and will.

In response to the *fourth* argument we reply by denying the major premise. For some positive destructive agent concurs in the destruction of habits of the intellect, the will, or the sense-appetite, as SAINT THOMAS shows in q.53, aa.1 and 3. For in a.1 he speaks as follows:

> A form is said to be of itself destroyed by its contrary, but accidentally destroyed through the destruction of its subject. If, then, there is a habit whose subject is destructible and whose cause has a contrary, it can be destroyed in either way, as is clear in the case of bodily habits such as health and sickness. But habits whose subject is indestructible cannot be accidentally destroyed. However, there are some habits which, even though they are present primarily **{304}** in an indestructible subject, are nevertheless present secondarily in a destructible subject; for example, the habit of science is present primarily in the possible intellect, but secondarily in the powers of sensitive apprehension, and hence it cannot be accidentally destroyed from the side of the possible intellect, but only from the side of the lower sensitive powers. We must, then, consider whether such habits can of themselves be destroyed.
>
> If there is a habit which has a contrary, whether for its own part or on

> the part of its cause, it can of itself be destroyed; but if a habit does not have a contrary, it cannot of itself be destroyed. Now it is clear that an intelligible species existing in the possible intellect has no contrary; nor again can there be a contrary to the agent intellect that is cause of the intelligible species. Hence, if there is a habit present in the possible intellect that is immediately caused by the agent intellect, it is not, either of itself or accidentally, destructible. Now such are the habits of speculative and practical first principles, which cannot be destroyed by any forgetfulness or error, just as THE PHILOSOPHER says of prudence in *Ethics* 6 that it is not lost through forgetfulness.
>
> But there is another habit in the possible intellect which is caused by reasoning, namely the habit concerning conclusions that is called science; and there can be a contrary of this habit's cause in two ways. In one way on the part of the propositions from which the reasoning proceeds: for, according to THE PHILOSOPHER in *De interpretatione* 2, the contrary of the statement "The good is good" is the one which says "The good is not good." In another way with respect to the process of reasoning, as a sophistical syllogism is opposed to a dialectical or demonstrative one; and hence it is clear that a habit of true opinion, or of science, can be destroyed through false reasoning, which is why THE PHILOSOPHER says that "error is the destruction of science."
>
> Now some virtues are intellectual and are present in reasoning itself, as is said in *Ethics* 6; the explanation of them is the same as that of science or opinion. Some virtues, namely the moral ones, are present in the appetitive part of the soul, and the explanation is the same concerning the opposite vices. Now the habits of the appetitive part are caused by reason naturally moving the appetitive part; hence a habit of virtue or of vice is destroyed by the judgment of reason moving in a contrary way, whether from ignorance or passion, or even choice.

Thus SAINT THOMAS. From this text it is clear that destruction of the virtues has a positive cause. Again, in a.3, SAINT THOMAS shows how cessation of an act only accidentally destroys a habit or virtue; for he speaks as follows:

> As is said in *Physics* 8, there are two ways in which something can be a mover: in one way of itself, that is, because it moves by reason of its own form, as fire causes heat; in another way accidentally, as when something removes an obstacle.
>
> It is in the latter way that cessation of an act causes destruction or diminution of a habit, inasmuch as the cessation removes the act that was hindering the causes that destroy or diminish the habit. For a habit is of it-

> self destroyed by a contrary agent. Hence, any habits whose contraries increase during a lapse of time, and should be removed by the act proceeding from the habit, are diminished or even totally removed by a long cessation of the act, as is clear in the case of science and virtue. For it is clear that a moral habit makes a man ready to choose the mean in his operations and passions. But when someone does not make use of his habit of virtue for moderating his operations or passions, many operations and passions of an unvirtuous manner must occur from the inclination of the sensitive appetite and of other things which move the sensitive appetite from without. Hence virtue is destroyed or diminished through cessation of the act.
>
> It is similar in the case of the intellectual habits by which a man is ready to judge rightly concerning what is imagined. For when a man ceases to make use of an intellectual habit, images arise that come from without and sometimes lead him to the contrary of judging rightly, so that unless these images are in some way removed or repressed by the frequent use of the intellectual habit, the man is made less apt for judging rightly, and sometimes is entirely disposed to the contrary of judging rightly. Hence, intellectual habit is diminished or destroyed by cessation of the act.

Thus SAINT THOMAS.

In response to the *fifth* argument we say that both the major and the minor premises are false. On this point SAINT THOMAS, in I–II, q.50, a.3, ad 2, speaks as follows:

> The sensitive powers in brute animals do not operate by the command of reason; rather, if left to themselves, brute animals operate by an instinct of nature; thus there are in them no habits directed to operations, although there are in them certain dispositions directed to their nature, such as health and beauty. But because human reason disposes brute animals to act in one way or another by accustoming them, habits in a way can be posited in brute animals. Hence AUGUSTINE says in *The Book of 83 Questions* that "we see the most enormous beasts abstain from the greatest pleasures from fear of pain, and when this {305} becomes customary with them, we call them 'tame' and 'gentle.'" However, the nature of habit, with respect to the will's act of exercising habit, is missing in the brutes, because they do not have mastery over the exercise or non-exercise, and so, properly speaking, habits cannot be present in them.

Thus SAINT THOMAS. From this text it is clear, first, that the case of the irrational powers and that of the rational ones are not similar; and second, that in brutes governed by human reason customary dispositions can be caused that are true absolute forms belonging to the first kind of quality, and can in a way be called "habits" and not merely "relations."

In response to the *sixth and seventh* arguments we reply just as we did to the first argument of AUREOLUS. For they conclude that virtue includes a relation in its nature, and we concede this, but not that virtue is a pure relation. All this is conceded.

III. To the Arguments of Others AUREOLUS responds very well to the third group of arguments brought against the second conclusion [p. 14] in his *Quodlibetal Questions,* q.11, a.2, where, having set forth many premises, he finally concludes as follows:

> Virtue is not a relation of agreement, nor essentially a relation at all, as some have thought; nor is it an absolute quality prescinded from a relation, as others have said; nor is it an essence constituted out of an absolute quality and the relation mentioned, as others have thought: rather, it is a quality and essence united to the relation mentioned. Now a union made up out of a quality and a relation is necessarily different from a quality united to a relation. For the former is not in a category, and is an accidental being, and is neither the quality nor the relation, but something constituted out of both. The latter, however, is in a category, is not an accidental being, and is, precisely, a quality, although it is not prescinded from, but rather joined to something else. For the term "precisely," taken syncategorematically, is different from the term "prescinded from," taken categorically. For that which is a quality, and nothing more, is "precisely" the quality; but such is a quality united to a relation, for it is a quality, and nothing more, because it is not the relation to which it is united, nor is it anything but the quality; it is, therefore, "precisely" an absolute quality. However, it is not "prescinded," because a quality united to a relation is not a "prescinded" but rather a united quality, and it would be a contradiction to say that it is a quality simultaneously "prescinded" and united.
>
> The above-mentioned persons, then, were unaware that, in addition to a pure relation, something purely absolute, and something constituted out of something absolute and a relation, there is a fourth possibility, namely something absolute united to a relation. But THE PHILOSOPHER makes this clear. For everything which is "a relative in speech" *(relativum secundum dici),* whether it be a substance or a quality, is like this. For it is "precisely" in the category of substance or that of quality, but it is not a substance or a quality "prescinded" from a relation, but rather one united to it, and by reason of this union, such a substance or quality cannot be understood or signi-

> fied as being apart from the relation; for this reason it is a relative in speech, and is spoken of with reference to something correlative to it, as "hand" is spoken of with reference to something handled and "knowledge" with reference to something knowable. All this is made clear in the *Categories*.
>
> Virtue, accordingly, inasmuch as it is something befitting, is a quality which befits the nature in which it resides. But "virtue" is not, concretely, "what is made befitting" or "what befits," because then it would be an accidental being; for example, whiteness in a tooth is beauty because it is befitting, not because beauty is something constituted out of whiteness and beauty.

Thus AUREOLUS, who speaks well throughout this text, except in that he posits no relation in the nature of virtue apart from the agreement of the quality with its subject, making no mention of the virtue's directedness to an end or an act. In this respect his remarks are insufficient, as is clear from the above solution of the second argument against the second conclusion. For the rest, however, his remarks can stand.

Having set forth these premises, in response to the *first* argument we say, following the same AUREOLUS:

> A thing can be understood to involve two categories in two ways: first, in the way in which what is constituted as a union out of two categories, such as "snub," "father," etc., and all concrete accidents; second, in the way in which one category is united to another, as "snubness" is united to "nose," and a category of relation is united to a term belonging to another category.
>
> In the first sense, the major premise is true, because what involves two categories, such as "snub," is an accidental being; but the minor premise is false, because virtue does not include two categories in this way. In the second sense, however, the major premise is false, for "snubness," and every relation, would be accidental beings, and thus would not belong to a category; but in this sense the minor premise is true.
>
> And when the opponent says that what involves one category directly and another indirectly seems to be no less an accidental being than if it included both directly, this is completely false: for in the latter case one would be speaking of something constituted out of two things, whereas in the former case one is speaking of "precisely" one category, although it is not "prescinded," but a category united to another; and the relation expresses this union indirectly.

Thus AUREOLUS, who speaks well here.

In response to the *second* argument AUREOLUS speaks as follows:

It proceeds from something insufficient: for the essence of virtue does not consist in something absolute taken "precisely," whether in whole or in part or in any manner; rather, it consists in something absolute united to a relation. For although the essence of virtue is something "purely" absolute *(absolutum pure),* since it is something absolute and nothing more, it is not, nevertheless, a "pure" absolute something *(absolutum purum),* but a united one. For example: "snubness" is {306} "purely" and "precisely" a quality; but it is not "pure" and "prescinded," but rather united with a substance, namely a nose. Thus, the form of the argument commits the fallacy of figure of speech by changing a "how" *(qualiter)* into a "what kind" *(qualem),* as well as the fallacy of the consequent by arguing from an insufficient premise.

When it is concluded that a relation partially belongs to and is included in the essence of virtue, we must respond that the relation is in no way a part of the essence, but is rather a term united to it, just as neither is the subject a part of the quality united to it: for a nose is not a part of the essence of snubness, but a term united to it.

From this it is clear how the first and the third kinds of quality differ essentially, although the same absolute thing can be found in both: thus, whiteness can be an essence in the first kind of quality; this essence as united to a relation of likeness is in the second kind of quality; but this essence in the third kind of quality is prescinded and not united to something. Now it is obvious that an essence united to something and one not so united are diverse, and are of different natures and diverse in mode. Hence SIMPLICIUS says that it is possible for the same thing to be referred to different categories if we reduce an individual thing either to diverse objects of signification, or to different concepts, or to diverse characteristics.

From the same conclusion it is evident that virtue and vice differ essentially, because the essence of each is united to something different, that of virtue to a relation of fittingness, and that of vice to a relation of unfittingness. Now it is impossible that essences united to contraries be the same essence; rather, they must be contraries.

Nor does the following form of argument hold: "Whiteness is beauty in a tooth, but deformity in the pupil of an eye, and yet it is essentially the same; therefore beauty and deformity are essentially the same." For the major premise is false if whiteness is taken in itself, prescinding from the relation. But if whiteness is taken as united to the relation, then the major premise is true, but the minor premise—namely that the whiteness united to the fittingness and the whiteness united to the unfittingness are, as united and under the aspect of being united, the same essence—is false. Hence, one would conclude rather the opposite, arguing as follows: "Whiteness, not as

> whiteness, but as whiteness united to the relation of fittingness, is beauty in a tooth; whiteness, not as whiteness, but as whiteness united to the relation of unfittingness, is deformity in a pupil; but as united to the former and to the latter, it is not the same essence, although the whiteness is the same; therefore, beauty and deformity are never the same." The minor premise is proved as follows: to be united to this and to be united to that are not the same being-united; therefore, an essence united both to this and and to that is not the same united-essence in both cases, arguing *per locum* from the things to which it is united.
>
> From the foregoing it is clear that the absolute something that is the same with respect to its absolute specific nature is not a virtue in one man and a vice in another, the opposite of which was assumed. Rather, according to its specific nature, it is neither a virtue nor a vice, and it is not in the first species of quality, but in the third. But according as it is united to this or that relation, it is a virtue or a vice; as such, however, it does happen to be one kind of absolute specific nature or the other: because whatever it is, while it is united to the one relation it will be a vice, and if it is united to the other, it will be a virtue.

Thus AUREOLUS, who speaks well enough as far as the facts are concerned, although his logic does not seem to be very strong. For he says that this form of argument is invalid: "Whiteness is beauty in a tooth and deformity in a pupil, and this whiteness is essentially the same; therefore, beauty and deformity are essentially the same"; but this form of argument certainly *is* valid for concluding, from the demonstration that the whiteness is numerically the same, that beauty and deformity are numerically the same; or, if the preliminary discussion demonstrates not that the whiteness is numerically, but only that it is specifically, the same, the same form of argument is valid for concluding that deformity and beauty are specifically the same essence.

Nor is the supplement or addition that he makes in the conclusion valid, because it argues with four terms; for the conclusion should contain only what was present in the premises.

But to the form of that argument we can say that the major and minor premises are never simultaneously true, although they may be true at successive times, if it is a case of a whiteness numerically the same. Hence it cannot be concluded that at the same time the same whiteness is beauty and deformity, although this perhaps might be conceded at successive times.

In response to the *third* argument AUREOLUS speaks as follows:

> To be united to a relation, or to be in relation, or to provide the foundation of a relation in actuality, can be understood to add—beyond what is united, or is in relation, or provides the foundation of a relation in actuality—an intermediary, whether real or conceptual *(secundum rem vel secundum rationem),* between what is absolute and the relation, or between what is absolute and an extrinsic term, namely the one to which it is united.
>
> If this is taken in the first sense <i.e. such that a real intermediary is added>, this is false, and sets up an infinite regress. If it is taken in the second sense <i.e. such that a conceptual intermediary is added>, then it is true. Consider the example of snubness.
>
> Being-united, then, will be said to be present in or absent from that which is united, merely by the presence or absence of the relation to which it is united, and not because there is some intermediary which possesses presence or absence. The prepositions "in" and "together with," and the expression "to be a foundation in actuality," do not express a prescinded foundation, nor a foundation only, nor an intermediary: rather, they express a foundation intrinsically and a relation as an extrinsic term.
>
> And when the opponent adds in the minor premise that whatever involves two things, one of which can be present to or absent from the other, is an accidental being etc., this is true, if it involves as a third thing composed out of the two somethings such as **{307}** "the snubbed." But it is not true if <he is speaking of> one thing that is united and the other as the term to which it is united—unless the whole category of relation is accidental being, as are masculinity, femininity, and any qualities united to anything.

Thus AUREOLUS, who speaks well here.

In response to the *fourth* argument AUREOLUS speaks as follows:

> Either the relation of fittingness can be associated with what is absolute in a virtue, as it might be with whiteness itself insofar as it is whiteness; and thus the relation exists as an affection present in the virtue, which is its foundation and subject. Or the relation of fittingness can be associated with the very nature of a virtue, for instance with the essence of beauty, which consists in a being-united; and thus the relation is not an affection, but something pertaining to the essence—not as a part, but rather as a term, in the way that the term in a relation is something pertaining to the relation, as a nose is something pertaining to snubness. According to this second alternative, then, it is not necessary that one be able to understand virtue and vice apart from the relation; rather, this is impossible.
>
> When the opponent later argues that virtue has an essential difference

> because it differs from vice merely in the relation, and through the latter alone is altered and acquired, we say that something can be considered or distinguished by means of something else in two ways. In one way, by means of something intrinsic and formal, as "man" is distinguished by "rational." In another way by means of something extrinsic that is a term, as "snubness" is distinguished by "nose," a relation by its term, habits by their acts, and an act by its object. Now, to apply this to the argument: extrinsically virtue is distinguished from vice, as well as altered and acquired, by means of a relation that serves as its term; but intrinsically it is distinguished by its union with the relation. Hence, formally speaking, whiteness is not beauty, and whiteness differs intrinsically from deformity not by means of its fittingness, but rather by means of its union with fittingness; just as the concavity of the nose which is snubness differs from the concavity or curvedness of the leg which is bowleggedness not by means of the nose itself, but by means of the curvedness's union with the nose.
>
> When the opponent adds that what varies when there is a variation merely in the absolute extrinsic relation is itself either a pure relation or something constituted out of something absolute and a relation, we say that he omits the third member. There is the relation; that which is constituted out of the something absolute and the relation; and the something absolute united to the relation.

Thus AUREOLUS, who speaks well here, except that it would be better if he said that the union of the something absolute to the relation is an existence left over *(quoddam esse derelictum)* in the something absolute by the relation.

In response to the *fifth* argument AUREOLUS speaks as follows:

> "The white" *(album)* does not signify the subject indirectly and the quality directly, because otherwise it would never be predicated of a subject. Hence, just as it is not true to say "the nose is snubness," so it would not be true to say "the body is 'white'"; rather, one would speak of "'the white' of the body" as of "the snubness of the nose."
>
> Therefore, "the white" signifies something constituted out of a subject and an accident: but the accident, namely whiteness, is included actually and determinately in what is signified, while the subject is included only potentially and indeterminately. This is because it is not determined what the white thing is, whether it is a rock, or a man, or something else. It is also because what is actually and determinately signified is signified principally, for it is the reason why what is potentially and indeterminately signified is signified at all, as "the white" is anything in which "whiteness" is present. This is

> why THE COMMENTATOR says in *Metaphysics* 5 that "'the white' signifies primarily an accident and secondarily a subject." Similarly, this is also THE PHILOSOPHER'S understanding when he says that "the white" signifies quality alone, which is true with respect to what is determinate and actual.

Thus AUREOLUS, who speaks well here.

In response to the *sixth* argument AUREOLUS speaks as follows:

> Justice and friendship are qualities united to relations. Hence AUGUSTINE says in his *Categories* that "injustice is contrary to justice"; as is shown in what follows: "justice is a quality; therefore, injustice is a quality." Thus AUGUSTINE.
>
> Now justice and friendship are said to be more "toward another" than are the other virtues, because they are united to a relation to which the others are not united. For the other virtues are united to a relation of fittingness and propriety with respect to a man in himself, but friendship and justice to a relation of propriety belonging to one man in his being directed to another. For this reason, then, friendship is a virtue "toward another," but temperance a virtue "toward oneself."

Thus AUREOLUS, who speaks well here.

In response to the *seventh* argument AUREOLUS speaks as follows:

> Something absolute in a relation, or as united to a relation, is, in addition to the something absolute, something else which is not a part, but a term; but there is not for this reason some one thing constituted out of the two. For example: a relation together with its term is something more than the prescinded reality of the relation, and this something more is not nothing, although it is not a part, but a term.

Thus AUREOLUS, who speaks well here.

In response to the *eighth* argument AUREOLUS speaks as follows:

> We must say that, since "to signify" is "to form an understanding," as is said in *De interpretatione* 1, we must speak of what is signified with reference to the understanding. Now "snubness" is conceived by one simple act of understanding, an act which simultaneously covers "concavity" and "nose." But it covers "concavity" principally and directly, and "nose" as a term and indirectly. Therefore, "nose" is said to be "co-understood," with the "co-understanding" referring not to the act of understanding but to the object: for if it referred to the act of understanding, "nose" is not "co-understood," but "understood," since it is the same act of understanding which understands "nose" and "concavity." The being-signified is similar:

> for by the same signification the word "snubness" signifies both "concavity" and "nose," but, from the point of view of what is signified, does not signify both in the same way or in the same order. For {308} this reason, "nose" is said to be "consignified" as a term, while "concavity" is signified principally and directly. Accordingly, when it is asked whether a relation signifies in the way that "twice" signifies "half" or in the way that "twice half of twice" signifies "half," we must answer that the name and the expression signify the same thing, according to THE PHILOSOPHER in *Metaphysics* 7, but do so in different ways: for the expression does so explicitly, the name implicitly. Hence "snubness" implicitly says "nose," but "concavity of nose" says it explicitly. Accordingly, the difference is not trivial, as THE COMMENTATOR says in *Metaphysics* 7: "The name 'snubness' signifies 'nose' only as a container; hence when one explicitly says 'snubness of nose', there does not follow what is impossible here, namely triviality." In this way "virtue" signifies "relation."

Thus AUREOLUS, who speaks well here.

In response to the *ninth* argument AUREOLUS speaks as follows:

> There are two kinds of relation. One is the relation of active and passive principles, and qualities of the second kind, called "powers," are united to this kind of relation. The other is the relation of fittingness or unfittingness, and qualities of the first kind, called "habits," are united to this kind of relation.
>
> Now the latter kind of relations, inasmuch as they are directed to their foundations, possess a unique feature, namely that the foundations are united to them, and they get their names from the foundations. There are two reasons for this.
>
> *First*, because the qualities united to such relations denominate and qualify the substances underlying them in a special way, a way belonging to a nature that is different from the nature of other qualities: for these qualities denominate and qualify the substances with respect to "well or badly" and "having ability or debility," something which does not at all pertain to these qualities when they are taken as not united, and does not pertain to pure relations, which do not qualify or refer. Thus whiteness qualifies a tooth and makes it beautiful, inasmuch as it befits the tooth; but it makes a pupil deformed inasmuch as does not befit it. Absolutely taken, however, "whiteness" does not denominate a substance.
>
> *Second*, because such relations, by reason of the end, are in a way prior to their foundations. For these qualities have as their end one of two things: either, with respect to the first kind ("well or badly"), the nature to which

> they are adapted and for the sake of whose beauty they are brought about; or, with respect to the second kind ("having natural ability or debility"), second actuality and operation.

Thus AUREOLUS, who speaks well here, except that he says that the relation which is of the nature of virtue is only befittingness to a nature, which is not always true, unless we are speaking only of bodily virtues and habits.

In response to the *tenth* argument AUREOLUS speaks as follows:

> If the relation of fittingness exists in complete actuality outside the intellect, as many say, then the argument does not hold. However, if it does not, but rather there is only the ultimate necessity of such a relation outside the intellect, one which the intellect reduces to actuality, then the nature of virtue is united to the relation of fittingness not in actuality, but according to the ultimate necessity of such actuality. Hence virtue is something absolute underlying a relation, or providing the foundation of a relation, not according to complete actuality, but according to ultimate necessity.
>
> However, this ultimate necessity is not immediately present in God; God is not the foundation, but rather the term. For example, setting aside all acts of understanding, God is exemplar. He is so because "the aspect *(ratio)* of exemplar" signifies the divine essence united to a relation not in actuality—for the relation is purely a relation of reason—but according to ultimate necessity; the divine essence is united to the relation not as a foundation, but rather as the term of the creature's ability to imitate.

Thus AUREOLUS, and this conforms well enough to what SAINT THOMAS says in *Questions on Truth,* q.4, a.5, ad 1, where he distinguishes two kinds of relations, some called "actual" and some "habitual":

> A relation is called "habitual" that does not require a creature to simultaneously exist in actuality. Such are all relations which follow upon acts of the soul, because there can be will and intellect even of what is not actually existent.

Thus SAINT THOMAS. And he gives as an example the relation implied in the name "Word," which implies an eternal relation to creatures. Thus it can be said that, since the names "virtue" and "power," which are said of God, imply a relation to an act or effect, whether it exists or not, such a relation of being to non-being cannot be a real or "actual" relation, but must be a relation of reason or "habitual" relation.

Now when the opponent says that the whole nature of virtue is outside the intellect, etc.—we answer that this is true with respect to what "virtue" principally and directly signifies, but not with respect to what it secondarily and indirectly speaks of. On this point SAINT THOMAS, in *Questions on Truth*, q.4, a.5, speaks as follows:

> Among relative names we find that some, such as "likeness," are given to signify the relations themselves; some, however, are given to signify something from which the relation follows, as the name "knowledge" is given to signify a quality from which a relation follows. Now it may happen that something absolute can have a relation to many things, and hence the name given to signify the absolute thing from which a relation follows can be used in a relative way with reference to many things. Thus "knowledge" as knowledge is used in relation to what is knowable; but as an accident or form, it refers to the knower.

Thus SAINT THOMAS. Again, in *In 3 Sent.*, d.33, q.1, a.2, qla.4, ad 4, he distinguishes between an "actual" relation and an "original" relation, where he speaks as follows:

> Although the final end does not cause specific identity, it does cause {309} diversity in the way that diversity of genus causes diversity of species. However, it must be known that it is not an "actual" relation to the remote end which causes the above-mentioned difference, but an "original" relation to it, namely inasmuch as from diversity in the end there follow diverse proportions to the end in acts and habits.

Thus SAINT THOMAS.

To the argument on the negative side of the question [p. 1], SAINT THOMAS responds in *ST* I–II, q.49, a.4, ad 2, where he speaks as follows:

> Sometimes a power is related to many things, and hence must be determined by something else. If, however, there were a power not related to many things, it would not need a determining habit. For this reason, natural powers do not perform their actions by means of habits, because they are of themselves determined to one thing.

Thus SAINT THOMAS.

This suffices for the question.

Blessed be God.

Amen.

Q.II (on d.24)

Whether Faith Is a Virtue Infused by God

In relation to the twenty-fourth distinction of the third book of *The Sentences,* the question is raised: Whether faith is a virtue infused by God.

It is argued that it is not, as follows. An infused virtue is more perfect than an acquired one; but acquired faith, on account of its imperfection, is not counted among the acquired intellectual virtues, as is clear from THE PHILOSOPHER in *Ethics* 6; therefore, much less can it be counted as an infused virtue.

Argument is made for the opposite conclusion as follows. It is said in *Ephesians* 2 that "by grace you are saved through faith, and not of yourselves, so that no-one should glory; for the gift is God's."

In this question there will be three articles: in the first the conclusions will be presented, in the second the objections, and in the third the solutions.

Article I: Conclusions

First Conclusion: Faith Is a Virtue

SAINT THOMAS presents this conclusion in *ST* II–II, q.4, a.5, where he speaks as follows:

> Human virtue is that through which a human act is made good. Hence, any habit which is of itself a principle of a good act can be called a human virtue. But formed faith is a habit of this kind. For, since to believe is an act of the intellect assenting by command of the will, two things are required in order for this act to be perfect: one is that the intellect infallibly intend its good, which is the true; the other

> is that the will be infallibly directed to its ultimate end, which is that for the sake of which one assents to the true. Now both of these are found in the act of formed faith: for by the nature of faith itself the intellect is always brought to the true, since the false cannot come under faith; and by charity, inasmuch as it forms faith, the soul is so disposed that the will is infallibly directed to the good. Therefore formed faith is a virtue.
>
> Unformed faith, however, is not a virtue, because even if the act of unformed faith has the required perfection on the side of the intellect, it does not have the required perfection on the side of the will. Similarly, if temperance were present in the concupiscible power and prudence were not present in the rational power, temperance would not be a virtue: because for an act of temperance there is required both an act of reason and an act of the concupiscible power, just as for an act of faith there is required both an act of the intellect and an act of the will.

Thus SAINT THOMAS. From this text one can argue as follows: every habit that is always a principle of a good human act is a virtue; but formed faith is such; therefore, etc.

Second Conclusion: Formed Faith, and Unformed Faith As Well, Are Infused into Man by God

SAINT THOMAS proves this conclusion in *ST* II–II, q.6, a.1, where he speaks as follows:

> Two things are required for faith: one is that the objects of belief be proposed to man, which is required in order that he believe something explicitly; the other thing required for faith is the assent of the believer to the things proposed.
>
> With respect to the first of these, it is necessary that faith be from God: for the things which pertain to faith exceed human reason, and hence they do not fall under human contemplation unless God reveals them. But to some they are immediately revealed by God, as they were revealed to the Apostles and the Prophets; while to others they are proposed by God's sending preachers of faith, in keeping with *Romans* 10: "How will they preach if they are not sent?"
>
> With respect to the second requirement, namely the assent of man to the things of faith, two causes can be considered. One is external inducement, such as a miracle seen or the persuasiveness of a man who leads one to faith. Neither of these is a sufficient cause: for among those who see one and the same miracle, and among those who hear the same preaching, some

> believe and some do not believe. {310} Therefore it is necessary to posit another, interior cause, which moves a man inwardly to assent to the things of faith. Now the Pelagians held this cause to be merely the man's free choice. For this reason they said that the beginning of faith comes from ourselves, inasmuch as it is from ourselves that we are prepared to assent to the things of faith; but that the confirmation of faith comes from God, by Whom the things which we must believe are proposed to us. But this is false, because, since a man in assenting to the things of faith is raised above his nature, this must occur in him by a supernatural principle moving inwardly, namely God. Therefore faith, with respect to the assent which is the principal act of faith, comes from God moving inwardly through grace.

Thus SAINT THOMAS. From this text the following argument can be formulated: that habit is infused in man by God through whose act man is elevated above his nature; but faith is such; therefore, etc.

Third Conclusion: No Man Who Stubbornly Disbelieves an Article of Faith Possesses the Habit of Infused Faith

SAINT THOMAS presents this conclusion in *ST* II–II, q.5, a.3, where he speaks as follows:

> A heretic who disbelieves one article of faith does not possess the habit of faith, whether formed or unformed. The reason for this is as follows. The species of any habit depends on the nature of its object, and when this is removed, the species of the habit cannot remain. Now the formal object of faith is the First Truth, according as it is manifested in the Sacred Scriptures and the doctrine of the Church, which proceed from the First Truth. Hence, whoever does not adhere, as to an infallible and divine rule, to the doctrine of the Church, which proceeds from the First Truth manifested in the Sacred Scriptures, does not possess the habit of faith, but rather holds what belongs to faith in a manner other than through faith; just as, if someone holds a conclusion in his mind without knowing the middle term of the demonstration, it is clear that he does not have scientific knowledge of the conclusion, but merely opinion. But it is clear that one who adheres to the doctrine of the Church as to an infallible rule assents to everything that the Church teaches; otherwise, if he holds what he wants to of the things that the Church teaches, and does not hold what he does not want to, he does not adhere to the doctrine of the Church as to an infallible rule, but rather adheres to his own will. Hence it is clear that the heretic who stubbornly disbelieves one article is not prepared to follow the doctrine of the Church in all

> things; if he does not do so stubbornly, he is not yet a heretic, but one who errs. Hence it is clear that such a heretic with respect to one article does not possess faith in the case of the other articles, but an opinion in keeping with his own will.

Thus SAINT THOMAS. From this text the following argument can be formulated: no-one who does not adhere to the doctrine of the Church as to an infallible rule possesses the habit of faith; but any heretic is such; therefore, etc.

Fourth Conclusion: Faith Is One Virtue, Not Many, and One Habit, Not Many Specifically Distinct Habits

SAINT THOMAS proves this conclusion in *ST* II–II, q.4, a.6, where he speaks as follows:

> If the term "faith" is taken for the habit, it can be considered in two ways. In one way, from the point of view of the object, and in this respect there is only one habit of faith; for the formal object of faith is the First Truth, by adhering to Which we believe whatever is included under faith. In another way, from the point of view of the subject, and in this respect faith is diversified according as it belongs to diverse subjects. For it is clear that faith, like any other habit, takes its species from the formal essence of its object, but is individuated by its subject. Hence, if "faith" is taken for the habit by which we believe, faith is specifically one but numerically different in diverse subjects; but if it is taken for that which is believed, again faith is one, because it is the same thing which is believed by all, and if there are diverse objects of belief which all believe in common, nevertheless they are all reducible to one.

Thus SAINT THOMAS. From this text the following argument can be formulated: that habit of virtue is one and not many which has one formal object, not many; but faith is such; therefore.

Here the first article terminates.

Article II: Objections

§1. Against the First Conclusion

Arguments of Durandus In the second article arguments are raised against the conclusions.

DURANDUS (d.23, q.6) argues against the first conclusion, arguing *first* that faith, however much formed by charity, is not properly speaking a virtue inasmuch as virtue is said to be a habit placing a power in the ultimate state of perfection required for its act; for in this way virtue is something ultimate in a power. Accordingly, he argues as follows.

> Every virtue properly so-called that perfects the intellect perfects it for an object that is seen either in itself or through analysis to something that is seen in itself: for in this consists the efficacy of the act of intellection, an efficacy that the virtue gives to the intellective power. But faith does not perfect the intellect for {311} an object that is seen either in itself or through analysis to something that is seen in itself. Therefore, it is not, properly and simply speaking, a virtue.

Second, he argues as follows:

> Faith is not more a virtue when charity is present to or existing in the will than when it is not so existing. For a habit that does not elicit a more perfect act is not more perfect. But faith does not elicit a more perfect act when charity exists in the will than when it does not so exist. For the act of faith, which is to assent to supernatural truth, is not more perfect with respect to anything pertaining to cognition of truth, which alone is the concern of the intellect that faith perfects—although it may be more perfect with respect to the aspect of merit, which is an extrinsic perfection, since it is the concern of charity, which perfects the will. Therefore, faith is no more or less a virtue when charity exists in the will than when it does not so exist.

Third, he argues as follows:

> The case of faith and charity is not similar to that of prudence and moral virtue. For prudence cannot be acquired without moral virtue, nor moral virtue without prudence. And because both are acquired by acts, an act of either gets its perfection from what is joined to it, so that it is impossible for an act of prudence to be perfect unless moral virtue is present in the appetite, and impossible for an act of moral virtue to be perfect unless prudence is present in the intellect. But faith as a habit does not depend on charity, since it is prior in the order of nature; and faith in its act does not receive any perfection from charity. Hence faith can possess the nature of virtue equally when charity does not exist in the will and when it does so exist: for although the will does incline the intellect to believe, the will need not be informed by charity.

Thus DURANDUS argues in form.

§2. Against the Second Conclusion

I. Arguments of Scotus SCOTUS (d.23, q.1) argues against the second conclusion by arguing that no other, infused faith is required besides acquired faith.

First, as follows.

> In the first one to whom the articles were revealed, as in the case of SAINT PAUL, acquired faith was sufficient for him firmly to adhere to them: for AUGUSTINE, in commenting on *Psalm* 71, 3, would have "The mountains bring peace to the people, etc.," mean that those who are lower are illuminated by those who are higher, and they are not more illuminated than are the higher ones who illuminate.
>
> The inference is clear; but the antecedent is proved as follows.
>
> By purely natural means, one can assent that the one who asserts and reveals such articles is truthful, because by purely natural means one knows and gives assent that God is more truthful than all men; and SAINT PAUL could have known and given assent to this. Thus, through a faith acquired by purely natural means one person could firmly and without hesitation assent to everything revealed by God, and consequently so could anyone else. Therefore, no other faith is necessarily required for assent beyond acquired faith.

Second, he argues as follows.

> Although a science such as geometry might not, on account of the difficulty which it contains, be able to be known by a man through his own discovery and by his own natural light; nevertheless, once it has been discovered and taught in an orderly way, a man can acquire and know it by purely natural means. Similarly, therefore, although no-one could, by the natural light of his intellect and through his own investigation, come to the knowledge that "God is three and one"; nevertheless, once it has been revealed to one man, another could, through the speech of the one to whom it was revealed, firmly adhere to the proposition by acquired faith.

Third, he argues as follows:

> "If infused faith is posited, it will be more certain than acquired faith, because otherwise it would be posited in vain." But that it is in fact less certain is proved as follows. A conclusion is less certain than a premise, because the whole certitude of the conclusion comes from the certitude of the premise. Now I assent to the proposition "God is three and one" by means of infused faith, if the latter is posited, because it has been revealed by God. But I be-

> lieve that it has been revealed by God because John, or another apostle, said that it had been revealed to him. But if I heard him say that this had been revealed to him, I would believe him with an acquired faith, believing that he is truthful and would be unwilling to assert anything false. So, too, I now believe that "that God is three and one has been revealed to the apostle" with an acquired faith, from hearing the Scriptures or from reading the Scriptures myself. Therefore, the whole firmness which you now place in faith comes from acquired faith. Therefore, an infused faith should not be posited.

Thus SCOTUS.

II. Arguments of Aureolus AUREOLUS also argues against the second conclusion, arguing *first* as follows:

> Infused faith is not required on account of the supernaturalness of the object of faith. For either the supernaturalness of that object is understood in terms of indifference to true and false, so that the object of faith is of such a kind that it is not evident whether it is true or false, just as it is not evident whether the sands of the sea are even-numbered or odd-numbered; or the supernaturalness is understood in terms of inconsistence with evidence, as "that God is three and one" is said to be inconsistent with what is evidently true. But a supernatural habit is not required by either of these ways of understanding: not by the first way, because a man can, naturally speaking, most firmly adhere to this kind of indifferent object without a supernatural habit; and not by the second way, for a man sometimes most firmly adheres to things contrary to first principles, either on account of a badly drawn syllogism, or on account of a custom or a natural disposition in him, one caused by his imagination.
>
> And if you say that the truths of faith are about God, Who is a supernatural object and cannot naturally {312} be understood by us—this is invalid, because we can understand many things about God from things sensed, and we can hold firmly to many other things about Him from things not sensed. This is evident in the case of heretics: for a heretic who errs in one article of faith loses his infused faith, and nevertheless holds the other articles so firmly that he is willing to be beheaded for them. It is also evident in the case of the unbaptized boy raised among believers, who holds many things of faith as firmly as does someone who has been baptized and has infused faith.

Again, he argues as follows:

> Infused faith is indeed necessary to the one who reveals the things of faith. But if he reveals them by chance, or on purpose, but by natural means, he is not to be believed, and what he says is not to be adhered to: for he cannot

> reveal them with certainty unless he holds them through a higher cause and by means of an infused supernatural habit. But an infused supernatural habit is not necessary to the one who believes what the one who does the revealing says.

Thus AUREOLUS argues in form.

§3. Against the Third Conclusion

Arguments of Durandus DURANDUS (d.23, q.9) argues against the third conclusion by arguing that infused faith remains in heretics with respect to the articles in which they do not err. *First* as follows:

> Every habit renders a power apt for the act required in relation to an object, and consequently for avoiding or repressing what is contrary. However, if what is contrary is not avoided, the habit is not for this reason entirely removed, because even if one posits aptitude and readiness for the required act, and for avoiding what is contrary, one does not posit that the contrary necessarily cannot occur. This is clear in the case of acquired habits, and the foregoing argument concerns them as much as it does infused faith.

Second, as follows:

> He who now assents to objects of belief in a way similar to the way he did before now possesses faith in a way similar to the way he did before, because similar assent argues for a similar habit. But a believer recently led astray concerning some object of belief—whether through his own ignorance, for instance, because he has not understood Sacred Scripture well, or through the false teaching of another, for example, the teaching that it is not permissible to swear—now assents to the other objects of belief in a similar, indeed an altogether similar, way as he did before. Therefore, he assents by the same habit by which he assented before. But before he possessed infused faith. Therefore, he does now as well. And nevertheless he is a heretic. Therefore, infused faith remains in the heretic.

Third, he argues as follows:

> Someone might pose the difficulty that if the objection were granted, it would seem to follow that one would be simultaneously a believer and an unbeliever. But this is not a difficulty, because faith as a habit can indeed co-exist with actual error concerning some object of belief, just as science as a habit can co-exist with actual error concerning some object of science. And if the habit were formed in someone that one must in no way swear, it could still co-exist with infused faith, because it would not be about the same object as

> the latter. For although the object of infused faith extends to everything contained in Sacred Scripture, still, faith itself could proceed to the act required in relation to some of these objects, although the intellect of the one possessing the infused faith might be deceived with respect to others. Similarly, one can possess true scientific knowledge concerning some properties of a certain subject, and be deceived concerning other properties of the same subject. Thus it does not seem improbable that the habit of faith can remain in heretics who have recently erred concerning some particular object of faith.

Thus DURANDUS.

§4. *Against the Fourth Conclusion*

I. Arguments of Scotus SCOTUS (*In 3 Sent.*, d.23, q.1) argues against the fourth conclusion that it is not the case that, just because faith considers all objects of belief as revealed by God, it follows that there is one faith concerning all objects of belief. *First*, as follows:

> If infused faith considers the First Truth as the revealer of the articles and as the one who causes assent to the objects of belief, but not as that with which faith is concerned as an object, it follows that the believer would never assent to the proposition "God is three and one." For, according to you, I assent to the proposition "God is three and one" because it has been revealed by the First Truth. I ask you, then, how do I assent to the proposition "This has been revealed by God"? For if I assent to the proposition "God is three and one" for this reason, namely "Because it has been revealed by God," as assenting to a conclusion because of a premise, it follows that I give greater assent to what stands as the premise than to what stands as the conclusion. If you answer, as you must, that <I assent> "Because it has been revealed that God is three and one," I further ask, how do I assent to the proposition "It has been revealed by God that it has been revealed that God is three and one"? If again, it is "Because it has been revealed," I shall proceed to infinity, and consequently I shall never believe anything firmly concerning the articles of faith, just as, if knowledge of conclusions were resolved into principles, and those principles into others, and so on to infinity, one would never know anything, and just as nothing can exist that essentially depends on an infinity of causes. If you say that I assent to the proposition "That God is three and one has been revealed by God" by acquired faith, I say to the contrary that then infused faith, in adhering to any article, depends in its being and firmness on acquired faith as on a premise; for you will not be able to say that it adheres to it through science, because the proposition "That God is three and one has been revealed by

> God" is no more evident from the terms than is the proposition "God is three and one."

Second, as follows:

> The formal essence of the object of a real habit {313} is not a relation, or a being of reason. But the proposition "It has been revealed by God that God is three and one" adds nothing beyond the proposition "God is three and one" except a relation of reason, just as "It is known that" adds only a relation of reason to the thing that is known. If, therefore, you assent to the above-mentioned article "Because it has been revealed by God," then the formal reason why you give assent through a real habit is a being of reason—which is inconsistent, since a real habit has a real formal object, just as a real power has a real object. This is evident. Therefore something which is capable of being revealed, in the passive sense, since it is a being of reason, cannot be the formal reason for believing [reading *credendi* for *tendendi*] in the proposition "God is three and one."

II. Arguments of Aureolus

AUREOLUS also argues against the fourth conclusion, arguing that the First Truth is not what is formal in the object of faith, precisely because faith adheres to anything by reason of the First Truth. *First,* as follows.

> It belongs to the essence *(ratio)* of a formal object that it not be reduced to a higher cause in the same science. But such is not the case in the conclusion proposed. For if it asked, "Why do you believe the articles of faith?" the response is given, "Because this is what the First Truth, Which cannot lie, says." It is further asked, "Why can It not lie?" and one must say "Because It is God." And thus reduction is made to another formal object, and the First Truth stands as the material object.

Second, as follows:

> Either it is by means of the First Truth that you understand what is said by the First Truth—which is not possible, because the truths that are the material object of faith are complex truths—or you understand some special attribute in God—and this cannot be said, because the attribute adds nothing to the divinity; or, if it does add something, then what it adds is not an end, and thus faith will not have the same thing for its formal object and for its end. Therefore it remains that the formal object is God under the aspect *(ratio)* of divinity, and not the First Truth.

Thus AUREOLUS.

Here the second article terminates.

Article III: Solutions

§1. To the Arguments Against the First Conclusion

To the Arguments of Durandus [*p. 55*] In the third article we must respond to the objections stated above.

In response to the arguments of DURANDUS against the first conclusion, we say *first* that SAINT THOMAS, in *In 3 Sent.*, d.23, q.2, a.4, qla.1, apparently takes the way that DURANDUS follows, namely that faith is not a virtue strictly speaking, but only broadly speaking. Nevertheless, it cannot definitively be proved from his own words that faith is not a virtue properly speaking, but only that it is not an intellectual virtue in the sense that philosophers speak of intellectual virtue. This is clear from his manner of speaking. For what he says is this:

> Given that it belongs to virtue to render an operation good, an operation can be called good in two ways: either formally, inasmuch as it proceeds from a power which is moved toward the good according to the essence *(ratio)* of the good; or materially, inasmuch as it is congruent and connatural with the power. Now the act of faith is good in both ways: for it is congruent with the intellect inasmuch as it is about what is true; and again, it proceeds from the will, which is moved toward the good as an object.
>
> Now from the point of view of the intellect, although there is goodness with respect to the object, there is not perfection, for the manner is deficient inasmuch as the intellect does not possess an evident truth to which it adheres. But from the point of view of the will, there can be perfection inasmuch as a will perfected in its desire for the good causes firmness and certitude in faith. This is why BERNARD says that faith is "a willing and certain foretaste of a truth not yet made plain."
>
> Hence it is clear that faith is not indeed an intellectual virtue, but a virtue in the sense in which we commonly speak of virtue, namely, as what produces a good act proceeding goodness of will. However, faith is not a moral virtue, because what it directs as its matter or object is not the sensitive appetite with respect to pleasures, pains and operations. Rather, it is a theological virtue, a kind of virtue which the philosophers did not know.

Thus SAINT THOMAS. Again, in a.3, qla.3, he speaks as follows:

> Since a virtue brings a power to completion *(in ultimo)* with respect to its act, it does not suffice for the essence *(ratio)* of virtue that the power be brought to completion with respect to its object. Rather, it must be brought to com-

> pletion with respect to the manner of acting, that is, in such a way that the act is good not only by the fact that the good is what is done, but also by the fact that it is done well, as is clear in the case of the moral virtues.
>
> Now the good of the intellect is the true, which is the intellect's end and perfection. Hence it does not suffice for the essence of intellectual virtue that by means of it the true be known; rather, the act by which the true is considered must also be perfect in its manner, which must be such that one understand well. Now the intellect's operating well does not come about by the operation proceeding from one's good will, but by the effectiveness of the intellect in seeing its proper object either in itself or by means of analysis to what the intellect does see in itself.
>
> Now faith, through its act, brings the intellect to completion in relation to its object, inasmuch as it causes the intellect to assent to the First Truth; but it does not bring the intellect to completion in relation to its own manner of understanding, because faith does not make our intellect so powerful as to be able of itself to see what it believes, or to reduce what it believes to what it can see. Hence faith is not **{314}** an intellectual virtue.

Thus SAINT THOMAS.

From these texts it is clear that DURANDUS constructed his opinion out of SAINT THOMAS's remarks in his commentary on the third book of *The Sentences;* and that SAINT THOMAS seems to support DURANDUS's opinion that faith is not a virtue properly speaking. But in fact he does not support it, because he does not assert that faith is not a virtue properly speaking, but only that it is not an intellectual virtue properly speaking because it does not place the power which it informs in a state of ultimate perfection in relation to its act. However, it can be called a virtue in a general and broad sense.

Second, we say that, even granting that SAINT THOMAS in his commentary on *The Sentences* was of such an opinion, nevertheless he later corrected that opinion in the *Summa,* as is evident in his proof of the conclusion, where, without qualification, he concedes that faith is a virtue; and again in *Questions on Truth,* q.14, a.3, obj.7, where he presents the following argument:

> A virtue is the completion *(ultimum)* of a power, as is said in *De caelo* 1. But faith is not the completion of a human power, because the latter is capable of something more, namely direct vision. Therefore faith is not a virtue.

This is the argument on which DURANDUS bases himself, and on which SAINT THOMAS seems to base himself in the third book of his *Sentences* commentary. The response is as follows:

> It must be said that faith is said to be the completion of a power in that it completes the power for choosing a good and meritorious act. But it is not required for the essence of virtue that by the virtue there be elicited the best act that can be elicited from the power; for it can happen that there are several virtues in the same power, one of which elicits a nobler act than does another, as, for instance, magnificence elicits a nobler act than does generosity.

Thus SAINT THOMAS.

From these texts the response to the *first* argument of DURANDUS is clear. But here it should be further noted that faith is in one respect more properly a virtue than is science. Thus SAINT THOMAS, in *Questions on Truth,* the text quoted above, a.3, ad 5, speaks as follows:

> In the sense in which we are speaking of virtue at present, neither science nor opinion can be called a virtue. Rather, only faith can be called a virtue, and faith, inasmuch as it pertains to the will—that is, inasmuch as it falls under the genus of virtue in the above-mentioned way—is not intermediary between science and opinion. For in science and opinion there is an inclination that comes not from the will, but from the reason alone.
>
> But if we were speaking of all these with respect to what pertains to knowledge alone, neither opinion nor faith, but only science, would be a virtue, since the other two do not possess complete knowledge.

Thus SAINT THOMAS.

From these texts it is clear that, although faith cannot properly be called a virtue according to the philosopher, it can still be called a virtue according to the theologian. This will be discussed more fully in the following response.

In response to the *second* argument we say that it answers itself, since it says that, when charity is present, the act of faith is not more perfect in knowledge *(in genere cognitionis),* although it is more perfect in merit *(in esse meriti).* Concerning this point SAINT THOMAS, in the text quoted above, speaks as follows:

> I say that "virtue"—as this name indicates—signifies completion of an active power. But there are two kinds of active power: one whose action terminates in something done externally, as the action of the building power terminates in something built; and one whose action does not terminate externally, but remains within the agent, as the act of sight remains in the one seeing. THE PHILOSOPHER maintains this in *Metaphysics* 9.
>
> Now "completion" is taken in different ways in the case of these two kinds of powers. For the acts of the first kind of power, as THE PHILOSO-

PHER says in the same place, are not in the doer, but in what is done; hence, in this case, the completion of the active power is taken to be in what is done. Thus, the virtue of what carries weights is said to consist in carrying the greatest weight, as is clear from *De celo* 1; and similarly the virtue of a builder consists in the fact that he makes the best house. But because the act of the other kind of power remains in the agent himself, and not in something done, the completion of this kind of power is taken with respect to the manner of acting, that is, inasmuch as something is done well and befittingly, from which the act of the power is said to be good. Hence it is that in the case of this kind of power, virtue is said to be that which makes the deed good.

Now the ultimate good that the philosopher considers is different from the one that the theologian considers. For the philosopher considers as good what is proportioned to human powers and consists in an act of man himself; hence the philosopher says that happiness is a certain operation. This is why, according to the philosopher, a good act, whose principle is called a virtue, is, absolutely speaking, called good inasmuch as it befits the power as perfecting it. Hence, the philosopher calls a virtue any habit he discovers that elicits such an act: whether the habit be in the intellective part, as are science, understanding, and similar intellectual virtues, whose act is the good of the power itself, namely consideration of the true; or whether the habit be in the affective part, as are temperance, fortitude, and the other moral virtues.

But the theologian considers as the ultimate good what exceeds the capacity of nature, namely eternal life. Hence he considers the good in human acts not to be absolute, because he places the end not there, but rather in the directing of these acts to the good that he does hold to be ultimate. He claims that only that act is completely good which is directed from the proximate to the final good, that is, which is meritorious of eternal life. He says that every such act is an act of virtue, and he calls a virtue any habit that elicits such an act.

Now no act can be called meritorious {315} except according as it is established in a power of the one who acts: for one who merits must offer something, and he can offer only what is in some way his own, that is, something of himself. But an act stands within our power according as it belongs to the will, whether as elicited by the will, as are loving and willing, or as commanded by the will, as are walking and talking. Hence, a virtue can be posited in relation to any such act, a virtue that elicits more perfect acts within the genus of all such acts.

Now belief gets its assent only by a command of the will; hence, accord-

> ing to what it is, it depends on the will. This is why belief itself can be meritorious, and why faith, which is the habit that elicits belief, is, according to the theologian, a virtue.

Thus SAINT THOMAS.

From these texts it is clear that although, according to the philosopher, an act is called virtuous only inasmuch as it is proportioned to human powers, and an act is more perfectly an act of virtue inasmuch as it is thus proportioned; nevertheless, according to the theologian, a human act can be called virtuous even though it is not proportioned in that way, that is, as bringing a power to its state of completion, as long as it is proportioned to the ultimate supernatural end. But the act of faith possesses this latter proportion if charity is present, and does not possess it if charity is not present. Consequently, formed faith more fully possesses the essence of virtue than does unformed faith.

In response to the *third* argument we say that it assumes something manifestly false, namely that the act of faith receives no perfection from charity. In this regard SAINT THOMAS, in *Questions on Truth,* q.14, a.2, ad 10, speaks as follows:

> The act of faith essentially consists in knowledge; and in this consists its perfection as regards the form or species which it gets from its object. But as regards its end, it is perfected in affection, because it gets its meritoriousness from charity.

Thus SAINT THOMAS.

Again, it is amazing that the opponent says that faith possesses the essence of virtue equally when charity is present and when it is absent, since AUGUSTINE expressly says, in *Contra Julianum,* that without charity there is no true virtue. And concerning this point SAINT THOMAS, in *ST* II–II, q.23, a.7, speaks as follows:

> Virtue is directed to the good. But the good is principally the end: for those things which are for the sake of an end are called good only in their being directed to the end. Now inasmuch as there is a twofold end, one ultimate and the other proximate, so too there is a twofold good, one ultimate and principal, the other proximate and particular.
>
> Now the ultimate and principal good of man is the enjoyment of God, according to the *Psalm:* "It is good for me to adhere to God"; and man is directed to this end by charity. But the secondary and particular good of man can be twofold: one is truly good, capable, in itself, of being directed to the

> principal good that is the ultimate end; the other is an apparent, not true, good that leads away from the final good.
>
> Accordingly, it is clear that true virtue, simply speaking, is virtue that directs to the principal good of man, just as THE PHILOSOPHER also says in *Physics* 7 that "virtue is the disposition of the perfect to the best." Thus there can be no true virtue without charity. But if virtue is taken according as it consists in a directing to a particular end, then there can be said to be a true virtue without charity, inasmuch as the virtue is directed to some particular end. But if that particular good is not a true good but an apparent one, the virtue that is directed to this good is not true virtue but a false likeness of virtue: for instance, the prudence of the avaricious, which thinks up different kinds of hiding places, is not true virtue; nor is the justice of the avaricious, by which, for fear of heavy losses, they do not respect what belongs to others; nor is the temperance of the avaricious, which restrains the appetite for luxury that is too costly; nor is the fortitude of the avaricious, by which, as HORACE—according to AUGUSTINE in *Contra Julianum* 4—says, "They flee poverty through the sea, through stones, through fire." But if a particular good is a true good, for instance the preservation of a republic or something of this kind, there will certainly be true virtue, although it will be imperfect unless it is referred to the end and perfect good. And in this respect, there cannot be true virtue simply speaking without charity.

Thus SAINT THOMAS. Again, in *ST* I–II, q.65, a.4, he speaks as follows:

> Faith and hope, like the moral virtues, can be considered in two ways: in one way with respect to the initial stage, and in another with respect to the perfect being of virtue. For since virtue is directed to a good deed to be done, it will be called perfect virtue in being capable of a deed which is perfectly good. A deed is perfectly good when what is done is not only good, but also done well; otherwise, if what is done is good but not done well, it will not be perfectly good; hence neither will the habit which is the principle of this act possess the essence of virtue perfectly. For instance, if someone does just things, he does what is good; but there will not be a perfect act of virtue unless he does this well, that is, according to right choice, which is made by prudence; hence, justice without prudence cannot be a perfect virtue.
>
> Accordingly, faith and hope can in a way exist without charity, but they do not possess the essence of perfect virtue without charity. For since the act of faith is to believe in God, and to believe is to give assent to someone with one's own will, accordingly, if one does not will in due measure, there will not be a perfect act of faith. But to will in due measure comes from charity, which perfects the will: **{316}** for every right movement of the will proceeds

> from right love, as AUGUSTINE says in *The City of God* 14. Therefore, faith does exist without charity, but not as a perfect virtue, just as temperance or fortitude exist without prudence.
>
> Hope must be spoken of in the same way. For the act of hope is to look for future blessedness from God, and this is a perfect act if it occurs on the basis of the merits that one possesses, which cannot exist without charity. But if one looks for blessedness on the basis of merits that he does not yet possess, but proposes to acquire in the future, it will be an imperfect act; and this can exist without charity.
>
> Therefore faith and hope can exist without charity, but without charity they cannot be, properly speaking, virtues: for it pertains to the essence of virtue that by it something good not only be done, but be done well, as is said in *Ethics* 2.

Thus SAINT THOMAS.

From these texts it is clear that the act of faith gets perfection, its greatest perfection, from the presence of charity, especially when it takes place not only with charity, but out of charity, because then it is directed to the ultimate end, and to seeing the First Truth as it is in itself. Hence, according to all Catholic doctors, faith without charity is said to be "unformed," because the act of faith is directed by charity to the First Truth as to the ultimate end, and that directedness is related to the act of faith as form of the latter; similarly, the end of the act is its form—not its intrinsic, but its extrinsic form. Concerning this point SAINT THOMAS speaks in *ST* II–II, q.4, a.3, and q.23, a.8; in *In 3 Sent.*, d.23, q.3, a.1; and in many other places.

Nevertheless, we do concede that faith is no more an intellectual virtue when charity is present than when it is absent, because neither in the latter case nor in the former is it an intellectual virtue, as was said above. For not every virtue that is present in the intellect as in its subject can be called an intellectual virtue; nor can every virtue that is present in the will be called a moral virtue.

§2. To the Arguments against the Second Conclusion

I. To the Arguments of Scotus [*p. 57*] We must now respond to the arguments brought against the second conclusion.

In response to the *first* argument from SCOTUS, we deny the antecedent with respect to its first part.

In response to the argument for the antecedent, we say that although Paul, or another apostle who was a hearer of Christ, might, by his merely natural powers—that is, without a supernaturally infused habit—assent to the sayings of Christ or to divine revelation, he would not do so with an assent that is perfect, discriminating, and exactly like the assent of infused faith. Concerning this point SAINT THOMAS, in *In 3 Sent.*, d.23, q.3, a.2, speaks as follows:

> Habits are necessary in order that powers that are not by nature determined to a perfect act might be determined by the habit. Now it can sometimes happen that a lower power is not determined to the perfect act, but a higher power is determined to it: for example, the concupiscible power is not by its own nature determined to keeping to the mean in pleasures, but the reason is by its own nature determined to this; this is why the habit of temperance is acquired in the concupiscible power through the force of the higher power. But no power is of its own nature determined to what is above the nature of human reason, and faith concerns what is such. Hence, for this act we need a habit that is not acquired, and that helps us in two respects: against hardness, it makes the intellect ready to believe; and against error, it makes the intellect discriminating, in order that it might avoid what should not be believed.

Thus SAINT THOMAS. Again, in a.3, qla.2, he speaks as follows:

> The habit of infused faith helps us in two matters, namely to believe what should be believed, and to in no way assent to what should not be believed. Man is capable of the first of these by judgment *(aestimatio)*, without an infused habit; but he possesses the second, namely to incline with discernment to this and not that, by the infused habit alone. This is the discernment by which we do not believe every spirit; and because it is not present in the heretic, it is clear that the habit of faith does not remain in him, and if he does believe some things which should be believed, this is by human reason: for if he were inclined to believe these by the habit of faith, he would reject what is contrary to faith, just as every habit resists what is contrary to that habit.

Thus SAINT THOMAS. Again, in *Quodlibetal Questions*, q.6, a.6, he speaks as follows:

> If someone takes what is common to many as proper to one, he is necessarily deceived. But certitude of adherence is not peculiar to the virtue of faith. First, because it belongs to the intellectual virtues, namely wisdom, science, and understanding. Secondly, because it belongs not only to true faith, but also to false faith: for just as there are true and false opinion, so it is with

> faith, and one may adhere to falsity no less than to truth, as THE PHILOSOPHER says in *Ethics* 7. Third, because certitude of adherence does not always come from a habit; rather, one can, by his own choice *(arbitrium)*, establish assent to something true or false before he possesses the habit. Fourth, because certitude of adherence belongs not only to informed faith, which is a virtue, but also to unformed faith, which is not a virtue.
>
> It must be said, therefore, that in the heretic the certitude of adherence is an act of false faith, and also that in the bad Catholic it is an act of unformed faith; and so in neither of them is it an act of the virtue of faith.

Thus SAINT THOMAS.

From these texts it is clear that, although a disciple or apostle might be able to assent to the sayings of Christ without the infused habit of the virtue of faith, he would still need the infused habit, not in order to assent simply speaking, but in order {317} to assent with discernment, and for the sake of the other features that the act receives from the habit.

The response to the *second* argument is clear from the foregoing; for it proves no more than does the first argument.

In response to the *third* argument, we deny the minor premise.

In response to the argument for the minor premise, we say that I assent to the article "God is three and one" because God has revealed it, and not by the fact that John, or another man, says that this has been revealed to him; I am speaking of the assent caused by the habit of faith.

Nor should one imagine, as the opponent does, that two or three assents are necessary in this case: one by which I assent to this: "God is three and one"; another by which I assent to this: "God has revealed this"; and another by which I assent to this: "John says that it has been revealed to him that. . .". Rather, by a single act I give assent that God is three and one and that God has revealed this, just as it is the same act by which I believe God *(credo Deo)*, believe about God *(credo Deum)*, and believe unto God *(credo in Deum)*. Hence SAINT THOMAS, in *In 3 Sent.*, d.23, q.2, a.2, qla.2, speaks as follows:

> The act of one who believes depends on three things: the intellect, which terminates in one thing; the will, which determines the intellect by its command; and the reason, which inclines the will. The three acts of faith are distinguished accordingly. For according as the intellect terminates in one thing, the act of faith is to believe about God *(credere Deum)*, because the object of faith is God according as He is considered in Himself, or something concerning Him or coming from Him. According as the intellect is determined by the will, the act of faith is to believe unto God *(credere in Deum)*, that is, to be

> directed to Him by loving: for loving belongs to the will. But according as the reason inclines the will, the act of faith is to believe God *(credere Deo):* for the reason why the will is inclined to give assent to what it does not see is that God speaks of such things, just as a man, in the case of things which he does not see, believes the testimony of a good man who does see what he himself does not. And what is named from all of the foregoing is only a single complete act of faith, but one named in various ways from the various features that are found in faith: for by that act by which he believes about God *(credit Deum),* he believes God *(credit Deo)* and believes unto God *(credit in Deum).*

Thus SAINT THOMAS. Again, in *ST* II–II, q.2, a.2, he speaks as follows:

> The act of any power or habit is understood with reference to the ordering of the power or habit to its object. But the object of faith can be considered in three ways. For since to believe pertains to the intellect inasmuch as it is moved by the will to assent, the object of faith can be understood either from the point of view of the intellect or from the point of view of the will moving the intellect. If from the point of view of the intellect, two things can be considered in the object of faith. One of these is the material object of faith, and thus the act of faith is held to be "to believe about God" *(credere Deum),* because nothing is proposed for us to believe except according as it pertains to God. The other is the formal essence of the object, which is like a middle term because of which assent is given to such an object of belief; and thus the act of faith is held to be "to believe God" *(credere Deo),* because the formal object of faith is the First Truth, to which man adheres in order that, because of it, he may give assent to what is believed. But if the object of faith is considered in the third way, namely according as the intellect is moved by the will, the act of faith is held to be "to believe unto God" *(credere in Deum).* For the First Truth, according as it has the aspect of an end, is referred to the will. And what is designated from these three is not several acts of faith, but one and the same act, which has several relations to the object of faith.

Thus SAINT THOMAS.

From these texts it can be grasped how by the same act of faith the intellect adheres to the First Truth for its own sake, and gives assent to an article of faith on account of God; and that it is not necessary to form two propositions, one of which says, "God is three and one," and the other, "God has revealed that God is three and one."

Second, we say that, granted that these three propositions are formed—the first that "God is three and one," the second that "God has revealed that

God is. . . ," and the third that "John preaches that God has revealed to him that God is three and one"—in that case, I say that assent to the first does not effectively and principally depend on assent to the third, but precisely on the habit of faith and on the intellect and will, although the three of them may be required for some other purpose, such as persuasion by the preacher and the hearing of him. Concerning this point, SAINT THOMAS, in *In 3 Sent.*, d.23, q.3, a.2, obj.1, presents the following argument:

> AUGUSTINE says that "faith is acquired, nourished, and protected" through knowledge. But no habit acquired through knowledge is an infused habit. Therefore, etc.

Thus the argument; the solution follows:

> An infused habit is like an innate habit, because just as a natural habit is given in creation, so an infused habit is given in redemption. But a natural habit, such as the understanding of principles, requires that the knowledge be determined through the sense-power (which is something an acquired habit does not need, because it gets its determination through its own act while it is being acquired). Similarly, the habit of faith must get its determination from our side. And with respect to that determination, faith is said to be "acquired" through the science of theology, which distinguishes articles, just as the habit of first principles is said to be acquired through the sense-power with respect to the distinction of principles, but not with respect to the light in which the principles are known.

Thus SAINT THOMAS. Again, in ad 2, he speaks as follows:

> Four things are considered in faith: what must be believed; reason, which determines the will to believe; the will, which commands the intellect; and the intellect, which carries out the command. Accordingly, faith, with respect to its determination and with respect to its act, {318} which comes from us although the habit is infused, is said to come "from" four things present in us. With respect to what must be believed, it is said to come "from hearing," because the determination of things to be believed occurs within us either through an interior speech by which God speaks to us or through an outer voice. With respect to reason, which leads the will to believe, faith is said to come "from the vision of something that shows God to be He Who is speaking in the one who proclaims the faith." With respect to the command of the will, faith is said to come "from the will." And with respect to the carrying out of the command by the intellect, the act of faith is said to come "from the intellect."

Thus SAINT THOMAS.

From these texts it is clear that the act of faith, which is assent, depends, with respect to its being carried out, on the habit of faith, and on the intellect as its proximate cause. But external persuasion or preaching is required for the determination of what is to be believed, and for proposing to the intellect its material object—for instance some complex statement—but not for causing assent.

Again, in *ST* II–II, q.6, a.1, ad 1, ST. THOMAS speaks as follows:

> Faith is generated and nourished through knowledge by way of external persuasion, which is caused by knowledge; but the principal and proper cause of faith is what inwardly moves one to assent.

Again, in ad 3, he speaks as follows:

> To believe is present in the will of those who believe; but the will of man must be prepared by God through grace in order to be raised up to what is above nature.

Thus SAINT THOMAS.

From these texts it is clear that infused faith depends effectively on acquired faith neither as a habit nor with respect to its principal act, which is to assent to the objects of belief. Nor does its certitude depend on the certitude of acquired faith in the way that the certitude of a conclusion depends on the certitude of a principle. Consequently, the whole fantasy of the opponent is worthless.

Third, we say that, conceding the opponent's final conclusion—namely that a man might assent to the three above-mentioned propositions by his merely natural powers—nothing opposed to the conclusion follows from this, because the infused habit of faith is still necessary in order to assent with discretion, readily, firmly, and with pleasure, a point which was touched on before.

II. To the Arguments of Aureolus [*p. 58*] In response to the *first* argument of AUREOLUS we say that it proves nothing except that someone without the infused habit can assent to supernatural truths; and this we concede, but not that without such a habit he can assent with discretion, etc., that is, in the manner frequently mentioned. Therefore the heretic, and the unbaptized child raised among believers, can, without the infused habit, have an assent to the things which should be believed, but not an assent which is with discretion, ready, easy, and firm.

The response to the *second* argument of the same opponent is clear from the foregoing. Accordingly, acquired faith without infused faith suffices neither the preacher nor his hearer for believing perfectly and securely.

§3. *To the Arguments against the Third Conclusion*

To the Arguments of Durandus [*p. 59*] In response to the *first* argument of DURANDUS against the third conclusion we say that the case of acquired faith and that of infused faith are dissimilar: for the first is lost neither soon, through cessation of its proper act, nor immediately, by the contrary act; however, the case of infused faith is otherwise. Concerning this point SAINT THOMAS, in *ST* II–II, q.24, a.12, where he asks "Whether charity is lost through one act of mortal sin," speaks as follows:

> Anything is removed by something else that is contrary and supervenes. Now any act of mortal sin is opposed to charity according to the proper essence of charity, which consists in this: that God is loved above all things, and that man submits himself to God entirely and directs everything which belongs to him to God. Therefore, it is of the essence of charity that one love God in such a way that one wills to submit to Him in all things, and to follow the standard of His precepts. This is why anything that opposes the precepts of charity is clearly opposed to charity itself, and hence of itself is able to remove charity. And if charity were an acquired habit, dependent on a power of its subject, it would not necessarily be removed at once by a single contrary act: for an act is directly opposed not to a habit, but to an act; but the preservation of a habit in a subject does not require a continual act; hence, an acquired habit is not immediately removed by a supervening contrary act. But charity, since it is an infused habit, depends on the action of God infusing, Who is related to the infusion and preservation of charity as the sun is to light in the air. Hence, just as the light would immediately cease to be present in the air by the placing of some obstacle to the illumination of the sun, so too charity immediately ceases to be present in the soul by the placing of some obstacle to the infusing of charity by God into the soul. Now it is clear that any mortal sin, which is opposed to the divine precepts, places an obstacle to the aforementioned infusion: for by the very fact that man, in choosing, prefers sin to divine friendship, which requires that we follow the will of God in all things, the habit of charity is consequently lost immediately by a single act of mortal sin.

Thus SAINT THOMAS. And what he says concerning the habit of charity—that it is removed by any act of sin that is opposed to it, because such an act places an obstacle to the divine infusion—must also be said of an act of sin opposed to faith or hope. **{319}** Thus the habit of faith is removed by any act of mortal sin opposed to it, such as unbelief; and similarly the habit of hope is immediately removed by an act of mortal sin opposed to it, such as despair. But faith or hope are not removed by other sins, which are not opposed to them, as SAINT THOMAS himself says, in the same article, ad 5. Again, in *Questions on the Virtues*, "On Charity", q.2, a.6, he speaks as follows:

> Things which are caused by divine infusion have need of divine action not merely in their beginning, so as to begin to be, but throughout their whole duration, so that they might be preserved in being; just as the illumination of the air needs the presence of the sun not merely when the air is first illuminated, but as long as it remains illuminated. This is why, if any obstacle is interposed that cuts off the air's immediate openness to the sun, the light ceases to be present in the air; and similarly, at the arrival of mortal sin, which cuts off the soul's immediate openness to God, the influence of God is cut off, etc.

Thus SAINT THOMAS. And he presents the same point in many other places. From these texts it is clear that the comparison made by the argument between acquired and infused virtues is invalid.

In response to the *second* argument we say that, if the minor premise is taken with reference to one who errs with stubbornness, that is, a heretic, it is false. But if it is taken with reference to one who is not a heretic, we concede the entire argument, but it is not opposed to the conclusion. Thus SAINT THOMAS presents a similar argument in *Quodlibetal Questions*, q.6, a.6:

> Everything which acts according to a likeness to something else seems to act in virtue of the latter. But the heretic, who through his certitude adheres to the things which he believes, acts according to a likeness to faith, inasmuch as he does adhere with certitude, and inasmuch as he judges that he has a faith which is correct. Therefore, he acts in virtue of faith.

Thus the argument; the response is as follows:

> It must be said that a thing can act according to a likeness to something else in two ways: in one way according to a true likeness, and thus it truly does in a way act in virtue of the other; in another way according to an apparent likeness, and thus it apparently acts in virtue of the other. And the latter is the case in question. Hence, in the heretic, certitude of adherence is an act of apparent faith, not of true faith.

Thus SAINT THOMAS. And the dissimilarity between the adherence of the Catholic and that of the heretic to an article to which they both assent is shown by SAINT THOMAS in *ST* II–II, q.5, a.3, ad 1, where he speaks as follows:

> A heretic does not hold the other articles of faith, those concerning which he is not in error, in the way in which a believer holds them—namely by simply adhering to the First Truth, which is something to which man needs to be helped by the habit of faith; rather, he holds the things which are of faith by his own will and judgment.

Thus SAINT THOMAS.

From these texts it is clear that one who was formerly a believer, and later fell into heresy, does not believe any article of faith in the way in which he did before, and that he does not believe it through the same middle term, but a different one.

The response to the *third* argument is now clear from what was said in response to the first: namely, that the case of the infused habit, which is removed by a single act, and that of the acquired habit are dissimilar. Hence, an erroneous judgment concerning a conclusion of a science can co-exist with the habit of that science, but an error concerning one article cannot co-exist with faith concerning another. Concerning this point SAINT THOMAS, in *ST* II–II, q.5, a.3, presents the following argument:

> Just as many articles are contained under faith, so many conclusions are contained under one science, for instance geometry. But a man can possess the science of geometry concerning some geometrical conclusions, while others are unknown. Therefore, a man can have faith concerning some articles of faith while not believing others.

Thus the argument; the response is as follows:

> It must be said that in the various conclusions of a single science there are various middle terms by which they are proved, one of which can be known without another. Therefore, a man can know some conclusions of a single science, while not knowing others. But faith adheres to all of the articles of faith because of one middle term, namely the First Truth, which is set forth for us in the Scriptures as they are rightly understood according to the doctrine of the Church. Hence, one who cuts himself off from this middle term is entirely lacking in faith.

Thus SAINT THOMAS.

§4. *To the Arguments against the Fourth Conclusion*

I. To the Arguments of Scotus [*p.* 60] In response to the *first* argument of SCOTUS against the fourth conclusion we say *first* that faith regards the First Truth not only as the middle term that is the reason why one assents to the objects of belief, but also as the object of faith. SAINT THOMAS presents this point explicitly in *ST* II–II, q.1, a.1, where he speaks as follows:

> A habit of any cognitive power has two objects: that which is known materially, which is, as it were, the material object; and that through which it is known, which is the formal essence *(ratio)* of the object. For instance, in the science of geometry, what are known materially are the conclusions; but the formal essence of the knowing is constituted by the middle terms of the demonstrations through which the conclusions are known.
>
> Accordingly, if in faith we consider the formal essence of the object, it is nothing other than the First Truth, for the faith of which we are speaking assents to something only because it is revealed by God; hence, it rests upon the Divine Truth itself as a middle term. But if we consider that to which faith assents materially, it is not only God Himself but also many other things, which, however, come under the assent of faith only according as they are directed to God, that is, inasmuch as man is helped by certain effects of the divinity to tend toward enjoyment of the divine. Hence, from this point of view also, the object of faith is in a way the First Truth, inasmuch as a thing comes under faith only in being directed to God; similarly, the object of medicine {320} is health, because medicine considers nothing except in terms of directedness to health.

Thus SAINT THOMAS. He says something similar in *In 3 Sent.*, d.24, q.1, a.1, qla.1, where he speaks as follows:

> Three things can be considered in the object of any power: what is formal in the object, what is material, and what is accidental. This is clear in the case of the object of sight: for what is formal in it is light, which causes color to be visible in actuality; what is material is the color itself, which is visible in potentiality; what is accidental is quantity and other such features that accompany color. Now everything acts through its form; and the object is active in the case of the passive powers. Therefore, the essence of the object to which a passive power is proportioned is what is formal in the object; and it is according to this that powers and habits, which are specified by the essences of their objects, vary according to what is formal in the objects.
>
> Now these three can be found in the object of faith. For since faith assents to something only because of the object of belief that is the First Truth,

> something is in actuality an object of belief only because of the First Truth, just as color is visible because of light. Hence the First Truth is what is formal in the object of faith, and is that from which the whole essence of the object comes. But whatever is believed about God, such as that He suffered, or anything of this sort, is what is material in the object of faith. And whatever follows from these objects of belief is, as it were, accidental. Hence it must be conceded that the object of faith, properly speaking, is the First Truth.

Thus SAINT THOMAS.

Second, we say that it does not follow from our conclusion that assent to the article "God is three and one" depends, as the opponent imagines, on an infinity of prior assents. Nor is it necessary to go through an infinite number of middle terms in order to assent to this article.

In response to the opposing argument we say that through faith I primarily and directly assent to the proposition "God has revealed that God is three and one," in the sense that sight is primarily directed to light; and secondarily I assent to the proposition "God is three and one," in the sense that sight is secondarily directed to color, although it is by the same single act.

Further on, the opponent asks: How do I assent to the proposition "God has revealed this, namely etc."? To this we say that faith assents to it because of faith itself, and not because of some other proposition, assent to which causes assent to the proposition "God has revealed this." For this is the first object of belief: "God, or the First Truth, has revealed whatever is contained in Sacred Scripture and in the teaching of the Church." And assent to this proposition is not caused by another preceding assent, but by God inwardly moving the intellect through the habit of faith to this assent. However, for this first assent of faith there is required the presentation of this complex proposition through internal or external speech, or through the reading of Sacred Scripture, or through preaching. We have discussed this at sufficient length in responding to the arguments against the second conclusion, which touched upon a similar difficulty.

The opponent asks: How do I assent to the preceding propositions, for instance the proposition "It has been revealed by God that it has been revealed that God is three and one"? And in response he says that assent is given to all these propositions by an assent caused by the free choice or by acquired faith. But here we deny the reasoning by which it is inferred that infused faith effectively depends on acquired faith, either as a habit or with respect to its principal act, which is to assent.

In response to the *second* argument we say *first* that, if we are speaking of the formal essence from the point of view of the thing itself, the formal essence of the object of faith is not a being of reason, but a real being—although it is not greatly inappropriate to say that the formal essence, from our point of view, is a being of reason, or involves a being of reason such as a negation or a relation of reason. Concerning this point SAINT THOMAS, in *ST* II–II, q.1, a.6, ad 2, speaks as follows:

> The formal essence of the object of faith can be considered in two ways. In one way from the point of view of the thing itself believed, and thus the formal essence of all objects of faith is one thing, namely the First Truth; and from this point of view the articles are not distinguished from one another. In another way the formal essence of the objects of faith can be considered from our point of view, and thus the formal essence of the object of belief is that it be unseen; and from this point of view the articles are distinguished from one another.

Thus SAINT THOMAS. From this text it is clear that the formal essence of the object of faith, from the point of view of the believer, is that it be unseen. But this is a negation, which is only a being of reason. One can speak this way of what is revealed: however, I do not read in what SAINT THOMAS says that "having been revealed" is the formal essence of the object of faith, and neither does this follow from what he says.

The opponent says that if I assent to the proposition "God is three" because it has been revealed by God, then a relation of reason is the cause of my assenting, and consequently is the formal essence of the object. In response to this, we deny the inference. For although I assent to the proposition "God is three" because it has been revealed by God, this is not to say that the relation of revelability is cause of the assent; rather, it is the First Truth, which is the term of that relation, that causes movement toward assent. Similarly, when a student assents to what a teacher says because the teacher says it, it is not that the relation of reason involved in "having been said by the teacher" causes assent in the student; what causes the assent is rather the authority and perfect knowledge, or the "word," of the teacher, which is the term of the relation mentioned. So it is in the present question: what causes the assent of faith is the First Truth, as primary cause, and His word, as proximate cause, and not the relation of reason that terminates in God, or in His Word, a Word that, having been taken on by humanity, has been spoken through the Prophets or Apostles. However, as I have said, **{321}** it is not inappropriate if the formal essence of the object of faith have, from our point of view, something of a being of reason; for the proximate material object of faith is a complex proposition, formed by an operation of the soul. Concerning this point SAINT THOMAS, in *In 3 Sent.*, d.24, q.1, a.1, qla.2, ad 3, speaks as follows:

> The object of charity is the good, which, according to THE PHILOSOPHER in *Metaphysics* 6, is in things; but the object of faith is the true, which is brought to completion by an operation of the soul. And because the composition and division that are present in enunciations exist only by means of the soul, something complex is the object of faith, although something incomplex is the object of charity.

Thus SAINT THOMAS. He presents the same point in *ST* II–II, q.1, a.2, where he speaks as follows:

> Things known are present in the knower according to the mode of the knower. But the proper mode of the human intellect is to know the truth by composing and dividing. Hence the human intellect knows what is in itself simple by means of what is complex, just as, conversely, the divine intellect knows what is in itself complex in an incomplex way.
>
> Accordingly, the object of faith can be considered in two ways. In one way, from the point of view of the thing itself believed, and thus the object of faith is something incomplex, namely the thing itself about which faith is held. In another way, from the point of view of the believer, according to which the object of faith is something complex with the mode of an enunciation.

Thus SAINT THOMAS.

II. To the Arguments of Aureolus [*p. 61*] In response to the *first* argument of AUREOLUS, we deny the minor premise.

Nor is the argument for the minor premise valid: for the proposition "The First Truth cannot lie" is not resolved into the proposition "God cannot lie"; rather, conversely, God cannot lie because He is the First Truth. Nevertheless, when SAINT THOMAS says that the formal object of faith is the First Truth, he does not mean to deny that God or the divinity is the formal object; rather, he expressly says this, in *ST* II–II, q.1, a.1, which was quoted in the response to the first argument of SCOTUS against the fourth conclusion.

In response to the *second* argument, we say that by "the First Truth" we understand the divine essence inasmuch as it assumes the aspect *(ratio)* of the First Truth. Moreover, we do not say that such an attribute adds anything to the divinity in reality, but only that it does so in relation to our mode of understanding and considering.

The opponent says that the divinity is not an end under the aspect of First Truth, etc. We respond that this is false. For since faith is in the intellect, and the good and end of the intellect is the true, it is manifestly clear that the divinity is the end of faith and of the intellect under the aspect of truth more than under any other aspect—although it is not the end of the will or of charity under that aspect, but rather under the aspect of the First Goodness. Concerning this point, a remark of SAINT THOMAS in *ST* II–II, q.2, a.2, was quoted above:

> If the object of faith is considered according as the intellect is moved by the will, then the act of faith is held to be "to believe in God": for the First Truth is referred to the will according as it has the aspect *(ratio)* of an end.

Thus SAINT THOMAS. Understand, too, that "the First Truth" is referred to the will according as it has the aspect of an end—not, indeed, the end of the will, but the end to which the will moves the intellect by its command.

SAINT THOMAS responds to the argument on the negative side of the question [p. 52] in *ST* II–II, q.4, a.5, ad 2, where he speaks as follows:

> The faith of which THE PHILOSOPHER speaks is based on human reason concluding without necessity, which may include the false; therefore such faith is not a virtue. But the faith of which we are speaking is based on Divine Truth, which is infallible, and hence cannot include the false. Therefore, such faith can be a virtue.

Thus SAINT THOMAS.

This suffices for the question.

Blessed be God.

Amen.

Whether Faith Is of Things Seen

In relation to the twenty-fifth distinction of the third book of *The Sentences,* the question is raised: Whether faith is of things seen.

It is argued that it is, as follows. The light of faith is related to the articles of faith as the natural light of the mind is to naturally known principles; but the natural light of the mind causes one to see the principles which are known of themselves; therefore, too, the light of faith causes one to see the articles of faith.

Argument is made for the opposite conclusion as follows. It is said in *Hebrews* 11.1 that "faith is the evidence of things unseen"; therefore, it is not of things seen.

In this question there will be three articles: in the first the conclusions will be presented, in the second the objections, and in the third the solutions.

Article I: Conclusions

First Conclusion: Faith Cannot Be of Things Seen

SAINT THOMAS presents this conclusion in *ST* II–II, q.1, a.4, **{322}** where he speaks as follows:

> Faith implies the assent of the intellect to what is believed. But the intellect can assent to something in two ways. In one way because it is moved to do so by the object itself, which is something either known through itself, as is clear in the case of first principles, or known through something else, as is clear in the case of conclusions, with which science is concerned. In another way the intellect assents to something not because it is sufficiently moved by its proper object, but because, through a voluntary choice, it inclines more to one side

> of a question than to the other. If this occurs with doubt and unease concerning the other side, it will be opinion; but if it occurs with certitude and without such unease, it will be faith. Now we are said to "see" those things that of themselves move our intellect or sense-power to knowledge of them. Hence it is clear that neither faith nor opinion can be of things seen either by the sense-power or by the intellect.

Thus SAINT THOMAS. Again, in article 6 of the same question, in his solution to the second objection, he speaks as follows:

> The formal essence of the object of faith can be considered in two ways: in one way, from the point of view of the thing believed, and thus there is one formal essence of all objects of belief, namely the First Truth; in another way the formal essence of objects of belief can be considered from our point of view, and thus the formal essence of an object of belief is that it be "unseen."

Thus SAINT THOMAS.

From these texts the following argument can be formed: that object which does not of itself suffice to move the sense-power or the intellect to knowledge cannot be said to be seen; but the object of faith is such; therefore . . .

Second Conclusion: Faith Is Not of Things Known Scientifically

SAINT THOMAS presents this conclusion in *ST* II–II, q.1, a.5, where he speaks as follows:

> All science is possessed through certain principles that are of themselves known, and consequently seen; hence whatever is known must be in some way seen. But it is not possible for the same thing to be believed and seen by the same man. Hence it is impossible for the same thing to be known and believed by the same man. It can, however, happen that what is seen or known by one is believed by another. For we hope that we shall see those things that we believe concerning the Trinity, according to 1 *Corinthians* 13.12: "Now we see through a glass, darkly, but then we shall see face to face." This vision the angels have now; hence, they see what we believe. In a similar way, it can happen that what is seen or known by one man, even in the present life, is believed by another who does not know it by way of demonstration. Nevertheless, what is generally proposed to all men as an object of belief is generally not known; and such are those things which simply speaking fall under faith. Hence faith and science are not of the same thing.

Thus SAINT THOMAS. Again, in the same article, in his solution of the fourth objection, he speaks as follows:

> It is altogether possible that opinion and science of the same thing be possessed by different men, as was said just now concerning faith and science. Indeed, it is possible that opinion and science of the same thing be possessed by the same man in a certain way, namely by being a thing that is the same in subject, but not taken in the same respect: for it is possible for someone to know one conclusion and opine another concerning one and the same object. Similarly, one can know demonstratively of God that He is one and believe that He is triune. But in one man science cannot co-exist with either opinion or faith concerning the same thing taken in the same respect; for the essence of these is different. For science cannot co-exist with opinion of the same thing simply speaking, because it is of the essence of science that what is known scientifically is judged impossible to be otherwise, while it is of the essence of opinion that what is opined is judged possible to be otherwise; hence the same thing cannot be by the same man simultaneously known and opined. But that which is held by faith is, on account of the certitude of faith, judged impossible to be otherwise. But the same thing cannot be in the same respect simultaneously believed and known, for the reason that the known is seen, but the believed is unseen.

Thus SAINT THOMAS.

From these texts we argue as follows: nothing that is unseen is known scientifically; but everything that is believed is unseen; therefore, nothing that is believed is known scientifically; and consequently faith is not of things known scientifically.

Third Conclusion: Faith Is Simply Speaking More Certain Than Science, although in Relation to Us and in a Certain Respect It Is Not

SAINT THOMAS presents this conclusion in *ST* II–II, q.4, a.8, where he speaks as follows:

> Of the intellectual virtues, two concern contingent things, namely prudence and art; faith excels these virtues in certitude by reason of its matter, because it is of eternal things, which cannot be otherwise. The three other intellectual virtues, namely wisdom, science and understanding, are of necessary things. But one should note that science, wisdom and understanding are spoken of in two ways: in one way insofar as they are counted as intellectual virtues by THE PHILOSOPHER in *Ethics* 6; in another way insofar as they

> are counted as gifts of the Holy Spirit. With respect to the first way, we must say that certitude can be considered in two ways. One is from the point of view of the cause of certitude, and thus that is said to be more certain which has a more certain cause; in this way faith is more certain than the three virtues mentioned above, because faith depends on the Divine Truth, while the three above-mentioned virtues depend on human reason. In another way certitude can be considered from the point of view of the subject, and thus that is said to be more certain which the understanding of man more fully grasps; and according to this way of considering, because the things of faith are above the understanding of man, while the things which come under the three above-mentioned virtues are not, faith is, from this point of view, less certain. And because anything is judged simply speaking {323} according to its cause, but judged in a certain respect according to a disposition on the part of the subject, faith is simply speaking more certain, but the other virtues are more certain in one respect, namely in relation to us. Similarly, if the three above-mentioned virtues are taken as gifts of the Holy Spirit in the present life, they are compared to faith as to a principle which they presuppose; hence, in this respect, too, faith is more certain than they are.

Thus SAINT THOMAS. Again, in *In 3 Sent.*, d.23, q.2, a.2, qla.3, he speaks as follows:

> Certitude is nothing other than the determination of the intellect to one thing. But certitude is greater to the extent that what causes the determination is stronger. Now the intellect is determined to one thing in three ways. For in the understanding of principles, determination is caused by the fact that something can of itself, by the light of the agent intellect, be sufficiently seen; in scientific knowledge, which is of conclusions, determination is caused by the fact that a conclusion is by an act of reason resolved into principles that are seen of themselves; in faith, determination is caused by the fact that the will commands the intellect. Now because the will does not determine the intellect so as to cause what is believed to be seen in the way that principles known of themselves or conclusions that are resolved into them are seen, but rather in such a way that the intellect firmly adheres to one side of a question, the certitude in scientific knowledge and understanding is of things that are called certain from their evidence; but the certitude of faith comes from firm adherence to what is believed. Accordingly, in the case of the things that we believe through faith, the reason that inclines the will is the First Truth itself, or God, Who is believed, and Who possesses greater firmness than the light of the human intellect in which principles are

> seen, or than the human reason by which conclusions are resolved into principles. Hence faith, with respect to firmness of adherence, possesses a certitude greater than that of science and understanding, although in science and understanding there is a greater evidence of the things to which assent is given.

Thus SAINT THOMAS.

From these texts the following argument can be formed. That is simply speaking more certain whose proximate and principal cause is more efficacious, more certain, and less susceptible of being turned into its contrary; but the proximate and principal cause of the assent of faith is more efficacious, more determinate, more certain, and less susceptible of being turned into its contrary than is the cause of the assent of science, wisdom, or understanding; therefore, etc.

Here the first article terminates.

Article II: Objections

§1. Against the First Conclusion

I. Arguments of Aureolus In the second article arguments are made against the conclusions.

AUREOLUS argues against the first conclusion by arguing that obscurity or lack of evidence is not of the nature of the formal object of faith. *First,* as follows:

> The object of faith is an immediate object of the intellect. Therefore, it has as its formal essence only what is immediately contained under the formal object of the intellect. Now lack of evidence, since it is a privation, is not immediately contained under the object of the intellect.

Second, as follows:

> Lack of evidence denotes an object taken as directed to a power, and it is a relation of reason, namely a privation; and something of this kind cannot be an object of faith, which is a theological virtue.

Third, as follows:

> It is impossible for a privation to be the formal condition of the object of a positive habit, because a habit is directed toward a positive nature. Now faith is a positive habit, but lack of evidence is a privative nature.

Fourth, as follows:

> The object of faith is the true to which adherence is given on account of authority; but authority may happen to be evident or to be lacking evidence.

II. Arguments of Durandus DURANDUS (*In 3 Sent.*, d.24, q.1) also argues against the first conclusion. *First,* as follows:

> The formal essence of the object of a cognitive habit cannot be negative or privative. But faith is a cognitive habit, while the essence of "the unseen" is a negative one. Therefore, the essence of "the unseen" cannot be the formal essence of the object of faith.
>
> The minor premise is evident of itself.
>
> The major premise is proved as follows. The primary object to which a cognitive habit is directed cannot be a negation or a privation, because privations are known only through what is possessed, and negations only through affirmations. But the primary object to which a cognitive habit is directed is the object according to its formal essence. Therefore, the formal essence of the object of a cognitive habit cannot be negative or privative. Therefore, the conclusion follows.

Second, he argues for the same conclusion as follows:

> The formal essence of the object of any cognitive habit comes not from the side of the one who possesses the habit, but from the side of the object, as is clear through induction from all instances. But the essence of "the unseen" comes from the side of the one who has faith. Therefore, it is not the essence of the formal object of faith.
>
> The minor premise is made evident as follows. The object is seen or unseen because the act of sight of the one seeing does or does not fall upon it.

Third, he argues as follows:

> If the formal essence of the object of faith were "to be unseen," a fortiori the formal essence of the object of sight would be "to be seen." But the latter is false. Therefore, so is the former.
>
> The major premise is made evident as follows. Opposite habits should have formal objects that have opposite natures. But faith and sight are, according to you, opposite habits. Therefore, if the formal essence of the object of faith is "to be unseen," the opposite essence, namely "to be seen," would be {324} the formal essence of the object of sight. That this is false is proved as follows. The object in its formal essence is prior to the act. But "to be seen" is not prior to the act of sight—rather, something is said to be seen because an act of sight falls upon it. Therefore "to be seen" is not the formal essence of the object of sight.

Fourth, he argues as follows:

> Whatever falls under the consideration of any cognitive habit is referred to the formal essence of the object of the habit. But not everything that is considered by faith is referred to the essence of "the unseen." Therefore, etc.

Fifth, he argues as follows:

> The end of any cognitive habit is perfect knowledge of its object with respect to its formal essence and whatever is referred to it. If, therefore, the formal essence of the object of faith were "to be unseen," it would follow that the proximate and intrinsic end of faith would be to know perfectly of God both how He is unseen and whatever is referred to Him as unseen. But this is false. Therefore, the formal essence of the object of faith is not the essence "unseen."

Thus DURANDUS argues in form.

§2. *Against the Second Conclusion*

Arguments of Durandus The same DURANDUS (*In 1 Sent.*, Prologue, q.1) argues against the second conclusion that the faith that is a habit infused by God can, simply speaking and entirely, co-exist with scientific knowledge in the same subject and in relation to the same object. *First,* as follows:

> The habit of infused faith extends to everything that has been taught to us by divine revelation, and especially to those points that have not been deduced from others. But some believers have true scientific knowledge of such things. Therefore, in them, there are simultaneously faith and scientific knowledge of the same thing.
>
> The major premise is self-evident. The minor premise may be made clear by a similar argument. That God is one is taught in Sacred Scripture as something revealed by God, and not as deduced from something else: "Hear, O Israel, the Lord your God is one" (*Deut.* 6.4). But many believers have true scientific knowledge of this point by means of an acquired demonstration. Therefore, the habit of infused faith and the habit of true scientific knowledge can co-exist.

Second, as follows:

> Not only the habits of scientific knowledge and of faith, but also the acts of these habits, can co-exist in the same man in relation to the same thing. For acts of scientific knowledge and of faith in relation to matters concerning which true scientific knowledge may be had by someone in the present life

can co-exist—not, indeed, in such a way that they are different acts, but rather because divine authority and demonstrative reason can simultaneously concur in causing a single assent to the fact that God is one.

This is made clear as follows. It is only the opposition between the clear and the obscure, between the evident and the non-evident, that can hinder the concurrence of the above-mentioned acts. But that opposition does not hinder it. Therefore. . . .

That that opposition does not hinder the concurrence is proved as follows.

Here we must note that two things that, taken separately, have effects whose features are incompatible can concur in producing a single effect that is common to both. For example, the light caused by the sun and the light caused by the moon or by a single star have incompatible features, namely "bright" and "dim" respectively; and nevertheless, when the sun and the star are in the same part of the celestial sphere, they concur in causing a single light in the medium. For it is not the sun alone that then shines, while the star does nothing, since every shining body present to a transparency necessarily causes light; rather, a single light is caused by both of them acting simultaneously, as a single agent, not individually and separately. And since, in this light, the light and the brightness are not, in the thing itself, different, but one and the same, both the sun and the star are causes—not total, but partial causes—of the light and of the clarity, although they are not equally so: for the more perfect and, so to speak, "total," nature of causality is in the sun, while that in the star is inferior, minimal, and imperceptible to sense, although reason does convince us that it is not nothing. And on account of this excess of illuminating power in the sun in comparison to the star—which is evident when they act by themselves, because then the sun causes a bright light and the star a dim one—when they simultaneously cause one bright light, the brightness is, by an appropriation of reason, attributed to the causality of the sun and not that of the star, even though, in the thing itself, the whole is produced by both as by partial causes that simultaneously concur and take the place of one whole cause. Thus it is clear that two things that, taken separately, have effects whose features are incompatible, can sometimes concur in producing the same effect which is a common effect of both.

Now the reason why such concurrence is possible is as follows. "Bright" and "dim" here are not understood as, respectively, possession and privation in a common subject that differ from one another in reality—as "light" and "darkness" in the air are understood, because the causes of light and darkness, understanding "darkness" as pure privation, can never concur in causing the same effect, since the effect of the one is formally the privation of the other. Rather, "bright" and "dim" here are understood as, respectively, degrees of perfection and of imperfection in the essence of light; and such degrees do not differ from light in reality; and such perfection and imperfection are present in an effect from the perfection or imperfection of its cause, not from any formal opposition in the causality. Thus, an imperfect cause, acting by itself, causes an imperfect, that is, a "dim" light because of deficiency of perfection in the force; but when it is united to a more perfect power and togther with it takes the place of one perfect whole cause, {325} it causes a perfect, that is, a "bright" light, because now the perfection that previously was deficient is no longer so.

To return to the question. Every knowledge of truth is a certain light, and is called a light by THE APOSTLE in *Ephes.* 3.8–9, where he speaks as follows: "To me, least of all the saints, has been given the grace to illuminate," that is, to give knowledge, which is a kind of spiritual light. Now some knowledge is "bright" and some is "dim." And this brightness and dimness are not, respectively, a possession and a privation having knowledge as their subject, because then the cause of the dimness could not concur with the cause of the brightness in causing one act of "bright knowledge," as was explained with respect to the causes of light and of darkness. Rather, this brightness and dimness are degrees of greater or lesser perfection that do not in reality differ from the essence of knowledge. Thus these degrees of knowledge according to degree of perfection and imperfection follow from perfection and imperfection in the middle term that causes knowledge, and not from some formal opposition in the causality. Accordingly, if a middle term taken from authority and a necessary middle term should each separately cause a different knowledge of the same conclusion, these knowledges will have incompatible features: for one—namely, that possessed through the necessary middle term—will be "bright" and evident on account of its perfection in truth and its link with the conclusion; the other, however—namely, that which is possessed through authority alone—will be "dim" and lacking evidence on account of a lack of the above-mentioned perfection in the necessary middle term. But if the necessary middle term is joined to the authority, the perfection that was previously lacking in the middle term will no longer be lacking; nor, consequently, will the "brightness" and evidence that were previously lacking in the knowledge be lacking: rather, there will be a single "bright" and evident knowledge caused by both middle terms concurring as partial causes and together taking the place of one whole cause. Nevertheless, that brightness and that evidence, with reference to the thing itself,

> ought to be attributed more to the necessary middle term than to the authority, because the former is more perfect, and of itself naturally causes "bright" and evident knowledge, something that human or divine authority does not of itself cause.

Third, he argues as follows:

> It seems rather harsh to say that the believer who has recently acquired the scientific knowledge that God is one does not hold that He is one because God Himself has revealed this in Sacred Scripture.

Fourth, he argues as follows:

> There can simultaneously be opinion and scientific knowledge of the same conclusion in the same man. For a contingent middle term and human authority by themselves alone cause doubtful assent; but a necessary middle term causes certain assent. These two assents cannot be simultaneously present in the same man with respect to the same conclusion. This, however, does not prevent the above-mentioned middle terms from being able, in an argument through middle terms, to concur in causing a single assent which will be, not both certain and doubtful, whether simultaneously or successively, but rather simply certain. Thus in the assent there will be no opposition or contradiction with respect to the certain and the doubtful, the bright and the dim, or the evident and the lacking in evidence, as has been explained. Thus, too, it is clear that although the necessary middle term removes the need for human authority or for any contingent middle term, it does not remove their compatibility in an argument through <several> middle terms causing a single assent. In this way scientific knowledge on the one hand, and opinion or the faith that depends upon human authority on the other, can be simultaneously present in the same man with respect to the same conclusion: they are so present not as distinct habits causing distinct acts, but rather because the middle terms, which of themselves would naturally cause distinct acts by which distinct habits would be formed in us, are able to concur in causing a single assent.

Fifth, he argues as follows:

> THE COMMON DOCTRINE, which says that one man can simultaneously know the same conclusion through a probable and a demonstrative middle term, agrees with the point. And elsewhere THE COMMON DOCTRINE says that opinion can co-exist with demonstrative science, which cannot be according to a plurality of acts, but only in the way described.

Sixth, he argues as follows:

> The proper distinction between scientific knowledge and opinion is as follows. Scientific knowledge is the habit of conclusions concluded through necessary middle terms whose necessity is evident to the one possessing the scientific knowledge; opinion is the habit of conclusions concluded through middle terms that are or are judged to be contingent. Now taking scientific knowledge and opinion in this way, it is clear that if the acts of scientific knowledge and of opinion—namely, to know scientifically in actuality and to opine in actuality respectively—are acts different in reality, they cannot co-exist, because several acts of understanding cannot, in the course of nature, co-exist in the same intellect. Therefore, when to know scientifically and to opine are several and distinct acts, they cannot co-exist in the same intellect, whether with respect to the same or with respect to different conclusions. In this sense it is not possible for one and the same man simultaneously to know scientifically and to opine either the same thing or different things.
>
> If, however, several acts of understanding could be simultaneous, nothing would prevent the same man from sometimes simultaneously knowing scientifically and opining the same conclusion; and sometimes this would not be possible. That it would sometimes be possible is clear from the following. To assent to a necessary conclusion through a contingent middle term that is judged to be necessary is to opine. But such assenting can co-exist with knowing scientifically, since it contains nothing contradictory to knowing scientifically. Therefore, such opining and scientific knowing can co-exist in the same man.
>
> The major premise is made clear as follows. Such assenting is not scientific knowing, since it comes about through a middle term which is contingent in reality. Nor is it the act of any habit other than opinion, because if I ask what {326} other habit it might be, no answer can be given, unless some new habit, besides those mentioned by THE PHILOSOPHER, is invented. Therefore, etc.
>
> Nor is it an objection that the man, in judging that the middle term that is contingent is necessary, is deceived. For it is not contrary to the nature of opinion that one be deceived, whether about the conclusion opined or about the middle term through which it is concluded, for by opinion it is possible to say both what is true and what is false, as is maintained in *Ethics* 3. Thus the major premise is clear.
>
> The minor premise is proved as follows. There is no formal contradiction between those acts that are similarly related to a conclusion: rather, they can be simultaneously present in the same man with respect to that

conclusion. But to know scientifically a certain conclusion and to opine the same conclusion by means of a contingent middle term judged to be necessary are acts similarly related to the conclusion, because by both acts the conclusion is judged to be necessary and incapable of being otherwise. Therefore, there is no contradiction between knowing scientifically and opining thus understood: rather, they can be simultaneously present in the same man and with respect to the same conclusion.

The following argument might be made. To be deceived is opposed to knowing scientifically. But to opine in the way described is to be deceived. Therefore, it is opposed to knowing scientifically, and thus the two cannot be present simultaneously.

In response to this we must say that to know scientifically and to be deceived concerning the same point cannot occur simultaneously. But to know scientifically and to be deceived concerning different points are not opposed and are not incompatible in the same man: otherwise, someone who scientifically knows one conclusion could not be deceived concerning any other conclusion, which is false. Now in the case in question, the scientific knowing and the being deceived do not concern the same point. For the man, in opining, is not deceived concerning the conclusion, which is the same in the case of both acts, namely that of knowing scientifically and that of opining, because in opining he judges that the conclusion is necessary, as it truly is: rather, he is deceived only concerning the middle term, which he judges to be necessary although it is contingent. But the middle term of the scientific knowing and that of the opining are not the same, but different, which is why the being deceived is not opposed to scientifically knowing the conclusion through a different middle term. Thus it is clear that if several acts of understanding could be present simultaneously, nothing would prevent the same man from knowing scientifically and opining the same conclusion when, in opining, he judged a middle term which is contingent to be necessary. But if, in opining, he were to judge the middle term to be contingent, then the opining could not be present simultaneously with the scientific knowing in the same man.

Seventh, he argues as follows:

> The habits of scientific knowledge and of opinion can be present simultaneously in the same man with respect to the same conclusion. For those habits are compatible that are caused by compatible acts. Now it is not possible, in the course of nature, for several acts of understanding to be present simultaneously in the same intellect, whether with respect to the same object or

with respect to different ones; however, the supposition is that the scientific knowing and the opining are not different acts of understanding, because the contingent middle term, which of itself would naturally cause opinion, and the necessary middle term, which of itself naturally causes a man truly to know scientifically, can concur in causing one and the same assent concerning the same conclusion, so that scientific knowledge and opinion are said to be present simultaneously if the necessary middle term, which causes scientific knowledge, and the contingent middle term, which naturally causes opinion, are able to concur in causing one assent concerning the same conclusion.

Here we must note that the contingent middle term is judged either to be necessary or to be contingent.

1. If it is judged to be necessary, then it can concur with another middle term that truly is necessary in causing the same assent concerning the same conclusion. The reason for this is as follows. In the case of every assent, a judgment based on two necessary middle terms is the same as a judgment based on two middle terms of which one is necessary and the other contingent, if the contingent one is judged to be necessary. But two necessary middle terms can concur in causing one assent. Therefore, too, a necessary middle term and a contingent one that is judged to be necessary can concur in causing one assent.

The major premise is made clear as follows. Assent to a conclusion as deduced from middle terms or principles depends entirely upon assent to and judgment concerning the principles or middle terms, and not upon the nature of the middle terms taken in themselves, except insofar as they fall under the judgment of the one making the deduction. Therefore middle terms judged to be similar, granted that they are not similar in reality, can similarly concur in causing the same assent.

The minor premise is also clear of itself. For if someone had several necessary middle terms for the same conclusion, he could join them together to take the place of a single middle term in the same demonstration, and so he would get from them a single assent concerning the same conclusion.

2. If the contingent middle term is judged to be contingent, such a middle term can still concur with a necessary middle term in causing the same assent. For, although one who has a necessary and evident middle term needs neither an authority nor a contingent middle term, nevertheless, the necessary middle term does not exclude the compossibility of a contingent middle term.

This is made clear as follows. If the contingent middle term were unable to concur with the necessary middle term in causing the same assent, this would be on account of opposition between the evident and the lacking evidence, between the certain and the doubtful. But this opposition does not hinder the concurrence. For, as was demonstrated above, the necessary middle term and the contingent middle term, when taken separately, naturally cause assents whose features are incompatible, since one is certain and the other is doubtful; but when they are taken together, they cause a single assent which is certain and in no way doubtful.

From the foregoing it is clear that a scientific assent and an opined assent can concur in the same conclusion. Therefore, similarly, **{327}** the habits of science and of opinion can also do so, in the manner explained above.

§3. Against the Third Conclusion

Arguments of Durandus DURANDUS (*In 3 Sent.*, d.23, q.7) argues against the third conclusion that faith ought not to be called more certain than scientific knowledge on account of the adherence which it involves. *First,* as follows:

> Firmness of adherence is improperly called certitude. For certitude does not co-exist with falsity. But firmness of adherence is sometimes present in falsity, as is clear in the case of heretics and others who stubbornly adhere to their false opinions. Therefore, firmness of adherence does not properly possess the nature of certitude.

Second, as follows:

> Even firmness of adherence seems to be greater in the act of scientific knowledge than in the act of faith. For we adhere more firmly to that from which we separate ourselves with greater difficulty. But a man separates himself from scientific knowledge—if he truly does know scientifically, and knows that he knows—with greater difficulty than he does from faith, for we frequently see a man separate himself from faith. Therefore, firmness of adherence seems to be greater in the act of scientific knowledge than in the act of faith.

Third, against what was said concerning what is more certain in itself as distinct from what is more certain in relation to us, he argues that this distinction is not valid, as follows:

> Although the distinction in a way has a place in the case of the objects of belief and of scientific knowledge—as when THE PHILOSOPHER says in *Metaphysics* 2 that separate substances are in themselves better known than

sensible substances, although to us they are not so, but are rather less well known—nevertheless, the distinction has no place in the case of acts and habits. The reason for this is that a habit is a disposition of the one who has it, and an act is his perfection in relation to an object. Therefore, an act or a habit is "more certain" only inasmuch as it makes the object more certain to us, although it can be called "more noble" from the nobility of the object alone. This is clear from the text of THE PHILOSOPHER at the beginning of the *De anima,* where he divides nobility of scientific knowledge into nobility that corresponds to certitude and the nobility that comes from the nobility of the object. This would not be so if the certitude of scientific knowledge corresponded to the certitude of the object, for then every science that is nobler in relation to its object would be nobler with respect to certitude, because objects that are nobler, such as divine things, are of themselves more certain. Therefore, the certitude of an act or habit does not come from the certitude of the object taken in itself, but from the manner that the habit posits in the one who has the habit and in his act. Therefore, an act or a habit is in no way called "more certain" unless it is more certain in relation to us.

Fourth, he argues as follows:

The distinction made with respect to objects in *Metaphysics* 2—that some are better known simply speaking and of themselves and some are better known to us—does not seem to be true unless it is intelligently understood. For one might oppose it as follows. Just as nothing is called a potential or an actual object of science except in relation to science *(scientia),* so nothing is called a potential or an actual object of knowledge except in relation to knowledge *(notitia).* But science and knowledge are features of the one who possesses science or knowledge, not of the thing that is the object of science or of knowledge. Therefore, nothing is an object of science or of knowledge of itself, but only in relation to us who possess science and knowledge. Therefore, the distinction according to which a thing is said to be either known of itself or known in relation to us does not seem to be a good one.

To this we must say that nothing is called a potential or actual object of science, or a potential or actual object of knowledge, except by reason of the one who possesses science and knowledge. But it is not only man—who is rather on the lowest level of intellectual creatures—who possesses science or knowledge. Hence not everything that is better known to man is better known simply speaking—such things are rather known to the lowest degree; what is better known to God is better known simply speaking, because it is better known with respect to the highest knowledge; and what is better known to an angel is better known at a second level, just as the knowledge of the angel is intermediate between the knowledge of God and that of man.

Now the remark of ARISTOTLE can be shown to be true as follows. Whatever is of a higher nature in being is first known to God and to the angel, who have a higher power of knowing. For God first knows His own essence, and through it He knows other things; ARISTOTLE, in *Metaphysics* 12, says the same thing of every intelligence. For this reason things that have more elevated being are said to be better known of themselves than are sensible things, which are better known to us, for it is the former that are known first and to the highest degree by the highest knowers, namely God and the angels. Simply speaking, however, nothing is said to be an object of science or of knowledge of itself and absolutely, but only from the relation which some science or knowledge has to it.

Fifth, as follows:

Although an object of belief, such as that God is both three and one, is, in the way explained, of itself better known and more certain than many things scientifically known about creatures, nevertheless, many habits and acts of scientific knowledge are, both extensively and intensively, more certain and better known to us than are faith and its act:

—extensively, because that which has several modes of certitude is extensively more certain; but such is the case of scientific knowledge in relation to faith, because scientific knowledge and its act have the certitude of evidence and the certitude—if it may be called "certitude"—of adherence, while faith has only the certitude of adherence; therefore, etc.

—intensively, because that is more certain which is less mixed with doubt; but scientific knowledge can in no way have doubt mixed in with it, while faith can have a kind of doubt mixed in with it, even while the faith is preserved; therefore, it seems that scientific knowledge is intensively more certain than is faith.

Sixth, as follows:

It is clear that the scientific knowledge of the blessed is more certain than the faith of believers. But this is not by {328} reason of the object, namely the Divine Essence and Divine Truth, which is the same in both cases, but only by reason of the different manners in which the intellect is directed to the God Who is both seen and believed in. Therefore, with respect to the present question also, the scientific knowledge that we have of God, for instance that He is one, is more certain than the faith by which we believe of

> Him that he is triune because of the more certain manner in which the intellect is directed to Him through scientific knowledge than through faith.

Seventh, as follows:

> Sight is more certain than hearing. But faith comes from things heard, or "by hearing," as is said in *Romans* 10.17. Scientific knowledge, however, is intellectual vision, and the principles of some sciences can be resolved into things seen with the bodily eyes, as in the case of mathematics. Therefore, it seems that such sciences are more certain than faith.

Eighth, as follows:

> Hugh, in *On the Sacraments* 1, says that "faith is a voluntary adherence or a certitude that is set above opinion and below science." Therefore, the certitude of faith is below the certitude of scientific knowledge and inferior to it.

Thus DURANDUS.

Here the second article terminates.

Article III: Solutions

§1. To the Arguments against the First Conclusion

I. To the Arguments of Aureolus [*p. 86*] In the third article, it remains to respond to the foregoing objections.

Although the response to the arguments against the first conclusion is evident if one examines its proof and the meaning of the conclusion, nevertheless, we say to the *first* argument, which is from AUREOLUS, that the first inference which it makes is correct with reference to the formal object, or formal essence of the object, taken from the point of view of the thing understood. For what is in this way the formal essence of the object of the intellect itself, or of the intellect's habit, is immediately and at first sight intelligible, and by means of this object the intellect is directed to other objects, which are material or accidental. However, it is not in this way that we posit "the mysterious" or "the lacking in evidence" as the formal essence of the object of faith.

If, however, the above-mentioned inference is understood with reference to the formal object of faith from the point of view of the one understanding and believing, it must be denied. For it is not necessary that the formal essence of the object of the intellect, or of the object of its habit, be understood at first sight, as is clear in the case of the essence of "the true" and "the intelligible," and similarly of "the non-apparent," "the seen," "the absent," "the mysterious," and similar essences. It is in this way, not in the former way, that we say that "the mysterious" is the formal essence of the object of faith. Hence the formal essence, taken in this way, is an essence belonging to the object not according to the first manner of perseity, but rather according to the second. It is not an essence which moves or is capable of moving; it is not what is primarily determinative, but is rather concomitant; and, to speak in conformity with what has been said elsewhere, such an essence is not one "to which" or "through which," but one "under which" an object comes under an act, or a habit, or a power.

On this point SAINT THOMAS, in *Questions on Truth,* q.14, a.8, ad 3, speaks as follows:

> The First Truth as appearing in its own form is the object of the heavenly vision, but as not so appearing it is the object of faith. Hence, even if the object of both is the same, it is not the same in aspect. Thus, in being formally different, the object causes different kinds of acts.

Thus SAINT THOMAS. Again, in a.9, he speaks as follows:

> According to AUGUSTINE, in his book *On Seeing God,* "Things absent from our senses are believed if the witness given of them seems to be sufficient. But things present either to the soul or to the senses of the body are seen." This difference is evident in the case of things that are present to the bodily senses, for here it is clear which things are present to the bodily senses and which are not. But in the case of the senses of the soul, which things are present is more obscure. Nevertheless, those things are said to be present to the intellect that do not exceed its capacity, so that its insight may be fixed upon them: for one assents to such things not on account of the testimony of others, but on account of the testimony of one's own intellect. But those things that exceed the faculty of the intellect are said to be absent from the senses of the soul. Hence the intellect cannot be fixed upon them. Hence we cannot assent to them through our own testimony, but only through the testimony of others. And such things are properly said to be believed. Hence the object of faith is properly that which is absent from the intellect,for "things absent are believed, but things present are seen," as AUGUSTINE says in the same book. Or again, the object of faith is what does not appear, that is, what is not seen, because, as is said in *Hebrews* 11.1, "faith is the substance of things hoped for, the argument of things that do not appear." But whenever the essence of a proper object is lacking, the act must also be lacking.

> Hence, as soon as anything begins to be present, or to appear, it cannot come under an act of faith as an object. But whatever things are, in the proper sense, scientifically known are known through resolution into first principles, which are of themselves present to the intellect. Thus all scientific knowledge is perfected in the vision of a thing present to it. Hence it is impossible for there to be faith and scientific knowledge of the same thing.

Thus SAINT THOMAS. **{329}**

In response to the *second* argument, we deny the minor premise with respect to the formal essence of the object from the point of view of the knower or of the knowing power. For the formal essence of the object, taken in this sense, might be something privative or something involving a relation of reason, as is clear in the case of the true, which is the formal object of the intellect, and the good, which is the formal object of the appetite or the will. Nevertheless, we concede that the formal essence of the object of a theological virtue or of a real power taken in a different sense, namely from the point of view of the thing, as the essence that primarily moves or terminates the act of the power, is neither a relation of reason nor a pure privation, but something real, positive, and absolute.

The response to the *third* argument is made clear by the same reasoning. For privation can be a feature of the object of a positive habit—not, indeed, as primarily moving or determining, but as concomitant. For example, uncertainty, uneasiness, and unsteadiness belong to the essence of opinion, which is a positive habit. And irrational belongs to the essence of ass, which is a positive species of substance, and nevertheless irrational is called a privation, although, as a constitutive difference, it is spoken of as something positive to which a negation or privation is inseparably joined.

To the *fourth* argument we say that the object of faith is the true to which adherence is given on account of authority—not, however, to anything true whatsoever, but to the true that is absent and not present, as has been explained above. This is so with respect to the faith that is a theological virtue.

II. To the Arguments of Durandus [*p. 87*] The response to the *first* argument is clear from what has been said above, because the major premise is false with respect to the formal concomitant essence.

In response to the argument for the major premise, we say that its conclusion concerning the formal moving or determining essence of the object is correct, although we do not say that this essence is "the unseen" or "the non-appearing" in relation to faith. But the argument concludes nothing at all with respect to the formal concomitant essence of the object, because the act of the power is neither immediately, nor primarily, nor principally directed to this kind of essence.

Hence, both in this argument and in the previous one there is an equivocation concerning the formal essence of the object. For the "form" or "essence" *(ratio)* of the object can be taken in two ways: in the first way as a moving or determining formal principle that is, in the object, the cause of and reason for the act of the power or habit being directed to its material object; in the second way, "the formal essence" can be taken as the concept or definition of the object. Now these arguments are directed against the first sense of "formal essence," not against the second; but our conclusion is understood with reference to the second sense, not the first, and hence it is untouched and unharmed by the opponent.

In response to the *second* argument we say that the major premise is false with respect to "formal essence" in the second sense, which is the sense in which our conclusion speaks of it, although the major premise is true if one takes "formal essence of the object" in the first sense, which is not the sense in which our conclusion speaks of it, as has been said.

Again, we say that the minor premise can be denied. For that something is seen or unseen comes not entirely from the side of the one who does or does not see, but also from the side of the object which is present to or absent from the power. Hence, as we said in the solution of the first argument of AUREOLUS, quoting the words of SAINT THOMAS in *Questions on Truth*, q.14, a.9:

> The object of faith is, properly speaking, that which is absent from the intellect; for things absent are believed, but things present are seen, etc.

Again, in *In 3 Sent.*, d.24, q.1, a.2, qla.3, ad 4, he speaks as follows:

> That is properly said to be present whose essence is presented to the sense-power or to the intellect. Hence, because this causes vision, AUGUSTINE says that "things present are seen, but things absent are believed." For this reason, faith is likened to hearing, which is of things absent; for by hearing we know things that, though they are absent, are described to us.

Thus SAINT THOMAS. Again, at the same place, in qla.1, he speaks as follows:

> Vision, properly speaking, is the act of the sense of sight. But because of the nobility of this sense, the term "vision" has been transferred to the acts of the other cognitive powers according to their likeness to the sense of sight.

> Now the likeness can be taken with respect to the genus of knowledge alone, and thus, in a large sense and improperly, every act of knowledge will be called an act of vision; in this sense faith, as THE MASTER says, is of things in some way seen, not, indeed, by external, but by internal vision.
>
> In addition, however, the likeness can be taken not merely with respect to the genus of knowledge, but also with respect to the manner of knowing. Now the way in which the sense of sight sees is this: a visible form made actual by light is formed in the sense of sight. Hence, transferring the term "vision" to the intellect, we properly "see" by understanding when, by an intellectual light, an intelligible form comes to be present in our intellect, whether that light is natural, as when we understand the quiddity of man or of any such thing, or whether it is supernatural, as is the light by which we shall see God in heaven.
>
> Moreover, we are said to "see" through the intellect complex objects the knowledge of which arises from the "vision" described: as when by a natural light we see first principles that we know at once because we know their terms; or as in the case of prophetic vision, which comes about through a supernatural light. And we are also said to "see" those things that we can resolve into these principles through reason, as in the case of things which are scientifically known and demonstratively proved.
>
> Now it is clear that faith cannot be of things "seen" in this second sense, because the intelligible form which is principally the object of faith, namely God, escapes formation by our intellect and is not accessible to our intellect in the present life, as AUGUSTINE says. Nor, again, are we able by demonstration to reduce the things of faith to principles which are seen.

Thus SAINT THOMAS.

From these texts it is clear that to be seen or unseen comes not entirely from the side {330} of the one seeing, but also from the side of the thing that is or is not seen and that can, through its own essence or its proper likeness, be present to or absent from the power of sight: for the act of seeing is caused by the power of sight and the visible object being united, because the sense-power in actuality and the sense-object in actuality are one, as is said in *De anima* 3.

To the *third* argument we respond by denying the inference. Furthermore, the argument is invalid because its minor premise is false. For it is not faith and sight, but faith and scientific knowledge, which we call opposite habits.

But granted that actual faith and actual sight are opposite acts, we concede, both in the case of the acts and in the case of the habits, the inference drawn, namely that, just as the formal essence of the object of faith—speaking of "formal essence of the object" in the second sense mentioned above—is "to be absent and unseen," so, similarly, the formal essence of the object of scientific knowledge is "to be seen, and deduced from principles seen in the light of the agent intellect."

To the argument against this point we say that the object, with respect to its formal essence, is prior to the act, taking "formal essence" in the first sense, not in the second. For the essence taken in the latter sense, as has been often stated, does not move the power.

Furthermore, we say that something can be said "to be seen" in two ways: in one way in its first actuality, that is, because it is present to the power of sight through its proper likeness; in another way in its second actuality, that is, because it determines the act of the power of sight. What I am saying about what is said "to be seen" I also understand of what is said "to be unseen." Now when we say that "the unseen" is the formal essence of the object of faith, this can be understood in either way, but more properly in the first way, such that it is of the essence of the object of faith, as such, that the principal form of the object is given, not in the essence of the intelligible object of the believing power, but only through the form and likeness of its effect, by which it is imperfectly represented. Hence SAINT THOMAS, in *In 3 Sent.*, d.24, q.1, a.2, qla.3, speaks as follows:

> Three things are required for the perfect nature of intellectual knowledge: first, that what is known be set before the intellect; second, that the intellect adhere to it; and third, that it see it. Accordingly, the things of faith are set before the intellect—not, to be sure, in themselves, but in words that do not suffice to express them and in likenesses that fall short of representing them. This is why they are said to be known "in a glass" and "darkly"; and this is why they are not, properly speaking, seen. Nevertheless, the intellect assents to them, and for this reason they are imperfectly known, and are not altogether unknown.

Thus SAINT THOMAS.

In response to the *fourth* argument we say that the major premise is true with respect to the formal essence of the object in the first sense mentioned, but is false if understood of the formal essence in the second sense mentioned. For it is not necessary that everything that falls under the consideration of a habit be attributed to the formal essence; rather, it is enough that such an essence belong to all such things as a feature without which they would not fall under the consideration of that habit, as is clear in the case of the essence of "the true," which is the formal essence, in this second sense, of the object of the intellect.

In short: all of these arguments presuppose one point that is false, namely that we are saying that "the unseen" or "the non-appearing" is the formal essence of the object of faith from the point of view of the thing believed, as the "that which" is believed or the "that through which" it is believed. But this is not what our conclusion means, as is clear from its proof; what it does mean is only that "the unseen" or "the non-appearing" is the formal essence from the point of view of the one who believes, and who receives the object believed in under this condition alone. Hence SAINT THOMAS, in *ST* II–II, q.4, a.1, speaks as follows:

> The First Truth is the object of faith according as it, and the things adhered to for its sake, are unseen. Accordingly, the First Truth must be related to the act of faith as an end according to the essence of "a thing unseen," which pertains to the essence of a thing hoped for, according to the saying of THE APOSTLE in *Romans* 8.25: "We hope for what we do not see." For to see the truth is to possess it.

Thus SAINT THOMAS.

In response to the *fifth* argument we say that it is clear from what has been said above that the major premise is not true with respect to the formal essence of the object from the point of view of the cognitive power, but only with respect to the formal essence of the object from the point of view of the thing. For perfect knowledge of the object according to the latter formal essence—not perfect knowledge of the formal essence on the side of the power that underlies the habit—is the end of the habit. SAINT THOMAS, in *Questions on Truth*, q.14, a.8, ad 16, discusses this point as follows:

> The First Truth is said to be the object of faith because faith is of it. Nevertheless, not all statements formulated about God need be an object of belief, but only those attested by Divine Truth. So, too, "moveable body" is the subject of natural philosophy, but not all statements that can be formulated about moveable body are objects of scientific knowledge in natural science, but only those that are shown from the principles of natural philosophy. For the testimony of the First Truth is in faith what a principle is in the demonstrative sciences.

Thus SAINT THOMAS.

Furthermore, we should note that it can be said in response to all of the foregoing arguments that the object of faith can be considered in two ways: in one way in itself, and thus its formal essence is the First Truth; in another way inasmuch as it falls under the act or the habit of faith, and thus its formal essence is "the obscure" and "the unseen." This distinction comes down to what was said above.

§2. *To the Arguments against the Second Conclusion*

To the Arguments of Durandus [*p. 88*] In response to the *first* argument against the second conclusion we say that the major premise, simply speaking, must be denied. For faith, properly speaking, is not of all things revealed by God, but only of those things revealed by God to which one adheres {331} solely and precisely on account of the divine revelation. Of those things to which the believer adheres not solely on account of the divine revelation, but rather on account of clear deduction from first principles known of themselves, he has not faith, but scientific knowledge. Of this point SAINT THOMAS, in *Questions on Truth*, q.14, a.9, speaks as follows:

> Hence the object of faith is properly that which is absent from the intellect, for "things absent are believed, but things present are seen," as AUGUSTINE says in the same book. Or again, the object of faith is "things that do not appear," that is, things that are not seen, because, as is said in *Hebrews* 11.1, "faith is the substance of things hoped for, the argument of things that do not appear." But whenever the essence of the proper object is lacking, the act must also be lacking. Hence, as soon as anything begins to be present, or to appear, it cannot come under an act of faith as an object. But whatever things are, in the proper sense, scientifically known are known through resolution into first principles, which are of themselves present to the intellect. Thus all scientific knowledge is perfected in the vision of a thing present to it. Hence it is impossible for there to be faith and scientific knowledge of the same thing.
>
> Now it must be known that a thing can be an object of belief in two ways. In one way it is so simply speaking, in the case of what exceeds the power of all men in the present life, as that God is one and triune; of these things it is impossible to have scientific knowledge, and every believer assents to such things rather on account of the testimony of God, to Whom these things are present and known.
>
> However, a thing can be an object of belief not simply speaking, but in

> relation to someone, in the case of what exceeds the power not of all men, but only of some, as do those things that can be demonstratively known of God, such as that He exists, or that He is one, or that He is incoporeal, and other such things. Nothing prevents these from being scientifically known by some, who have demonstrations of them, and believed by others, who do not grasp the demonstrations of them. But it is impossible for them to be scientifically known and believed by the same man.

Thus SAINT THOMAS. Again, in the same article, ad 8, he speaks as follows:

> Inasmuch as "that God is one" is something demonstrated, it is not called an article of faith, but something presupposed by the articles. For the knowledge of faith presupposes natural knowledge, as grace presupposes nature. But the unity of the divine essence as it is posited by believers, namely together with omnipotence, omniprovidence, and other such things that cannot be proved, does constitute an article of faith.

Thus SAINT THOMAS. Again, in *ST* II–II, q.1, a.5, ad 3, he speaks as follows:

> Things that can be demonstratively proved are included among the things to be believed, not because there is simply speaking faith in them in the case of everyone, but because they are prerequisites to the things of faith, and they must at least be presupposed through faith by those who do not have a demonstration of them.

Thus SAINT THOMAS. He says something similar in *In 3 Sent.*, d.24, q.1, a.2, qla.2, where he speaks as follows:

> Faith may be related to a thing in two ways, namely of itself and accidentally. Because what of itself pertains to faith pertains to it always and everywhere, therefore, what pertains to faith under this or that aspect belongs to faith not of itself, but accidentally. Accordingly, what simply speaking exceeds the human intellect, as pertaining to God and having been divinely revealed to us, of itself pertains to faith; but what exceeds the intellect of this or that man, but not of every man, pertains not of itself, but accidentally, to faith. Now those things that exceed every human intellect cannot be proved by demonstration, because demonstration is founded on the understanding of principles; this is why such things cannot be scientifically known. But there are certain preambles to faith concerning which there is faith only accidentally, namely inasmuch as they exceed the intellect of a particular man, but not of man simply speaking. Such things can be demonstrated and scientifically known. An example is that God exists, which indeed is something believed in the case of one whose understanding does not grasp the demon-

> stration. For faith, of itself, sufficiently inclines one to everything that accompanies faith, whether as a preliminary or as a consequence.

Thus SAINT THOMAS.

In response to the *second* argument we say that nothing follows from the whole business except that divine authority and a necessary middle term can concur in causing one and the same clear and evident assent; and this we concede. Nevertheless, in such a case, the assent based on evidence will not be an act of faith properly speaking, that is, a believing act that lacks evidence, but rather an act of scientific knowledge. The reason for this is as follows. The evident and necessary middle term takes away the formal essence of the object of faith, since it makes the proposition to which it concludes something appearing and seen. But the act of faith does not occur where the essence of its object is not preserved. Concerning this point a comment was made in the immediately preceding solution, namely that as soon as something begins to be present, or to appear, it cannot come under the act of faith as an object.

In response to the *third* argument we say that the believer who acquires the scientific knowledge that God is one holds this point through two middle terms, namely the authority of God and a demonstrative middle term. But it does not follow from this that the assent caused by these two middle terms is an act both of scientific knowledge and of faith, but only that it is an act of scientific knowledge. For not every assent caused by authority is one of belief—it is so only if the authority is the whole and precise cause, or if another middle term concurs with the authority without taking away the formal essence of the object of faith, as has been stated. But a necessary middle term does take away that essence, and therefore takes away the act of faith. **{332}** SAINT THOMAS speaks on this point as follows in *ST* I–II, q.67, a.3, where he asks whether faith remains after the present life:

> Opposition is the per se and proper cause that one thing is excluded by another, inasmuch as every opposition maintains or involves an opposition of affirmation and negation. Now in some cases there is found an opposition according to contrary forms such as, in the case of colors, black and white. In other cases, however, there is found an opposition according to perfect and imperfect. Thus, in the case of alterations, "more" and "less" are taken as contraries, as when "hotter" comes to be out of "less hot," as is said in *Physics* 5. And because perfect and imperfect are opposed, it is impossible for there to be perfection and imperfection simultaneously in the same respect.

Now it must be considered that imperfection is sometimes of the essence of a thing and belongs to its species, as lack of reason pertains to the essence of the species of horse or cow. And because a thing that remains numerically one and the same cannot be changed from one species to another, when such imperfection is taken away, the species of the thing is taken away as well: thus, if it became rational, it would no longer be a cow or a horse. Sometimes, however, imperfection does not pertain to the essence of the species, but befalls the individual for some other reason. For instance, sometimes lack of reason befalls a certain man inasmuch as the use of reason is impeded in him on account of sleep, drunkenness, or something similar. And it is clear that when such imperfection is taken away, the substance of the thing still remains.

Now it is clear that imperfection of cognition is of the essence of faith, for it is part of its definition. For faith is "the substance of things hoped for, the argument of things that do not appear," as is said in *Hebrews* 11.1. And hence AUGUSTINE says: "What is faith? Believing what you do not see." Now it pertains to the imperfection of cognition that cognition occur without any appearing or vision. Thus imperfection of cognition is of the essence of faith. Hence it is clear that faith cannot become perfect cognition while remaining numerically the same.

Further, it must be considered whether faith can be present simultaneously with perfect cognition. For nothing prevents some kinds of imperfect cognition from sometimes being present simultaneously with perfect cognition. Accordingly, it must be considered that cognition can be called imperfect in three ways: in one way from the point of view of the object of cognition; in another from the point of view of the middle term; and in a third way from the point of view of the subject. From the point of view of the object of cognition, it is matutinal and vespertinal cognition in the angels that differ as perfect and imperfect respectively. For matutinal cognition is of things according as they have being in the Word, but vespertinal cognition is of things according as they have being in their own natures, a being that is imperfect in comparison to the first kind of being. From the point of view of the middle term, it is cognition of a conclusion through a demonstrative middle term and cognition of it through a probable middle term that differ as perfect and imperfect respectively. From the point of view of the subject, it is opinion, faith, and scientific knowledge that differ as perfect and imperfect. For it is of the essence of opinion to assent to one of two contraries together with uneasiness concerning the other, and hence opinion does not involve firm adherence. It is of the essence of scientific knowledge to involve firm adherence

> accompanied by intellectual vision, for scientific knowledge has a certitude that proceeds from understanding of principles. Faith, however, is intermediary, for it is greater than opinion in involving firm adherence, but lesser than scientific knowledge in not involving vision.
>
> Now it is clear that perfect and imperfect cannot be simultaneously present in the same respect. But things that differ as perfect and imperfect can, in a respect that is somewhat the same, be simultaneously present in a thing that is somewhat the same. Thus there can in no way be perfect and imperfect cognition of the same object from the point of view of the object itself. They can, however, come together in the same middle term in the same subject: for nothing prevents one man from possessing, at one and the same moment, through one and the same middle term, cognition of two things, one of which is perfect and the other imperfect, such as health and sickness, or good and evil. Again, it is impossible, from the point of view of the middle term, for perfect and imperfect cognition to come together in a single middle term. But nothing prevents them from coming together in a single object and a single subject: for one man can know the same conclusion through both probable and demonstrative middle terms. Similarly, it is impossible, from the point of view of the subject, for perfect and imperfect cognition to be simultaneously present in the same subject. But faith includes in its essence imperfection from the point of view of the subject, inasmuch as the one who believes does not see what he believes; blessedness, however, includes in its essence perfection from the point of view of the subject, inasmuch as one who is blessed sees that in which he is made blessed. Hence it is clear that it is impossible for faith to remain simultaneously with beatitude in the same subject.

Thus SAINT THOMAS. From this text it is clear that, since the knowledge of belief is imperfect from the point of view of the subject, and since scientific, as well as beatific, knowledge is perfect from the point of view of the subject, it is thus impossible for the act of faith and the act of scientific knowledge to be simultaneously present in the same subject. Secondly, it is clear that not every assent caused by a probable middle term is an assent of opinion, since such assent sometimes implies perfection from the point of view of the subject, just as does the beatific vision. This will be more fully explained in what follows, both in this question and in others: for, as will become clear, this is not the work of a single day.

The response to the *fourth* argument is clear from what has been said above. For a probable middle term, when it concurs with a necessary one in causing assent with respect to the same {333} conclusion, does not cause an assent that is in actuality one of opinion, because the necessary middle term takes away the formal essence of the object or subject of opinion. ("The essence of the object" of opinion from the point of view of the subject I call "uneasiness" or "unfirm adherence," just as "unseen" or "non-appearing" is the formal essence of the object of faith from the point of view of the believer.) This is why, in such a case, assent of scientific knowledge alone is caused, and an assent of opinion is caused only virtually, namely inasmuch as the probable middle term would naturally cause an assent of opinion if it did not concur with the necessary middle term.

Furthermore, we respond to this argument, as we did to the second argument above, that "bright" and "dim," according to which assent of belief and assent of scientific knowledge differ, differ not merely as perfect and imperfect in the essence of light or of vision, but rather as privation and possession, or as involving privation and possession, with respect to the same subject, namely the intellect. For assent of belief involves privation of vision in the subject, but assent of scientific knowledge, as is clear from what has been said, involves the positing of vision.

In response to the argument against this point we say that, although the cause of assent of belief, taken in itself and alone, produces an effect united to privation of brightness and evidence; and although the cause of assent of scientific knowledge produces an effect united to possession of brightness and evidence; nevertheless, this does not prevent them from being able to concur in causing the same effect, one that involves possession, not privation, of brightness. For the cause of assent of faith, namely the First Truth or its witness, causes privation not of itself but accidentally, namely because of imperfection in the subject on which it acts, the human intellect, which, on account of its distance from the First Truth, imperfectly participates in the influence of the First Truth. This is why the First Truth can concur in causing an assent that involves a possession opposed to the privation mentioned, when the subject, acting through something else, is disposed to participate in the effect of brightness and evidence. On this point BLESSED THOMAS, in *Questions on Truth*, q.14, a.9, ad 2, speaks as follows:

> Although the supernaturally infused light is more efficacious than the natural light, we do not in the present state participate in it perfectly, but imperfectly. Because of our imperfect participation in it, we are not led by that infused light to a vision of the things for the knowledge of which the light is given.

> But this will be the case in heaven, when we shall participate in that light perfectly, and shall see the light in the light of God.

Thus SAINT THOMAS.

However, we must note that in such an assent, caused by the concurrence of divine authority and a necessary middle term, there are two features, namely firmness of adherence and the evidence of the complex object to which assent is given. Now the cause of the assent of belief immediately contributes to the first of these, because, by means of the will, it moves the intellect to assent; but it does not contribute to the second.

Similarly, the argument says that "certain" and "doubtful," according to which the assent of scientific knowledge and the assent of opinion differ, differ not merely as perfect and imperfect in the species or genus of "the evident," but rather as possession and privation with respect to the same subject, namely the intellect. For understanding based on opinion is unsteady and involves no firm adherence to what is opined; but the understanding of one who knows scientifically involves firm adherence.

Nor is the attempted argument against this point, an argument like the foregoing one, valid. For although the probable middle term will of itself and in isolation cause an assent united to a privation, when it concurs with the necessary middle term it does not cause such a privation, nor, properly, does it cause the possession opposed to such a privation, namely the possession of evidence or firmness; rather, it causes a certain appearing, inclines the intellect more to one side than to the other, and in so doing co-operates with the necessary middle term.

In response to the *fifth* argument we say that the doctrine of SAINT THOMAS, which the opponent calls "the common doctrine," does not hold that the same man simultaneously possesses scientific knowledge and opinion concerning the same conclusion. For although, as was mentioned in the solution of the third argument, SAINT THOMAS does say that the same man can know the same conclusion both through a probable and through a demonstrative middle term, it does not follow that he both scientifically knows and opines the same conclusion, because, as was said above in response to the third argument, not every assent caused by a probable middle term is an assent of opinion. Rather, as SAINT THOMAS says in the same place, opinion and scientific knowledge differ, from the point of view of the subject, as imperfect and perfect respectively. This is why, according to his argument, they cannot be simultaneously present in the same subject with respect to the exact same composite object.

But the opponent further claims that SAINT THOMAS himself says elsewhere that opinion can co-exist with demonstrative scientific knowledge, etc.

In response to this we say that nowhere in the *Summa* does he either say this explicitly or say anything from which this might be concluded. However, in *ST* III, q.9, a.3, ad 2, he does speak as follows:

> A disposition is related to a perfection in two ways: in one way as a path leading toward the perfection, and in another way as an effect proceeding from the perfection. For through heat matter is disposed to receive the form of fire; but when the form arrives, the heat does not cease, but remains as an effect of the form. Similarly, an opinion caused by a dialectical syllogism leads toward the scientific knowledge acquired through demonstration. But when the scientific knowledge is acquired, knowledge by means of the dialectical syllogism can remain as a consequence of the demonstrative scientific knowledge, which is knowledge through the cause: for one who knows the cause is by that fact also better able to know the probable signs on which the dialectical syllogism is based.

Thus SAINT THOMAS. Now from these words it does not follow that opinion and scientific knowledge concerning the same conclusion can be simultaneously present in the same {334} subject, as is clear from two considerations.

First, because, as is clear from SAINT THOMAS's comparison, the knowledge caused by the dialectical syllogism remains when the scientific knowledge arrives, in the way that the heat that precedes the form of fire in matter remains when the form of fire arrives. But it is clear that, according to him, no accident preceding a substantial form remains numerically the same when the substantial form arrives, as is explained in *In 2 Sent.*, where the plurality of substantial forms in the composite is treated: rather, if the accidents that precede and those that follow are the same, they are not numerically, but specifically or generically the same. Thus, in the present case, the knowledge caused in the intellect by a dialectical syllogism prior to the arrival of scientific knowledge remains not numerically, but specifically or generically the same as that which follows upon the arrival of scientific knowledge.

Secondly, the same point is made clear as follows. Just as SAINT THOMAS says that the heat that follows upon the substantial form of fire is an effect of the form of fire, so he says the same of the knowledge caused by the dialectical syllogism that remains after the arrival of scientific knowledge. But it is clear that it is not the heat that is an effect of the substantial form of fire, but a heat specifically similar to it, which precedes the form of fire in time, because an effect does not precede its efficient cause in time, but rather follows upon it both according to nature and in time. Thus, similarly, the knowledge that could be had through a dialectical syllogism, but which follows upon a demonstration as the effect of the latter, is not numerically, but specifically or generically the same as that which preceded the demonstration and was then an opinion. Therefore, the meaning of the words quoted above is that the demonstrative scientific knowledge leads to a knowledge, whether actual or virtual, of everything that had been known through the dialectical syllogism, and not that the act or habit of opinion remains after the arrival of scientific knowledge. Hence, in *Questions on Truth,* q.14, a.9, ad 6, SAINT THOMAS speaks as follows:

> It does not seem to be possible for anyone to have scientific knowledge and opinion of the same thing, because opinion is accompanied by uneasiness concerning the other side, but scientific knowledge excludes this uneasiness. Similarly, it is not possible for there to be faith and scientific knowledge of the same thing.

Thus SAINT THOMAS.

From these texts it is clear how all other arguments can be resolved that seem to claim that, according to the words of SAINT THOMAS, opinion can be present together with scientific knowledge in the same man and with respect to the same complex object.

The response to the *sixth* argument is clear from what has been said above. For the argument is founded upon something false, namely the claim that the difference between opinion and scientific knowledge consists merely in the fact that opinion is caused by a probable and contingent syllogism or middle term, while scientific knowledge is caused by a necessary one. But there is something more in the essence of opinion, namely its being accompanied by uneasiness, as has just been said. On this point SAINT THOMAS, in *In 3 Sent.*, d.23, q.2, a.2, qla.1, speaks as follows:

> As THE PHILOSOPHER says in *De anima* 3, there are two operations of the intellect. One apprehends the simple quiddities of things, and this operation is called "formation" or "simple understanding" by the philosophers. Corresponding to this understanding is the single word that signifies this operation of the intellect. Hence, just as truth and falsity are not found in the

single word, so neither are they found in this operation of the intellect. This is why, just as the single word, because truth and falsity are not present in it, is neither affirmed nor denied, so, by this operation, the intellect neither assents nor dissents. For this reason, faith, to which assenting pertains, is not found in this operation, but in the other operation, by which the intellect composes or divides, and in which the true and the false are found, as they are in a statement. Again, for this reason, the intellect in this second operation assents or dissents, just as a statement is affirmed or denied. Hence, faith, which involves assent, is found in this operation.

Now since *"sententia"* ("a thought"), which, as ISAAC says, is the acceptance of one side of a contradiction, comes from *"assentiendo"* ("assenting"), one who assents must determine his intellect to one side of a contradiction. This can happen in three ways, corresonding to the three ways in which our intellect can be considered. For in one way our intellect can be considered in itself, and thus it is determined by the presence of an intelligible object as matter is determined by the presence of form. This occurs in the case of those objects that are immediately made intelligible by the light of the agent intellect, namely the first principles that are the object of understanding. Similarly, the judgment of the sensitive part of the soul is determined by the fact that the sensible object lies under one of the sense-powers, the chiefest and most certain of which is sight, which is why the above-mentioned knowledge by the intellect is called "vision."

In another way our intellect can be considered as directed to reason, which terminates in understanding when, by resolving conclusions into principles known of themselves, reason causes certitude in conclusions. This is the assent of scientific knowledge.

In a third way the intellect is considered as directed to the will, which moves all of the forces of the soul to their acts. Now the will determines the intellect to something that neither is seen in itself nor can be resolved into what is seen of itself. It does so by an argument which makes it seem good to adhere to that side of the contradiction, although the argument does not suffice to determine the understanding. Such insufficiency is due to the weakness of the understanding, which neither sees that to which the argument judges assent should be given in itself, nor is able to resolve it into principles known of themselves. This assent is properly called "belief." Hence, too, faith is said to "capture" the intellect, inasmuch as {335} the intellect is terminated by or determined to something not by its own movement, but by a command of the will. Thus, in the one who believes, the argument determines the intellect not of itself, but only through the mediation of the will.

But when an argument that moves to one side of a contradiction neither

> suffices to determine the understanding, because it does not resolve the conclusion into principles known of themselves, nor suffices to determine the will by making it seem good to adhere to that side of the contradiction, then the man "opines" that to which he adheres; and the understanding is not determined to one side, because there still remains a movement toward the contrary, for he accepts one side together with uneasiness about the other, which is why one who opines does not assent.
>
> But when a man has no greater argument for one side than for the other—whether because he has an argument for neither, in the case of the "ignorant" man, or because he has equal arguments for both sides, in the case of the "doubtful" man—then he does not assent in any way whatsoever, since his judgment is not determined at all, but is equally related to different things.
>
> It is clear, therefore, that what separates the believer from all of the others mentioned is "thinking combined with assent." For since "thinking" *(cogitatio)* implies discourse of reason, in one who "understands" there is assent without "thinking," because understanding is of principles, to which anyone agrees at once on hearing them, as BOETHIUS says in his *De hebdomadibus*. In one who "scientifically knows" there is both assent and thinking—not thinking combined with assent, but thinking preparatory to assent, because thinking is reduced to understanding by a resolution, as has been said. In one who "believes" there are assent and thinking simultaneously, because the understanding is not reduced to principles known of themselves, and hence, of itself, it still moves toward different things, though by something extrinsic, namely the will, it is determined to one thing. In one who "opines" there is thinking without perfect assent, although there is a kind of assent, inasmuch as he adheres to one thing more than to another. In one who "doubts" there is no assent, but only thinking. And in one who is "ignorant" there is neither assent nor thinking.

Thus SAINT THOMAS. He says something similar in *ST* II–II, q.2, a.1 and in *Questions on Truth*, q.14, a.1.

From this text it is clear that uneasiness and weakness of assent belong to the essence of opinion. Hence we say to the opponent that assent caused by a contingent middle term, whether it be judged to be contingent or to be necessary, in one who possesses scientific knowledge of the same conclusion through a necessary middle term, if it is an assent distinct from the scientific assent, is an assent of opinion not in actuality, but only virtually or potentially, as was said above in the solution of the fourth argument. The reason for this is as follows. The necessary middle term takes away what is the formal essence of the object of opinion from the point of view of the subject, as well as the privation and imperfection that are of the essence of opinion.

With reference to the question, it is not necessary to discuss whether two acts of understanding can be present simultaneously. I believe that they can, as long as either they have a certain order between them or one is an argument for the other. This is clear in the case of the straight and the bent, in the case of knowledge of principles and of conclusions, and in the case of matutinal and vespertinal knowledge.

The response to the *seventh* argument is clear from what has been said above. For a contingent middle term that concurs with a necessary middle term with respect to the same conclusion never causes an actual or a habitual assent that is truly and formally an assent of opinion: rather, it causes an assent that is potentially one of opinion, in the sense that the assent caused by the contingent middle term would be one of opinion if it did not concur, in the same subject, with the necessary middle term. For, as was said above, the subject of opinion and the subject of scientific knowledge have contrary features with respect to possession and privation, because the subject of scientific knowledge assents firmly, but the subject of opinion is unsteady. But it is impossible for the same intellect, simultaneously and with respect to the same thing, both to have a firm assent and to be unsteady or uneasy.

§3. To the Arguments against the Third Conclusion

To the Arguments of Durandus [*p. 95*] In response to the *first* argument against the third conclusion we say that not every firmness of adherence is properly called "certitude" as the argument indeed proves: rather, only that firmness that has "the firm and stable" as object can be called certitude. But only the true, not the false, can be firm and stable. Hence the firm assent of heretics or of others who err cannot properly be called "certitude," because such assent, although it possesses firmness on the side of the subject, does not do so on the side of the object, where it rather has every kind of frailty and weakness, since it is false and contrary to firm truth. Similarly, such assent or adherence does not possess firmness on the side of the middle term on account of which assent is given. It is otherwise with faith, whose adherence is firm both on the side of the object to which assent is given and on the side of the cause on account of which assent is given, and which is the First Truth, as has often been said.

Again, when we say that firmness of adherence is certitude, we understand this not of any firmness whatsoever, nor of any adherence whatsoever, nor of adherence to any object whatsoever, but only of firmness of adherence of the intellect to its knowable object. But this is nothing other than "the true," for the false is not a knowable object. On this point SAINT THOMAS, in *In 3 Sent.*, d.26, q.2, a.4, speaks as follows:

> What is properly called "certitude" is firmness of adherence of the cognitive power to its object, etc.

as will be stated in the following distinction. And this second response is better than the first. **{336}**

In response to the *second* argument we say that the major premise is true with reference to the firmness of adherence that arises from the evidence of that to which adherence is given; but not with reference to the firmness of adherence that depends on the will, which is the kind of firmness present in the assent of faith. Hence SAINT THOMAS, in *Questions on Truth*, q.14, a.1, speaks as follows:

> In faith, assent and thinking are equally present. For the assent is caused not by the thinking, but by the will. But because the understanding is determined to one thing, in the sense that it is led to its proper term, namely the vision of an intelligible object, its movement is not yet brought to rest, but still involves reasoning about and inquiry into what it believes, even though it gives its most firm assent to it. For it is not given satisfaction or determined to one thing of itself, but is so determined from without. This is why the understanding of one who believes is said to be "captivated," because it is held by extrinsic determinations, and not its own. As is said in 2 *Corinthians* 10.5, "Leading every understanding into captivity, etc." This is why a movement contrary to what he most firmly holds can arise in one who believes, but not in one who understands or knows scientifically.

Thus SAINT THOMAS. Again, in *In 3 Sent.*, d.23, q.2, a.2, qla.3, he speaks as follows:

> A movement of doubt can occur in one who believes, from the fact that his understanding is determined in the vision of its intelligible object not by itself, as it is in the case of scientific knowledge or understanding, but only by the command of the will. Hence, with respect to both features, the one who knows scientifically is farther from the one who doubts than is the one who believes. But with respect to firmness of adherence alone, the one who believes is farther from the one who doubts than is the one who, with respect to both features, knows scientifically.

Thus SAINT THOMAS. He shows what those features are, according to which the one who knows scientifically stands apart from the one who doubts, in the same text, ad 1, where he says:

> The certitude of faith is said to be intermediary between scientific knowledge and opinion not intensively, in the manner of continuous quantity, but extensively, in the manner of number. For the certitude of scientific knowledge consists in two features, namely evidence and firmness of adherence; but the certitude of faith consists in only one, namely firmness of adherence; while the certitude of opinion consists in neither. Nevertheless, the certitude of faith of which we are speaking is, with respect to that one feature, more vehement than the certitude of scientific knowledge with respect to the two.

Thus SAINT THOMAS.

From these texts it is clear that, although it is easier to separate oneself from the assent of faith than from the assent of scientific knowledge, it is still the case that the assent of faith is firmer than the assent of scientific knowledge. For the essences of the two firmnesses are not properly speaking the same, but different, since the firmness of adherence of faith has its principal cause in the will, while the firmness of scientific knowledge is in the understanding as the evidence of the complex object, to which assent is sometimes given against the will. Therefore, the understanding of one who believes, since it is inclined to give assent to the things believed both by its own habit and by a command of the will, adheres more firmly and more intensively—though perhaps not more rootedly—than does the understanding of one who knows scientifically. Nevertheless, just as it is impossible for one who knows scientifically to dissent from a conclusion scientifically known and demonstrated while the habit of scientific knowledge is present, so it is impossible for one who believes to dissent from an article of belief while the habit of belief is present, as is self-evident.

Apart from all this, the assent of faith is said to be firmer by reason of its cause, and by reason of the infallibility of the middle term on account of which assent is given to what is adhered to, as has been said, and as will be discussed at greater length.

In response to the *third* argument we say that the distinction between what is more certain to us and what is so in itself is found not only in the objects believed or scientifically known, but also in the acts and habits of scientific knowledge and of faith.

Concerning the first argument against this point, we say that, although a habit or act is not called more certain on the basis of the certitude of the object alone, it can nevertheless be called more certain on the basis of the certitude of the object and that of the middle term or cause, even though the certitude is imperfectly participated by the subject of the habit or act. Such is the present case. For it is not merely the object of faith that is more certain than the object of scientific knowledge; but the First Truth, on which faith rests, is more certain than the natural light, on which scientific knowledge rests. Thus it is clear that the opposing argument is invalid.

In the same way the response to what is said concerning *De anima* I is clear. For we concede that the nobility, whether of scientific knowledge or of a cognitive habit, that follows from the nobility of the object is different from that which follows from certitude—we concede this where the object of the habit is different from the middle term on which the habit rests. But where the object and the argument leading to the object are the same, as is the case in the present discussion, the two nobilities are the same, or at least inseparable. Hence it is clear that the opponent does not grasp the words of SAINT THOMAS very well. For he thinks that SAINT THOMAS means that faith is of itself, and by reason of its object alone, more certain than scientific knowledge; but SAINT THOMAS does not say this, but rather that faith is more certain by reason of the cause and middle term on which it rests.

In response to the *fourth* argument we say that the distinction concerning objects—some being better known to us and some better known by nature—is correct not merely in the way that the opponent explains when he distinguishes a threefold knowledge, namely divine, angelic, and human: rather, it is also true, from the point of view of the object of knowledge and according to more and less, with respect to the known and the unknown.

The opponent says that nothing is called an actual or potential object of knowledge, or an actual or potential object of science, except through knowledge or science, etc.

In response to this we say that, although nothing is called an actual or potential object of knowledge except by its being directed to knowledge, or knowledge to it, nevertheless, that directing need not be merely with respect to the act or the active potency of the one who knows: rather, it can also be with respect to the passive potency of the object, that is, because the object has more or less knowability according as it has more or less being. On this point BLESSED THOMAS, in *In 1 Phys.*, speaks as follows: **{337}**

> It must be noted that "to be known by us" and "to be known simply speaking" do not mean the same thing. Things are simply speaking better known that are better known of themselves. But things are better known of themselves that have more being, because anything is an object of knowledge inasmuch as it is a being. But those things are to a greater extent beings that are to a greater extent in act; hence, such things are by nature best able to be known. But in relation to us it is the converse, because in understanding we proceed from potency to act, and the beginning of our knowledge is in sensible things, which are material and [are] intelligible only in potency. Hence they are known to us prior to the separate substances, which are by nature better known, as is clear from *Metaphysics* 2. Accordingly, ARISTOTLE says they are "better known by nature" not as if one knew them by nature, but because they are, in themselves and in their own nature, better known.

Thus SAINT THOMAS. From this text it is clear how certain things are said to be better known "by nature," or in their own nature and of themselves: it is not that they are actually known by an act of knowledge, but that, in their own nature, they have more knowability because they have more actuality, just as a thing has more visibility that has more light.

In response to the *fifth* argument we say that nothing that is known in natural science, and no act or habit of knowledge in natural science, is intensively more certain, simply speaking, than the act or habit of faith.

In response to the argument against this point we say that the admixture of doubt with faith indeed shows that the act or habit of faith is less certain from the point of view of the subject and with respect to us. But this is consistent with the fact that this act or habit is more certain from the point of view of the cause and middle term on which it rests, and which has a greater infallibility than does that on which science rests. This is why this act or habit is, simply speaking, more certain. Hence BLESSED THOMAS, in *ST* II–II, q.4, a.8, obj.1, argues as follows:

> Doubt is opposed to certitude. Hence that seems to be more certain which involves less doubt, just as that is more white which is less mixed with black. But understanding, scientific knowledge, and wisdom are incompatible with doubt concerning their objects. One who believes, however, can experience a movement of doubt, and doubt concerning the objects of faith. Therefore, faith is not more certain than are the intellectual virtues.

Thus the argument; the response is as follows:

> We must say that the doubt comes not from the side of the cause of faith, but in relation to us, inasmuch as we do not fully grasp with our understanding the things of faith.

Thus SAINT THOMAS.

In response to the *sixth* argument we say that the scientific knowledge of the blessed is not more certain than the faith of believers from the point of view of the cause or middle term on which it rests, because in both cases this is the First Truth. But it is more certain from the point of view of the subject, who more fully grasps the things that he sees than does the believer the things that he believes.

Similarly, we concede, with respect to the faith and scientific knowledge of those in the present life, that scientific knowledge is more certain from the point of view of the subject. However, it is less certain from the point of view of the cause or middle term.

SAINT THOMAS responds, in form, to the *seventh* argument, in *ST,* II–II, q.4, a.8, ad 2, where he speaks as follows:

> Vision, or the power of sight, is, other things being equal, more certain than hearing. But if what is heard exceeds the power of sight of one who sees, then hearing will be more certain than sight, just as a man of little scientific knowledge is more certain of what he hears from someone extremely wise than he is of what he sees for himself through his own reason. And so much more is a man more certain of what he hears from God, Who cannot err, than of what he sees with his own reason, which can err.

Thus SAINT THOMAS.

BLESSED THOMAS responds to the *eighth* argument in *In 3 Sent.,* d.23, q.2, a.2, qla.3, ad 1, where he speaks as follows:

> The certitude of faith is said to be intermediary between the certitude of scientific knowledge and that of opinion, etc.

—as was quoted above in the solution of the second argument.

SAINT THOMAS responds to the affirmative argument for the question [p. 82] in *In 3 Sent.,* d.24, q.1, a.2, qla.1, ad 2, where he speaks as follows:

> The terms of principles that are naturally known are comprehensible to our intellect; and hence the knowledge of those principles that arises is vision.

But it is not so concerning the terms of the articles of faith. Hence, in the future, when God will be seen in His essence, the articles will be known of themselves just as principles of demonstration are now.

Thus SAINT THOMAS.

This suffices for the question.

Blessed be God.

Amen.

Whether Hope Is a Theological Virtue Really Distinct from Faith and Charity

In relation to the twenty-sixth distinction in the third book of *The Sentences,* the question is raised: Whether hope is a theological virtue really distinct from faith and charity.

It is argued that it is not, as follows. Hope is not a theological virtue. Therefore, etc.

The major premise is made clear as follows. A theological virtue is one that has God for its object. But hope has for its object not merely God, but also other goods, which we hope to obtain from God. Therefore hope is not a theological virtue. **{338}**

Argument is made for the opposite conclusion as follows. In *1 Corinthians* 13, hope is enumerated together with faith and charity, which are theological virtues. From this it is apparent that it is a theological virtue, one counted together with faith and charity.

In this question there will be three articles: in the first the conclusions will be presented, in the second the objections, and in the third the solutions.

Article I: Conclusions

First Conclusion: Hope Is a Virtue

SAINT THOMAS presents this conclusion in *ST* II–II, q.17, a.1, where he speaks as follows:

> According to THE PHILOSOPHER, in *Ethics* 2, the virtue of anything is that which makes what possesses it, and the operation of what possesses it, good. Accordingly, wherever

> there is a good human act, there must be a corresponding human virtue. Now in the case of everything that is ruled and measured, we take the good to be the thing's conformity to its appropriate rule, as we say an article of clothing is "good" which neither exceeds nor falls short of its appropriate measure. But there are two measures of human acts: one that is close and connatural to such acts, namely reason; and another that is exalted and transcends such acts, namely God. Hence every human act that conforms to reason or to God Himself is good.
>
> Now the act of hope, of which we are now speaking, does conform to God. For the object of hope is an arduous future good which it is possible to possess. But a thing may be possible to us in two ways: in one way through ourselves, and in another way through others, as is clear from *Ethics* 3. Now inasmuch as we hope for something as possible for us through divine help, our hope conforms to God Himself, on Whose help we rely. Hence it is clear that hope is a virtue, since it causes a human act to be good, and to conform to the required rule.

Thus SAINT THOMAS. Again, in *Questions on the Virtues,* "On Hope", a.1, he speaks as follows:

> Habits are known through acts, and acts through objects. Hence, in order to know whether hope is a virtue, we must consider the nature of its act.
>
> Now it is clear that "hoping" implies a movement of the appetitive part or of a virtue, a movement that is directed to a good: not, like joy and pleasure, to a good as already possessed, but rather, like desire and longing, to a good as something to be attained. However, hope differs from desire in two respects. First, because desire is universally related to any good whatsoever, and so is attributed to the concupiscible power, while hope concerns an arduous good, that is, one attained with difficulty, and so is attributed to the irascible power. Secondly, because desire concerns a good taken absolutely, with no consideration of its possibility or impossibility, while hope is directed to a good as to something possible of attainment, for it implies, in its very essence, a certain assurance of attainment. Accordingly, there are four things to consider in the object of hope: first, that it is a good, by which hope differs from fear; second, that it is a future good, by which hope differs from joy or pleasure; third, that it is an arduous good, by which hope differs from desire; and fourth, that it is a good possible to obtain, by which hope differs from despair.
>
> Now there are two ways in which it is possible for a good to be obtained by someone. One is through his own power; the other is through the help of

> another, for whatever is possible through our friends is possible for us, as is made clear by THE PHILOSOPHER in *Ethics* 3. Accordingly, sometimes a man hopes to obtain something through his own power, but sometimes he hopes to obtain something through the help of others. This latter kind of hope "has an expectation," "looks out" *(expectationem habet)*, inasmuch as a man "expects," "looks to" *(respicit)*, the help of another, and in such a case the movement of hope must be directed to two objects, namely the object to be obtained and the one on whose help the man relies.
>
> Now man cannot obtain the highest good, which is eternal blessedness, except through divine help, as is said in *Romans* 6: "Eternal life by the grace of God." Hence the hope of obtaining eternal life has two objects, namely the eternal life that one hopes for, and the divine help from which it is hoped for. Similarly, faith has two objects, namely the thing that is believed, and the First Truth that is believed in. Faith, however, has the essence of a virtue only inasmuch as it adheres to the witness of the First Truth, believing in it with respect to what has been revealed by it, according to the remark of *Genesis* 15: "Abraham believed in God, and was held to be just." Hence, too, hope has the essence of a virtue by the fact that a man adheres to the help of divine power in the attainment of eternal life. For if someone should rely on human help, whether his own or that of another, this would be a vice, according to the remark of *Jeremiah* 17: "Cursed is the man who trusts in man, and who makes the flesh his strength." Accordingly, just as the formal object of faith is the First Truth through which, as through a middle term, one assents to the things which he believes and which constitute the material object of faith; so, the formal object of hope is the help of divine power and pity, by which the movement of hope is directed to the good things that are hoped for and that constitute the material object of hope. And just as the things that we believe as material objects of faith are all referred to God, although some of them are creaturely, such as that all creatures come from God, or that the Son of God took on flesh in the oneness of his person; so, the things that we hope for as material objects of hope are ordered to one final object of hope, which is the enjoyment of God: for in {339} the directing of things to this enjoyment, we hope to be helped by God not merely to spiritual benefits, but also to bodily ones.

Thus SAINT THOMAS.

From these texts the following argument can be formulated. Every habit that causes an act to be good and to conform to the rule required is a virtue. But the hope of which we are speaking is such. Therefore, etc.

Second Conclusion: Hope Is a Theological Virtue

SAINT THOMAS presents this conclusion in *ST* II–II, q.17, a.5, where he speaks as follows:

> Since specific differences of themselves divide a genus, we must note whence hope gets its essence as a virtue in order to know the specific difference of virtue under which it is placed. Now it is clear that hope has the essence of a virtue by the fact that it conforms to the supreme rule of human acts, namely God, to Whom it conforms both as a first efficient cause, inasmuch as it relies on His help, and as an ultimate final cause, inasmuch as it looks for blessedness in the enjoyment of Him. Thus it is clear that the principal object of hope, inasmuch as it is a virtue, is God. Since, therefore, the essence of a theological virtue consists in its having God as its object, it is clear that hope is a theological virtue.

Thus SAINT THOMAS. He presents a similar opinion in *In 3 Sent.*, d.26, q.2, a.2.

From these texts the following argument can be formulated. Every virtue that has God as its object is theological. But hope is this kind of virtue. Therefore, it is a theological virtue.

Third Conclusion: Hope Is a Virtue Distinct from Faith and from Charity

SAINT THOMAS presents this conclusion in *In 3 Sent.*, d.26, q.2, a.3, qla.1, where he speaks as follows:

> The theological virtues are for directing us to our last end. Now in order for someone to begin to act for the sake of an end, he must first know that end, and secondly desire it. But because the will may be directed to both things possible and things impossible, and because no-one acts for the sake of something that is impossible to obtain, even if he desires it, therefore, in order for the will to begin to act, it must be directed to the object as something possible. This inclination of a will directed to an eternal good as something possible to it through grace, is the act of hope. This is why hope is something distinct from faith and from charity. For faith causes knowledge of the end, and inasmuch as faith shows that the end is good, there arises the movement of charity; but inasmuch as it shows that the end is possible, there arises the movement of hope; for faith is the foundation of all the virtues, and precedes all of them in the natural order of their acts.

Thus SAINT THOMAS. Again, in the same place, ad 1, he speaks as follows:

> The object of all the theological virtues is the same in reality, but differs in aspect. For inasmuch as it is the First Truth, it is the object of faith; inasmuch as it is the highest good, it is the object of charity; and inasmuch as it is what is most difficult to obtain, it is the object of hope. Now because "blessedness" names what is most difficult to obtain—for it is a state made perfect by the aggregation of all goods, as BOETHIUS says—blessedness enters into the definition of hope. But the way in which virtues and powers differ on the basis of objects is not according to a real difference of object, but according to the different aspects of an object that together constitute it as a formal object.

Thus SAINT THOMAS. Again, in *ST* II–II, q.17, a.6, he speaks as follows:

> A virtue is called "theological" by the fact that it has God as the object to which it adheres. But someone can adhere to a thing in two ways: in one way, on account of the thing itself; in another way, inasmuch as through it one reaches something else. Accordingly, charity causes a man to adhere to God on account of God Himself, uniting the man's mind to God through the affection of love; hope and faith, however, cause a man to adhere to God as a principle whereby certain things may come to us. Now it is from God that both knowledge of truth and attainment of perfect goodness come to us. Accordingly, faith causes a man to adhere to God as a principle, for us, of knowing truth, inasmuch as we believe that those things are true that have been said by God. Hope, however, causes a man to adhere to God as a principle, for us, of perfect goodness, inasmuch as through hope we rely on divine help in obtaining blessedness.

Thus SAINT THOMAS.

From these texts the following argument can be formulated. Those habits are really distinct that have distinct formal objects. But this is true of faith, hope, and charity. Therefore, etc.

Here the first article terminates.

Article II: Objections

§1. Against the Second Conclusion

Arguments of Durandus In the second article, argument is made against the foregoing. DURANDUS (*In 3 Sent.*, d.26, q.2; *In 1 Sent.* d.1, q.2) argues against the second conclusion, as well as certain points contained in its proof, that it is not God, but rather created blessedness, that is the immediate object of hope. *First,* he argues as follows:

> Hope pertains to the love of concupiscence, by which we will a good for ourselves. But {340} the proximate and immediate object of the love of concupiscence is not God Himself in Himself, for in that case He would be loved for His own sake, and with the love of friendship. Therefore, the proximate and immediate object is something created, and nothing other than created blessedness, as is clear from the description of hope as the expectation of future blessedness, etc.

Second, he argues as follows:

> The object of hope and that of joy or pleasure are the same, differing only with respect to what is present and what is future. But the proximate object of joy or pleasure is not God in Himself, but created blessedness. Therefore the same is true of hope.
>
> The minor premise can be proved in many ways. *First,* as follows. The immediate object of the love of concupiscence is not a thing that is different in subject from the one who desires. But since enjoyment is a pleasure taken in God possessed, it is a love of concupiscence. Therefore the immediate object of enjoyment or pleasure is not God, Who is a thing different from us in subject, but the act by which He is attained or possessed by us.
>
> Both of the premises of this argument will now be proved.
>
> First, the major premise will be proved by induction and demonstration.
>
> The proof by induction is evident. I love wine with a love of concupiscence. Is the immediate object of this love the wine itself? Of course not: it is rather the use and the enjoyment of the wine, which is an act. For it is not the wine itself, but the enjoyment of the wine, that I immediately love. It is the same in all other cases.
>
> The same thing is made clear by reasoning, as follows. What is loved with the love of concupiscence is a good or a perfection that we will or love for ourselves. But a thing different in subject from us is never our good except by reason of the act by which it is united to us; for instance, nourishment, such as bread or wine, would never be our good except by reason of the act by which it is united to us, namely, eating and drinking, and it is this union which is the immediate good. Therefore, a thing different in subject from the one who desires is not the immediate object of the love of desire. And this was the major premise.
>
> The minor premise, namely that the enjoyment that is pleasure in God and in God possessed is a love of concupiscence, is proved as follows. It is either a love of concupiscence or one of benevolence. Now it cannot be called a love of benevolence, that is, one by which we would wish some good to God. For pleasure in God possessed corresponds to a desire to possess

Him. But in such a desire we do not desire that some good be possessed by God, for such a desire would be foolish, since nothing that is yet to be can come to God. Rather, we desire that He be possessed by us, and this pertains to the love of desire, by which we desire a good for ourselves, such as the possession of God, or the seeing of Him, or something similar. Therefore, the love of God possessed is not a love of benevolence toward God, but a love of concupiscence turned back upon ourselves.

This point is confirmed as follows. The love that has as the formal essence of its object a useful or a pleasurable good is love of concupiscence. But such is the case under discussion. Therefore. . . .

Thus both the major and the minor premises have been proved.

Second, the minor premise of the second principal argument can also be proved as follows. The object of an antecedent desire and of a subsequent pleasure are the same in the way that the terminus in which there is rest and the terminus toward which there is movement are the same. But the immediate object of desire is not God, but an act by which we attain God. Therefore, the immediate object of enjoyment or pleasure is not God, but an act by which God is attained.

The major premise is evident.

The minor premise is proved as follows. The object of desire is something that is "going to be." But God in Himself is not "going to be": rather, the vision or revelation of Him is "going to be" for us. Therefore, it is the latter that we desire, and not God in Himself, except inasmuch as He is included in the latter as object.

Third, we also argue for the same point as follows. Desire and pleasure are related to a good as fear and sorrow are to an evil. But the greatest sorrow, which the damned experience, concerns, not God in Himself and immediately, but the absence of the vision of God. Therefore, the greatest pleasure or enjoyment, which the blessed experience, concerns not God in Himself and immediately, but the vision of God.

This is confirmed as follows. Just as God in Himself does not have the nature of something evil in relation to the damned except by reason of the punishment He causes, so God in Himself is good to the blessed only by reason of the reward He causes. For there is no extrinsic good of anything except by reason of an intrinsic good.

Fourth, we also argue for the same point as follows. According to THE PHILOSOPHER, pleasures are distinguished, and are judged to be good or evil, according to the operations upon which they follow. Now this remark might be understood in two ways. It might be understood with reference to operations that are antecedent to pleasures but are not the objects of the pleasures, such as thinking about objects: for such thinking always precedes the pleasures that concern things thought about, although the thinking itself is not always the object of the pleasures. Or again, the remark might be understood with reference to operations that precede the pleasures as their objects. Now the remark cannot be understood in the first way: for, in the case of the thinking that precedes pleasure, no such thinking can be judged to be evil, because all thinking, even about evil things, is good. Therefore, the remark must be understood in the second way, namely with respect to operations that precede the pleasures as their objects, in this case as objects of thinking. Hence it is clear that the immediate object of any pleasure is an operation that is, or is judged to be, the formal good of the one operating. And this is what THE PHILOSOPHER says in *Ethics* 7, namely that pleasure is an unimpeded connatural operation; this is a "predication by cause," because the operation is the cause of the pleasure, and is so in the manner of an immediate object.

Fifth, we also argue for the same point as follows. Two things are required for pleasure, **{341}** namely the presence of one's proper good and the knowledge of the good that is present. From this we argue as follows. That alone can be the proper and immediate object of pleasure which either is or is able to be the proper good of the one who takes the pleasure. But neither God nor anything different in subject from man can be man's proper good: rather, nothing can be his proper good except by reason of the operation by which he attains it. Therefore, neither God nor anything different in subject from man can be the immediate object of human pleasure.

The major premise is made clear as follows. No-one takes pleasure in any good except inasmuch as he judges it to be in some way his own. Hence THE PHILOSOPHER says in *Ethics* 8: "The good that is an object of love is, to each one, what belongs to him." For no affection follows upon knowledge of the good in itself, which is speculative knowledge.

The minor premise is proved as follows. When something is said to be "such" by extrinsic denomination, and something else is said to be "such" by formal denomination, that which is said to be "such" by extrinsic denomination agrees with the something else in the "suchness" only by reason of the formal denomination. For example: "healthy" may be said of a medicine, of a diet, and of an animal, but it is said of the medicine and the diet by extrinsic denomination, and of the animal by formal predication; hence both the medicine and the diet are called "healthy" only by reason of the health that is formally present in the animal. Similarly, something can be called "good for man" by extrinsic denomination, namely because it is the cause of some good in man. For example, the sun is good for one who is getting cold be-

> cause it causes in him the heat that is formally his good; and the sun could never be called "good for one who is getting cold" except by reason of the heat that is formally his good. Now it is in this way that God, or anything that is different from man in subject, cannot be called "the good of man" formally speaking, but only by extrinsic denomination, whatever the latter may be. Therefore, to be the good of man cannot pertain to God except by reason of the formal good that is formally present in man. Rather, just as the health that is formally present in man and the health from which medicine is denominated "healthy" are not numerically different, but one and the same, so the goodness by which God is called "the good of man," or fire "the good of one who is getting cold," is none other than the good by which man is, formally speaking, good, or the good by which the one who was getting cold is said, formally speaking, "to be well." Thus the minor premise is clear.
>
> The conclusion therefore follows, namely that the immediate object of pleasure is not God in Himself, but an act by which He is reached by or united to us.

Thus DURANDUS.

From these arguments, DURANDUS says, the minor premise of the second principal argument against our conclusion—namely that the proximate object of joy or pleasure is not God in Himself, but created blessedness—is clear. And thus it seems that not God, but created blessedness, is the immediate object of hope.

§2. *Against the Third Conclusion*

Arguments of Scotus SCOTUS (*In 3 Sent.*, d.26, q.1) argues, against the third conclusion, that hope is not a third habit, distinct from faith and charity.

First he argues that it is not a habit different from faith. *First,* he does so as follows:

> A habit regarding what is universal is not formally different from a habit regarding what is particular, as is clear in the case of all intellectual virtues. But faith regards what is universal, because by faith I hold that everyone who is in the end just is to be saved; and hope regards what is particular, because by hope I hold that I, being just in the end, am to be saved. Therefore the two are not formally different habits.
>
> This is confirmed as follows. One who despairs is said not to hate, but to be mistaken; and he does not need to be persuaded to love or to choose, because he would do so if he believed that the object were possible; rather, he needs to be persuaded to believe that the object is possible for him to attain.

Second, he argues as follows:

> If hope were a habit different from faith, this would be either because hope has for its object things pertaining to it alone, while faith has for is object things pertaining to all of the theological virtues; or, secondly, because futurity belongs to the essence of the object of hope, but not that of faith; or, thirdly, because hope has to find the intermediary between hoping too much, which is presumption, and hoping too little, which is despair, while faith has to do no such thing. But none of these is a sufficient explanation.
>
> The first is not, because a specification of the kind mentioned does not make for a difference of habit, as is clear in the case of the other intellectual habits. Therefore, it does not do so in this case.
>
> Nor can the second explanation be given. For in that case hope would not be a theological virtue, because it would not regard the eternal as its object, but something temporal, for temporality would be the formal essence of its object. On the one hand, if futurity requires a habit of its own, so, with equal reason, will pastness, and thus the habit of faith concerning things past will not be the same as that concerning things future. On the other hand, faith concerns the future proposition "Everyone who is just will be saved" in the way that hope concerns the future proposition "If I am just in the end, I shall be saved," and the only difference here is between universal and particular, which does not make for a difference of habit.
>
> Nor can the third explanation be given, for two reasons. On the one hand, because hope would then be an acquired moral virtue, not an infused theological one, because a virtue which moderates the passions is an acquired moral one. On the other hand, because there would then be an infused fear; but fear is not a theological virtue; and fear does not regard an uncreated object, but only an evil, while a theological habit regards an uncreated good.

Thus SCOTUS.

Furthermore, he argues that hope is not a theological virtue different from charity. *First,* he argues as follows:

> A plurality is to be avoided where there is no need for positing it. But so it is in the present question, where there seems to be no need for positing a third theological virtue different from faith and charity. Therefore, etc. **{342}**
>
> The minor premise is proved as follows.
>
> *First* because the same virtue suffices to dispose the will both to will what has been ordained to be willed and to reject what has been ordained to be rejected. This is proved as follows. There cannot be willing of what has

been ordained to be willed unless there is rejection of what has been ordained to be rejected. This is confirmed by the statement in *De anima* 1: "The straight is judge both of itself and of the crooked."

Again, the same virtue is sufficient to dispose one to love a present good and to desire an absent good, as may be proved by argument and by authority. By argument as follows: it is by the same virtue that a thing both tends to a terminus not yet reached and rests in one that has been reached, as is clear in the case of something heavy. Then there is the authority of AUGUSTINE, in *De trinitate* 9: the appetite of one who desires becomes the love of one who enjoys. If, therefore, there is a habit that suffices to dispose the will to willing, or, in the case of a present good, to enjoying, what has been ordained to be willed or enjoyed, then that habit also suffices for rejecting everything that has been ordained to be rejected, as well as for the desire that is hope. But charity alone suffices to dispose the will to supernaturally love every present object of enjoyment. Therefore, it also suffices to dispose the will to hope for what is not possessed.

Second, the minor premise is proved as follows. Acquired friendship suffices for willing everything that has been ordained to be willed concerning the friend: for the willing which is loving a present good, and for the rejecting of the evil that is opposed to the one loved, and for the desiring of an absent good which is hoping. But infused friendship suffices no less than does acquired friendship with respect to the multiplicity of objects, since by charity the will extends itself as widely as possible to loving all things.

Thus SCOTUS argues in form.

Here the second article terminates.

Article III. Solutions

§1. To the Arguments against the Second Conclusion

To the Arguments of Durandus [*p. 127*] In the third article it remains for us to respond to the foregoing objections.

In response to the *first* argument of DURANDUS against the second conclusion we say that the major premise can be conceded, but the minor premise must be denied.

The former is evident from the words of BLESSED THOMAS in *ST* II–II, q.17, a.8, where he speaks as follows:

> There are two kinds of order. One follows to the way of generation and of matter, according to which the imperfect is prior to the perfect; the other fol-

> lows the way of perfection and of form, according to which the perfect is naturally prior to the imperfect.
>
> According to the first kind of order, then, hope is prior to charity. This is made clear as follows. Hope, as well as every movement of appetite, is derived from love. But one kind of love is perfect, and another imperfect. Perfect love is that by which something is loved for itself, as when one wishes good to another in himself, for instance when a man loves a friend. Imperfect love is that by which one loves something not in itself, but rather inasmuch as it provides him with a good, as when a man loves a thing that he desires. Now the first kind of love, when it is love of God, pertains to charity, which adheres to God in Himself. But hope pertains to the second kind of love, because one who hopes is intent upon obtaining something for himself. Hence, in the way of generation, hope is prior to charity. For just as one is led to love God by the fact that, fearing to be punished by Him, one ceases from sin, as AUGUSTINE says in his commentary on the Canon of John, so, too, hope leads to charity, inasmuch as, hoping to be rewarded by God, one is enflamed to love God and keep His precepts.
>
> But according to the order of perfection, charity is naturally prior. Hence, when charity is added, hope is made more perfect, because we have the greatest hope in the case of friends. This is the sense in which AMBROSE says that "Hope comes from charity."

Thus SAINT THOMAS. He says something similar in *Questions on the Virtues*, "On Hope", a.3, where he speaks as follows:

> All of the affections of the soul, which are movements of appetite, are comparable to natural movements. For natural movement proceeds from a natural inclination called "natural appetite"; similarly, the movements of the affections of animals proceed from a natural inclination that is "animal appetite." Now in natural movements, there is, first, a principle of movement, which is the informing of the mobile thing by its natural form, as when what is heavy or light is brought into being; second, there is the natural movement that proceeds from such a form, as when a light body rises or a heavy one falls; third, there is rest at the place proper to the body. Similarly, in animal appetite, there is first an informing of the appetite by the good, and this informing is the love that unites the thing loved to the one loving; from this, if the good that is loved is remote, it follows, second, that the appetite tends toward it by a movement of desire or hope; third, when one obtains the thing loved, there follows joy or pleasure. Hence, just as natural movement and rest proceed from a form, so every affection of the soul pro-

> ceeds from love. Accordingly, {343} differentiation among other affections of the soul must be according to differentiation of love.
>
> Now there are two loves, one perfect and the other imperfect. There is imperfect love of a thing when one loves the thing not as wishing good to it in itself, but as wishing its good for oneself, and this love is what some call "concupiscence" or "love of concupiscence"; for instance, when we love wine, wishing to enjoy its sweetness, or when we love a man for the sake of our own profit or pleasure. But the other is the perfect love by which the good of someone is loved for his own sake, as when, in loving someone, I wish that he may possess the good even if I get nothing out of it; this is said to be "the love of friendship" by which someone is loved for himself.
>
> Now in order that someone might love the divine good in or for itself, he is led to this by the goods that come to him from God and that he desires for himself, and by the evils that he avoids by adhering to God. With respect to the avoidance of evils, fear pertains to this love; but with respect to the attainment of goods, hope, which is a movement directed to obtaining something, pertains to it. Hence both fear and hope, according to their proper essence, are derived from an imperfect love of God.

Thus SAINT THOMAS.

From these texts it is clear that hope pertains to, and is derived from, the love of desire, not that hope itself is the love of desire.

Similarly, the falsity of the minor premise is clear from what has been said. For, as has been seen, God can be loved with two loves, namely an imperfect love called "love of concupiscence," and a perfect love called "love of friendship." Neither of these is a sin: rather, if charity and grace are present, they are both good, licit, and meritorious; and the second one does not rule out the first, because the first leads to the second, as has been said above. However, the first love of God, that of concupiscence, is meritorious only if the second love of God, the love of friendship by which God is loved for His own sake, is also present. SAINT THOMAS shows that it is not inappropriate to love God on account of something else in *ST* II–II, q.27, a.3, where he speaks as follows:

> The term "on account of" *(propter)* implies a relation to some cause. But there are four genera of causes, namely final, formal, efficient, and material; the material disposition, which is a cause not simply speaking, but in a certain respect, is reduced to the last of these.
>
> Now one thing is said to be loved "on account of" something else with

> respect to each of these four genera of causes: with respect to the genus of final cause, as we love medicine "on account of" health; with respect to the genus of formal cause, as we love a man "on account of" his virtue, that is, because he is formally good through virtue, and therefore loveable; with respect to the efficient cause, as we love certain men inasmuch as they are sons of a great father; and with respect to the disposition that is reduced to the genus of material cause, we are said to love something "on account of" the fact that it disposes us to love it, for instance "on account of" benefits that we have received, although afterwards, once we have begun to love, we may love the friend not "on account of" those benefits alone, but "on account of" his virtue.
>
> In the first three ways, accordingly, we love God not "on account of" something else, but "on account of" Himself. For He is not ordered to something else as to an end, but is Himself the ultimate end of all things; and He is not informed by something else in order to be made good, but rather His substance is His goodness, a goodness by which, as by an exemplar, all things are good; and again, goodness is not present in Him from something else, but rather from Him it is present in all other things. In the fourth way, however, He can be loved "on account of" something else, because it is through certain other things—such as the benefits received or things hoped for from Him, or the punishments we wish to avoid through Him—that we are disposed to make progress in the love of God.

Thus SAINT THOMAS.

In response to the *second* principal argument of DURANDUS we say *first* that the major premise, namely that the object of hope and the object of the subsequent enjoyment or pleasure are entirely the same, is, if taken universally, false. This is made clear as follows. As has been said before, hope has, so to speak, two objects, or rather, it regards two features in its object: one is material, namely what is hoped for; the other is formal, namely that by whose help one hopes to obtain it. These two are sometimes really distinct, as when someone hopes to obtain something with the help of friends; but this real distinction does not occur in the object of enjoyment or pleasure.

Again, difficulty and possibility belong to the essence of the object of hope, but not to the essence of the object of pleasure. Hence, when enjoyment arrives, hope is removed.

Again, inasmuch as they are passions, hope is in the irascible power, while enjoyment or pleasure is in the concupiscible power. Now it is true that the object of desire and the object of pleasure are the same, with a difference only according to what is present and what is future; but desire and hope are different, as SAINT THOMAS shows in many places, especially *ST* I–II, q.40, a.1. We can, however, concede that the material object of the hope that precedes and of the pleasure that ensues are the same in reality.

Second, we say that the minor premise is false. For God in Himself is the proximate and immediate object of enjoyment and pleasure. But He is not the total or complete object, because every pleasure has for its partial or total object some operation. Concerning this point SAINT THOMAS, in *ST* I–II, q.32, a.1, speaks as follows:

> Two things are required for pleasure, namely attainment of an appropriate good and knowledge of this attainment. Now each of these consists in an operation. For actual knowledge is an operation; and similarly, we obtain an appropriate good {344} by means of an operation; and furthermore, one's own operation is an appropriate good. Hence every pleasure must follow upon an operation.

Thus SAINT THOMAS. And in the same place, ad 1, he speaks as follows:

> The objects of operations are objects of pleasure only inasmuch as they are united to us: whether through knowledge alone, as when we take pleasure in the consideration or the vision of certain things; or in some other way accompanied by knowledge, as when someone takes pleasure in knowing that he possesses some good, for example riches, honors, or other such things, which are objects of pleasure only inasmuch as they are known as possessed. For, as THE PHILOSOPHER says in *Politics* 2: "It gives great pleasure to think that something is one's own," a fact which follows from the natural love that one has for oneself. Now this kind of possessing is nothing other than a use, or an ability to use, the things possessed. But this use comes about through an operation. Hence it is clear that pleasure is reduced to operation as its cause.

Thus SAINT THOMAS. Again, in *In 4 Sent.*, d.49, q.3, a.2, he speaks as follows:

> The formal cause of a passion or operation is its object. Now the object of pleasure is an appropriate good that has been obtained: for by the fact that pleasure is in the appetitive part, its object must be a good; and by the fact that it is an appetite that has reached its term in its object, the object must be appropriate and obtained. Now this good that is the proper object of pleasure is, taken precisely, an operation, for three reasons.
>
> First, because, since pleasure consists in bringing appetite to rest, and since the movement of appetite is toward a good, the rest and pleasure of ap-

> petite must be in an ultimate good. But what is ultimate and most perfect in anything is its operation. Hence every inherent form is, in a way, related to its operation as is potency to act; and this is why form, such as the possession of scientific knowledge, is called "first act," while operation, such as the consideration of the objects of scientific knowledge, is called "second act," as is clear from *De anima* 2.
>
> Second, because, since pleasure is present in appetite, and since every passion, or operation of appetite, demands a prior apprehension, the good obtained that causes pleasure must be apprehended. But a disposition that is already present is not apprehended by us in the way that one that is still coming into being is, as AVICENNA says in *De naturalibus* 6. This is why those with a hectic fever feel the fever's heat less than do others with a fever even though the fever is more intense in the former: because in the former the heat has been spread through their bodily members as, so to speak, part of their constitution. This is because our sensing and our understanding come about through alteration of the understanding and of the sense-power by their objects. But nothing is altered by what is already at rest within it. Hence, since our being, and our being alive, and all such first acts, are present in us as having come to rest in us, and operation alone is present in us as coming into being, it is in our operation that we also perceive our being and our being alive. This is why it is in performing operations that we take pleasure, for example in vegetating, in sensing, and in other such operations by which our being, and our being alive, are in some way manifested to us, as is made clear by THE PHILOSOPHER in *Ethics* 10.
>
> Third, because operation proceeds from good things that are present in us, and in a way contains them within itself as an effect contains its cause; and by means of operation we are also united to external goods. Hence, every good that is an object of love for us brings our appetite to rest through the mediation of an operation. Therefore, operation is of itself the cause of pleasure.

Thus SAINT THOMAS. Again, in ad 1, he speaks as follows:

> Although many things other than operation are appropriate, nevertheless pleasure arises from none of them except through the mediation of operation. For external things appropriate to us are united to us through an operation; and internal things appropriate to us are apprehended in operations.

Thus SAINT THOMAS.

From these texts it is clear that every pleasure has an operation as its whole or partial object.

SAINT THOMAS says that enjoyment and pleasure, whether of this life or of heaven, have God in Himself as a partial object in *ST* I–II, q.11, a.3, ad 3, where he speaks as follows:

> The term "end" can be used in two ways: in one way to name the thing itself, and in another way to name the attainment of the thing. These are not two ends, but one end considered both in itself and as applied to something else. Accordingly, the ultimate end is: God as the thing that is ultimately sought after, but enjoyment as the attainment of this ultimate end. Accordingly, just as God and the enjoyment of God are not different ends, so it is the same essence of enjoyment by which we enjoy God and by which we enjoy the enjoyment of the divine; and the essence of created blessedness, which consists in the enjoyment, is also the same.

Thus SAINT THOMAS. From this text it is clear that it is in the same essence that enjoyment regards both God and the attainment of God through vision and enjoyment, and that it has each of them as a partial object.

SAINT THOMAS shows that the enjoyment more principally has God than any creaturely act as object, and that it has the latter as object only inasmuch as it is an act with God as object, in *In 1 Sent.*, d.1, q.2, a.1, ad 2, where he speaks as follows:

> The object of an operation determines and perfects it, and is its end. Hence, it is impossible for an operation to have the essence of an ultimate end. But because we grasp the object only by means of an operation, the appetite for the operation and the appetite for the object are the same. Hence, if we in some way enjoy the enjoyment itself, this is inasmuch as the enjoyment unites us to God, and it is by the same operation that we enjoy both the end and the operation whose object is the ultimate end.

Thus SAINT THOMAS. From this text it is clear that the enjoyment more principally and directly {345} regards God than any operation concerning God.

From the foregoing texts the falseness of the minor premise of the second argument is clear.

In response to the *first argument* for this minor premise, then, we say, *first,* that its major premise is false. For love of desire can have as object not only something inhering in the one loving, but also a subject or supposit distinct from the one loving.

Second, we say that the minor premise of this argument is also false. For enjoyment is neither love of concupiscence nor love of friendship, but rather pleasure, which is specifically distinct from love.

SAINT THOMAS addresses the *first* point in *In 4 Sent.*, d.49, q.1, a.2, qla.1, ad 3, where he speaks as follows:

> There are two kinds of objects of dilection or love. One is what is loved by way of benevolence, when we wish the good of someone for his own sake, as when we love our friends even if we get nothing from them. The other is what is loved with love of concupiscence, and this is either a good that is present in us, or something from which a good comes to be present in us, as we love either pleasure, or wine inasmuch as it causes pleasure. Now whatever is loved with love of concupiscence cannot be an ultimate object of love, since it is directed to the good of something else, namely the good of the one for whom it is desired. But what is loved with love of benevolence can be an ultimate object of love. Accordingly, the creaturely blessedness that is present in us is loved only with love of concupiscence. Hence we direct the love of it to ourselves, and subsequently we also direct it to God, since we ought also to direct ourselves to God; thus it cannot be an ultimate object of love. It is, however, an ultimate object of concupiscence in that it is the greatest good that comes to us from union with God. Hence it is said to be something "sought after" or "desired" "for its own sake." For both descriptions imply an ultimate among the things that are loved with love of desire, namely a good that is present in us, and that from which a good comes to be present in us. Hence it is the same thing to desire God and to desire the greatest good that comes to us from God, just as it is the same thing to desire wine and to desire its effect in us, namely pleasure.

Thus SAINT THOMAS. From this text it is clear that a thing that is subsistent and is different from a man in subject can be desired and loved with love of concupiscence, as is illustrated in the case of God and that of wine.

The argument for the major premise (a premise that we have already denied) by means of induction is invalid. For the immediate object of the love or dilection with which wine is loved is as much the wine itself as its use, and in fact the use is loved only on account of the wine, although both are directed to the one who loves. For, as SAINT THOMAS says in *In 2 Sent.*, d.36, q.1, a.5, the proximate end of any act is its object, and consequently the goodness and desirability of an act come from its object.

Nor is the argument by means of demonstration valid. For the major premise is false, because in love of concupiscence it is not only a perfection present within us that is loved, but also the good that causes that perfection in us, as was said above.

Concerning the *second* point that we made above—that enjoyment or pleasure is not love, but an act specifically distinct from love—SAINT THOMAS speaks in many places. For he shows that pleasure is an act specifically distinct from love in *In 3 Sent.*, d.26, q.1, a.3, and in *ST* I–II, q.23, a.4; and he holds that enjoyment is pleasure in *ST* I–II, q.11, aa.1 and 4, and q.4, a.3, and in many other places.

Thus it is clear that both the major and the minor premises of the first attempted proof of the second principal argument are false.

In response to the *second argument* for the minor premise, I say, *first*, that it presupposes something false, namely that hope and desire are the same thing. SAINT THOMAS shows the contrary in *In 3 Sent.*, d.26, q.1, a.3 and in *ST* I–II, q.23, a.4, both of which have been quoted above. In *ST*, I–II, q.40, a.1, he speaks as follows:

> The species of a passion is taken from its object. Now there are four features to be noted in the object of hope. First, it is a good, for hope, properly speaking, is only for a good; in this respect hope differs from fear, which is of an evil. Second, it is something future, for hope is not for something present already possessed; in this respect hope differs from joy, which is of a present good. Third, it must be something arduous, or attainable only with difficulty, for no-one is said to hope for something trivial which it is immediately in his power to possess; in this respect hope differs from desire or cupidity, which concerns a future good taken absolutely, and which thus pertains to the concupiscible power, while hope pertains to the irascible power. Fourth, that arduous thing is something possible to attain, for no-one hopes for what he can in no way attain; in this respect hope differs from despair.

Thus SAINT THOMAS.

Second, we say that the minor premise is false. For God can be the immediate object of desire, although He is sometimes not the whole, but rather a partial object. For, as was said above, just as it is the same thing to desire wine and to desire its effect in us, so it is the same thing to desire God and to desire our vision or possession of Him.

In order to prove this point, we say that, although God in Himself is not "going to be," but rather is present, He is nevertheless, in a special way, "going to be" present in us, namely as object of the operations of vision and enjoyment—or rather, prior to every act of intellect and will, the divine essence will be united to our intellect as an intelligible form, as we have elsewhere shown at length, namely in d.14, when treating of scientific knowledge in the soul of Christ. Thus it is clear that not only the vision or revelation of God, but also God's special presence in us, is "going to be"; and that God is "going to be" present in us in the special way in which the vision and enjoyment of Him will be caused in us.

Again, even granting that God will not be possessed by us and that He is not "going to be" present in us by means of those acts of vision and enjoyment, **{346}** the inference that not He, but those acts, are the immediate object of desire is still invalid. For it is by the same act, and equally or more directly, that the will of one who desires is directed to the thing and to possession or acquisition of the thing; and the thing and its possession are not two objects, but one, as was said in the comparison made above.

Third, we say that even positing—although not conceding—that the immediate object of desire is not God, but the vision or enjoyment of Him, the case of hope, which immediately attains God as rule and measure, and as first efficient cause and ultimate end, is different. Concerning this point SAINT THOMAS, in *ST* II–II, q.17, a.4, speaks as follows:

> Hope regards two things, namely the good that it intends to obtain, and the help by which the good is to be obtained. Now a good that one hopes to obtain has the essence of a final cause, while the help by which one hopes to obtain that good has the essence of an efficient cause, etc.

And he presents the same opinion in aa.2 and 5.

The response to the *third argument* for the minor premise of the principal argument is clear from what has been said above. For the argument demonstrates only that beatific pleasure or enjoyment has for its object not God alone, but the vision of Him, and this has frequently been conceded. But it does not demonstrate that beatific pleasure is in a more primary and immediate way directed to the vision of God than to God Himself as its object: rather, we must say the contrary. For since pleasure, and most especially beatific enjoyment, regards an ultimate end, it is proximately and more immediately directed to what to a greater extent has the essence of an ultimate end. But it is clear that God to a greater extent has the essence of an ultimate end than does the vision or enjoyment of Him, since creaturely blessedness, or any part of it, is directed to God as an end, as has been said above. Nor is vision or enjoyment the end of a rational nature or substance except inasmuch as the vision or enjoyment is joined to God. Concerning this point SAINT THOMAS, in *In 4 Sent.*, d.49, q.1, a.2, qla.1, obj.5, presents the following objection:

> Everything that is present in us either is present in us essentially or is an accident. But blessedness is not of the essence of man, because in that case every man would always be blessed. Therefore, if it is something present in man, it will be an accident. But an accident cannot be the end of a substance, since a substance is nobler than an accident. Therefore, it is impossible for blessedness to be something present in us, etc.

Thus the objection; the response is as follows:

> We must say that although any accident, as such, is less noble than a substance, nevertheless an accident can be nobler than a substance in a certain respect. For an accident can be considered in two ways. One way is according as it inheres in a subject, from which it gets its essence as an accident; and in this way any accident is less noble than a substance. In another way it can be considered as directed to something external; and in this way an accident can be nobler than a substance inasmuch as by means of it a substance is united to something nobler than itself. In this latter way grace, created blessedness, and the like are things by nature nobler than the soul in which they inhere.

Thus SAINT THOMAS.

In response to the confirmation of the argument we say, *first,* that the comparison is invalid. For God is united to the blessed in two ways: in the first way through His essence, as an intelligible form, and in the second way through His noblest effect, which is vision and enjoyment. Hence He is in two ways a good to the blessed. But He is united to the damned in only one way, namely through His effect of being opposed to them. Hence God is a good to the blessed both in Himself and through His effect; while He is an evil to the damned in only one way, namely through His effect.

Second, we say that, even positing—although not conceding—that God is a good to the blessed only by reason of His effect, it does not follow from this that the blessed more immediately and more proximately take pleasure in the vision of God than they do in God Himself. For the vision does not have the essence of a perfect good or of an ultimate end except inasmuch as it causes union with God, or is caused by union with God. Concerning this point SAINT THOMAS, in *In 4 Sent.,* d.49, q.1, a.2, qla.1, which was quoted above, speaks as follows:

> The good that all things desire is being, as is made clear by BOETHIUS in the *Consolation.* Hence the ultimate object of desire of each thing is perfect being, inasmuch as this is possible in a nature. But everything that has its

> being from another has its perfection from the other. For anything more perfectly receives being to the extent that it is more truly united to the principle of being. Thus the lower bodies, because they are very remote from the first principle, have a corruptible being, as is clear from *De generatione* 2. Hence, the ultimate end of anything that has its being from another consists of two things: one is external, namely that which is the principle of the desired perfection; and the other is internal, namely the perfection itself of the thing, which is caused by union with the principle.
>
> Thus, since blessedness is the ultimate end of man, his blessedness consists in two things. One is within him, namely the ultimate perfection which it is possible for him to reach; and this is created blessedness. The other is outside of him, namely that by which, in his union with it, the aforementioned blessedness is caused within him; and this is God Himself.

Thus SAINT THOMAS. Again, in the same question, a.2, qla.2, ad 2, he speaks as follows:

> There are two things to be considered in an act, namely the substance of the act and the form of the act, from which it gets its perfection. With respect to its substance, the principle of an act is a natural power; but with respect to its form, its principle is a habit. If, then, the habit is acquired, we shall be wholly the cause of our act; but if it is infused, its perfection will come from the external cause that causes the habit. Now blessedness is held to be our act {347} only by reason of the perfection by which it is able to unite us in a most noble way to an external end. Hence, we are not the cause of our blessedness, but rather God is.

Thus SAINT THOMAS.

From these texts it is clear that any created act properly speaking causes blessedness not on the side of the subject and inasmuch as the act flows from a created power, but only on the side of the object, and inasmuch as the act is a participation and a likeness of uncreated blessedness. This is why enjoyment or delectation is more primarily, in the order of nature, directed to God than to the vision of Him, and is directed to the vision only by reason of the object.

In response to the *fourth argument* for the minor premise we say that it demonstrates only that the whole or partial object of any pleasure is an operation, which we concede; but not that the operation more immediately determines the pleasure than does the object, which is the divine operation *(obiectum divinae operationis).*

It might be said that no object that is external and different in supposit or subject causes pleasure except through the intermediary of an operation, and that, therefore, the operation more immediately causes pleasure.

In response to this we say that in acts of intellect, for instance intellectual vision, two media can be distinguished. One is a medium "by which" *(quo)* something is seen, namely the intelligible form of the thing by which the intellect is determined to its special object, as it is determined by the form of a stone to the understanding of a stone. The other is the medium "in which" *(in quo)* or "from which" *(ex quo)* a thing is seen, namely that by the consideration of which the intellect is led to something else, as, for example, by looking into a mirror, we are led to the things represented in the mirror, and by seeing an image, we are led to what is imaged, and by understanding an effect, we are led to knowledge of a cause. And it is not the medium in the first sense, but only the medium in the second sense, that is more immediately understood than that with respect to which it is a medium.

Thus, we must say that acts of the will, for instance pleasure or enjoyment, are in their own way similar. For when it is said that "God causes pleasure only through the mediation of vision or knowledge of Him," this vision or knowledge is not a medium in the second sense, as that "from which" or "in which" we enjoy or take pleasure in God. But it is a medium in the first sense, as that "by which" we enjoy God. For just as an intelligible species perfects the intellect for understanding or being able to understand, so the vision of God perfects the one seeing for being able to enjoy God inasmuch as it unites him to God and shows him the possession of his ultimate end. Hence, just as an intelligible species is not more immediately understood than is the external object, so a blessed man does not enjoy the vision of God more immediately than he enjoys God Himself—although the two cases are not altogether similar, since the vision of God does not formally perfect the will as the intelligible species does the intellect.

In response to the *fifth argument* for the minor premise we say that its own minor premise is simply false. For God is able to be the proper good of man not simply by reason of the operation by which we attain Him, but rather by His essence, which is prior to every operation terminated by or attaining Him. For, as has often been said, especially in Distinction 14 of the present book, the divine essence is united to the intellect of every blessed man as an intelligible form which takes the place of an intelligible species; and no-one doubts that He is in this way the formal good of every blessed man.

Again, God in His essence is a good for every blessed man as the principle of being and of preservation in being, and as an ultimate end. Concerning this point SAINT THOMAS, in *ST* I, q.6, a.4, speaks as follows:

> Each thing is said to be "good" by the divine goodness as the exemplar, efficient and final first principle of the whole of goodness. Nevertheless, each thing is also said to be "good" by its inherent likeness to the divine goodness, a likeness that is formally the goodness by which it is called good. Thus there are both one goodness of all things, and many goodnesses.

Thus SAINT THOMAS. Again, in q.60, a.5, ad 1, he speaks as follows:

> Among things of which one is the whole essence of the being and the goodness of another, the latter naturally loves the former more than itself, just as any part naturally loves the whole more than itself, and just as any individual naturally loves the good of its species more than its own individual good. But God is not merely the good of one species, but the universal good itself. Hence each thing, in its own way, naturally loves God more than itself.

Thus SAINT THOMAS.

From these texts it is clear that God is the proper good of each thing and the universal good of all things, not only by reason of the operation by which He is attained, or by reason of the effect which He actually causes in each thing, but because He is the essence of the being and the goodness of each thing, and is related to other things as is the good of a whole to the good of a part.

Second, we say that even positing—although not granting—that God is the proper good, or any other kind of good, of something only by reason of an operation, or of an effect that He produces, the argument still does not demonstrate that His effect, or the operation by which we attain or are united to Him, is more immediately presented as an object to one taking pleasure or enjoying than is God Himself. BLESSED THOMAS says as much in a comparison that he makes; for in *ST* I, q.60, a.5, which was quoted above, he presents the following objection (obj.2):

> That on account of which a thing is such, is itself more so. But by natural love a thing loves another on account of itself: for anything loves something else inasmuch as the latter is a good for it. Therefore, by natural love, an angel does not love God more than itself.

Thus the objection; the response is as follows:

> We must say that, when it is said that "God is loved by an angel inasmuch as He is a good for the angel," if the "inasmuch as" refers to an end, the

> statement is false. For the angel naturally does not love God on account of the angel's own good, but on account of God Himself. But if the "inasmuch as" refers to the essence of the love from the point of view of the one loving, the statement is true. For it would not be in the nature of anything to love God were it not for {348} the fact that each thing depends on the good that is God.

Thus SAINT THOMAS.

Accordingly, in the present question, we say that, although the vision of God, or any other operation by which He is attained, is the essence of the pleasure and enjoyment on the part of the one who enjoys, it does not follow that the one who enjoys enjoys the operation by which he attains God more immediately, or more proximately, or more intensively, than he enjoys God Himself. For such an operation is not a medium "from which" or "in which," but one "by which." But the operation need not more immediately terminate in the latter kind of medium than, through the intermediary of such a medium, in something else. Rather, it follows only that such a medium disposes the one operating, and perfects him for being able to attain something else in the manner of an object, just as, as was said before, one who enjoys wine or money does not more immediately enjoy the use of the wine or the possession of the money than he does the wine or the money, even though he enjoys the latter only through the intermediary of a use or possession, whether actual or habitual. This is especially so because anyone who enjoys or takes pleasure in a subsistent thing more immediately thinks of the thing than of its use, or of the operation by which he attains it, because such an operation is known only through a reflexive act, as is clear in the case of the vision or the knowledge of God.

Third, we say that, whatever be the case concerning the object of pleasure, hope, as has often been said, attains God immediately as its formal object, inasmuch as it relies on His help for obtaining both created and uncreated blessedness.

This suffices for the objections to the second conclusion.

§2. To the Arguments against the Third Conclusion

To the Arguments of Scotus [*p. 131*] I. In response to the *first* argument of SCOTUS against the third conclusion, we say that both it and all of the other points which he introduces in the first stage of his objection to the third conclusion are based on something false. For they suppose that our conclusion says that hope and faith are distinguished as two intellectual or cognitive habits, one of which considers a universal and the other a particular object. But this we neither say nor mean: rather, we say that hope is distinguished from faith as is an appetitive from a cognitive habit, or as is a habit present in the will from one present in the intellect. Concerning this point SAINT THOMAS speaks in *In 3 Sent.*, d.26, q.2, a.3, qla.1, which was quoted in the proof of the third conclusion. Again, in *In 3 Sent.*, d.26, q.2, a.4, he speaks as follows:

> Some have said that hope has no other certitude than that which comes from faith, but that they differ in that the certitude of faith is universal, as is the certitude that every good man will have eternal life, while the certitude of hope is particular, as is the certitude that this man, if he acts well, will have eternal life. Hence the certitude of faith is universal and absolute, while that of hope is particular and conditional.
>
> But this cannot be maintained, because universal and particular do not make for a difference in the essence of habits. Hence, according to this position, hope would not differ from faith as a habit, and it would not be present in a different power, which is altogether false, etc.

Again, at the end of the article, in ad 5, he speaks as follows:

> The certitude of faith and that of hope differ in four ways. First, in that the certitude of faith is one of understanding, while that of hope is one of affection. Second, because the certitude of faith cannot fail, but that of hope sometimes does fail accidentally. Third, because the certitude of faith concerns a complex object, while that of hope concerns an incomplex object, namely an object of appetite. Fourth, because doubt is opposed to the certitude of faith, while despair or uncertainty is opposed to the certitude of hope.

Thus SAINT THOMAS. Again, in d.23, q.1, a.5, he speaks as follows:

> The theological virtues cause in us an inclination to the end, namely God. Now in everyone who acts for the sake of an end and who does so by a will, there must be present two things that he possesses in relation to the end before he can act in view of the end, namely knowledge of the end and an intention of reaching the end. But two things are required in order that he intend the end: possibility of the end, because nothing is moved toward the impossible; and goodness of the end, because intention can be directed only to a good. Hence there are required faith, which makes the end known; hope, by which there is a confidence in attainment of the end as something

> possible; and charity, by which the end is judged to be a good for the one intending, inasmuch as it causes a man's affection to be moved toward the end—for otherwise he would never be directed toward it.

Thus SAINT THOMAS. Again, in *ST* II–II, q.18, a.1, he speaks as follows:

> Habits are known through acts. Now the act of hope is a movement of the appetitive part, since its object is a good. But since there are two appetites in man—a sensitive appetite, which is divided into the irascible and the concupiscible powers, and an intellective appetite, called the will—movements present in the lower appetite together with passion are similar to movements present in the higher appetite without passion. Now the act of the virtue of hope cannot pertain to the sensitive appetite, because the good that is the principal object of this virtue is not a sensible, but a divine good. Hence hope is present in the higher appetite called the will, and not in the lower appetite to which the irascible power belongs.

Thus SAINT THOMAS.

From these texts it is clear that hope is distinguished from faith not as an intellectual habit regarding a particular object is from an intellectual habit regarding a universal object, but rather as an appetitive habit is from a cognitive one. We do, however, concede that the object of hope is more particular than that of faith, and concerning this point SAINT THOMAS, in *ST* II–II, q.17, a.3, speaks as follows:

> There can be hope of something in two ways: in one way absolutely, and thus hope is only for an arduous good pertaining to oneself; in another way on the basis of a presupposition, and thus hope can also be for what {349} pertains to another.
>
> For evidence of this point, it must be known that love and hope differ in that love implies a union of the one loving to what is loved, while hope implies a stretching forth of the appetite to an arduous good. Now union is between things that are different, and hence love can directly consider another whom one unites to oneself through love, regarding him as oneself. But movement is always toward a terminus proportioned to the mobile thing, and hence hope directly regards its own good, and not something pertaining to another. But if the union of love with another is presupposed, then one can hope and desire something for another as for oneself. In this respect one can hope for eternal life for another, that is, inasmuch as one is united to him through love. And just as it is the same charity by which one loves God, oneself, and a neighbor, so, too, it is the same virtue of hope by which one hopes both for oneself and for another.

Thus SAINT THOMAS.

In response to the confirmation presented in the first argument of SCOTUS, we say that one who despairs must be persuaded not only to believe, but also to hope, because, as SAINT THOMAS proves in *ST* II–II, q.20, a.2, despair can be present without unbelief; for he speaks as follows:

> Unbelief pertains to the intellect, but despair to the appetitive power. Now the intellect is concerned with universals, but the appetitive power is moved toward particulars, because it is a movement of appetite from the soul to things, which are in themselves particular. Now it can happen that one who has a right universal judgment concerning appetitive movement is not rightly disposed if his particular judgment has been destroyed. For one must proceed from a universal judgment to the appetite for a particular thing through the intermediary of a particular judgment, as is said in *De anima* 3; for instance, a particular conclusion is not drawn from a universal proposition except by taking a particular proposition as a minor premise.
>
> Accordingly, one who has a faith that is right in the universal may fail in appetitive movement concerning a particular if his particular judgment has been destroyed by habit or passion. For example, one who fornicates, choosing fornication as his good for the moment, has a destroyed particular judgment, although he may retain a universal judgment that is true according to faith, namely that fornication is a mortal sin. Similarly, while holding, in the universal, the true judgment of faith that there is remission of sins in the Church, one may nevertheless undergo a movement of despair according to which for him, existing in such a state, there is no hope of forgiveness, if his judgment concerning the particular has been destroyed. In this way there can be despair, just as there can also be other mortal sins, without unbelief.

Thus SAINT THOMAS. From this text it is clear that it is not sufficient for one who despairs to believe with the state of belief that is the act of faith, since one can despair even in that state of belief, and despair can co-exist with faith—although it cannot co-exist with the particular state of belief by which one believes that there is hope of forgiveness for him. But this particular state of belief is not an act of theological faith, but a judgment that comes from another source. Hence SAINT THOMAS, in the same place, ad 1, speaks as follows:

> An effect is removed not only when the first cause, but also when a secondary cause, is removed. Hence the movement of hope can be removed not

> only when the universal judgment of faith, which is like a first cause of the certitude of hope, is removed, but also when the particular judgment, which is like a secondary cause, is removed.

Thus SAINT THOMAS. From this text it is clear that hope is not a believing, but an appetitive habit, one whose act proceeds from two states of belief or judgments: one universal, which is an act of faith, and the other particular, which is an act not of faith, but merely of the understanding or cogitative power.

In response to the *second* principal argument we say that hope is indeed distinguished from faith in those three ways, although it is not a habit of the intellect.

In response to the argument concerning *the first way* of distinguishing them, we say that, although universal and particular do not make for a difference between intellectual habits, they can, nevertheless, differentiate and distinguish between appetitive habits, or between an intellectual and an appetitive habit. For example, just now we said that an act of faith regards something universal, but an act of hope or of despair regards something particular; and above, in response to the first argument, we said that hope regards only what pertains to oneself or to those united to oneself.

In response to the argument concerning *the second way* of distinguishing hope and faith, we say that hope regards something eternal and future. Accordingly, SAINT THOMAS, in *In 3 Sent.*, d.26, in his exposition of the text, presents the following objection:

> Hope is of what is future; but everything future is temporal; nothing temporal is eternal; therefore, hope cannot be of eternal things.

Thus the objection; the response is as follows:

> We must say that what is in itself eternal is future to the one who hopes, and thus there can be hope concerning God.

Thus SAINT THOMAS.

We can also respond in another way by saying that hope regards two objects. One is formal, namely God, Whose help is relied upon, and this object is eternal; the other is material, namely created blessedness and other things that are directed to acquiring it, and such objects can be future and temporal, a point which was touched upon in the proof of the first conclusion.

Again, SAINT THOMAS, in *In 3 Sent.*, d.26, q.2, a.2, ad 2, speaks as follows:

> Because what is directed to an end is directed by the end, the theological virtues, which have the ultimate end for their object, operate in relation to the end not only in itself, but also as it is directive of what is directed to the end. **{350}** Hence, they are, in a way, principles of other virtues. Faith, for example, knows not only the First Truth, but also other truths that are made clear by the First Truth and are directed to it; hence many things are contained in the articles of faith which pertain to creatures. Similarly, charity causes one to love not only God, but also one's neighbor for the sake of God. Similarly, hope causes one to be directed to God Himself not only as something arduous to be attained, but also as One from whom help comes concerning all other arduous things, whether they be goods to be acquired or evils to be avoided. Hence he who has hope hopes to attain God, and hopes to obtain, through God, all things necessary, however difficult they may be. For he also hopes to drive away all harmful things, however difficult they may be to drive away. In this respect, hope is a principle in man of all operations that are directed to an arduous good, just as charity is the principle of all operations that are directed to a good, and just as faith is the principle of all operations that pertain to cognition.

Thus SAINT THOMAS.

The opponent says further, "Futurity requires its own habit," etc.

In response to this we say that the proper habit required by "futurity" is not intellectual but appetitive, as is clear in the case of desire and concupiscence, of hope and despair, and of fear and boldness, all of which regard the future.

In response to the argument against this point—in which it is said that "pastness," with equal reason, would require its own habit—we say that the two cases are not alike. For the passions of the sensitive appetite and the acts of the will are movements of attraction and repulsion. But it is not something past as such that attracts or repels, but only something present or future. Therefore any appetitive act, properly speaking, regards not something past, but only something present or future—except, perhaps, anger and sorrow, which can regard things past, although this is accidental and does not proceed from the proper essence of the species of passion, for they can also be of what is not past, as will be said below. Concerning this point SAINT THOMAS, in *ST* I–II, q.23, a.4, speaks as follows:

> Passions differ according to the active things that are the objects of the passions of the soul. Now differences among active things can be understood in two ways: in one way, according to the species or natures of the active things

> themselves, as fire differs from water; in another way, according to different active powers. Differences among active or moving things from the point of view of power of moving can be understood in the case of the passions of the soul through their resemblance to natural agents. For everything that moves another in some way either draws what is acted upon to itself or repels it from itself. In drawing it to itself, it causes three effects in it. First, it gives it an inclination or aptitude to tend toward itself, as when a light body that is above gives to a generated body a lightness through which the latter has an inclination and aptitude to rise. Second, if the generated body is out of its proper place, it gives it movement toward its place. Third, it gives it rest in its place when it reaches it, because a thing rests in its place through the same cause by which it is moved to its place. And something similar is to be understood of the cause of repulsion.
>
> Now in movements of the appetitive part, a good has, so to speak, the power of attraction, and an evil the power of repulsion. Therefore, a good first causes in the appetitive power an inclination toward, or aptitude for, or connaturality with, the good, which pertains to the passion of love, to which there corresponds as a contrary, on the side of evil, hatred. Second, if the good thing is not yet possessed, it gives the appetitive power movement in the direction of obtaining the good thing that is loved; and this pertains to the passion of desire or concupiscence, to which is opposed, on the side of evil, avoidance or rejection. Third, when the good thing has been attained, it gives the appetite rest in the good obtained; and this pertains to pleasure or joy, to which is opposed, on the side of evil, pain or sorrow.
>
> Among the irascible passions there is presupposed on the part of the concupiscible power, which regards something good or evil absolutely, an aptitude for or inclination toward pursuing what is good and fleeing what is evil. Regarding a good not yet attained the irascible passions are hope and despair; regarding an evil not yet at hand they are fear and boldness. There is no passion in the irascible power regarding a good attained, because such a good no longer has the aspect of something arduous; but from an evil already at hand there follows the passion of anger.

Thus SAINT THOMAS. Again, in q.25, a.4, when discussing the four principal passions, he speaks as follows:

> The number of these passions is customarily taken according to the difference between what is present and what is future. For movement regards something future, but rest is in something present. Accordingly, joy concerns a present good, sorrow a present evil, hope a future good, and fear a future evil.

Thus SAINT THOMAS.

From these texts it is clear that no passion, properly speaking, regards what is past, but only what is present or future.

It might be urged that SAINT THOMAS, in *ST* I–II, q.35, a.2, ad 2, says that

> . . . inner sorrow can concern a present, a past or a future thing, just as there is repentance and sorrow concerning what is past and anxiety concerning what is future . . .

In response to this we say that sorrow does not concern a past thing in its essence as past formally, but materially, because nothing past or future causes sorrow unless it is in some way present and united to the appetite, either in itself or in its effect or cause. Concerning this point SAINT THOMAS, in *In 4 Sent.*, d.17, q.2, a.1, qla.1, ad 1, speaks as follows:

> Pain concerns only what is in some way present. But a past sin, even if it is not present in actuality, is nevertheless present in some one of its effects, such as the disposition to sin, or the guilt, or the stain, or the loss of time that can in no way {351} be recovered, even when repentance is completed, or the loss of the dignity of innocence, to which one can never return. Or, it might be said that a past sin arouses pain inasmuch as it remains present in the memory, just as, when we remember past sorrows, we are affected by them as if they were in the present.

Thus SAINT THOMAS.

It might, perhaps, be said that it is not only appetitive habits that regard what is past or future, but also intellectual habits, such as the part of prudence called the memory of things past. SAINT THOMAS responds to this in *ST* II–II, q.49, a.1, ad 1:

> Because prudence applies universal knowledge to singulars, which are considered by the sense-power, many things that pertain to the sensitive part are required for prudence, and among these is memory.

Thus SAINT THOMAS.

If it is asked why an appetitive habit can be concerned with what is future as future or with what is past as past, while an intellective habit cannot, SAINT THOMAS responds in *ST* I, q.79, a.7, ad 2, where, discussing something similar, he says:

> Past and present can be the proper differences of sensitive powers but not of intellectual powers.

This is because differences such as past and future are features of what is particular and individual, and it is not the intellect, but only the sensitive powers, that regard such features. Now reasoning from similarity, we can say that because an intellectual habit regards its object under a universal aspect and is directed to it in a universal way, while an appetitive habit is directed to its object with respect to the object's particular being, futurity can therefore be a formal feature of an appetitive habit, but not of an intellective one.

The opponent says further that faith is of future things, etc.

In response to this we say that it is materially true, but not formally true in the sense that futurity would belong to the essence of the object of faith as it does to the essence of the object of hope. For not every object of belief is future, as is, in some way, every object of hope, whether in itself or to the one hoping, as was said above.

In response to the argument concerning *the third way* of distinguishing hope and faith, we say that a theological virtue can be one that moderates passions, or acts resembling passions, with respect to secondary objects. Thus SAINT THOMAS, in *ST* II–II, q.17, a.5, obj.2, presents the following objection:

> A theological virtue does not consist in a mean between two vices. But hope does consist in a mean between presumption and despair. Therefore, it is not a theological virtue.

Thus the objection; the response is as follows:

> It must be said that the intermediary in things ruled and measured is taken according as the rule or measure is conformed to. According as there is a going beyond the rule, there is an excess, and according as there is a falling short of the rule, there is a deficiency; but in the rule or measure itself, no intermediary or extremes can be taken. Now moral virtue concerns, as its proper object, things regulated by reason. Hence it pertains to moral virtue of itself, from the point of view of its proper object, to be intermediary. But theological virtue concerns, as its proper object, the first rule itself, which is not regulated by another rule. Hence it does not pertain to theological virtue, of itself and with respect to its proper object, to be intermediary, although this can accidentally pertain to it by reason of what is directed to its principal object. Faith, for example, cannot have an intermediary or extremes inasmuch as it relies on the First Truth, which cannot be relied upon too much: but from the point of view of the things that it believes, it can have an intermediary and extremes in the sense that one true thing is intermediary between two false ones. Similarly, hope does not have an intermediary and ex-

> tremes from the point of view of its principal object, because no-one can rely too much on divine help: but with respect to the things that one hopes to obtain for oneself, there can be an intermediary and extremes inasmuch as one presumes concerning things disproportionately above him or despairs concerning things that are proportioned to him.

Thus SAINT THOMAS. From this text it is clear that it is not contrary to the essence of theological virtue for an intermediary state to be posited in them, and thus for hope to be a virtue intermediary between presumption and despair.

But when the opponent further says that such hope would be a kind of fear, we deny the inference. Concerning this point, SAINT THOMAS, in *Questions on the Virtues,* "On Hope", a.1, ad 6, speaks as follows:

> No virtue can be named, simply speaking, from a passion, except a theological virtue. For the intellectual virtues pertain to the cognitive power, while the passions are in the appetitive power. And the moral virtues constitute intermediaries in the passions. Hence a moral virtue is named, not from a passion absolutely speaking, but from the modification of a passion, as are temperance, courage, and similar virtues. But a movement of the human mind which in any way attains God pertains to virtue, and hence the names of simple movements or passions are applied to theological virtues. But because the object of the theological virtues is God, Who is the highest good, it is clear that passions whose object is an evil cannot give their names to theological virtues. Similarly, because theological virtue pertains to the state of pilgrimage, in which we are directed to God, the passions whose object is a present good, such as pleasure and joy, do not give their names to any virtues, but pertain rather to blessedness; hence pleasure is numbered among the gifts of blessedness. Desire, on the other hand, implies a movement toward something future, but without any present adherence to or special contact with it; hence, neither does desire give its name to a virtue. Thus, there remain only hope and love to give their names to theological virtues.

Thus SAINT THOMAS. Again, in *In 3 Sent.,* d.26, q.2, a.1, ad 1, **{352}** he speaks as follows:

> Hope is a virtue not inasmuch as it is a passion, but according as it is present in the appetite of the intellective part. And the names of the other passions cannot so aptly be transferred to a virtue as can the name "hope." For "hope" signifies a relation to a good, and further implies movement of an appetite directed to the good; thus it contains something like the choosing and

> tending toward a good that are required in every virtue. "Fear," on the other hand, signifies a relation to an evil; and although withdrawal from evil does pertain to virtue, nevertheless perfect virtue does not consist in this withdrawal, but in the choice of a good. And "joy" and "sorrow" signify rather the impression of a good or of an evil upon the appetite than movements of the appetite directed to a good or an evil; hence they do not resemble the choice made by virtue.

Thus SAINT THOMAS.

II. We must now discuss the second group of arguments that SCOTUS brings against the third conclusion, where he attempts to prove that hope is not a third habit distinct from faith and charity [p. 132].

In response to the *first* argument we deny the minor premise. For reason dictates with necessity, and the authority of Scripture compels us to posit, that faith, hope, and charity are three habits and three virtues.

Then, in response to the first attempted proof of the minor premise, we say that, although the will indeed can, by the same habit of perfect virtue, be disposed both to will what it is ordained to choose and to reject what it is ordained to reject; and is, similarly, sufficiently disposed to loving and desiring what it is ordained to love and desire; nevertheless the same habit does not always suffice for both loving and hoping, because, as was said above (in the preceding section, in response to the second argument for the minor premise of the second principal argument), hope differs from desire. Concerning this point SAINT THOMAS, in *In 3 Sent.*, d.26, q.2, a.3, qla.2, speaks as follows:

> An act of faith precedes desire, because every act of an affective power presupposes an act of a cognitive power. But desire precedes hope, etc.

This point has been sufficiently discussed above. But the reason why the habit of charity suffices, as a first and proximate principle, to incline one to desire God and blessedness, but does not suffice, as a proximate principle, to incline one to hope for God and blessedness, is as follows. In hoping for God, one encounters special difficulty and a special aspect of arduousness. Hence a special habit of virtue is required that causes one to be well disposed concerning this arduousness. Concerning this point SAINT THOMAS, in *In 3 Sent.*, d.26, q.2, a.2, speaks as follows:

> Hope of its essence signifies a stretching forth of the appetite to something arduous that does not altogether exceed the ability of the one who hopes. For things that do exceed one's ability, and are apprehended as so exceeding

> it, cause despair rather than hope. Hence, according as there is present in someone an ability with respect to something arduous, there is also present in him an inclination toward that arduous thing. Therefore, the inclination of the sensitive appetite toward an arduous thing proportioned to the sensitive nature causes the hope that is a passion; while the inclination of the intellective appetite toward an arduous thing proportioned to the intellective nature causes the hope that is an act of the will. But because there is something arduous that exceeds the ability of nature, but that man can reach through grace, namely God Himself inasmuch as He is our blessedness, the inclination toward that arduous object must come from a gift of grace superadded to nature, and that gift is the habit of hope. And because it has God Himself as its object, it must be a theological virtue, etc.

Thus SAINT THOMAS. The habit of hope and that of compassion are similar in that both are distinct habits different from charity. Thus SAINT THOMAS, in *ST* II–II, q.30, a.3, obj.3, presents the following objection:

> Joy and peace are not special virtues, because they follow from charity. But compassion follows from charity, for it is out of charity that we weep with those who weep, as we rejoice with those who rejoice. Therefore, compassion is not a special virtue.

Thus the objection; the response is as follows:

> It must be said that joy and peace add nothing to the essence of the good that is the object of charity. Hence they do not require virtues other than charity. But compassion does regard a special aspect, namely the pitiful state of the one to whom compassion is extended.

Thus SAINT THOMAS. Thus it is in the case at hand. For hope regards a special aspect of the good that charity does not formally regard as its adequate object, namely the arduousness of what is divine. Therefore, hope must be a special habit distinct from the habit of charity. Concerning this point SAINT THOMAS, in *ST* II–II, q.17, a.6, obj.3, presents the following objection:

> Through hope man tends toward God. But this properly pertains to charity. Therefore, hope is not distinct from charity.

Thus the objection; the response is as follows:

> It must be said that hope causes one to tend toward God as a final good to be obtained and as a help whose support is efficacious. But charity, properly speaking, causes a man to tend toward God by uniting his affection to God, so that he lives no longer for himself, but for God.

Thus SAINT THOMAS. He says something similar in *In 3 Sent.*, d.26, q.2, a.3, qla.1, obj.4, where he presents the following objection:

> It pertains to hope to tend toward God. But this is proper to charity. Therefore, hope does not differ from charity.

Thus the objection; the response is as follows:

> It must be said that to tend toward something desirable belongs both to the irascible and to the concupiscible powers, but in different ways. For to tend toward a good inasmuch as it is, simply speaking, good belongs to the concupiscible power; but to tend toward a good inasmuch as it is arduous and difficult belongs to the irascible power. Thus hope and charity tend toward God in different ways.

Thus SAINT THOMAS. Again, in d.23, q.1, a.5, obj.5, he presents the following objection:

> For operation {353} concerning the end there are required only knowledge of the end, which faith causes, and desire for the end, which charity causes. Therefore, it seems that there are only two theological virtues.

Thus the objection; the response is as follows:

> It must be said that knowledge and affection do not suffice for a man to begin to act for the sake of an end if he does not have confidence concerning his attainment of the end. For otherwise one would never begin to act, especially when the end is above the nature of the one acting.

Thus SAINT THOMAS.

From these texts it is clear that the habit of charity does not, as a proximate principle, suffice to incline the will of a man to hope without some other special intermediate habit. It can, however, suffice in the manner of a first principle. Concerning this point SAINT THOMAS, in *Questions on the Virtues*, "On Hope", a.4, obj.7, presents the following objection:

> A principle of movement toward a terminus is the same as the principle of rest in the terminus. But hope is a principle of movement toward blessedness, according to the remark of *Hebrews* 6 that "We have hope which advances," that is, which causes us to advance, "to within the veil." Therefore, hope is a principle of rest in blessedness, and thus hope must be present in the blessed.

Thus the objection; the response is as follows:

> It must be said that, in the case of a first principle of movement, the principle that causes movement toward the terminus and the principle of rest in the terminus are the same. But among secondary and instrumental principles, there are some principles of movement that cease once the terminus has been reached, as a ship and the wind's pushing of it cease once port has been reached. Thus charity, which is a first mover, remains once the terminus of blessedness has been reached, but hope, which is a secondary principle proper to the movement itself, does not.

Thus SAINT THOMAS. These texts suffice for response to the first argument.

In response to the *second* argument we say that the comparison between infused and acquired friendship is not applicable to the case at hand. For one who loves with an acquired and political friendship neither loves nor has the intention of attaining anything arduous that is above the natural ability of the one who loves. Hence he does not require a special gift or a special habit other than the friendship itself, which causes a confidence in and an assurance of obtaining what is loved. But it is otherwise in the case at hand. Concerning this point, SAINT THOMAS, in *In 3 Sent.*, d.26, q.2, a.1, obj.2, presents the following objection:

> Just as the infused virtues are ordered to the arduous object that is eternal life, so the acquired virtues are ordered to the arduous object that is either civil or contemplative happiness. But the philosophers, who treat of the acquired virtues, do not hold that hope is a virtue. Therefore, hope should not be held to be a virtue by the theologians.

Thus the objection; the response is as follows:

> It must be said that the arduous object to which the acquired virtues are ordered is an end proportioned to the ability of nature. Thus nature of itself has been determined to hope for that end, and hence it does not require any superadded habit through which it would be determined to it. But the arduous object that is eternal life does exceed the ability of nature. Hence, since nature has not of itself been determined to hope for it, it must be so determined by an infused habit, and this is the hope that is a virtue.

Thus SAINT THOMAS. He says something similar in d.23, q.1, a.5, ad 5, which has been quoted in the solution of the first argument immediately above. Again, in a.4, qla.3, ad 3, he speaks as follows:

> Speculative principles are known through a natural habit other than that through which conclusions are known: that is, principles are known through understanding, but conclusions through science. But in affection, there is no preliminary natural habit: rather, from the very nature of the power there is an inclination toward an ultimate end proportioned to the nature. On the other hand, in relation to the end that is above nature, there must be a habit, given by grace, that is preliminary to other habits: in the intellect there must be faith; and in the affection there must be charity and hope, in order to incline one to an end to which the natural inclination does not pertain.

Thus SAINT THOMAS.

SAINT THOMAS responds to the opposing argument [p. 123] in *ST* II–II, q.17, a.5, ad 1, where he speaks as follows:

> Whatever else hope looks forward to obtaining, it hopes in being ordered to God as something final and as a first efficient cause.

Thus SAINT THOMAS.

This suffices for the question.

Blessed be God.

Amen.

Whether a Man Ought, out of Charity, to Love God More Than Himself

In relation to the twenty-seventh, twenty-eighth, twenty-ninth, and thirtieth distinctions of the third book of *The Sentences,* the question is raised: Whether a man ought, out of charity, to love God more than himself.

It is argued that he should not, as follows. THE PHILOSOPHER says, in *Ethics* 9, that feelings of love toward another come from feelings of love toward oneself. But what is first in any genus is most important. Therefore, the love that one has toward oneself {354} is more important than the love that one has toward another. Thus anyone loves himself more than he loves God according to nature, and hence according to charity as well, since grace does not destroy nature.

Argument is made for the opposite conclusion as follows. An end is to be loved more than what is directed to the end. But God is the end of all things that can be loved out of charity. Therefore, He is to be loved most of all.

In this question there will be three articles: in the first the conclusions will be presented, in the second the objections, and in the third the solutions.

Article I: Conclusions

First Conclusion: Charity Is a Virtue

SAINT THOMAS, in *ST* II–II, q.23, a.3, proves this conclusion as follows:

> Human acts have goodness according as they are governed by a due rule and measure. Hence human virtue, which is a prin-

> ciple of the good acts of man, consists in conformity to the rule of human acts, a rule which is twofold, namely human reason and God Himself. Thus, just as moral virtue is defined by being according to right reason, as is clear in *Ethics* 2, so the attaining of God constitutes the essence of theological virtue, as has been said above with respect to faith and hope. Hence, since charity attains God, because it joins us to God—as is made clear by AUGUSTINE, who, in *De moribus ecclesiae*, says that "Charity is a virtue that joins us to God by a true and perfect feeling with which we love Him"—consequently charity is a virtue.

Thus SAINT THOMAS. Again, in the same place, ad 1, he speaks as follows:

> THE PHILOSOPHER does not deny that friendship is a virtue, but says that "it is a virtue or accompanies virtue." For one could say that it is a moral virtue concerning operations directed to another, but that it is so under a different aspect than is justice. For justice concerns operations directed to another under the aspect of legal debt, while friendship concerns such operations under the aspect of a debt that is moral and one of friendship, or rather under the aspect of a gratuitous benefit, as is made clear by THE PHILOSOPHER in *Ethics* 8. However, it can be said that friendship is not a virtue in itself, distinct from other virtues. For it gets the aspect of something praiseworthy and fine only from its object, that is, only according as it is founded upon the fine quality of virtue. This is clear from the fact that not every friendship has the aspect of something praiseworthy and fine, as is clear in the case of a friendship of usefulness or one of pleasure. Hence, virtuous friendship is more a result of virtues than it is a virtue. But the case of charity is different, because charity is principally founded not on human virtue, but on the divine goodness.

Thus SAINT THOMAS.

From these texts the following argument for the conclusion can be formulated. Every habit that of its nature elicits an act conforming to the divine rule of human acts, and that conforms to the divine rule as its immediate object, is a theological human virtue. But charity is such a virtue. Therefore, etc.

Second Conclusion: The Object of Charity Is God inasmuch as He Is the Cause or the Object of Blessedness

SAINT THOMAS presents this conclusion in *ST* II–II, q.23, a.4, where he speaks as follows:

> Acts and habits are specified by objects. Now the proper object of love is a good. Hence, where there is a special aspect of good, there is a special aspect of love. But the divine good, inasmuch as it is the object of blessedness, does have a special aspect of good. Hence the love of charity, which is the love of this good, is a special love. Hence, too, charity is a special virtue.

Thus SAINT THOMAS. Again, in I–II, q.109, a.3, ad 1, he speaks as follows:

> Charity loves God above all things more outstandingly than does nature. For nature loves Him above all things inasmuch as He is the end and the principle of natural good, but charity loves Him above all things according as He is the object of blessedness, and according as man has a spiritual companionship with Him. For charity adds, over and above the natural love of God, a readiness and a choice, just as any virtuous habit adds something over and above the good act that is done through the mere natural reason of a man who does not possess the habit of virtue.

Thus SAINT THOMAS. Again, in II–II, q.23, a.1, he speaks as follows:

> According to THE PHILOSOPHER, in *Ethics* 8, not every love has the essence of friendship, but only love that is accompanied by benevolence, which occurs when we love someone in a such a way that we wish him good. But if we do not wish good to things loved, but rather wish their good for ourselves, in the way that we are said to love wine, or a horse, or something of this kind, this is love not of friendship, but of concupiscence. For it is ridiculous to say that someone has friendship toward wine or a horse. But neither does benevolence suffice for friendship: rather, there is required a reciprocated feeling of love, because a friend is the friend of his friend. Now such reciprocal benevolence is based on some sharing. {355} Since, therefore, there is a certain sharing by man in relation to God, inasmuch as He shares His blessedness with us, there must be a friendship based on this sharing. This sharing is spoken of in the remark of *1 Corinthians* 1: "The faithful God through Whom you have been called into the companionship of His son. . . ." Now the love based on this sharing is charity. Hence it is clear that charity is a friendship of man toward God.

Thus SAINT THOMAS. Again, in q.26, a.1, he speaks as follows:

> The love of charity is directed to God as to the principle of blessedness, and the friendship of charity is founded on a sharing in this principle.

Thus SAINT THOMAS.

From these texts one can argue as follows. The formal essence of the object of charity is that according to which charity is directed to its object, namely God, in a way different from that in which other habits and practices are so directed. But the essence "causative of blessedness," or "object of blessedness," or "principle of blessedness," pertains to God in such a way that charity is directed to Him. Therefore, etc.

Third Conclusion: By Charity Man Ought to Love God More Than Himself

SAINT THOMAS presents this conclusion in *In 3 Sent.*, d.29, q.1, a.3, where he speaks as follows:

> The object of love being a good, there are two ways in which one can be directed to the good of a thing. In one way, such that the good of the thing is referred to something else, as when I choose the good of one thing for the sake of another, if the other does not already possess the good, or am pleased by it, if the other does possess it. For instance, one loves wine inasmuch as he wants its sweetness, and is made glad by enjoying it, but he does not want the wine itself to have some good. This love is called by some "love of concupiscence." Now this love does not terminate in the thing that is said to be loved, but is turned back toward the thing for whose sake the good of the first thing is chosen.
>
> In another way there is love for the good of a thing in such a way that the love terminates in that thing itself, being pleased that the thing has the good that it does have, and wanting it to have the good that it does not. This is love of benevolence, which is the beginning of friendship, as THE PHILOSOPHER says in *Ethics* 9. Hence the degrees of charity should be understood with reference to this kind of love, because charity implies friendship.
>
> Now each most of all wants that good to be preserved that pleases him more, because such a good conforms more to his appetite, which has been informed by love. But such a good is his own good. Hence, the more the good of a thing is, or is judged to be, the good of the one who loves, the more the latter will want the good to be preserved in the thing loved. Now the good of the one who loves is found to a greater extent where it is more perfect. Hence, because any part is imperfect in itself, and has its perfection in its whole, a part, by natural love, tends more to the preservation of its whole than of itself. This is why an animal will naturally expose a limb in defense of its head, for the health of the whole depends on the latter. It is also why individual men will expose themselves to death for the preservation of the community of which they are parts.
>
> Accordingly, because our good is made perfect in God as the first, universal and perfect cause of goods, we are naturally more pleased that good

> should be present in Him than in ourselves. Hence, through love of friendship, God is naturally loved by man more than man is loved by himself. And because charity perfects nature, man through charity loves God above himself, and above all other particular goods. Now charity adds, over and above the natural love of God, a companionship in the life of grace.
>
> But some say that man naturally loves God more than himself through love of concupiscence, inasmuch as the divine good is more pleasing to him than his own; but that man naturally loves himself more than God through love of friendship, since he wants himself to be, and to live, and to have other goods, more than he wants God to do so, although charity elevates nature to the point that, even by friendship, a man loves God more than himself. But the former opinion is more probable, because the inclination of the nature of man as man never contradicts the inclination of virtue, but rather conforms to it.

Thus SAINT THOMAS. Again, in *ST* II–II, q.26, a.3, he speaks as follows:

> There are two goods that we can receive from God, the good of nature and the good of grace. Now there is a natural love based on God's sharing of natural goods with us, a love by which not only man, in the incorruption of his nature, loves God above all things and even more than himself, but also every creature does so in its way, whether by an intellectual love, an animal love, or at least, in the case of stones and other things that lack knowledge, a natural love. For any part naturally loves the common good of the whole more than it does its particular proper good. This is clear from the working of the part: for the principal inclination of any part is toward a common action directed to the advantage of the whole. This is also clear in the case of the political virtues, by which citizens will sometimes sustain the loss of their private goods and persons on behalf of a common good. Hence, all the more is this true in the case of friendship of charity, which is based on the sharing of gifts of grace. Therefore, by charity, a man should love God, Who is the common good of all things, more than himself. For blessedness is present in God as in the common and original principle of all things that are capable of sharing in blessedness.

Thus SAINT THOMAS. {356} He makes similar remarks in I–II, q.109, a.3, and in I, q.60, a.5; and in many other places he makes use of a similar proof.

From these texts the following argument can be formulated. Charity loves God no less than does human nature while the latter remains in its state of incorruption. But the uncorrupted nature of man naturally loves God above all things, even more than itself. Therefore, so does charity.

Fourth Conclusion: Charity Inclines One to Love God with a Twofold Love, Namely the Love of Friendship and the Love of Concupiscence

SAINT THOMAS implicitly presents this conclusion in *In 3 Sent.*, d.27, q.2, a.1, where he speaks as follows:

> Love is a coming to rest of appetite. Hence, just as appetite is found both in the sensitive and in the intellective parts, so is love. Now things that pertain to the sensitive appetite, such as the names of the passions, are used in a transferred sense with respect to the intellect; but what is proper to the intellective appetite, such as the name "will," is not applicable to the sensitive appetite. Hence, love is found in both appetites. But according as it is found in the sensitive appetite, it is properly called "love," because this name implies a passion; while according as it is found in the intellective appetite, it is called "dilection," which implies the "election" or choice that pertains to the intellective appetite. Nevertheless, the name "love" is transferred to the higher part, but the name "dilection" is never transferred to the lower.
>
> Now all other names that seem to be related to love either are implied by "love" and "dilection," or imply them while adding something over and above them. For because love in a way unites the one who loves to what is loved, the one who loves is related to what is loved as to himself, or as to something pertaining to his own perfection. But he is related to himself and to the things that are his in such a way that, first, he wants whatever pertains to his own perfection to be present to him; hence, love implies a "concupiscence" for what is loved by which the presence of the latter is desired. Second, a man, through his feeling, turns other things toward himself, and desires for himself whatever is useful to him; and inasmuch as this is done for the sake of a beloved, love implies "benevolence," by which one desires good things for what is loved. Third, by acting a man acquires for himself the things that he desires for himself; and inasmuch as this is done for another, "beneficence" is implied in love. Fourth, a man is agreeable to providing whatever seems to be good for himself; and inasmuch as this is done for a friend, love implies "concord," by which one is agreeable in matters concerning what seems good to the friend—not, indeed, in speculative matters, because in such matters, concord, as THE PHILOSOPHER says in *Ethics* 9, does not pertain to friendship, and there can, on the contrary, be discord without prejudice to friendship, because concord and discord do not submit to the will, since the understanding is compelled by argument.
>
> Love, however, adds something over and above the four features mentioned, namely the "coming to rest" of appetite in the thing loved, without which there can still be any of these features.

> In addition, there are other things that add something over and above love or dilection. For "being enamored" *(amatio)* adds, over and above love, an intensity of love that is like a heat. "Friendship" adds two features. One is a companionship of lover and beloved in the love, so that they mutually love one another and know that they love one another; the other is that they act from choice, and not from passion alone. Hence THE PHILOSOPHER says that being enamored is like a passion, while friendship is like a habit. Thus it is clear that friendship is the most perfect of the things related to love, and implies all of the things mentioned above. Hence, it is in the genus of friendship that we must place charity, which is a friendship of man in relation to God by which man loves God, and God man, so that a fellowship between man and God is brought about, as is said in *1 John* 1: "If we walk in the light, as He is in the light, we shall have fellowship with one another."

Thus SAINT THOMAS. Again, in the same place, obj.1, he presents the following objection:

> AUGUSTINE says that charity is the virtue by which we desire to see God and to fully enjoy Him. But this is a concupiscence. Therefore, charity is concupiscence.

Thus the objection; the response is as follows:

> It must be said that any friendship implies concupiscence or desire, and adds something over and above it.

Thus SAINT THOMAS. Again, in *ST* II–II, q.26, a.3, obj.3, he presents the following objection:

> Inasmuch as anyone loves God, he loves the enjoyment of God. But inasmuch as anyone loves the enjoyment of God, he loves himself alone, because this is the highest good that anyone could want for himself. Therefore, a man ought not, out of charity, to love God more than himself.

Thus the objection; the response is as follows:

> It must be said that the fact that someone wants to enjoy God pertains to the love by which God is loved with a love of concupiscence. But we love God to a greater extent with love of friendship than with love of concupiscence, because the good of God is in itself greater than the good which we are able to share by enjoying Him. Hence, man, out of charity, simply speaking loves God more than himself.

Thus SAINT THOMAS.

From these texts, we argue as follows. Any fine and perfect friendship loves a friend with two loves: with a love of friendship, in wanting good for the friend; and with love of concupiscence, in desiring the friend's presence and companionship. But charity is perfect friendship toward God. Therefore, etc.

Fifth Conclusion: In One's Love of God, a Regard for Reward Can in Some Way Be Present

SAINT THOMAS presents this conclusion in *In 3 Sent.*, d.29, **{357}** q.1, a.4, where he speaks as follows:

> "Reward," properly speaking, is said to be the prize that one in some way earns by work or activity. But a prize is something given to someone as his good. Hence, as such, "reward" implies something capable of being referred, through love, to the one to whom reward is given, for anyone loves reward for the sake of himself. Nevertheless it is not of the essence of reward to be the end of an intending, because in general the one to whom reward is given is not looking for reward for his work. Now the things that someone loves for his own sake are either, formally speaking, perfections of himself such as health, virtue, activity, pleasure, and the like; or they cause or preserve these perfections, or prevent their contraries. Hence, if someone loves something outside himself for the sake of himself, that can be called a "reward" inasmuch as by it something is given to him or preserved within him. But it is of the essence of friendship that the friend be loved for his own sake. Hence, in friendship, the friend does not have the essence of a "reward," properly speaking, although the things we get out of the friendship can have the essence of reward. Such things are the pleasures and useful benefits that the one who loves gets from the friendship, and by reason of which his friend is himself called a "reward," by way of his causality, just as God is called our "reward" by reason of what we get from Him.
>
> It is clear, therefore, that to posit reward as the end of love on the side of the one loved is against the essence of friendship. Hence charity, in this sense, cannot have its eye on a reward, for this would be to hold that not God, but the goods obtained from Him, are the ultimate end. But it is not against the essence of friendship to posit reward as the end—though not the ultimate end—of love on the side of the one loving, namely inasmuch as the love itself is an operation of the soul. For the very operation of love, since it is an accident, cannot be said to be loved except for the sake of its subject, and there can be an order among the things that one loves for their own

> sakes while the friendship is still preserved. Thus, I can love the very operation of love for the sake of something else without hindrance from the friendship. It will, however, be against the essence of virtue, if the operation of virtue is loved for the sake of something else inferior to the virtue, such as temporal goods.
>
> It is clear, therefore, that one who possesses charity cannot have his eye on reward in such a way as to posit that what is loved, namely God, has any further end, for this would be against the essence of charity as a kind of friendship; nor, again, in such a way as to posit that the love itself has any temporal good as its end, because this would be against the essence of charity as a virtue. Nevertheless, charity can have its eye on reward in such a way as to posit that created blessedness is the end of the love (though not of what is loved), for this is neither against the essence of friendship nor against the essence of virtue, since blessedness is the end of virtue.

Thus SAINT THOMAS. From this text we argue as follows. It does not detract from charity for it to direct the operation of virtue to its own end, namely blessedness. But in so directing it, charity has its eye on reward, since blessedness is the reward of the acts of the virtues. Therefore, etc.

Sixth Conclusion: In One's Love of God, No Limit Is to Be Set

SAINT THOMAS presents this conclusion in *ST* II–II, q.27, a.6, where he speaks as follows:

> As SAINT AUGUSTINE says in his *Literal Commentary on Genesis,* a "mode" *(modus)* is that which pre-establishes the proper measure *(mensura)* of each thing. From this authoritative text it is clear that "mode" implies determination of an amount.
>
> Now this determination is found both in the measure and in what is measured, but in different ways. For in the measure it is present in an essential way, because a measure, as such, determines and "moderates" other things. In what is measured, however, measure is present with respect to something else, namely inasmuch as what is measured conforms to the measure. Hence, no "immoderation" can be found in the measure itself, but a thing measured is "immoderate" if it does not conform to the measure, whether by falling short of or by going beyond it.
>
> Now in all objects of action and of appetite, the measure is the end, because the proper essence of what we do and what we desire must be taken from their end, as THE PHILOSOPHER makes clear in *Ethics* 2. Hence, the

> end has a "mode" of itself, while what is directed to the end has a "mode" from the fact that it is proportioned to the end. Hence, as THE PHILOSOPHER says in *Politics* 1, desire for the end is without limit or end in all of the arts, although there is a limit of what is directed to the end. For a doctor does not impose a limit on health, but rather makes health as perfect as he can; but he does impose a limit on medicine, for he does not give as much medicine as he can, but gives it in proportion to health, and if the medicine should exceed or fall short of this proportion, it would be "immoderate."
>
> Now the end of all human actions and feelings is love of God, through which we attain, to the greatest extent, the ultimate end. Hence, in love of God, a "mode" cannot be had in the way in which it is present in a thing measured, so that more and less can be taken in it: rather, "mode" is present as it is found in measure, in which there can be no excess, but rather the more the rule is conformed to, the better it is. Thus, the more one loves God, the better the love is.

Thus SAINT THOMAS. Again, in *In 3 Sent.*, d.27, q.3, a.3, he speaks as follows:

> "Mode" implies a measure. Now an act is measured by the essence of the acting; for instance, pity is measured, with respect to what is to be done to help the miserable man, {358} by the quantity of misery that moves one to pity. But the cause of loving God is the divine goodness, which is infinite; but the act of a creature is finite, since it proceeds from a finite power, and hence it cannot be commensurate with the essence of the love. Thus, in the love of God, no "mode" is set beyond which one should not go: rather, however much one loves, one always reaches out to more. This is why it is said that love of God does not have a "mode," that is, a pre-established one, beyond which it should not go.

Thus SAINT THOMAS.

From these texts one can argue as follows. An act that has the essence of an end and measure has no pre-established mode beyond which it passes into excess. But the love of God is such an act. Therefore, etc.

Again, an object of infinite lovability cannot be loved excessively. But God is such an object. Therefore, etc.

Seventh Conclusion: Not All Neighbors Are to Be Loved out of Charity Equally

SAINT THOMAS presents this conclusion in *ST* II–II, q.26, a.7, where he speaks as follows:

Every act must be proportioned to its object and to its agent, getting its species from the object and its mode of intensity from the power of the agent. For instance, movement gets its species from the terminus toward which it is directed, and its intensity of speed from the character of what is moved and the power of the mover. Accordingly, love gets its species from its object, but its intensity from the side of the one who loves.

Now the object of love of charity is God, while the one who loves is a man. Accordingly, the specific differentiation of charitable love, with respect to the various neighbors to be loved, must be taken with reference to God, in such a way that through charity we desire a greater good for a neighbor who is closer to God. For although the good that charity desires for all men, namely eternal blessedness, is in itself one, it has different degrees according to the different ways of participating in it; and it pertains to charity to want to observe the justice of God, according to which those who are better participate more perfectly in blessedness. This pertains to the species of love, for the different species of love follow from the different goods that we desire for those whom we love.

Intensity of love, however, must be taken with reference to the one who loves. In this regard, a man loves those who are closer to him, with respect to the good that he wishes for them, with an intenser feeling than he loves those who are better, with respect to a greater good.

But there is also another difference to be noted here. For some neighbors are close to us by a natural origin from which they cannot depart because it is that by which they are what they are. But the goodness of virtue by which some men grow close to God can approach and recede, and grow and diminish. Hence, I can, by charity, want someone close to me to be better than someone else, and thus to be able to reach a greater degree of blessedness.

But there is another way in which we by charity love those close to us to a greater extent, namely because we love them in a greater number of ways. For toward those who are not close to us we have only the friendship of charity; but toward those who are close to us we have other friendships, according to the manner of their closeness to us. Now since the good upon which any other fine friendship is based is directed, as to its end, to the good upon which charity is based, consequently charity commands the act of any other friendship, just as the art concerning an end commands the art concerning things directed to the end. Hence, the loving of someone because he is related by blood, or is close, or is a fellow-citizen, or for any other licit reason capable of being directed to the end of charity, can itself be commanded

> by charity; and thus, by charity, which chooses and commands, we love those who are closer to us in a greater number of ways.

Thus SAINT THOMAS. He presents something similar in *In 3 Sent.*, d.29, q.1, a.6, and in many other places.

From these texts one can argue as follows. A habit that inclines us to love some more and others less intensely, and to want a greater good for one than for another, inclines us to love in unequal degrees. But charity is such a habit. Therefore, etc.

Eighth Conclusion: Charity More Fervently Loves Friends than Enemies, and Love of a Friend Is Better than Love of an Enemy

SAINT THOMAS presents this conclusion in *ST* II–II, q.27, a.7, where he speaks as follows:

> The reason for loving one's neighbor out of charity is God. Since, then, the question is raised, "Whether it is better or more meritorious to love a friend than to love an enemy," the response is that there are two ways in which these loves can be compared: in one way, from the point of view of the neighbor who is loved, and in the other way from the point of view of the reason for which he is loved.
>
> Now in the first way, love of a friend stands above love of an enemy, because a friend is something better and closer, and hence is more suitable matter for love, which is why an act of love performed upon such matter is better. Hence its opposite is worse: for it is worse to hate {359} a friend than to hate an enemy.
>
> In the second way, however, love of an enemy is better, for two reasons. First, because there can be another reason for love of a friend than God, but God alone is the reason for love of an enemy. Second, because, assuming that both are loved on account of God, the love of God that extends the soul of man to what is more remote, that is, to love of enemies, shows itself to be more powerful, just as the strength of fire shows itself to be greater the more it diffuses its heat to more remote things. Also, our love for the divine shows itself to be greater to the extent that we accomplish more difficult things for its sake, just as the strength of fire is greater to the extent that it is able to burn material that is less combustible. But just as the same fire acts more strongly on what is closer than on what is more distant, so charity more fervently loves those who are close than those who are distant, and in this respect, love of friends is, considered in itself, more fervent and better than is love of enemies.

Thus SAINT THOMAS. From this text one can argue as follows. Love that is directed to a better object, and is, on the side of the subject, more intense, is of itself better. But love of a friend is related to love of an enemy in this way. Therefore love of a friend is, simply speaking and in itself, better.

Here the first article terminates.

Article II: Objections

§1. Against the First Conclusion

Arguments of Aureolus and Henry In the second article, argument is made against the conclusions.

AUREOLUS (*In 3 Sent.*, d.27, a.3) argues against some points contained in the proof of the first conclusion that moral friendship is truly and properly a virtue. *First,* as follows:

> Such friendship has a contrary vice, namely untrustworthiness or faithlessness, which is the greatest vice.

Second, he argues as follows:

> Any act that is distinct from acts of the other virtues and has both its own praiseworthiness and its own circumstances, different from circumstances of acts of the other virtues, will, if repeated, generate a virtuous habit. But so it is with the act of friendship, which is the identification of another with oneself in conversation, daily life, feeling, and activity: for this act has its own praiseworthiness and its own circumstances, and it is distinct from the acts of other virtues such as affability, benevolence, and beneficence. Therefore, etc.

Third, HENRY, in *Quodlibet* 10, q.12, argues as follows:

> Although friendship is based on virtue, nevertheless, no virtue is perfect with regard to exercise without friendship. Hence CICERO says: "For friendship was given by nature as a help-mate of the virtues, in order that, since virtue could not reach what is highest by itself alone, it might be able to do so in union and companionship with another." For this reason, with regard to performance of deeds and in relation to the other virtues, friendship is a general virtue, and a principal part of general justice, one that renders to each what is his and fulfills the precept, "Do to another what you would have done to you, and do not do to another what you would not have done to you."

Fourth, he argues as follows:

> THE COMMENTATOR, in treating the beginning of *Ethics* 8, says that friendship is one of the virtues, just as are fortitude, temperance, and each of the moral virtues. For friendship, like the others, is concerned with actions and passions, namely with actions such as loving and with passions such as being enamored.

Thus HENRY and AUREOLUS.

§2. Against the Second Conclusion

Arguments of Scotus SCOTUS (*In 3 Sent.*, d.27, q.1) argues against the second conclusion that God is not the object of charity under the aspect by which He is causative of blessedness in the rational nature. *First* he argues as follows:

> An act of charity, if it is perfect, regards God under His most perfect aspect as an object of love. But this most perfect aspect in God is not a relation of God to a creature, but an aspect of His that is absolute in itself, for what is absolute is in itself better than any relation to another could be.

Second, he argues as follows:

> One may ask, What is it to be "causative of blessedness"? Either it is a relation of capacity by which something is naturally capable of causing blessedness; or it is a relation of actuality by which it does cause blessedness.
>
> If one answers in the first way, we respond that a capacity is an essence that perfectly determines a perfect act only by reason of that to which the capacity belongs, just as, universally speaking, a perfection does not exist by itself, but necessarily involves in itself the nature in which it is present. To say, therefore, that it is as "causative of blessedness" in this sense that God is the object of charity, is to say that He is the object of charity inasmuch as He has a nature in which a capacity is present.
>
> If one answers in the second way, we respond that this answer does not seem probable, because that relation that is present in the object inasmuch as it actually causes blessedness follows upon an act. For there is no difference in the object itself between a relation of actuality and one of capacity, unless because an act is elicited in relation to the object. Therefore, to give this second answer would be to hold that **{360}** it is inasmuch as He determines an elicited act of charity that God has the formal essence of the object of that act.

Third, he argues as follows:

> To seek a good as something for this particular man pertains to the feeling of the pleasant; and it is not with respect to this feeling that the will is perfected by charity.

Fourth, he argues as follows:

> Actual and dispositional causing of blessedness, if they name something in God, name an actual or a dispositional relation of reason, taken precisively. But no relation of reason can be the formal essence that determines an act of charity.

Fifth, he argues as follows:

> A power directed to a common object proportioned, whether as a determining or as a moving essence, to the power, can most perfectly be brought to rest only in that in which the essence of the adequate object is most perfectly present. But every volitional power regards as its first and proportioned object the whole of being. Therefore, it can be perfectly brought to rest in no being, whether created or uncreated, except that being in which the essence of being is most perfectly present. But the only such being is the particular first being, not under some relative aspect, but under the aspect by which it is this particular being.

Thus SCOTUS argues in form.

§3. Against the Third Conclusion

I. Arguments of Scotus The same SCOTUS (d.27, q.1) argues against the third conclusion that nature does not suffice for loving God more than oneself without a supernatural habit. *First,* he argues as follows:

> A nature is determined to one object. But what it is determined to, according to *De generatione* 2, is a desire for its own being. Therefore, whatever else may be held concerning a nature, it cannot desire its own non-being, unless it were to be said that it is only conditionally determined to a desire for its own being, which does not seem probable. Accordingly, any intellectual nature is determined to a desire that it itself exist rather than to a desire that God exist if the two are incompatible. For it is determined to the desire that it itself exist as to the one natural object toward whose contrary it cannot be inclined, whatever presupposition may be made or condition posited with respect to it or to anything else. Otherwise, it would only conditionally desire that it itself exist.

Second, he argues as follows:

> A natural desire seems to regard only what befits the one desiring, and consequently to regard first of all the one for whom the appetite desires what is befitting. But this is the very one who loves, and thus, his desire first of all regards himself. Therefore, it cannot to a greater extent regard another.

Third, he argues as follows:

> If any thing were inclined more to the being of another than to its own being, this would be the case, it would seem, because a part loves the being of its whole more than its own being: for a hand will expose itself to protect the head, and water will leave its proper place for the good of the universe, that is, in order to eliminate a vacuum. But these examples are irrelevant, because they show only that a whole loves its own being more than it does that of its part: for it is not the hand that exposes itself, but the man who exposes his hand; and it is not that water moves itself upwards for the good of the universe, but rather that the governing power of the whole loves the well-being of the whole above that of the part.

II. Arguments of Others Others also argue against the third conclusion. *First* as follows:

> The cause of love is unity of the thing loved with the lover. Now anyone has greater unity with himself than with God.

Second, they argue as follows:

> Just as natural knowledge precedes supernatural knowledge, so anyone's natural love of himself precedes the supernatural love that occurs when he loves God above all things.

Third, they argue as follows:

> If what the conclusion says were possible, then charity, which is posited in order that God be loved above all things, would overflow.

Fourth, they argue as follows:

> ARISTOTLE, in *Ethics* 9, says that feelings of friendship toward another come from feelings of friendship toward oneself.

Fifth, they argue as follows:

> It is clear that the heretic who allows himself to be burnt, apparently for the sake of God although he does not have charity, does so for the sake of love of himself; and that it is because he loves his own honor and will, and not for the sake of love of God, that he allows himself to be burnt. This seems to

be the meaning of THE APOSTLE in *1 Corinthians* 13: "If I give all my goods for food for the poor," he says, "and if I deliver my body to be burned, but have not charity, it availeth me nought." This is so because he would not love God above all things; for he would not be able to know whether he did love God above all things. For sometimes someone believes that he loves God above all things, and thinks that he is exposing himself to death for the sake of God, but in fact does so for the sake of accomplishing his own will, in order to maintain what he affirms.

III. Arguments of Durandus DURANDUS (*In 3 Sent.*, d.29, q.2) also argues against the third conclusion. *First* as follows:

> The comparison with the citizen who exposes himself to death for the sake of the common good is invalid, because the citizen exposes himself for the community, not as loving the community more than himself, but because he loves the good of virtue more than health of body.
>
> Such seems to be the meaning of ARISTOTLE in *Ethics* 9, as is clear from the whole development of the chapter beginning "But one might ask whether one should . . . ," where he treats of this matter. Thus, he there says that, in exposing himself for his friends or homeland, a citizen wants the greatest good for himself, namely the good of virtue, while giving most other goods to friends and homeland. ARISTOTLE concludes that, in all praiseworthy matters, such a citizen seems to be someone more zealous for himself than devoted to the good.
>
> Hence, {361} the following interpretation, given by some, is not true: "When Aristotle says that the zealous man who exposes himself for the sake of his friends or his homeland wants the greatest good for himself and thus loves himself most of all, he is not making a comparison between the love by which a man loves himself and the love by which he loves the common good, but rather a comparison between the love by which a man loves himself in one way and the love by which he loves himself in another way. The meaning is rather that a man, by exposing himself to death for the common good, loves himself to a greater extent by doing this than by doing the contrary or by doing something else."
>
> This is not true: it is rather the first, not the second, comparison which is being made, as is clear from the development of the text.

Second, he argues as follows:

> Anyone ought to be more sorry if he himself has done something against the good of virtue than if the whole rest of the city has done so. Therefore, anyone ought to love his own possession of the good of virtue more than that of

> a community; and if he exposes himself for a community, he does so in giving a lesser good, namely a good of the body, to the community and a greater good, namely the good of virtue, to himself.

Third, he argues as follows:

> It is clear that anyone ought to love himself more than a friend, and nevertheless, as THE PHILOSOPHER says in *Ethics* 9, one should suffer many things, and even die, if necessary, for one's friends. Therefore, the fact that someone exposes himself to death for another does not suffice as an argument that he loves the other more than himself, whatever the other may be, whether private person or commonwealth. For this reason, the manner of proof that is used, namely that "a citizen loves the common good more than himself except insofar as he is included in the common good," is insufficient, because it assumes something false.

Fourth, he argues as follows:

> Something false is assumed in the proof, namely that charity elevates nature to love God under a special aspect, namely that of "being causative of blessedness." For it is not charity that does this, but faith, which shows us His aspect as causative of blessedness in His being itself.
>
> Nor, again, is infused faith required for this, since we can conceive of His aspect as causative of blessedness without infused faith.
>
> And even given that charity does elevate nature to love God with love of concupiscence, one would have to hold equally that it also elevates nature to love God with love of friendship, and this with respect to another special aspect present in the God Who is loved, not with respect to the manner of loving on our part, according to which He is loved above all things. For love of friendship arises from a good apprehended in the one who is loved, as we love a virtuous friend on account of the good of virtue that exists in him. Hence, if that essence of goodness is through grace conceived to exist absolutely in God beyond that which we by nature conceive to exist in Him, there is no reason why nature should be elevated by grace to love God with love of concupiscence, unless it is also elevated to love Him with love of friendship with respect to the above-mentioned manner of loving.

IV. Arguments of Others Others, according to DURANDUS *(ibid.),* argue thus. *First,* as follows:

> God is loved by us both with love of concupiscence and with love of friendship. But charity elevates the will to love God with love of concupiscence, beyond what the will could do by its natural powers. For, while by natural

powers we love God inasmuch as He is the universal productive and preservative principle of all things, charity elevates us to love Him inasmuch as He is the good that causes blessedness. Similarly, then, charity elevates nature to love God with love of friendship, beyond what nature could do to love Him by its natural powers. But this is only with respect to the mode and order of loving that charity observes, according to which God is loved for Himself and above all things. Therefore, etc.

This argument is confirmed as follows. Through grace man is in a way elevated to divine being. Accordingly, just as natural love follows upon natural being, so gracious love follows upon the gracious being that is divine being. Hence, just as natural love causes a man to love himself more than anything else, so grace causes him to love God, to whose being he is elevated through grace, more than himself. Thus the order in natural love is the converse of the order in gracious love. For just as in natural love feelings of friendship toward another come from feelings of friendship toward oneself, so in gracious love, feelings of friendship toward oneself and toward one's neighbor come from feelings of friendship toward God.

Again, the argument is confirmed as follows. The case of natural and supernatural knowledge is like that of natural and supernatural love. But natural knowledge starts from creatures and terminates in God, while supernatural knowledge does the reverse. Therefore, it is similar in the case of natural and supernatural love.

Second, they argue as follows:

BERNARD, in *On Loving God,* distinguishes four levels of loving: the first is when a man loves nothing except himself; the second is when he loves nothing except for the sake of himself and his own advantage; the third is when he loves God for the sake of God; the fourth is when he loves himself and all other things for the sake of God. He also says that the third and fourth levels come by grace, and that the fourth level is reached in this life by few and very briefly. Now because to love oneself for the sake of God is to love God more than oneself, it is not to be attributed {362} to natural love, since one can scarcely reach this level by grace in the present life. Therefore by natural love everyone loves himself more than God; but through grace and charity he is elevated to love God more than himself.

§4. Against the Fourth Conclusion

Argument of Durandus DURANDUS (d.29, q.2) argues against the fourth conclusion that for us the immediate object of love of concupiscence cannot be God in Himself, but only the act by which He is attained by us. He argues as follows:

> What is loved with love of concupiscence is, from the point of view of the end, loved for the sake of the one for whom it is desired, as we love wine for the sake of ourselves. But God, of and in Himself, should not be loved, from the point of view of the end, for the sake of anything else. Therefore, God, inasmuch as He is something in Himself, should not be loved with love of concupiscence. Nevertheless, we do love with love of concupiscence the act by which we attain God, namely the vision or the subsequent enjoyment, which we love as directed to ourselves and for the sake of ourselves. Yet because God is the object of such acts, consequently He is the remote object of this love of concupiscence, because He is the object of the object. For this reason, the masters sometimes say that God is loved by us with love of concupiscence, just as we say that we love wine although what we love immediately is not the wine, but the tasting of it.

§5. *Against the Fifth Conclusion*

Argument of Durandus DURANDUS (d.29, q.3) argues against the fifth conclusion that, in some cases, to direct one's love of God to blessedness as reward would be illicit, and consequently that the distinction made in the argument for the conclusion is insufficient. He speaks as follows:

> If we take reward to be the end of the love, but not the end of God as loved, there is still a distinction to be made.
>
> If, on the one hand, the reward is regarded as wholly the end for which God is loved and without which He would not be loved, it is then not licit to have one's eye on the reward, because we ought to love God for His own sake, even given that we should get no advantage out of such a love. And we ought to love Him much more than any virtuous man ought to love another virtuous man. For everyone who is good is to be loved, setting aside everything else, since the object of love is the good in all its amplitude.
>
> If, however, the reward is intended as not wholly the end of the love—since God would still be loved without it, and since it is through the love by which God is loved that we intend to attain blessedness although we would love God even if we were certain of not attaining blessedness—then it is licit, in the love of God, to have regard for the reward.

§6. Against the Sixth Conclusion

Argument of Durandus DURANDUS (d.27, q.2) argues against the sixth conclusion that the love of God ought to have a "mode." He speaks as follows:

> There are three "modes" to consider in the love of God, and in the act of any virtue: one according to the limitation of essence; a second according to the determination of circumstance; and a third according to the relation of intermediary to what is excessive and what is defective.
>
> If we take the first "mode," we must say that the love of God does have a "mode." The reason is as follows. What belongs to a certain genus and a certain species has a "mode" with respect to limitation of essence. But the love of God does belong to a certain genus and a certain species. Therefore, it has a "mode" with respect to limitation of essence.
>
> If we speak of "mode" with respect to determination of circumstance, here again, love of God has a "mode." This is made clear as follows. Evil is related to a vicious act as goodness is to a virtuous act. But evil consists in a vicious act on account of a deficiency of determinate and proper circumstance in the latter. Similarly, therefore, goodness consists in a virtuous act on account of proper circumstances being present to or informing the act.
>
> But if we take the limit according to the relation of intermediary to what is excessive and what is deficient, then love of God has no "mode."

§7. Against the Seventh Conclusion

Argument of Durandus DURANDUS (d.29, q.1) argues against the seventh conclusion that, with respect to rational creatures, to whom charity is directed, we ought to want an equal good of grace and glory for all of them.

He says that the reason for this is as follows:

> Through charity we desire divine good for creatures inasmuch as they are capable of receiving it and of being directed to God through it. But all intellectual creatures are capable of receiving an equal amount of the good of grace and glory—as is very commonly held and is doubtless true of creatures of the same species—and all of them are equally capable of being directed to God. Therefore we ought through charity to want an equal amount of good for all.
>
> This is confirmed by what is said in *1 Corinthians* 13: "Charity is not envious." Now there would be envy if one did not desire for each as great a good as he is capable of receiving, especially when one good does not diminish or hinder another, {363} as is the case with the goods of grace and glory which charity regards. Or rather, it would seem to be prejudicial to what is

> divine. For since charity is, first of all and simply speaking, related to God, and desires a good for someone only in order that he might be directed to God as an end, it would be prejudicial to divine love if charity did not desire for anyone a good by which he might more efficaciously tend toward God. But such a good is the highest good of grace and glory, which a pure creature is capable of receiving, and in which there are no levels, as has been said. But this desire is conditioned, since the divine ordering and will, to which charity first adheres and according to which it wants all things to occur, are presupposed.

Thus DURANDUS.

§8. *Against the Eighth Conclusion*

Arguments of Durandus DURANDUS (d.30, q.2) argues against the eighth conclusion, *first* as follows:

> Love of an enemy is in some cases better and more meritorious than love of a friend, for example when love of an enemy neither excludes nor includes love of a friend. For instance, when one man is directed by an act of love toward a friend without thinking of his enemy, and another is on the contrary directed by an act of love to an enemy without thinking of his friend, here it seems that, other things being equal—namely the habit of charity in each, and the intensity of the act on both sides—love of an enemy is more meritorious than love of a friend.
>
> This is made clear as follows. When two good acts are so related that they proceed from identical habits and are equally intense, although, by the nature of the act, greater effort is required for one act than for the other, the one for which greater effort is required is more meritorious. But, by the nature of the act, greater effort is required for love of an enemy, if it is equally intense as love of a friend. Therefore, it is more meritorious.
>
> The major premise is made clear as follows. When greater effort is required only from the point of view of one who is disposed to act badly, the effort does not increase the merit: for otherwise an incontinent man would be more meritorious than a temperate man who performs an act that is similar with respect to kind of virtue, because the incontinent man must make greater effort, on account of his disposition to act badly, than the temperate one. But this is not true, because, if it were, the virtues would be more harm than help. But when greater effort is required, not on account of the disposition of the one acting, but on account of the difficulty of the act itself, then greater effort causing a more difficult act to be just as intense as an easier one, does increase the merit.

> The minor premise is clear of itself. Greater effort is required to love an enemy just as intensely as one loves a friend, since there is more that is disagreeable and less that is attractive. Therefore, etc.

Second, he argues as follows:

> An act whose entire intention is based on charity is more meritorious than an act whose intention, though similar, is not entirely based on charity, the cause of this being that merit depends principally on charity. But love of an enemy is such an act, for the entire reason for loving an enemy is charity toward God. But the entire reason for loving a friend is not always charity, since another reason, namely the sharing of familial good, civil good, or some other such good, can also be present. Therefore, etc.

Third, he argues as follows:

> A good that includes another good is better than the first good alone. But love of an enemy does include love of a friend. Either it does so in actuality, as when one loves, for the sake of God, both friend and enemy. Or it does so by habit, from the nature of the case, and not merely on the basis of a supposition. For when anyone loves an enemy, it follows, from the nature of the act and of the object, that he loves his friend by habit, and would love him in actuality, both in feeling and in deed, if the occasion arose and there were need. But the converse does not follow in the same way. Therefore, love of an enemy is better, other things being equal.

Thus DURANDUS.

Here the second article terminates.

Article III. Solutions

§1. To the Arguments against the First Conclusion

To the Arguments of Aureolus and Henry In the third article we must respond to the foregoing objections.

To the *first and subsequent* arguments against the first conclusion [p. 174], we say that, concerning the question there touched on, namely whether friendship is a political virtue, SAINT THOMAS apparently spoke in different ways in different places. For in *Questions on the Virtues,* "On Charity", a.2, he seems to mean that such friendship is not a virtue, since, in ad 8, he speaks as follows:

> Friendship is held to be not a virtue, but something that follows from virtue. For from the very fact that one possesses virtue and loves the good of reason, it follows, from the very inclination of virtue, that he loves those like himself, namely virtuous men, in whom the good of reason flourishes. But friendship toward God inasmuch as He is blessed and the author of blessedness must be established prior to the virtues that order one to that blessedness. Hence, since it is not something that follows from other virtues, but is a preamble to them, it must of itself be a virtue.

Thus SAINT THOMAS. Again, in *In 3 Sent.*, d.27, q.2, a.2, ad 1, he speaks as follows:

> The friendship of which THE PHILOSOPHER treats is caused either by an inclination of nature, in the case of friendships of pleasure and advantage, or by the inclination of a virtuous habit in which an inclination of nature is presupposed, in the case of fine friendship, inasmuch as {364} everything that causes resemblance to something also causes inclination toward love of that thing. Hence, friendship is not held to be a virtue, but something following from the virtues. But the friendship that we have toward God cannot have any such basis, since it exceeds the limits of nature. Hence one must be raised up to this friendship through a special gift, a gift that we do call a virtue.

Thus SAINT THOMAS.

Now in these texts he seems to mean that political friendship is not a virtue distinct from others. But in *ST* II–II, q.23, a.3, ad 1, which was quoted in the proof of the first conclusion, he seems to want to say that it is properly speaking a virtue. And he says something similar in *Commentary on the Ethics* 8.1, where he speaks as follows:

> Friendship is a certain equality, inasmuch as it requires mutual love, and this seems to add something over and above the mode of virtue. For the act of one who is virtuous is enough in the case of any virtue, but is not enough in the case of friendship, where, rather, the acts of two who love one another must concur. Therefore THE PHILOSOPHER does not without qualification say above that friendship is a virtue, but adds "or it accompanies virtue," because it seems to add something over and above the essence of virtue.

Thus SAINT THOMAS.

From these texts it is apparent that there is, properly speaking, no contradiction in what SAINT THOMAS says. For his thought is that friendship of this kind is not a virtue in the way that the other political virtues are: first, because it has the other virtues as a basis, and is born out of an inclination arising from antecedent habits; again, because an act or habit existing in another subject is of the essence of this kind of friendship; again, because the habit of this kind of friendship sometimes ceases to be friendship toward a particular person, for instance when a friend has turned to incorrigible evil, and can afterwards begin again to be friendship toward him if, at another moment, he truly or apparently becomes better; and again, because friendship of this kind can be lost, not because of any vice of him in whom it is present, but merely by deficiency in his friend. And many other dissimilarities between the habit of friendship and the habits of the moral virtues can be given.

From this, the solution to all of the arguments against the first conclusion is clear. For they demonstrate only that a habit of this kind is in some way a virtue, since it is chosen and praiseworthy, and consists in an intermediary, all of which we concede. But they do not demonstrate that it is a virtue in exactly the same sense as are the other virtues. This is SAINT THOMAS's meaning with respect to the friendship of which THE PHILOSOPHER speaks in *Ethics* 8 and 9. It is otherwise with the other "friendship" of which he speaks in *Ethics* 4, which is also called "affability" or "friendliness," and which holds to the intermediary between fawning on the one hand, and quarrelsomeness or discord on the other.

§2. *To the Arguments against the Second Conclusion*

To the Arguments of Scotus To the *first and other, subsequent* arguments of SCOTUS against the second conclusion [p. 175], we say that the formal essence of the object of charity can be understood in two ways. One way is from the point of view of the thing that charity principally loves, and to which its act is principally directed; and thus the formal essence of the object of charity is "highest good," or "good of divine blessedness." The other way is from the point of view of the volitional power that loves God; and thus the formal essence of the object of charity is "principle of the rational nature's blessedness," or "essence that is causative of blessedness."

Concerning the first way, BLESSED THOMAS, in *Questions on the Virtues*, "On Charity", a.2, speaks as follows:

> Charity is without doubt a virtue. For since a virtue "is what makes the one who possesses it good and renders his act good," it is clear that a man is directed to his proper good by his proper virtue. Now the proper good of man

must be taken in different ways according as man himself is taken in different ways. For the proper good of man as man is the good of reason, because to be man is to be rational; but the good of man as artificer is the good of an art; so, too, the good of man as political is the common good of a city.

Since, then, virtue is exercised with reference to a good, the virtue of anything requires that the thing be in such a state as to act well—that is, voluntarily, readily, and with pleasure and constancy—with respect to the good. For these are the features of virtuous action, and they cannot belong to any action unless the one acting loves the good for whose sake he acts, because love is the principle of all affections of the will. For what is loved is desired while it is not yet possessed and brings pleasure when it is possessed; and what hinders the possession of what is loved brings sorrow; furthermore, what is done out of love, is done with constancy, readily, and with pleasure. Virtue, therefore, requires love of the good with respect to which virtue is exercised.

Now the good with reference to which the virtue belonging to man as man is exercised is connatural to him. Hence, love of that good of his that is the good of reason is naturally present to his will. But if we take the virtue of man with respect to some other consideration that is not natural to him, such virtue will require that the love of the good to which such virtue is ordered be something superadded over and above the natural will. For the artificer does not operate well unless there supervenes in him a love of the good that {365} is aimed at through the operation of art. Hence THE PHILOSOPHER says, in *Politics* 8, that in order for one to be politically a good man, it is required that he love the good of a city.

Now just as, to the extent that a man is admitted to participation in the good of a city, he is made a citizen of that city, and there pertain to him certain virtues for doing the things proper to citizens and for loving the good of the city; so, when a man, through divine grace, is admitted to participation in the heavenly blessedness that consists in the vision and enjoyment of God, he is made, so to speak, a citizen and companion of that blessed city that is called the heavenly Jerusalem, according to the remark of *Ephesians* 2: "You will be citizens of the saints and of the household of God." Hence, to the man thus enrolled in the heavenly city there pertain certain virtues of grace, which are infused virtues, and whose appropriate exercise requires a prior love of the common good of the whole society, namely the divine good inasmuch as it is the object of blessedness.

But one can love the good of a community in two ways: in one way with the aim of obtaining that good, and in another way with the aim of preserving it. Now to love the good of a city with the aim of obtaining and possess-

> ing that good does not make a man politically good, because this is the way in which even a tyrant loves the good of a city with the aim of dominating it, which is to love himself more than the city, since he desires that good for himself, not for the city. But to love the good of a city with the aim of preserving and defending it is truly to love the city: this makes a man politically good to the extent that, with the aim of preserving or enlarging the good of the city, he exposes himself to mortal dangers and neglects his private good.
>
> Similarly, then, to love the good participated by the blessed with the aim of obtaining or possessing it does not make a man to be rightly related to blessedness, because even the evil desire that good. But to love that good in itself, with the aim that it continue and be diffused, and that nothing be done against it, does make a man to be rightly related to the company of the blessed. And this love is charity, which loves God for His own sake and loves as oneself one's neighbors who are capable of receiving that blessedness, and which strives against all impediments to blessedness both in oneself and in others. Hence it can never co-exist with mortal sin, which is an impediment to blessedness. Accordingly, it is clear that charity is not only a virtue, but the most important virtue.

Thus SAINT THOMAS. From this text it is clear that the formal object of charity, from the point of view of the thing loved, is "divine good as object of blessedness." Concerning this point, SAINT THOMAS, in the same question, a.7, speaks as follows:

> Since the question concerns what falls under the act of a certain power or habit, we must consider the formal essence of the object of that power or habit. For it is according as things are related to that essence that they are related to what falls under the power or habit. For instance, it is according as things are related to the essence "visible" that they are, in themselves or accidentally, objects of sight. Now since the object of love, universally speaking, is a good, universally speaking, the object of a special kind of love must be a special kind of good. For instance, the proper object of natural friendship toward one's siblings is the natural good received from one's parents; and in political friendship, the object is the good of a city. Hence, charity, too, has a special kind of good as its proper object, namely the good of divine blessedness, etc.

Thus SAINT THOMAS. Again, in the tenth article of the same question, he speaks as follows:

> Since an act or habit gets its species from its object, the essence of its perfection must be taken from the object also. But the object of charity is the high-

> est good. Therefore, perfect charity is that which is directed to the highest good as something loveable, etc.

Concerning the second way of understanding mentioned above, which is that the formal essence of the object of charity from the point of view of the one who loves is the essence "causative of blessedness," or something similar, SAINT THOMAS shows that this is so in a similar passage of his, namely *ST* I, q.60, a.5, ad 2, where he speaks as follows:

> When it is said that God is loved by an angel inasmuch as He is good for the angel, if the "inasmuch as" indicates an end, the statement is false: for the angel naturally loves God not on account of the angel's own good, but on account of God Himself. But if the "inasmuch as" indicates the essence of love from the point of view of the one loving, then the statement is true: for it is not in the nature of anything to love God, except by the fact that each thing depends on the good which God is.

Thus SAINT THOMAS. Again, in ad 4, he speaks as follows:

> According as God is the universal good on which every natural good depends, He is loved by each thing with natural love; but inasmuch as He is the good which supernaturally makes everyone blessed with a supernatural blessedness, He is loved with love of charity.

Thus SAINT THOMAS. Again, in *ST* II–II, q.26, a.1, he says:

> Love of charity is directed to God as to the principle of blessedness, the friendship of charity being based on a sharing in blessedness.

Thus SAINT THOMAS.

From these texts it is clear that the formal essence of the object of charity from the point of view of the one who loves is "principle of blessedness," or "principle that is causative or communicative of blessedness," in the following way: because this essence is present in God the rational nature is, by the habit of charity, directed to God, and disposed and inclined to love God. It is not that God is loved for the sake of this essence as for the sake of an end: rather, this essence belongs to the genus of material cause.

Now, as to the form of the *first* argument, we concede the major premise.

In response to the minor premise, we say that the most perfect **{366}** essence of the loveable in God, from the point of view of what is loved and in the genus of formal or final cause, is not any relation of God to the creature, but rather God's own goodness and blessedness. But it is not inappropriate that the most perfect essence of the loveable in God, from the point of view of the one loving and, through the disposition to the love of God, in the genus of material cause, does include a relation to the creature. For anything that loves loves only what is good for it or appropriate to and perfective of it, and it is clear that all such terms describe a relation.

In response to the *second* argument we say that, by "causative of blessedness," we understand not merely a relation of actuality in which God actually makes blessed, nor merely a relation of capacity by which He is capable of making blessed: rather, we understand and imply something absolute under a relation. It is just as when we say "good," for the essence of good as a whole is neither absolute nor relational, but partly the one and partly the other. Hence, when we say "God Who is causative of blessedness" or "the principle that is causative of blessedness," we are understanding in God the highest goodness and blessedness according as it is the source of all created blessedness and is a principle in three genera of causes, namely formal, efficient, and final.

The opponent says that "a relation of capacity is not an essence that determines an act unless it involves the nature," etc.

In response to this we reply that we are not saying that the relation of being "causative of blessedness" of itself or directly determines the act of charity, but rather that it disposes one toward and incites the act. For this relation does not pertain to the formal essence of the object of charity considered in itself, but rather to the formal essence of the object from the point of view of the one loving. Now the former essence determines the object of charity, but the latter does not. For the latter is not an essence "to which" *(in quam),* or "by which" *(qua),* or "on account of which" *(propter quam)* charity is directed, but rather an essence "along with which" *(cum qua)* from the point of view of the subject, a subject that would not be directed to God if there were not some sharing between God and man by way of gifts of grace and of glory. And it is this sharing that is expressed by such relations as are implied in my expressions "principle of blessedness," "causative of blessedness in a rational nature," and the like.

In response to the *third* argument we say that charity does not seek a good as something for this particular man in such a way as to want the good principally for a particular subject, or in such a way as to refer the divine good to a particular subject as to an end. Nevertheless, it is compatible with this that, if the divine good were something neither befitting the subject of charity nor capable of being shared with it, charity would not incline its subject toward the divine good. Accordingly, charity does not love God because He is good for man or because He is causative of blessedness in man if the "because" names a final cause, for this would be to refer God to the creature as to an end. But if the "because" names a material cause, or a disposition reducible to the genus of material cause, then it is true that charity loves God because He is causative of blessedness in man or because He is good for man. Concerning this point many things have been said in the preceding remarks.

In response to the *fourth* argument we respond just as we did to the second.

In response to the *fifth* argument we say that if we are referring to the formal, proper and per se object of the will, this object is not being but good. With respect to this sense, therefore, the minor premise is, simply speaking, false.

Second, we say that a volitional power cannot be perfectly brought to rest in anything, whether created or uncreated, other than that in which the essence of "good" is most perfectly present.

Third, we say that the essence of "good" is most perfectly present in God not under the aspect by which He is this particular being, but under the aspect by which He is this particular good. For neither the essence of "a being" nor the essence of "this particular being" formally includes the essence of "good," and consequently neither do they include the essence of "highest good."

Fourth, we say that even positing—but not conceding—that God determines the act of the will and perfectly brings the will to rest according to an essence that is absolute from His own point of view, nevertheless, that essence can be grasped by us in the present life not absolutely and apart from all relation, but only together with a relation. This is clear, for instance, with respect to the essence of "highest good," or "perfect good," or any good of this kind, and similar essences that imply relations or negations. And this is so because we grasp God not according as He is in Himself, but through His effects. Thus it is quite possible for an essence of some kind to be something absolute and positive from the point of view of the object thought about *(rationcinabilis),* and yet something relative or negative from the point of view of the subject which thinks about it *(ratiocinantis).*

SAINT THOMAS, wherever he speaks of this matter, asserts that the object of the will is not being, but good, especially in *ST* I–II, q.9, a.1, ad 2, where he speaks as follows:

Just as imagination of a form without a judgment concerning the befitting

> and harmful does not move the sensitive appetite, neither does apprehension of the true without the aspect of the good or desirable move the will. Hence it is not the speculative intellect, but the practical intellect that moves, as is said in *De anima* 3.

Thus SAINT THOMAS. Again, in the principal solution, he speaks as follows:

> Anything requires to be moved by something else inasmuch as it is in potency to several things. For what is in potency must be reduced to act, and this is to move. Now there are two ways in which a power of the soul is in potency to different things: in one way with respect to acting and not-acting, and in another way with respect to doing this or doing that. Sight, for instance, sometimes sees in actuality and sometimes does not, and sometimes it sees white and sometimes black. Thus the power requires a mover in both respects, that is, with respect to exercise or application of the act, and {367} with respect to determination of the act. The first of these movers is on the side of the subject, which sometimes is found to be acting and sometimes not; but the second is on the side of the object according as the act is specified.
>
> Now the motion on the side of the subject itself comes from an agent, and, since every agent acts for the sake of an end, the principle of this motion comes from the end. Hence an art to which an end pertains moves by its command an art to which what is directed to the end pertains. Now the good in general, which has the nature of an end, is the object of the will. Hence, on the side of the subject, the will moves all other powers of the soul to their acts. For we make use of the other powers because we will to do so, and this is because the ends and perfections of the other powers are included, as particular goods, within the object of the will. Now an art or power to which a universal end pertains always moves an art or power to which a particular end contained within the universal one pertains. Similarly, the leader of an army, who intends the common good that is the order of the whole army, moves by his command one of the tribunes, who intends the order of one regiment.
>
> The object, however, moves by determining the act in the manner of a formal principle that specifies action in natural things, as heat specifies the action of heating. Now the first formal principles are being and the universally true that is the object of the intellect. Hence, in this kind of motion, the intellect moves the will, as presenting to it its object.

Thus SAINT THOMAS.

From these texts the following points are clear. *First,* that a being, under the aspect by which it is a being, is the object not of the will, but of the intellect. *Second,* that if the intellect shows the will something under the aspect of a being, and not under the aspect of a good or evil, this showing causes no affection in the will. *Third,* that however much God may be apprehended under the aspect by which He is this particular being, unless He is apprehended under the aspect of a good, He does not cause movement toward delight in Himself; consequently, unless He is apprehended in some way other than the former, He neither causes delight nor brings the created will to rest; therefore, He does bring the will to rest by an aspect of His which is at once both absolute and relative, and such is the aspect of a good. *Fourth,* that the reason why God brings the will to rest when He is clearly seen is that it is then evident that He is the highest good and the essence of goodness. Concerning this last point SAINT THOMAS, in *ST* I, q.62, a.8, speaks as follows:

> The blessed angels cannot sin. The reason for this is as follows. The blessedness of the angels consists in the fact that they see God in His essence. But the essence of God is the very essence of goodness. Hence an angel who sees God is related to God in the way that one who does not see God is related to the common nature of good. Now it is impossible for anyone whatsoever to will and act without considering the good, or to want to turn away from the good as such. Therefore a blessed angel cannot will or act without considering God. But in so willing or acting he cannot sin.

Thus SAINT THOMAS.

§3. *To the Arguments against the Third Conclusion*

I. To the Arguments of Scotus [*p. 176*] To the *first* argument against the third conclusion we say that, just as a nature has been so determined to desire its own being that, whatever else may be held concerning it, it cannot of itself seek its own non-being; so, much more fully and more intensely, it has been so determined to desire the being of God that it can in no way seek the non-being of God: rather, just as it desires the divine being more than its own, so it rejects the non-being of God more than its own non-being.

The argument says "If the being of God and the being of a creature were incompatible. . . ."

In response to this I say that such a case is impossible, because the good of a creature is more powerfully preserved in God than in the creature itself, as is made clear in the proof of the third conclusion. Nor can one be opposed to the other, any more than the good of a species can be opposed to the good of one of its individuals, or vice-versa. Concerning this point SAINT THOMAS, in *ST* I, q.60, a.5, obj.3, presents the following argument:

> Nature is turned back upon or into itself, for we see that every agent naturally acts for its own preservation. But nature would not be turned back into itself if it were directed to something more than itself. Therefore, etc.

Thus the argument; the response is as follows:

> Nature is turned back into itself not merely with respect to what is singular, but to a much greater extent with respect to what is common. For each thing is inclined not merely to its own individual preservation, but also to that of its species; and each thing to a much greater extent has a natural inclination to what is simply speaking the universal good.

Thus SAINT THOMAS.

Furthermore, we say that, even positing per impossibile that the being of God and the being of a creature were incompatible, in such a case a nature would to a greater extent desire the preservation of God than that of itself, and would accidentally want its own non-being in order to prevent the non-being of God, like a part that exposes itself for the good of the whole body. Nor does it follow from this that nature has been only conditionally determined to desire its own being, because nature of itself, simply speaking and without condition, always desires its own being. It can, however, accidentally desire its own non-being, inasmuch as such non-being preserves some being that belongs to the same nature but is better than its own individual being, in the way that a part has a better and more perfect being in the whole than in itself. And, reasoning from likeness, any thing more perfectly has being in God than in itself. Thus, in the case mentioned, it would expose its less perfect being for the sake of its more perfect being.

To the *second* argument we respond by denying the first inference that it makes. For although a natural appetite is directed only to **{368}** what agrees with the one desiring, it does not follow that it regards first of all the one for whom it desires what is agreeable. Hence, the solution of this argument is clear from the foregoing. Concerning this point SAINT THOMAS, in *In 3 Sent.*, d.29, q.1, a.3, obj.2, presents the following argument:

> THE PHILOSOPHER says, in *Ethics* 8, that what is loveable to anything is that which is good for it. But whatever a man loves because it is good for

> him, he loves because of himself. Therefore, whatever a man loves, he loves on account of himself. Therefore, he loves himself more than any of the other things he loves.

Thus the argument; the response is as follows:

> We must say that, although what is loveable to anything is that which is good for it, the thing need not be loved on account of the fact that it is good for the one loving, as for the sake of an end. For friendship does not refer back to oneself the good that one wants for another, since we love our friends even if we get nothing out of the friendship.

Thus SAINT THOMAS. Similarly, in the present discussion, I say that, although natural desire is only for what agrees with the one desiring, it need not always refer the agreeable thing to the one desiring as to an end. This is especially so where the agreeable thing is the nature of being and of goodness for the one desiring and not the reverse, as, in the present discussion, God is the essence of being and goodness with regard to anything natural that desires. Hence natural appetite need not "first of all"—with reference to primacy of perfection—regard the one desiring.

To the *third* argument we respond by denying the minor premise. For the examples given are indeed relevant to the discussion, and, if rightly understood, make clear not only that a whole loves its own being more than the being of its part, but also that a part itself loves the being of the whole more than its own being.

Again, the remark that "a hand does not expose itself etc." is invalid. For a hand, as long as it is a part, does not have its own action: rather, the whole acts by means of the hand. Nevertheless, the hand's passive motion or exposing of itself on behalf of the head or of the preservation of the whole is not a violent, but a natural motion for the hand, because it is naturally disposed to this motion: for natural things act as they are naturally disposed to act, as is said in *Physics* 2. Hence, if the hand had its own movement and action, it would move itself to do what the whole to which it belongs moves it to do.

In response to the remark that "water does not move itself upwards etc.," we say that whatever the water is being moved by, whether an intrinsic or an extrinsic principle, the movement, according to the philosophers, is not violent, but natural to the water, even if it does not originate in an inclination of the particular nature of water, taken precisively, as its entire principle, but rather in a universal inclination of nature as a whole. For of these inclinations, the particular one subserves the universal one. Concerning this point SAINT THOMAS, in *Questions on the Power of God,* q.6, a.1, ad 17, speaks as follows:

> In any natural thing there is a natural order and relationship to all higher causes. Hence, what occurs in lower bodies through the influence of the heavenly bodies is not violent, although it might seem to be contrary to the natural movements of the lower bodies. This is clear in the case of the ebb and flow of the sea, which follow the movement of the moon. And much less is what is done by God in these lower bodies violent.

Thus SAINT THOMAS. From this text it is clear that water is naturally inclined to rise and to give up its place for the sake of the good of the universe, given that the causal principle of its movement is a heavenly body, or some other power governing the universe.

II. To the Arguments of Others [*p. 177*] SAINT THOMAS responds to the *first* argument in *ST* I, q.60, a.5, where he presents the following argument in obj.1:

> Natural love is founded upon natural union. But the divine nature stands as far as possible apart from the angelic nature. Therefore, by natural love, an angel loves God less than he does himself or another angel.

Thus the argument; the response is as follows:

> We must say that this argument is valid for the case of things divided from one another as equals, so that the one is not the nature of existing and of goodness for the other. For among such things, each naturally loves itself more than another, inasmuch as it is more at one with itself than with another. But in the case of things one of which is the whole nature of being and of goodness for the other, the latter naturally loves the former more than itself. For instance, as has been said, any part naturally loves the whole more than itself, and any individual naturally loves the good of its species more than its own individual good. But God is not merely the good of one species, but, simply speaking, the universal good itself. Hence, each thing in its way naturally loves God more than itself.

Thus SAINT THOMAS. From this text it is clear that the cause of natural love is not merely union or unity of what is loved with the one loving, but rather the lover's being contained in being and goodness by the thing loved. In this way God contains every creature in being and goodness more than the creature is contained by itself or by its intrinsic principles. And similarly God is the cause of the unity of anything, and of its union with itself or with anything else. Hence, although God is less united to the creature than the creature is to itself, it does not follow that He is less loved.

The response to the *second* argument is clear from what has been said above, because not every loving of God above all things is supernatural, but only that by which charity loves God as the first principle of blessedness. Hence SAINT THOMAS, in *ST* I, q.60, a.5, obj.4, presents the following argument:

> It seems to be proper to charity that one love God more than oneself. But the love of charity is not natural, but is poured into our hearts by the Holy Spirit. Therefore, the angels do not love God more than themselves by natural love.

Thus the argument; the response is as follows:

> We must say that according as God is the universal good on which every natural good depends, He is loved by everything with a natural **{369}** love; but inasmuch as He is the good that universally causes blessedness to all, He is loved with the love of charity.

Thus SAINT THOMAS.

The response to the *third* argument is made clear in the same way. Concerning this point SAINT THOMAS, in *ST* I–II, q.109, a.3, ad 1, speaks as follows:

> Charity loves God above all things in a more outstanding way than does nature. For nature loves God above all things inasmuch as He is the principle and the end of natural good. But charity does so according as He is the object of blessedness, and according as man has a spiritual companionship with Him. For charity adds, over and above the natural love of God, a readiness and a pleasure, just as any virtue adds something over and above a good act done through the natural reason of a man who does not have the habit of the virtue.

Thus SAINT THOMAS.

SAINT THOMAS responds to the *fourth* argument in *ST* II–II, q.26, a.3, ad 1, saying that:

> THE PHILOSOPHER is speaking of feelings of love toward another in which the good that is the object of friendship is found in a particular way, not of feelings of love toward another in which the good mentioned is found according to its whole nature.

Thus SAINT THOMAS.

To the *fifth* argument we say that such a heretic does not love God above all things with a love of charity, since he sins against God mortally.

Nor does he expose himself to death "for the sake of God," if the "for the sake of" indicates an ultimate end that is loved to the highest degree to which he refers himself and all other things. Still, perhaps he does expose himself to death "for the sake of God" if the "for the sake of" indicates a material cause, because the "matter" in defense of which he exposes himself to death does touch on an article of faith concerning God. And perhaps he also does so if the "for the sake of" indicates an end that is not ultimate but is desired, and is related to something else as an end. For such a heretic does want to attain God, but because he makes use of but does not enjoy God, he refers God to himself.

Furthermore, we say that because such a heretic does not have an uncorrupted nature, but rather one that has been corrupted in our first parent, he does not love God above all things with a natural love. But this is not opposed to our conclusion, which only means that every nature remaining in its state of incorruption loves God above all things. Concerning this point SAINT THOMAS, in *ST* I–II, q.109, a.3, speaks as follows:

> To love God above all things is in a way something connatural to man, and also to every creature, not only to the rational, but also to the irrational and the inanimate creature, according to the kind of love of which each is capable.
>
> The reason for this is as follows. What is natural to each thing is what it desires and what it loves according as it is by nature disposed to desire and love, for each thing acts according as it is by nature disposed to act, as is said in *Physics* 2. Now it is clear that the good of a part is for the sake of the good of a whole. Thus, by a natural appetite or love each particular thing also loves its own individual good for the sake of the common good of the whole universe, which is God. Hence DIONYSIUS also says, in the book *On the Divine Names,* that God turns all things toward love of Himself. Thus, man in the state of uncorrupted nature referred love of himself to love of God as to an end, and did likewise with his love of all other things, and so he loved God more than himself and above all things. But in the state of corrupted nature, man falls short of this with respect to the appetite of the rational will, which, because of the corruption of nature, follows its private good unless it is healed through the grace of God. Therefore, we must say that man in the state of uncorrupted nature did not need a gift of grace su-

> peradded to natural goods in order to naturally love God above all things, although he would need the help of God moving him in order to do so; but in the state of corrupted nature, man needs in addition the help of the grace that heals nature in order to do so.

Thus SAINT THOMAS. Again, in I, q.60, a.5, he speaks as follows:

> Some have said that an angel, by natural love, loves God more than itself by love of concupiscence, that is, because it desires the divine good more than the human good for itself; and that it also does so, in a way, by love of friendship, inasmuch as it naturally wants a greater good for God than for itself, for it naturally wants God to be God, but wants itself to have merely its own nature; but that, simply speaking, by natural love, it loves itself more than God, because it naturally loves itself more intensely and more primordially than God.
>
> Now the falseness of this position clearly appears if, in the case of natural things, one considers that toward which a natural thing is naturally moved: for natural inclination in things without reason may be used to illustrate the natural inclination in a will belonging to an intellectual nature. Now every natural thing, which by nature is an essence belonging to something else, more primordially and to a greater extent is inclined to that to which it belongs than to itself. And this natural inclination is shown from what it naturally does, because each thing naturally so acts as by nature it is disposed to act, as is said in *Physics* 2. For we see that a part naturally exposes itself for the sake of preservation of the whole, as a hand exposes itself without deliberation to a blow for the sake of preservation of the whole body. And because reason imitates nature, we find this kind of imitation in the political virtues. For it is proper to a virtuous citizen to expose himself to danger of death for the sake of preservation of a whole commonwealth, and if man were naturally a part of this city, this inclination would be natural to him. Because, therefore, the universal good is God Himself, and includes angel, man, and every creature, therefore, since every creature, according to what it is, belongs to God, it follows that by natural love an angel or a man to a greater extent and more primordially {370} loves God than himself. Otherwise, if he naturally loved himself more than God, it would follow that natural love would be perverse, and that it would not be perfected, but rather destroyed, by charity.

Thus SAINT THOMAS.

III. To the Arguments of Durandus [*p. 178*] In response to the *first* argument of DURANDUS we say, *first,* that the comparison with a citizen who exposes himself to death for the good of the city and commonwealth is good, and the objections brought against it are invalid.

The argument says that the citizen does not expose himself as one who, setting aside his own particular good, loves the common good more than his own particular good.

This is false. For political virtue inclines one to prefer an end to what is directed to the end. But it is evident that the common good of a commonwealth, whether such a good includes this particular citizen or not, is the end of this particular citizen. Therefore moral virtue inclines this particular citizen to love the good of the commonwealth, whether such a good includes the particular citizen or not, before his own private good.

Second, we say that a citizen who exposes himself to death for a commonwealth does not will a greater good for himself than for the commonwealth, but rather the reverse. For he wills his own being, action, and life, and his own destruction and ceasing to be, in order that the being, life, and action of the city may continue.

The opponent says that "In this way he acquires the greatest good for himself, namely the good of virtue etc."

We respond that this is utterly invalid.

First, because the citizen acquires the good more for the city than for himself, for the good of a part belongs more to the whole than to the part itself.

Then, because, if neither supernatural blessedness nor some other blessed life is presupposed—and many unbelieving virtuous citizens who expose themselves to death for a community do not presuppose such a life—, then the community will rejoice in the act of virtue longer than will the particular citizen who performs the act, for the community will rejoice and be honored for the act after the death of the citizen.

Then again, because even positing—but not conceding—that such an act of virtue would be more a good of the particular citizen than of the city, the argument still does not hold. For a virtuous citizen exposes himself to death for the city or the common good not in order that the city be well-off with respect to riches, or in order that it live well with respect to vegetative or sensitive life, but in order that it live well with respect to intellect and reason, that is, virtuously, for such is the end of a city and the good of a commonwealth, according to THE PHILOSOPHER in *Politics* 7. But it is clear that the virtuous action and happiness of a city outweigh the virtuous action and happiness of a particular citizen. And so the citizen, in dying for the happiness of the city, wills a greater good to the city than to himself.

Third, we say that, although ARISTOTLE, in the chapter of *Ethics* 9 beginning "But one might ask whether one should love oneself most of all . . . ," seems to say that a good man, in exposing himself to death for his friends and homeland, wills the greatest good for himself, in fact he there speaks hardly at all about the commonwealth and the common good of the commonwealth, but rather about friends. Thus one cannot argue from this text that his thought is that any virtuous man loves his private good more than the good of the commonwealth, since he expressly says in *Ethics* 1 that the good of a people and of a city is more loveable and more divine than the good of one man. He means, rather, that the virtuous man, in dying for an individual friend of his, chooses a greater good for himself than for the friend. Nevertheless, whatever may be the thought of ARISTOTLE in this text, it is not relevant to the present discussion, since the truth that he has in mind may be gathered from his remarks elsewhere.

In response to the *second* argument we say that it is indeed true that, other things being equal, one should be more sorry if one has oneself acted against the good of virtue than if the whole rest of the city has done so—that is, intensively, though not extensively, more sorry. But the subsequent inference, that one should will the good of virtue for oneself more than for a community, is invalid. The reason is as follows. To act against the good of virtue or against God is directly opposed to the love of virtue. But to be without the good of virtue is not a fault, but a punishment, unless it proceeds from a fault. Therefore, in some cases, it can be chosen, at least accidentally, in order to avoid a greater evil, for instance in order that the whole community not be deprived of the good of virtue. Hence it is not so directly opposed to love of virtue or of God as is acting against the good of virtue or of God, which must in no case be chosen. Therefore, we concede that one should love the good of virtue more for the community than for oneself, and similarly that one should love blessedness in the same way, especially the blessedness of the perfect community which is the community of all the elect. Concerning this point SAINT THOMAS speaks in *ST* II–II, q.26, a.4, where, in obj.3, he presents the following argument:

> In *1 Corinthians* 13 it is said that "Charity does not seek what is its own." But what we love most is that whose good we most seek. Therefore, by charity one does not love oneself more than one's neighbor.

Thus the argument; the response is as follows:

> As AUGUSTINE says in his *Rules*, when it is said that "Charity does not seek what is its own," this is understood to mean that charity places what is common before what is individual, not what is individual before what is common. But a common good is always more loveable to anything than is its own individual good, just as the good of a whole is more loveable to a part itself than is its own good as a part, as has been said.

Thus SAINT THOMAS. From this text it is clear that one should want the good of virtue for a whole community more than for oneself as a part, except in a case where privation of the good of virtue in the part would dishonor a good more universal than the whole community; such a good is God, and anything done against Him through sin dishonors Him. And I say the same thing of blessedness as I do of the good of virtue. For a man ought to prefer that the whole of human nature or a whole city of the elect have grace and glory without himself, than that he alone should have grace and glory, {371} as long as the privation in himself did not come from his own fault, for this would dishonor a more universal good, namely God. Concerning this point SAINT THOMAS speaks in a similar way in *Questions on the Virtues*, "On Charity", a.11, ad 6, where he shows that it pertains to the love of God to sometimes want to separate oneself from the enjoyment of God for the sake of the salvation of one's neighbor; for he speaks as follows:

> The difference between a fine friendship and a friendship of pleasure is that in a friendship of pleasure the friend is loved for the sake of pleasure, but in a fine friendship the friend is loved for his own sake, although pleasure follows as a result. Accordingly, it pertains to the perfection of friendship that one sometimes, for the sake of the friend, abstains even from the pleasure that one takes in his presence, since one is busy doing things for him. Therefore, one who absents himself from his friend for the friend's sake loves the other more, with respect to this kind of friendship, than does one who is unwilling to leave the presence of his friend, even for the friend's sake. But one who is gladly or easily separated from the presence of his friend because he takes more pleasure in other things, obviously loves his friend either not at all or scarcely.
>
> Accordingly, we find these three levels in charity. Now God should most of all be loved for His own sake. There are those who gladly, or without any great annoyance, are separated from the freedom of divine contemplation, since they are involved in earthly business, and these obviously have little or

> no charity. But some delight in the freedom of divine contemplation to such an extent that they are unwilling to leave it, even in order to offer up divine service for the salvation of their neighbor. But some rise to such a peak of charity that they forego even divine contemplation, although it is their greatest delight, in order to serve God in the salvation of their neighbors. This perfection appears in PAUL, who said, in *Romans* 9, "I was willing that I myself be anathema to," that is, be separated from, "Christ for my brothers"; and in *Philippians* 1: "I have a desire to be freed and to be with Christ, but it is necessary to remain in the flesh for your sakes, etc."

Thus SAINT THOMAS.

But should a man will that he himself alone offend God rather than that the whole rest of the human community do so?

In response to this we say no, for in no case should one will to dishonor the divine good. And although it would dishonor the divine good more if the whole of humankind offended God than if he alone did so, and the whole of humankind would suffer more than if he alone fell, notwithstanding this, we say "no," as we did above, because in the case described he would not dishonor the divine good inasmuch as it is his own good, since his being ordered to God as to an end remains correct; but if he himself should sin, this would dishonor the divine good inasmuch as it is his own good.

Again, if that man should offend God, this would accrue to him as evil of fault; but if the whole of humankind except him should offend God, this would accrue to him only as evil of punishment. But evil of fault is something incomparably more to be avoided than is evil of punishment in the same subject.

Again, because to offend God is prejudicial to divine love, but to be a part of a multitude which, with the exception of him, offends God is not.

In response to the *third* argument we say, *first,* that to expose oneself to death for another is not a sufficient sign that the one so exposing himself simply speaking loves the other more than himself. Concerning this point SAINT THOMAS, in *In 3 Sent.*, d.29, q.1, a.5, ad 3, speaks as follows:

> To give oneself up to death for the sake of a friend is the most perfect act of virtue. Hence a virtuous man desires this act more than he does his own bodily life. Hence to lay down one's own bodily life for the sake of a friend does not occur because one loves the friend more than oneself, but because, within oneself, one loves the good of virtue more than one does a good of the body.

Thus SAINT THOMAS. And he says something similar in *ST* II–II, q.26, a.4, ad 2.

Second, we say that to expose oneself to death for another, whether that other is a community or a private person, is a sufficient sign that the one so exposing himself loves the bodily life of the other more than his own, or loves the happiness of the other more than his own bodily life. This is sufficient to make the argument that a part of a political community loves the good of the whole more than it does its own good as a part, for a particular citizen loves himself, at least with respect to bodily life, less than he does the commonwealth—although it does not show that the particular citizen simply speaking loves the community more than he does himself.

Third, we say that a sufficient sign that a virtuous citizen does simply speaking love the good of the community more than his own individual good is that he is willing that his being, life, and action be destroyed for the preservation of the happiness of the city, the city to which he orders himself and what is his—whether his life or his death—as to a proximate end, just as a whole is the end of its part. But there have been many citizens who in this way exposed themselves to death for a city.

In response to the *fourth* argument we say *first* that, however much infused or acquired faith were to show that God is to be loved above all things under a special aspect, namely that of being causative of blessedness or the object of blessedness, the will would not easily, readily, with pleasure, and in a virtuous manner tend to God under that aspect unless it were habituated by a supernatural habit. Concerning this point SAINT THOMAS, in *ST* II–II, q.23, a.2, speaks as follows:

> No act is perfectly educed from an active power unless the act is connatural to the power through a form that is the principle of action. Hence God, Who moves all things to their due ends, endowed individual things with forms by which they are inclined to ends pre-established for them by God; and {372} it is in this regard that "He disposes all things sweetly," as is said in *Wisdom* 8. Now it is clear that the act of charity exceeds the natural power of will. Therefore, unless there were superadded to the natural power a form by which it is inclined to the act of love, as such the act would be less perfect than natural acts and the acts of other virtues, if it were not easy and delightful. But this is clearly false. For no virtue has as much inclination to its act, or is exercised with so much delight, as charity. Hence it is most necessary that there exist in us a habitual form directed to the act of charity, one superadded to the natural power, inclining it to the act of charity, and causing this act to be performed readily and with pleasure.

Thus SAINT THOMAS. Again, in q.24, a.2, he says:

> Charity is friendship of man toward God that is based on God's sharing of eternal blessedness. But this sharing is not among the goods of nature, but among the gifts of grace, for, as is said in *Romans* 6, "The grace of God is eternal life." Hence, charity itself also exceeds the ability of nature. But what exceeds the ability of nature cannot be something natural, or something acquired by natural powers, because a natural effect does not transcend its cause. Hence, charity cannot be given to us by nature or acquired by natural activity, but must come by an infusion of the Holy Spirit, Who is the love between the Father and the Son, and Whose participation in us is created charity itself, etc.

Thus SAINT THOMAS.

From these texts it is clear that charity is necessary for elevating the will to a supernatural act.

Second, we say that our position holds not so much that charity elevates nature to love God with a love of concupiscence, but rather that it more primordially elevates it to love God with a love of friendship. For through charity we will that God be supremely blessed in Himself, and that He pour out His blessedness on us. Thus nature and charity love God with love of friendship under different aspects. For nature desires and wills that God be supremely good by nature, and the principle of every natural good; but charity wants God to be supremely blessed, and the principle of blessedness.

IV. To the Arguments of Others [*p. 179*] In response to the *first* argument we say that it correctly concludes that charity elevates nature to love with love of friendship beyond what nature is capable of by purely natural means. But in the subsequent development there occurs the fallacy of affirming the consequent. For if charity elevates nature to love God with love of friendship beyond what nature is capable of without charity, it need not be that it elevate it solely with respect to the manner of loving God, namely above all things and for His own sake, because nature is sufficient for this without charity, as has been often said above. Rather, charity elevates nature with respect to the nature of loving, because charity loves God with love of friendship as Him Who is supremely blessed, and with love of concupiscence as the principle, object, and source of blessedness.

In response to the confirmation of the argument we say that it includes two false statements. The first is that by natural love man loves himself more than anything else. The second is that by grace alone, without any other principle, human nature, while remaining in its incorrupted state, is sufficient for loving God above all other things.

In response to the *second* confirmation we say that the comparison is utterly invalid. For God cannot be immediately known by us in the present life, but He can be immediately loved by us. Hence, natural love of God need not start from a creature: rather, both natural and supernatural love can start from God. Concerning this point SAINT THOMAS, in *ST* II–II, q.27, a.4, speaks as follows:

> The act of a cognitive power is accomplished by a being present of what is known in the knower, but the act of an appetitive power is accomplished by an inclination of the appetite toward the thing itself. Hence, the movement of an appetitive power must be present in things according to the features of things themselves, but the act of a cognitive power is according to the mode of the knower. Now the order of things is such that God is of Himself knowable and loveable as essentially existing truth itself and goodness itself, through which other things are known and loved. But because our knowledge has its origin in sense, to us objects of knowledge that are closer to sense are prior, and the ultimate term of knowledge is in what is farthest removed from sense. Accordingly, we must say that love, which is an act of an appetitive power, is, even in the present life, directed primarily to God, and from Him derived to other things, and accordingly, that charity loves God immediately, and other things through the intermediary of God. But in cognition it is the reverse: for we know God through other things, as a cause is known through its effect, or by way of eminence or negation, as is made clear by DIONYSIUS in the book *On the Divine Names*.

Thus SAINT THOMAS. Again, in ad 2, he speaks as follows:

> Love of God is something greater than knowledge of Him, especially in the present life. Therefore, it presupposes this knowledge. And because knowledge does not come to rest in created things, but is directed through them to something else, love begins in God, and from Him is derived to other things by way of a certain circulation. For knowledge, which begins as knowledge of creatures, is directed to God, and love, which begins as love of God as a final end, is derived to creatures.

Thus SAINT THOMAS.

From these texts it is clear that the second confirmation of the opponent's argument contains two false statements in the comparison that it presents. The first is that supernatural knowledge starts from God, which is completely false, for all knowledge of God in the present life starts from creatures. The second is that natural love of God always starts from creatures, {373} which is false because natural love sometimes starts from the final end, which is God.

The response to the *second* argument is clear from the solution of the fifth and sixth arguments. For to love God, oneself, and all things for the sake of God inasmuch as He is the object of blessedness is proper to charity. But to love God, oneself, and all things for the sake of God inasmuch as He is the principle of natural good is not proper to charity, since the rational nature, if it remains in a state of incorruption, is capable of this, as has often been said.

§4. To the Arguments against the Fourth Conclusion

To the Arguments of Durandus In response to the objections made against the fourth conclusion [p. 180] we say that if the major premise is taken universally, it is false. For we do not refer everything that we love with love of concupiscence to ourselves as to an end, because any friend loves his friend with love of concupiscence inasmuch as he wants to enjoy his presence, yet he does not refer the friend to himself as to an end. But it is quite true that we refer what we love only with love of concupiscence to ourselves as to an end. But it is not with such a love—namely love of concupiscence that excludes friendship—that we love God out of charity, as SAINT THOMAS says in *ST* II–II, q.26, a.3, ad 3, which was quoted in the proof of the conclusion.

§5. To the Arguments against the Fifth Conclusion

To the Arguments of Durandus In response to the objections made against the fifth conclusion [p. 181] we say that they do not contradict the conclusion, because the new distinction that the opponent introduces is understood in the distinction that SAINT THOMAS makes, although it is not made explicit. For SAINT THOMAS does not say that blessedness is the ultimate or principal end of divine love. Rather, he says that the operations of love and of blessedness, since they are accidents, are to be loved for the sake of their subject; and further, that the subject, with all its accidents, ought to be referred to God, as SAINT THOMAS himself shows in *In 4 Sent.*, d.49, q.1, a.2, qla.1, ad 3.

§6. To the Arguments against the Sixth Conclusion

To the Arguments of Durandus In response to the objections made against the sixth conclusion [p. 182] we say that they do not go against the intention of the conclusion. For the conclusion refers to the third sense mentioned, and not to the first or second. Nevertheless, even with reference to the second sense mentioned, the argument is invalid. For this second sense, namely that of determination of circumstance, has no place in the interior act of charity, nor in any interior act of virtue, since goodness of will does not depend on any circumstance, as SAINT THOMAS shows in *ST* I–II, q.19, a.2, obj.2, where he presents the following argument:

> The goodness of an act comes not only from the object, but also from circumstances. But there can be diversity of goodness and evil in an act of the will that follows from diversity of circumstance—for instance that someone wills when he should, where he should, how he should, or in the way that he should. Therefore goodness of will depends not only on the object, but also on circumstances.

Thus the argument; the response is as follows:

> We must say that, if we suppose that the will is directed to what is good, no circumstance can make it evil. Accordingly, the remark that "someone wills a good when he should not or where he should not" can be understood in two ways. In one way such that the circumstance is referred to the object of the will, and thus the will is not directed to what is good, because to will to do something when one should not do it is not to will what is good. In another way such that the circumstance is referred to the act of willing, and thus it is impossible for someone to will what is good when he should not, because man should always will what is good, except perhaps accidentally, inasmuch as someone, by willing a particular good, is prevented from willing another good that he should will, and then the evil comes about not from his willing the first good, but from his not willing the other good. And something similar is to be said concerning other circumstances.

Thus SAINT THOMAS.

§7. To the Arguments against the Seventh Conclusion

To the Arguments of Durandus In response to the objections made against the seventh conclusion [p. 182] we say that the major premise, as it stands, is false. For by charity we are required to desire for our neighbors not only the level of glory or blessedness of which they are capable simply speaking, and with respect to obediential potency, because this would be to desire against divine predestination and justice, which has predetermined different levels of blessedness for men, not only those who are already blessed, but also those in the present life who have not yet obtained blessedness but are being directed toward it, some slowly, some quickly. Rather, charity wills the observance of divine justice, according to which those who are better participate in a more perfect blessedness, as was said in the proof of the conclusion.

In response to the confirmation of the argument, we say *first* that there is no envy if unequal, rather than equal, goods of glory are desired for two men who are capable of receiving an equal good, but are not equally worthy or equally prepared for the good that comes from divine justice. **{374}** On the contrary, to desire equal goods for those for whom God desires unequal goods would be to disagree with the divine will and to will against the whole order of charity and justice, and would be an impious presumption and blasphemy.

Second, we say that it is no prejudice to what is divine to desire unequal movements and tendencies toward God for those whom God has disposed to move and tend toward Himself unequally. Rather, to choose the contrary would be prejudicial to the divine predestination, justice, and charity, and in addition would be vain and fanciful.

§8. *To the Arguments against the Eighth Conclusion*

To the Arguments of Durandus [*p. 183*] In response to the *first* argument against the eighth conclusion we say that it correctly concludes that love of an enemy in one man can be better and more meritorious than love of a friend in another subject or another man if other things are equal on both sides, but not if the one loving his enemy applies a greater effort than does the other in loving his friend; and all this we concede.

But the argument does not prove that in the same subject love of an enemy is more meritorious than love of a friend. For the same man never loves an enemy as intensely as he does a friend at one and the same time, unless he loves both in a single act and out of an inclination of charity. Indeed, if he were to love both equally intensely, he would be acting evilly, unmeritoriously, and against the order of charity. And this the opponent also concedes. Hence, with respect to the present question, he speaks as follows:

> If it is the same one who loves both, to love a friend more than an enemy is in keeping with the order of charity in a case of need, when affection and service cannot be given to both. For in such a case the same man who loves an enemy as much as a friend sins, acting as he does against the order of charity. But if it is different ones who are loving, and especially if it is not a case of need, it is not against the order of charity that one man, for the sake of God, will to an enemy as much good and as much affection as another

> wills to a friend; rather, this pertains to the perfection of charity. Also, in the same man, it is not against the order of charity for him, at different times and apart from cases of need, to will an equal good, and with equal affection, to a friend and to an enemy.

Thus DURANDUS.

In response to the *second* argument we say *first* that it is never the case that the same lover out of charity loves an enemy as intensely as he does a friend at the same time and in the same case. Hence, with reference to the same one loving, the minor premise is false. For the intensities of these acts of love are neither similar nor equal.

Second, we say that if, in different lovers, the two loves are equally intense, love of the enemy would not be better by this fact alone. For its whole intensity is reduced to charity, while the intensity of the other love has another cause in addition to charity. The reason for this is as follows. An act is judged to be better inasmuch as it is informed by a greater number of virtues. Now love of a friend is informed by habits of charity, justice, piety and many other virtues, but love of an enemy is informed by the habit of charity alone, and thus does not have as many principles of goodness as does love of a friend. And although merit depends in any case on charity alone, the goodness of an act does not depend on charity alone. Hence, the concurrence of other virtues with an equal charity and effort renders an act better, and consequently more meritorious, because an act better in itself, performed out of an equal charity, is more meritorious. Nevertheless, love of an enemy can be more meritorious from another point of view, if greater effort is applied to it and all other things are equal in the two cases.

Concerning efficacy of deserving, SAINT THOMAS, in *ST* I, q.95, a.4, speaks as follows:

> Quantity of merit may be measured in two ways. One is by the root of charity and grace, and such quantity of merit corresponds to the essential reward that consists in the enjoyment of God: for one who does something out of greater charity will enjoy God more perfectly. The other way in which quantity of merit can be measured is by the quantity of the deed, which in turn is twofold, namely absolute and proportional. For the widow who threw two small coins into the treasury performed a smaller deed, with respect to absolute quantity, than did those who made great offerings; but with respect to proportional quantity, the widow, in the judgment of the Lord, did more than they, because she went farther beyond what she could afford.

> Now these two quantities of merit correspond to the accidental reward that is joy in created good. Accordingly, we must say that the deeds of man were more efficacious in obtaining merit in the state of innocence than they were after sin, if one considers quantity of merit from the point of view of grace, which was then more abundant, since no obstacle to it in human nature had yet been encountered. And the same is true if absolute quantity of the deed is considered, for, since man was then of greater virtue, he did greater deeds. But if one considers proportional quantity, more of the nature of merit is found after sin, on account of human weakness. For a small deed exceeds the power of one who performs it with difficulty more than a great deed exceeds the power of one who performs it without difficulty.

Thus SAINT THOMAS. Again, and more to the point, in *In 3 Sent.*, d.30, q.1, a.3, he speaks as follows:

> The comparison between love of a friend and love of an enemy can be understood in two ways, namely with respect to acts and with respect to habits.
>
> With respect to acts, we must know that, when it is asked concerning two acts, "Which is the better and more meritorious?" the question must be understood of the acts in themselves, according to their kind. {375} For it can happen that what is less good or meritorious in its kind is made more good or meritorious by the addition of something, as a small deed performed out of great charity is more meritorious than a great deed performed out of small charity. Now the goodness of an act is measured by the two things from which it receives goodness, namely its terminus or object, and its principle, which is the will. From the terminus it gets its species of goodness; but from the will it gets the aspect of merit, because an act is in the power of the one acting according as it proceeds from the will.
>
> If, accordingly, we compare love of a friend and love of an enemy with respect to their termini or objects, then, since the friend is an object more in keeping with love than is the enemy, it is better to love the friend than the enemy.
>
> But if we compare the two loves with respect to their principle, which is the will, there must be more merit in loving the enemy. For the greater the effort of will, the more fervent the will in relation to the end for whose sake one attempts what is in itself more repugnant to oneself—although sometimes the will may be less intense in relation to that for which the greater effort is made. But merit consists in the will's being affected by the end. Hence, if we compare the acts of the two loves, love of an enemy is as such more meritorious, because, as such, it requires greater effort and greater fervor in relation to the end, even though love of a friend is more intense with respect

> to the object. But love of a friend is better with respect to essential goodness, which follows from the species of the act, which comes from the object.
>
> But if we compare these loves with respect to habits, the comparison must be understood either of the love of enemies that pertains to need, and thus there is no difference, because it is exactly the same habit in both cases; or of the love of enemies that pertains to perfection, and thus love of enemies includes love of friends, but not the reverse, so that love of enemies is better.

Thus SAINT THOMAS.

From these texts it is clear that, in the same one who loves out of charity, it cannot happen that love of an enemy be equally intense as love of a friend at one and the same time.

Second, it is clear that, in some cases, love of an enemy is of greater merit than love of a friend, if these two loves are present in different subjects, or are present in the same subject at different times or in relation to different kinds of cases.

In response to the *third* argument we respond by denying the minor premise with reference to actual love of a friend and love of an enemy. For in such love, the friend is more intensely loved than the enemy, whenever they are simultaneously in actuality loved, and thus love of a friend includes love of an enemy, and not the reverse.

But if we are speaking of the habitual love of an enemy that pertains to perfection, not that which pertains to need, then we concede that love of an enemy is better, as has been said above.

Response to the opposing argument [p. 162] has been made in the response to the seventh argument against the third conclusion.

This suffices for the question.

Blessed be God.

Amen.

Whether Faith Remains in Heaven

In relation to the thirty-first and thirty-second distinctions of the third book of *The Sentences,* the question is raised: Whether faith remains in heaven.

It is argued that it does, as follows. The cognition of faith and the cognition proper to the state of glory differ as perfect and imperfect. But perfect and imperfect cognition do co-exist. In an angel, for instance, matutinal cognition co-exists with vespertinal cognition; and a man can, with respect to the same conclusion, simultaneously have scientific knowledge by means of a demonstrative syllogism and opinion by means of a dialectical syllogism. Therefore, too, faith can, in the afterlife, co-exist with the cognition proper to the state of glory.

Argument is made for the opposite conclusion as follows. THE APOSTLE, in *2 Corinthians* 5, says: "While we are in the body, we travel in separation from the Lord; for we walk by faith, and not by sight." But those who are in the state of glory do not travel in separation from the Lord, but are present to Him. Therefore, faith does not continue after this life in the state of glory.

In this question there will be three articles: in the first the conclusions will be presented, in the second the objections, and in the third the responses.

Article I. Conclusions

First Conclusion: It Is Impossible for the Act of Faith and the Act of Beatific Vision to Co-Exist in the Same Subject

SAINT THOMAS presents this conclusion in *ST* I–II, q.67, a.3, **{376}** where he speaks as follows:

Opposition is the proper and per se cause that one thing is excluded by another, inasmuch as every opposition maintains or involves an opposition of affirmation and negation. Now in some cases there is an opposition according to contrary forms such as, in the case of colors, black and white. In other cases, however, there is found an opposition according to perfect and imperfect. Thus, in the case of alterations, "more" and "less" are taken as contraries, as when "hotter" comes to be out of "less hot," as is said in *Physics* 5. And because perfect and imperfect are opposed, it is impossible for there to be perfection and imperfection simultaneously and in the same respect.

Now it must be considered that imperfection is sometimes of the nature of a thing and belongs to its species, as lack of reason pertains to the essence of the species of horse or cow. And because a thing that remains numerically one and the same cannot be changed from one species to another, when such imperfection is taken away, the species of the thing is taken away as well: thus, if it became rational, it would no longer be a cow or a horse. Sometimes, however, imperfection does not pertain to the essence of a species, but befalls the individual for some other reason. For instance, sometimes lack of reason befalls a certain man inasmuch as the use of reason is impeded in him on account of sleep, drunkenness, or something similar. And it is clear that when such imperfection is taken away, the substance of the thing still remains.

Now it is clear that imperfection of cognition is of the nature of faith, for it is part of its definition. For faith is "the substance of things hoped for, the argument of things that do not appear," as is said in *Hebrews* 11. And AUGUSTINE says, "What is faith but believing what you do not see?" Now it pertains to the imperfection of cognition that cognition occur without any appearing or vision. Thus imperfection of cognition is of the nature of faith. Hence it is clear that faith cannot be perfect cognition while remaining numerically the same.

Further it must be considered whether faith can be present simultaneously with perfect cognition. For nothing prevents some kinds of imperfect cognition from sometimes being present simultaneously with perfect cognition. Accordingly, it must be considered that cognition can be called imperfect in three ways: in one way from the point of view of the object of cognition; in another from the point of view of the middle term; and in a third way from the point of view of the subject. From the point of view of the object of cognition, it is matutinal and vespertinal cognition in the angels that differ as perfect and imperfect respectively. For matutinal cognition is of things according as they have being in the Word, but vespertinal cognition is of things according as they have being in their own natures, a being that is imperfect

> in comparison to the first kind of being. From the point of view of the middle term, it is cognition of a conclusion through a demonstrative middle term and cognition of it through a probable middle term that differ as perfect and imperfect respectively. From the point of view of the subject, it is opinion, faith, and scientific knowledge that differ as perfect and imperfect. For it is of the nature of opinion to assent to one of two contraries together with uneasiness concerning the other, and hence opinion does not involve firm adherence. It is of the nature of scientific knowledge to involve firm adherence accompanied by intellectual vision, for scientific knowledge has a certitude that proceeds from understanding of principles. Faith, however, is intermediary, for it is greater than opinion in involving firm adherence, but less than scientific knowledge in not involving vision.
>
> Now it is clear that perfect and imperfect cannot be simultaneously present in the same respect. But things that differ as perfect and imperfect can, in a respect that is somewhat the same, be simultaneously present in a thing that is somewhat the same. Thus there can in no way be perfect and imperfect cognition of the same object <from the point of view of the object itself>. They can, however, come together in the same middle term in the same subject: for nothing prevents one man from possessing, at one and the same moment, through one and the same middle term, cognition of two things, one of which is perfect and the other imperfect, such as health and sickness, or good and evil. Again, it is impossible, from the point of view of the middle term, for perfect and imperfect cognition to come together in a single middle term. But nothing prevents them from coming together in a single object and a single subject: for one man can know the same conclusion through both probable and demonstrative middle term. Similarly, it is impossible, from the point of view of the subject, for perfect and imperfect cognition to be simultaneously present in the same subject. But faith includes in its nature imperfection from the point of view of the subject, inasmuch as the one who believes does not see what he believes; blessedness, however, includes in its nature perfection from the point of view of the subject, inasmuch as one who is blessed sees that in which he is made blessed. Hence it is clear that it is impossible for faith to remain simultaneously with beatitude in the same subject.

Thus SAINT THOMAS. From this text the following argument can be formulated. Several acts whose formal essences require incompatible dispositions in their subjects cannot co-exist in the same subject. But the act of faith, namely belief, and the beatific vision are such acts. Therefore, etc.

Second Conclusion: The Habit of Faith Does Not and Cannot Remain in Heaven Together with the Beatific Vision

SAINT THOMAS presents this conclusion in *In 3 Sent.*, d.31, q.2, a.1, qla.3, where he speaks as follows:

> The removal of anything that belongs to the substance of a thing leads to the destruction of that thing, but the removal of anything that is {377} accidentally related to the thing does not. Now the imperfection that the state of glory removes from faith belongs to the substance of faith and pertains to its species, as is clear from the fact that the imperfection is understood with reference to the nature of the object from which faith gets its species. For the obscurity implied by "mystery" pertains to the genus of cognition. Hence, once this imperfection is removed, the substance and the species of faith must be destroyed, as would be the substance and the species of "ass" if its irrationality were removed from it. But because faith is an accidental form, and is not composed of matter and form, but is simple, when it is destroyed what remains is not numerically, but rather generically the same as the faith. Similarly, it is clear that when white becomes black, or the reverse, what there is of color remains, not as numerically the same color, but as something generically the same. But it is numerically the same light that remains when it is perfect and then imperfect, for that perfection and imperfection do not pertain to the species of the light, but are accidental to it.

Thus SAINT THOMAS. From this text one can argue as follows. Where the nature of the object of faith is not preserved, the habit of faith does not remain. But in heaven the nature of the object of faith is not preserved, but rather removed. Therefore, the habit of faith does not remain there.

Here the first article terminates.

Article II: Objections

§1. Against the Second Conclusion

Arguments of Durandus In the second article, argument is made against the conclusions.

DURANDUS (*In 3 Sent.*, d.31, q.3) argues against the second conclusion, *first* by arguing as follows:

> It is neither heretical nor contrary to Sacred Scripture to posit that the habit of faith can remain in heaven. For Sacred Scripture says nothing against the possibility of its remaining, as is made clear by going through the whole of

> the thirteenth chapter of the first epistle to the Corinthians, where this topic is more particularly and explicitly touched on than it is in other passages, and by going through all of the other passages of Scripture. For there is never a single word that explicitly says, or from which it can be plausibly deduced, that the habit of faith cannot remain in heaven. If anyone says that there is such a word, let him quote the authoritative passage, because it has yet to be quoted by anyone. Therefore, to say that the habit of faith can remain in heaven is in no way heretical, because Scripture in no way says the contrary.

Again, he argues as follows:

> Scripture, rightly understood, is in no way opposed to the actual remaining of the habit of faith in heaven. For in the same chapter in which this point is discussed, it is said that "Whether prophecies are abolished, whether the gift of tongues ceases, whether scientific knowledge is destroyed. . . ." And the cause given is similar to that given with respect to faith. For the text says, with respect to scientific knowledge, "For we know in part, and we prophesy in part; but when what is perfect has arrived, what is in part will be abolished," just as it adds, with respect to faith, "Now we see through a glass, and in a mystery, but then we shall see face to face." On the basis of these passages we can argue in three ways.
>
> *First,* as follows. Just as Scripture says that faith is abolished in heaven, so the same Scripture, in the same chapter, says that the gift of prophecy, the gift of tongues, and scientific knowledge, cease and are destroyed. But according to THE DOCTORS, scientific knowledge is not destroyed as a habit; and the gift of tongues will not cease in itself, for the blessed know how to speak different tongues, whatever the case may be concerning actual use of them; and the gift of prophecy was present, according to THE DOCTORS, in Christ, Who called Himself a prophet in *Matthew* 13, where He said "No prophet is without honor, except in his homeland," and Who was blessed in His soul. Therefore, since these things are not abolished as habits, it seems that neither is faith. And at least it cannot be proved from Scripture that faith is so abolished, for Scripture speaks in the same way of all the foregoing and of faith throughout the whole of the chapter.
>
> *Second* as follows. THE APOSTLE compares the abolition of faith, the gift of tongues, and scientific knowledge to maturity, where he says, "When I was a child, I spoke as a child, I understood as a child, etc., but when I became a man, I set aside childish things." But when a child becomes a man, neither the power by which he spoke, understood, or thought, nor any good habit which he had in relation to these acts, is set aside. Therefore, neither will the above-mentioned habits be set aside in heaven.

It might be said that the case of faith is not similar to that of other habits, because imperfection is not of the essence of other habits, but is of the essence of faith. Hence, when perfection arrives, the other habits, since they are not opposed to perfection, will not be set aside, but faith alone, which is opposed to perfection, will be.

To this objection I say that it is not valid for the present question. For the difference mentioned is not based on Scripture, but rather—if the objection's conclusion is true—on the nature of the habits mentioned. Still, I believe that the conclusion is not true, and this will be made clear below. Therefore, since the difference is not at all based on Scripture, to say that "the habit of faith will not be set aside any more than the other virtues that are mentioned in the same way in the passage will be" is not contrary to Scripture, and hence is not heretical, which is all we are considering for the moment, for we shall later consider whether it is false.

Third as follows. When Scripture speaks of the setting aside of these things, it explains itself and shows that this setting aside is understood **{378}** with respect to act, where it says: "I spoke as a child, I understood as a child, etc.," and later, "Now we see in a glass, and in a mystery, etc. ." Therefore, on the basis of Sacred Scripture, it cannot be held that the habits are set aside, but only that the acts are, something which is also given an explanation, as will be said later. It is therefore clear that it is in no way contrary to Scripture rightly understood—that is, inasmuch as Scripture explains itself by context, which is the best kind of explanation according to AUGUSTINE in *Eighty-three Questions,* q.69—to say that the habit of faith can or does remain in heaven.

Furthermore, DURANDUS argues that the habit of faith can remain in heaven without an act. *First,* as follows:

> Paul in his rapture saw God, and yet the habit of faith remained in him according to THE DOCTORS. Therefore, the habit of faith can co-exist with vision.
>
> To this one might respond that it is not known whether Paul in his rapture was in or out of his body, since he himself did not know, as is said in *2 Corinthians* 12. But if his soul was out of his body, then he did not have faith, but vision alone; and when his body was restored, he then had faith again, but without vision; and thus faith and vision were never simultaneous.
>
> But this response is not valid. For if it is not known whether he was in or out of his body, why posit that he was out of his body rather than in it? And why not respond that, if he was in his body, faith co-existed with vision,

> just as, if he was out of his body, faith did not co-exist with vision? For if rapture were not possible while the soul is present in the body, Paul, knowing that he had undergone rapture, would not have wondered whether he was in or out of the body, but would have said without qualification that he was out of the body. And if rapture is possible while the soul is present in the body, why include Paul among the dead on account of his rapture? And if he is held to have been dead in fact, still, he could have undergone rapture while living. For Moses, too, like Paul, underwent rapture, or at least saw the divine essence, as AUGUSTINE says in his *Literal Commentary on Genesis,* but Moses was not dead. Also, THE DOCTORS hold that Paul in his rapture was not dead, but only abstracted from the use of the senses. And thus the argument stands.

Second, he argues as follows:

> The faith that is an acquired habit co-exists with bodily vision and with the assent of the intellect caused by vision. Therefore, the faith that is an infused habit can co-exist with the spiritual or blessed vision. The inference clearly follows, because the two cases seem to be altogether similar.
>
> The antecedent is proved as follows. If one has a habit of acquired faith by which one believes what a certain astrologer says concerning eclipses of the sun and moon, then, if one actually sees the moon eclipsed, just as the astrologer had foretold it would be, the former habit of faith will not be destroyed, but rather confirmed. For otherwise one's belief in what the astrologer has said would be easier and firmer because one has seen what he has predicted come to pass.
>
> One might object that the habit of faith contributes nothing to the vision of the eclipse, and that the act of this habit cannot concur in the vision.
>
> But this objection is invalid. For we are not asking here whether the act of faith can co-exist with vision, but only whether the habit of faith can. Hence, even granting that the habit of faith contributes nothing to the vision and that the act of faith cannot co-exist with the vision, it still does not follow that the habit of faith cannot co-exist with it.

Third, he argues as follows:

> A habit of opinion can co-exist with an act of science. Therefore, it can similarly co-exist with an act of vision; and the same is true of acquired faith, since it is a habit of opinion.
>
> The antecedent is made clear as follows. One and the same man can have, with respect to the same conclusion, both demonstrative middle terms,

which cause a habit of science, and topical or probable middle terms, which cause a habit of opinion. And when he performs the act of considering the conclusion according to the demonstrative middle terms, which cause him to know scientifically, he need not have forgotten the probable or topical middle terms, which cause the habit of opinion. And thus he simultaneously knows scientifically in act and possesses opinion in habit.

The inference is proved as follows. Just as believing and opining are opposed to seeing according to the evident and the non-evident, so they are opposed to knowing scientifically according to the certain and the doubtful. Hence, if opinion and faith can, in a state of habit, co-exist with the act of scientific knowledge in spite of the opposition between the doubtful and the certain, in the same way they can, in a state of habit, co-exist with the act of vision in spite of the opposition between the non-evident and the evident. And just as this is true with respect to acquired faith in relation to bodily vision, so it is true of infused faith in relation to the beatific vision.

One might say that faith cannot co-exist with the beatific vision, not because of any opposition that it has to the vision in itself, but because of the opposition that it has to the habit of the state of glory. Similarly, a vicious habit can co-exist with a virtuous act, but a virtuous habit cannot co-exist with a vicious habit, because a habit is not opposed to an act, but to a habit.

This response is invalid, for the following reason. Either the beatific vision can exist without the habit of the state of glory, or it cannot. If it can, then the habit of faith can co-exist with the beatific vision, since it is not opposed to it. If it cannot, then Paul in his rapture had the beatific vision, and consequently the habit of glory, together with the habit of faith, and consequently faith and the habit of the state of glory co-existed. Therefore, they are not opposed, because opposites cannot co-exist.

One might say that they co-existed in the manner of something passing, and not in the manner of a permanent habit.

This response is not valid either, for the following reason. Things that can co-exist for {379} one instant can co-exist always, because it is not length or shortness of time that hinders simultaneity, but the nature of opposition. Hence, if faith and the habit of the state of glory co-existed in Paul for that instant, they must be able to co-exist always.

Fourth, he argues as follows:

A lesser light is not destroyed when a greater one arrives. But the light of faith and the light of the state of glory are related as a lesser and a greater light. Therefore, etc.

§2. *Against the First Conclusion*

I. Arguments of Durandus In the second place DURANDUS (d.31, q.4) argues against the first conclusion. *First,* he speaks as follows:

> To posit the compatibility of the act of faith with the act of vision is not at all contrary to Sacred Scripture. For this compatibility is denied in no passage of Sacred Scripture, although in some passages, at least according to the surface meaning of the text, the de facto simultaneity of the two acts does seem to be denied.
>
> And let those who say the contrary, namely that the compatibility is denied by Scripture, quote an authoritative text for this point—as they quote the authoritative texts of THE COMMENTATOR and THE PHILOSOPHERS, who are more commonly and more frequently quoted. Such an authority has never yet been quoted, and I do not think that one could be quoted.

Second, he speaks as follows:

> Even to posit that the two are de facto simultaneous is not contrary to Scripture. For, just as Scripture says that faith will be set aside, so it says the same of scientific knowledge and of the gift of tongues, positing no difference with respect to either act or habit, and assigning the same reason, namely: "When what is perfect has arrived, what is in part will be set aside"; and again, "Now we see in a glass, and in a mystery, but then we shall see face to face."
>
> Now according to all of THE DOCTORS, scientific knowledge is set aside not with respect to actuality, but only with respect to the manner of its imperfection.
>
> I do not know whether the gift of tongues will be set aside in heaven with respect to actuality or with respect to manner, unless there is going to be vocal praise in heaven. For it is probable, if God is going to be praised there vocally, that the blessed man who has the gift of tongues will sometimes praise him in one tongue and sometimes in another, so that nothing in him is unoccupied with divine praise. This gift will, however, be set aside with respect to necessity, as THE GLOSS explains, because it will not be necessary to speak in tongues where each one will know in God whatever pertains to him.
>
> It is in this manner, as far as the text of Scripture goes, that the act of faith will be set aside in heaven: either because the imperfection of the act, and not the act itself, is removed, as was said of the act of scientific knowledge; or because, like the act of the gift of tongues, it will not be necessary,

for the blessed vision excludes the necessity of faith and its act. But as far as one can say from the words of Scripture, it excludes neither the possibility nor the actuality of the co-existence.

One might say the following to the contrary. Imperfection is necessarily set aside when perfection arrives. But imperfection is of the essence of the act of faith. Therefore, it will be destroyed when the perfection of vision arrives. But this is not so in the case of the act of scientific knowledge, for imperfection is not of its essence, although imperfection is joined to it in the present life.

In response to this we say that the argument is invalid. For this difference between the act of faith and the act of scientific knowledge is held nowhere in Scripture, which speaks of both in completely the same way, as is clear from the series of texts in the chapter *1 Corinthians* 13. Therefore, to say the contrary is not contrary to Scripture. Thus it is clear that it is in no way contrary to Scripture to say that the act of faith and the act of vision can co-exist.

Third, he says that although the two acts are not in fact simultaneous, they nevertheless could be simultaneous. He argues for the antecedent as follows:

If the two acts were simultaneous, they would be either two distinct acts or one act.

They are not two acts, for the following reason. The blessed in heaven clearly see what those in the present life believe. For this reason, just as we now believe that the Scriptures are inspired by God, so the blessed see that God has inspired the words of Scripture in holy men, and therefore, with respect to this point, the blessed have an act not of faith, but of scientific knowledge or of vision. Consequently the same is true of the truth of the words of Sacred Scripture. Hence, among the blessed, there is, as it were, this argument based on principles known per se: "Whatever God has said, or has inspired in those who speak, is true (this is known per se, even according to natural light). But God has spoken, or has inspired in holy prophets and apostles, the words of Scripture (this is also known per se to the blessed). Therefore, the words of Scripture are true." This conclusion is known by the blessed, and cognition of it is an act of scientific knowledge, and not of faith, which relies on an authoritative text that is not evidently spoken by God. Thus the act of faith, as of itself distinct from the beatific vision, is not present in the blessed.

Again, neither are the two one act, inasmuch as one of them concurs with the other. For two habits do not concur in one act except through the concurrence of the middle terms proper to the habits. But the proper middle term of infused faith cannot concur with the middle term that causes the beatific vision. Therefore, etc.

The minor premise is proved in two ways.

First, as follows. The proper middle term of infused faith is the authority of Scripture, which is not evidently spoken by God, for if it were evident that Scripture has been spoken by God, this authority would be a middle term of scientific knowledge rather than of faith. But to the blessed it is not non-evident, but rather evident, that Scripture has been spoken, or inspired, by God. Therefore, the proper middle term of the habit of faith is lacking in the blessed in heaven.

Second, as follows. Even granting that such a middle term is present in heaven, it would still not concur with the middle term that causes the blessed vision. For since the beatific vision is an act that, taken precisively, is supernatural, it arises wholly and **{380}** precisely from a supernatural cause. And hence it comes wholly and precisely from the divine essence, effectively and objectively, with nothing else concurring.

Thus the antecedent is clear.

He argues for the consequent as follows:

> If the blessed neither saw nor knew that Scripture is inspired by God, so that the proper middle term of the habit of faith remained in them, then believing and seeing, if they were held to be two acts in reality, could be simultaneous.
>
> This is made clear as follows. The act of vision or of acquired scientific knowledge and the act of faith have an opposition between themselves only with respect to the more and the less evident. For the act of vision simply and supremely possesses evidence; the act of scientific knowledge possesses moderate evidence; but the act of faith possesses evidence in the lowest degree—and yet it does possesses evidence in a way. For since it is a positive act of the intellect, it is a kind of vision, although an obscure one. THE APOSTLE agrees with this in his remark in *1 Corinthians* 13, where he speaks as follows: "Now we see through a glass, in a mystery, but then we shall see face to face." Note how he calls each of the acts "a seeing" or a vision, but says that one is clear, since it is "face to face," while the other is "obscure," since it is "in a glass" and "in a mystery."

Fourth, he argues as follows:

> The acts of scientific knowledge and of faith seem to be opposed to vision with respect to the more and the less evident, although, in this apparent opposition, the opposition of the act of faith to vision seems to be greater than that of the act of scientific knowledge. But the act of scientific knowledge, ac-

cording to THE DOCTORS, co-exists with the act of vision in heaven. Therefore, similarly, the act of faith will be able to co-exist with vision in heaven. For although the act of faith possesses less evidence than does the act of scientific knowledge, still, by the fact that the act of scientific knowledge is compatible with vision, the act of faith will be able to be compatible with the same vision. For vision is opposed either to both or to neither: if to both, then it can co-exist with neither, because every opposition, whether great or small, hinders co-existence; if to neither, then by whatever argument it is able to co-exist with one, it will also be able to co-exist with the other.

But I think that it is opposed to neither of them. For formal opposition is only between species that come under the same proximate genus. For instance, whiteness and the other colors come under color as their proximate genus, and are incompatible with one another in the same subject; but colors and flavors, because they are not in the same proximate genus, are not opposed to one another, and are not incompatible with one another in the same subject. But the beatific vision does not seem to be of the same proximate genus as any other act of understanding that we have in the present life, whether an act of scientific knowledge or an act of faith. For the beatific vision is an act that is supernatural not merely with respect to its cause, as was the sight given to the man born blind, but essentially. Hence, no act of understanding that we are able to have by purely natural means—whether knowing scientifically, or opining, or believing (for which infused faith is not necessarily required)—can be of the same proximate genus as the beatific vision. Hence, any such act can have no opposition—whether in itself or in its intrinsic features, whatever they may be—to the beatific vision, and therefore the two can co-exist. Thus it is clear that the act of scientific knowledge and the act of faith, given that they are different acts, can each co-exist with the beatific vision.

Again, things whose precise formal essences are compatible are themselves compatible. But the formal essences of the act of believing and of the act of seeing or scientifically knowing, each taken precisively, are compatible. Therefore, etc.

The major premise is self-evident.

The minor premise is proved as follows. To see is to assent to something that is present in itself; to know scientifically is to assent to something on account of a cause, or on account of knowledge of a cause; to believe is to assent to something on account of the authority of one who speaks. It is in what has just been stated that the formal essences of these acts, taken precisively, consist. Now it is clear that one can assent to a conclusion because he

> sees it in itself—for instance he sees the moon being eclipsed; and because he knows the cause—for instance he knows that by a certain movement the earth is interposed between the sun and the moon; and because he has heard it from an expert astrologer whom he is used to believing. Therefore, etc.

II. Other Arguments of Durandus DURANDUS (d.31, q.5) further argues that imperfection is in no way of the essence of the act of believing or of any other act. *First,* he argues as follows:

> No privation can be of the essence of anything positive, because everything positive is intrinsically and essentially constituted out of what is positive alone. Since, therefore, the act of believing, and every other act, is something positive, it is impossible that an imperfection, inasmuch as this describes a privation, be intrinsically of the essence of the act of faith or of any other act.
>
> Imperfection can, however, be a concomitant condition, for a lesser perfection falls short of a greater perfection. And thus imperfection is always and inseparably concomitant with the act of faith that is precisively and wholly caused by faith, for such an act falls short of the perfection of scientific knowledge and of vision. For the act of vision is directed to a thing that is actually and in itself present to the act; the act of scientific knowledge is directed to an object made present through a certain and evident middle term whose certainty is clear to the one who knows; and the act of faith—to which the object is present only through the authority of a speaker whose truthfulness is not evident to the one who believes—falls short of both of these. Thus this imperfection is always concomitant with the act which is of faith alone. I say "of faith alone" because the middle term on which faith relies can concur with the middle term that causes one to know scientifically, and with the presence of the object, and then one act is caused by the simultaneous concurrence of the three middle terms, {381} and this act does not have the imperfection that belongs to the act caused by "faith alone."

Second, he argues as follows:

> Just as the "mystery" that is assigned to faith connotes imperfection, so does the "being in part" that is assigned to scientific knowledge by THE APOSTLE in *1 Corinthians* 13. But imperfection is not of the nature of the act of scientific knowledge according to THE DOCTORS. Therefore, similarly, it is not of the nature of the act of faith.

Thus DURANDUS.

Here the second article terminates.

Article III: Responses

§1. To the Arguments against the Second Conclusion

To the Arguments of Durandus In the third article we must respond to the objections stated above.

Accordingly, to the objections made against the second conclusion [p. 216], we say, first of all, that many authoritative texts of Sacred Scripture seem to mean obviously and, as it were, to say explicitly that it is impossible for faith to remain in heaven, as is clear for the following reasons.

First, because in *Hebrews* 11 it is said that faith is "the argument of things that are not evident." Now it is clear that in heaven nothing that was the object of faith in the present life will be non-evident. And, since it is impossible for the same thing to be evident and non-evident to the same man at one and the same time, it is evident that, according to the mind of THE APOSTLE, faith is incompatible with vision and with the state of heaven.

Second, because in *2 Corinthians* 5 it is said that "While we are in the body, we travel in separation from the Lord, for we walk by faith and not by sight." From this authoritative text, taken together with the glosses of holy men, we may gather: first, that faith makes a man travel in separation from God; and second, that it makes him walk and direct himself towards God as towards something distant. Now it is clear that these two facts are incompatible with the state that causes blessedness. For the blessed do not travel in separation from God, but are present to Him, and God is present to them through His species; nor do they direct themselves or walk towards God, but rather they rest in Him. Hence THE GLOSS upon the passage quoted speaks as follows: "He who travels and walks by faith is not yet in heaven, but still on the way."

Third, because in *1 Corinthians* 13 THE APOSTLE compares the knowledge of faith to "reflected" and "mysterious" knowledge, and the knowledge of heaven to "direct" knowledge. Now it is clear that these two are incompatible with one another in the same man, with respect to the same object, and especially if both use the same middle term as the reason for giving assent. But faith and the beatific vision do give assent through the same middle term, namely the First Truth.

Again, in the same passage, THE APOSTLE compares the knowledge of faith to the thinking of a child and the knowledge of heaven to the wisdom of a man. Now it is clear that, according to THE APOSTLE, these two are incompatible, for he says that the latter casts out the former, which can only be because of their incompatibility.

Fourth, because to anyone who has faith there is something to be hoped for in the future, according to the remark of *Hebrews* 11: "Faith is the substance of things to be hoped for." But according to what THE APOSTLE says in *Romans* 8, vision excludes expectation and hope: "The hope that is seen is not hope." THE GLOSS comments as follows:

> A thing hoped for that is seen is not an object of the virtue of hope, which is only of things that are not evident. Hope is only of such things, because otherwise it would be against reason. For one might ask, "Why should someone hope for what he sees?" that is, "Why or how could he be said to hope in such a case?" as if to say, "For no reason whatsoever."

Thus THE GLOSS.

From these authoritative texts it is clear that to say that faith is compatible with the beatific vision does not agree with Sacred Scripture.

Much less does it agree with what THE SAINTS have said. Hence GREGORY, in his homily on the Gospel of John, while explaining the remark of *John* 20, "Because you have seen me, Thomas, etc.," speaks as follows:

> When THE APOSTLE PAUL says, "Faith is the substance of things to be hoped for, the argument of things that are not evident," this is certainly clear: because of things that are evident, there is no longer faith, but knowledge. When, therefore, Thomas saw, when he touched, why was it said to him, "Because you have seen me, Thomas, you have believed"? But he saw one thing, and believed another: he saw a man, and acknowledged God.

Thus GREGORY. And AUGUSTINE and other holy men say similar things, basing themselves on the remarks of THE APOSTLE in *1 Corinthians* 13, *Hebrews* 11, and other places. Hence it follows either that the holy men explain and understand THE APOSTLE incorrectly or that faith, according to THE APOSTLE, is a virtue incompatible with the state of blessedness and the vision of heaven.

From these remarks it is clear that the *first statement* of the opponent, in which he asserts that the compatibility of faith with the vision of heaven is opposed to neither the words of Sacred Scripture nor the conclusions of the saints, is altogether false and unprecedented.

Second, we say that the *second statement* of the opponent, in which he asserts that to say that faith co-exists with the beatific vision is not contrary to Sacred Scripture, or to the words of Scripture, is completely false.

This is made clear as follows. Since the compatibility of the habit of faith with the beatific vision is denied in Sacred Scripture, all the more is their actual co-existence, because whatever things cannot possibly co-exist never do co-exist.

In response to the *first* attempted proof of this argument we say that, although, from the words of THE APOSTLE in the thirteenth chapter of *1 Corinthians,* it cannot be concluded with evidence that the habit of faith will be removed any more than will be the habit of scientific knowledge, **{382}** or than the gift of prophecy or of tongues, still, from the words of THE APOSTLE in other passages, and from the glosses of saints who expound that chapter of THE APOSTLE and other words of his, it is perfectly clear that the habit of faith will be removed in a different way than will be the habit of scientific knowledge. Hence, THE ORDINARY GLOSS, in discussing that passage, speaks as follows:

> As AUGUSTINE says in the book *On Christian Doctrine,* "The vision that we shall see will replace faith, and the blessedness that we shall arrive at will replace hope; but charity will rather be increased," and nothing will replace it, although it will be destroyed inasmuch as it is imperfect, for it will cease to be imperfect and partial; but neither it nor its act will be destroyed. Therefore, everything that is partial will be destroyed: whether wholly, as in the case of faith and hope; or partially, as in the case of scientific knowledge, whose act and manner will be destroyed, and that of charity, whose manner will be taken away, but not itself, nor its act, nor indeed its manner.

Thus THE GLOSS.

a. SAINT THOMAS shows the way in which prophecy will cease in heaven in his *Postilla* on the thirteenth chapter of *1 Corinthians,* where he says:

> In the future state of glory, prophecy will have no place, for two reasons.
>
> First, because prophecy regards the future, while the future state of glory will not look for anything in the future, but will rather include the final fulfillment of everything that had been prophesied before. Hence, as is said in the *Psalm,* "As we have heard," that is, through the Prophets, "so we see," that is, by way of presence, "in the city of the Lord of powers."
>
> Second, because prophecy is accompanied by a figurative and obscure knowledge that will cease in heaven. Hence, as is said in *Numbers* 12, "If anyone among you is a prophet, I shall speak to him through a dream or in a vision."

Thus SAINT THOMAS. However, one should not rely too much on the second reason given here, for, as SAINT THOMAS himself says in *ST* III, q.7, a.8, ad 1:

> . . . These words do not show that the obscure knowledge that comes through a dream or in a vision is of the nature of prophecy. For divine knowledge reached Moses, who saw God clearly and not obscurely, and who is nevertheless called a prophet, according to the remark of *Deuteronomy:* "There has not arisen another prophet in Israel like unto Moses."

Thus SAINT THOMAS. And the objection concerning Christ, Who had the gift of prophecy together with blessedness, is resolved by SAINT THOMAS in the same place, ad 2, where he says:

> Faith is of things that are not seen by the one who believes; similarly, hope is of things that are not possessed by the one who hopes; but prophecy is of things that are far from the common understanding of the men with whom the prophet lives and shares in the present life. Hence, faith and hope are opposed to the perfection of the blessedness of Christ, but prophecy is not.

Thus SAINT THOMAS. Again, concerning the same point, in *ST* II–II, q.174, a.5, where he asks whether there is a state of prophecy among the blessed, he presents the following argument in obj.3:

> Christ was from the moment of His conception a seer *(comprehensor),* and yet He Himself called Himself a prophet in *Matthew* 13, where it is said, "A prophet is not without honor except in his homeland." Therefore seers and the blessed can be called prophets.

Thus the argument; the response is as follows:

> It must be said that Christ was simultaneously a seer and a pilgrim. Accordingly, the nature of prophecy was in Him not inasmuch as He was a seer, but only inasmuch as He was a pilgrim.

Thus SAINT THOMAS. But another explanation must be given with respect to the rest of those who are blessed; hence, in the same place, SAINT THOMAS speaks as follows:

> Prophecy implies a vision of supernatural truth as existing at a distance. This can happen in two ways.
>
> In one way, from the point of view of knowledge. For supernatural truth is known not in itself, but in certain of its effects; and it will be still more distant if it is known through the figures of bodily things than if it is known through intelligible effects; and prophetic vision, which occurs through the

> mere images of bodily things, is above all an instance of the former way of knowing.
>
> In another way the vision is far off from the point of view of the one who sees and who has not been completely brought to final perfection, according to the remark of *2 Corinthians* 5: "While we are in the body, we travel in separation from the Lord."
>
> But the blessed are not far off in either way. Therefore, they cannot be called prophets.

Thus SAINT THOMAS.

b. SAINT THOMAS shows the way in which the habit of scientific knowledge, and especially scientific knowledge of divine things, will be destroyed, in the above-mentioned *Postilla,* where, having stated and refuted certain opinions, he concludes as follows:

> Scientific knowledge remains in the soul after the death of the body with respect to intelligible species, but not with respect to the inspection of phantasms, which the separated soul, having a being and an operation without the participation of the body, does not need. It is in this respect that THE APOSTLE says that "knowledge will be destroyed," namely with respect to the turn towards phantasms. Hence, in *Isaiah* 29, it is said: "Wisdom will perish from the wise, and the understanding of the wise will be hidden."

Thus SAINT THOMAS. Again, in *ST* I, q.89, a.5, he determines that the habit of scientific knowledge, insofar as part of it is present in the sensitive powers, does not remain in the separated soul; but insofar as part of it is present in the intellect, it does remain in the separated soul. Again, in the same place, obj.1, he presents the following argument:

> THE APOSTLE says in *1 Corinthians,* "Knowledge will be destroyed."

Thus the objection; SAINT THOMAS responds as follows:

> It must be said that THE APOSTLE is there speaking of scientific knowledge not with respect to habit, but with respect to the act of knowledge. Hence, in order to show this, he adds: "Now I know in part."

Thus SAINT THOMAS. And understand that the act of scientific knowledge is destroyed in the separated soul inasmuch as such knowledge requires a turning {383} to phantasms. But the blessed, after taking on a body again, will in two ways be able to understand and to use the habit of scientific knowledge in the re-acquired body, namely both with and without a turning to phantasms. Hence SAINT THOMAS, in *ST* III, q.11, a.2, speaks as follows:

> Christ, in His state before the passion, was simultaneously a pilgrim and a seer. He had the features of a pilgrim especially from the point of view of the body, inasmuch as He was capable of being acted upon; but He had the features of a seer especially from the point of view of the intellective soul. Now it is a feature of the soul of a seer that it in no way is subject to or dependent upon its body, but rather dominates it entirely. Hence, too, after the resurrection, glory will redound from the soul to the body. But by the fact that the soul of man the pilgrim needs to be turned to phantasms, it is bound to the body, subject to it in a way, and dependent on it. Hence, the blessed souls, both after and before the resurrection, are able to understand without the turning to phantasms. And the same must be said of the soul of Christ, which had the power of a seer most fully.

Thus SAINT THOMAS. And in the same place, ad 3, he speaks as follows:

> Although the soul of Christ could understand without turning itself to phantasms, still it could also understand by turning itself to phantasms.

Thus SAINT THOMAS. And the same thing must be said of the rest of the blessed after the resurrection, namely that they will be able to use the habit of acquired scientific knowledge in both ways.

C. SAINT THOMAS shows the way in which the gift of tongues will be removed in heaven in his *Postilla* on the thirteenth chapter of *1 Corinthians,* where he says:

> When it is said "Tongues will cease," this is not to be understood with respect to the bodily members called "tongues," because, as is said in *1 Corinthians* 15, "The dead shall arise uncorrupted," without loss of members. Nor again is it to be understood with respect to the use of the bodily tongue, for there is going to be vocal praise in heaven according to the remark of the *Psalm,* "exaltations of God in their throats," as THE GLOSS on this remark explains. Therefore, it must be understood with respect to the gift of tongues, by which some in the early Church spoke in various tongues, as is said in *Acts* 2. For in the future state of glory, everyone shall understand every tongue. Hence it will not be necessary to speak various tongues. For it was also so at the beginning of humankind, as is said in *Genesis* 11: "There was one people and one language on all lips"; and this will be all the more true in the final state, in which there will be perfect unity.

Thus SAINT THOMAS.

The opponent's remark that the blessed will know how to speak various tongues etc. is not valid. For just as the blessed will know things that they knew before as pilgrims, but not with the same habit, as they know the articles in the present life through faith, but in heaven by the light of glory; so, correspondingly, while they were in the present life they had the habitual gift of tongues by which they were able to understand and to speak every tongue, but in heaven they will know how to speak and to understand every tongue, not by a prior habit, but in the light of the state of glory, by which they will know all things pertaining to their blessedness.

In response to the *second* argument for the opponent's *second statement* we say that, when a child becomes a man, neither natural powers nor perfect habits—if he previously had any when he was a child—are removed, because imperfection is not of the nature of such habits. Nevertheless, the imperfection of youth and that of powers, habits, and acts are removed. Acts and habits to whose nature imperfection pertains, such as false opinions and erroneous judgment, if any such were present before, are also removed. Thus, any preceding imperfection will be removed in heaven. And because imperfection is of the nature of faith and hope, but not of the nature of scientific knowledge or of charity, faith and hope must be removed, but charity and the habit of scientific knowledge must not, for the imperfection concomitant with charity and scientific knowledge in the present life were not of the nature of these habits, but came to them from something else. Concerning this point something has been seen in the proof of the first conclusion, and again in the proof of the second. Also concerning this point, SAINT THOMAS, in *ST* I–II, q.67, a.6, speaks as follows:

> When the imperfection of a thing is not of the nature of its species, nothing prevents the numerically same thing which earlier was imperfect from later becoming perfect, as a man becomes perfect through growth, and whiteness through intensification. Now charity is love, and no imperfection is of the nature of love, for love can be of what is possessed and what is not possessed, of what is seen and what is not seen. Hence charity is not removed by the perfection of the state of glory, but remains numerically the same.

Thus SAINT THOMAS. Again, in *ST* I–II, q.67, a.3, ad 1, he speaks as follows:

> Faith is nobler than scientific knowledge from the point of view of the object, because the object of faith is the First Truth. But scientific knowledge has a more perfect manner of knowing, namely vision, which is not opposed to the perfection of blessedness, as the manner of knowing of faith is opposed to this perfection.

Thus SAINT THOMAS.

The opponent says that the difference is not based on Sacred Scripture.

We respond that this is false. For Scripture says that faith is of things that are not evident, and consequently faith, by its formal essence, is accompanied by imperfection. Again, Scripture says that faith is accompanied by a travelling in separation from God, as was said above in response to the first argument.

In response to the *third* argument we say that Scripture explains itself not in the sense suggested by the opponent, according to which faith is abolished only with respect to act and not with respect to habit, but rather in the contrary sense. For on the basis of Scripture one holds that the habit of faith of its nature includes imperfection from the point of view of the subject, and that blessedness excludes imperfection from the subject, so that it must exclude the habits of faith and of hope. Concerning this point **{384}** SAINT THOMAS, in *ST* I–II, q.67, a.4, speaks as follows:

> That which of its nature implies imperfection of a subject cannot co-exist with a subject perfected by the opposite perfection. For instance, it is clear that movement of its nature implies imperfection of a subject, since it is "the act of what exists in potency as such"; hence, when this potency is reduced to act, the motion then ceases, for nothing is still being whitened after it has already been made white. Now hope implies a movement towards what is not possessed. Hence, when what is hoped for, namely enjoyment of divine things, is possessed, hope will no longer be able to exist.

Thus SAINT THOMAS. And he says something similar concerning faith in the preceding article:

> Faith of its nature contains imperfection from the point of view of the subject, etc.

—as was quoted in the first conclusion.

Furthermore, to what purpose would the habit of faith remain without an act and without the possibility of issuing in an act? Concerning this point, SAINT THOMAS, in the same question, a.5, obj.3, presents the following argument:

> The substance of a habit is not destroyed by the fact that its matter is removed, for a man can retain the habit of generosity even when he has lost his money, although he cannot perform the act. But the object of faith is the unseen First Truth. Therefore, when this object is removed by the fact that the First Truth is seen, the habit of faith itself can still remain.

Thus the argument; the response is as follows:

> It must be said that one who loses his money does not lose the possibility of possessing money, which is why it is appropriate that the habit of generosity remain in him. But in the state of glory, the object of faith, which is the unseen, is destroyed not merely in actuality, but, because of the stability of blessedness, even in its possibility, and hence this habit would remain in vain.

Thus SAINT THOMAS. He says something similar in *Questions on the Virtues,* "On Hope", a.4, where he presents the following argument in obj.11:

> The act of a virtue apparently is not only to do or will to do what pertains to the virtue when ability is present, but also to want to do it if ability were present. For the act of justice is to will to render money due, even if one is unable to get hold of the money. But the saints in heaven are so disposed as to will to look forward to blessedness even if they did not possess it. Therefore the act of hope is present in them. But an act proceeds from a habit. Therefore, the virtue of hope is present in them.

Thus the argument; the response is as follows:

> It must be said that the object of a virtue can be absent in two ways. In one way, together with the possibility of possessing it, and thus, even when the object is not possessed the virtue can exist, as can the act of the virtue under the condition "if ability were present." In another way, the object can be absent together with the impossibility of possessing it, and thus neither the habit nor the act remains. It is in this latter way that the object of hope is removed in heaven, for otherwise blessedness would never be possible.

Thus SAINT THOMAS. And what he says of hope can correspondingly be said of faith, as was made clear above.

Third, we say that the opponent's *third statement,* in which he says that the habit of faith can remain without act in heaven, is false and badly proved.

In response to his *first* argument we say *first* that not all THE DOCTORS agree that Paul in his rapture saw the divine essence, and in fact many of them deny this, saying rather that he had a vision that was intermediate between the knowledge of the blessed and the knowledge of those in the present life, an opinion that SAINT THOMAS quotes in *Questions on Truth,* q.13, a.2, and in *ST* II–II, q.175, a.3.

Second, we say that, granting that Paul in his rapture did see the divine essence—as BLESSED THOMAS holds in the passages quoted, following AU-

GUSTINE's *On Seeing God* 13 and *Literal Commentary on Genesis* 12; and as is held in THE GLOSS on *2 Corinthians* 12—it is still not very clear whether Paul and Moses—who, being alike in their raptures in the sense that both were still living, are both said by AUGUSTINE to have seen the divine essence clearly and without obstruction—still possessed the habit of faith or that of hope during their rapture, or whether these habits were taken away from them because of their rapture. For SAINT THOMAS, in *ST* II–II, q.175, a.3, seems to say that the habit of faith co-existed in Paul with vision of the divine essence, but that the act of faith did not. In obj.3 he presents the following argument:

> As is held in *1 Corinthians* 13, faith and hope cannot co-exist with vision of the divine essence. But Paul in his state of rapture had faith and hope. Therefore, he did not see the divine essence.

Thus the argument; the response is as follows:

> It must be said that, because Paul in his rapture was not blessed in a habitual way, but merely possessed the act of the blessed, consequently the act of faith was not present in him during that time, although the habit of faith was.

Thus SAINT THOMAS. And in order to clarify this solution, he prefaces it with something he says in ad 2, speaking as follows:

> The divine essence cannot be seen by a created intellect except through the light of glory, of which it is said in the *Psalm*, "In your light we shall see light." But the light of glory can be participated in two ways: in one way in the manner of an immanent form, as the blessed saints participate it in heaven; in another way in the manner of a passing affection, which is the way in which the light of glory was present in Paul when he underwent rapture. Hence, by this vision Paul was made blessed not simply speaking—that is, in such a way that there would be an overflow to his body—but only in a certain respect.

Thus SAINT THOMAS. He makes a similar point in *Questions on Truth*, q.13, a.2, where, in obj.5, he sets forth the following argument:

> Paul possessed faith and hope during his rapture. But these cannot co-exist with vision of God in His essence, for "faith is of things that are not evident," as is said in *Hebrews* 11, and "why should one hope for what he sees?" as is said in *Romans* 8. {385} Therefore . . .

Thus the argument; the response is as follows:

> It must be said that when complete vision arrives, faith departs. Hence, inasmuch as the vision of God in His essence was present in Paul, faith was not present in him. But the vision of God in His essence was present in Paul in its act, but not with respect to the habit of the state of glory. Hence, conversely, faith was present in him with respect to habit, but not with respect to act, and the case is the same concerning hope.

Thus SAINT THOMAS.

By these remarks SAINT THOMAS seems to mean that the habits of faith and hope can co-exist with that vision of the divine essence which is not simply speaking beatific, that is, the vision which is caused by the light of divine glory being present in the intellect as an affection, rather than as a habit; but that these virtues cannot co-exist with that vision of the divine essence which is simply speaking beatific, that is, the vision which results from the light of divine glory being present as a habit.

In many other places, however, he seems to say that the habit of faith can in no way co-exist with either kind of vision, but that, on the contrary, just as a thing ceases to be an object of sight as soon as it ceases to be colored or shining, so God, or a thing believed in, ceases to be an object of faith as soon as it begins to be evident or seen; and thus it is impossible for there to be faith of things seen or known, just as it is impossible for the power of sight to be related to what is not colored or not shining. This point was discussed at enough length in d.25.

Now this second way of understanding the question, which seems much more probable, would have to say that neither Moses nor Paul possessed the habit of faith during their raptures, but that it was removed from them during the time of the rapture, and restored to them after.

Or, if the habit of faith did remain during the time of rapture, there is no doubt that, in relation to God, Who was seen, the habit, during that time, did not have the nature of faith in actuality, but perhaps the nature of faith in potency: for during that time there was not in God the formal essence of an object of faith.

Nevertheless, the nature of faith could remain in relation to other objects, which were not seen. For instance, it is numerically the same habit that first has the nature of faith concerning the truth "God is one" in one who does not have a demonstration of it, but adheres to it merely on the authority of God's revelation; and that afterwards, when demonstrative proof of this truth is acquired, ceases to be faith in relation to this truth, because the truth has now lost the formal essence of the object of faith, which is to be unseen and non-evident.

In response to the *second* argument for the third statement we deny the antecedent as something completely false.

In response to the argument for the antecedent, we say that when one who has acquired a habit of faith in what an astrologer says concerning future eclipses of the sun does in the present see an eclipse predicted by the astrologer, the habit then loses the nature of faith with respect to the eclipse that is actually seen and made manifest, although it can still have the nature of faith with respect to other, future eclipses, or other things predicted by the astrologer. And although one with such a habit does assent more strongly to what the astrologer says than he did before, this does not come about through the preceding habit of faith, but from another source, namely through experience of the truth of what the astrologer said, or for other reasons. For, as has been said elsewhere, not every act of belief is caused by a habit of faith. Concerning this point, SAINT THOMAS, while treating of a similar point in *Questions on the Virtues,* "On Hope", a.4, speaks as follows:

> If the principal object of hope as a theological virtue is removed in such a way that eternal blessedness is no longer future, but possessed, the hope that is a theological virtue ceases. The saints can still, by relying on divine help, hope for certain things pertaining to themselves or to others according to the common nature of hope, but not according to the proper nature of the hope that is a theological virtue.
>
> This is made clear by a counterexample illustrating the point in a different case. The principal object of charity is God. Hence, as long as anyone loves God, he loves his neighbor in God by the same virtue of charity. But if he ceases to love God, he will still be able to love his neighbor according to another nature, but not by the virtue of charity, whose species is destroyed when its principal object is removed.

Thus SAINT THOMAS. And I say the same thing, in the present question, of faith and the act of believing.

It can also be said in response to the argument that it merely concludes that the habit of faith can co-exist with the vision that does not proceed from habit; and SAINT THOMAS concedes this, as was seen above. But the beatific vision proceeds from the light of glory inasmuch as it is present in the manner of a habit.

In response to the *third* argument we say that a habit of opinion in act, as is commonly held, cannot co-exist with an act of vision or with an act of scientific knowledge. Therefore, we deny the antecedent.

We have frequently responded to the proof of the antecedent in d.25. For in the subject of scientific knowledge, no topical middle terms can cause a habit of opinion in act. Rather, either they cause no new habit, but merely increase a pre-existing habit of scientific knowledge; or, if they do cause a different habit, the latter is a habit of opinion not in act, but only in potency, that is, one which would be in act if it existed apart from the habit of scientific knowledge.

Second, we say that, even granting that the habit of faith or of opinion can co-exist with the act of vision, it does not follow from this that it could co-exist with the vision that is simply speaking beatific. For the latter, as was said above, requires the perfection of the intellect by the light of the state of glory as a habit, not as an affection. But the habit of faith is more opposed to the habit of the state of glory than it is to the act of the state of glory unaccompanied by the habit.

Third, we say that the vision that is simply speaking beatific cannot exist without the habitual light of the state of glory, but that the vision of the divine essence that is not simply speaking beatific can exist without this habit—although not without the light being present as an affection. And it is the latter vision of the divine essence, not the former, that **{386}** Moses and Paul had in their raptures, as was said above.

Fourth, we say that the habit of faith cannot co-exist with the habit of the state of glory, whether for an instant or for a time, in the same subject. But the habit of faith, according to the first way of SAINT THOMAS, can co-exist in the same subject, both for an instant and for a time, with the light of the state of glory if the latter is present as an affection. Nevertheless, the other way of understanding touched upon above, which holds that the habit of faith is incompatible with the vision of the divine essence, whether this vision is beatific or not, seems, at least for now, more probable to me. For every vision removes the faith which regards the same object.

SAINT THOMAS responds to the *fourth* argument in *ST* I–II, q.67, a.5, where, in obj.2, he presents the following argument:

> Faith is a spiritual light of the soul, according to the remark of *Ephesians:* "The eyes of your heart enlightened for the knowledge of God." But this light is imperfect in comparison to the light of the state of glory, concerning which it is said in the *Psalm:* "In your light we shall see light." But imperfect light

> remains when perfect light comes, for a candle is not extinguished when sunshine arrives. Therefore, it seems that the light of faith remains together with the light of the state of glory.

Thus the argument; the response is as follows:

> It must be said that the imperfection of the light of the candle is not opposed to the perfection of the solar light, because they do not concern the same subject. But the imperfection of faith and the perfection of the state of glory are opposed to one another and do concern the same subject. Hence they cannot co-exist, just as brightness of the air cannot co-exist with its darkness.

Thus SAINT THOMAS.

§2. To the Arguments against the First Conclusion

I. To Arguments of Durandus It remains for us to address the arguments brought against the first conclusion [p. 221].

In response to DURANDUS's *first statement,* we say that it is expressly held in Sacred Scripture that the act of faith, which is belief, and the act of the state of glory, which is vision, have an opposition between them, and consequently an impossibility of being simultaneously present in a subject. The authoritative texts establishing this point have been quoted above, at the beginning of this article.

In response to his *second statement* we say that the response quoted in his argument suffices.

Something has been said above concerning his argument against this response. For the difference that we are positing between the act of faith and the act of the state of glory is explicitly held in Sacred Scripture. And although it cannot be explicitly held on the basis of the thirteenth chapter of *1 Corinthians,* it is maintained in many of the other passages quoted.

In response to his *third statement* we say that he badly and insufficiently proves the compatibility of the act of faith with the act of the beatific vision, because he relies on a false basis, namely the affirmation that the act of vision and the act of faith are opposed to one another only according to the more and less evident, and not at all by way of contrariety, or privation, or contradiction. SAINT THOMAS holds the opposite of this in many places. In *In 3 Sent.,* d.31, q.2, a.1, qla.1, obj.2, he presents the following argument:

> Nothing is driven out except by its contrary. But the state of glory is not contrary to faith. Therefore, when the state of glory arrives, faith is not removed.

Thus the argument; the response is as follows:

> We must say that, although the vision of glory is not contrary to faith with respect to what there is of cognition in faith, it is contrary to faith with respect to what there is of obscurity in it, and from this point of view, it drives out faith.

Thus SAINT THOMAS. Again, in obj.3, he presents the following argument:

> Perfect and imperfect with respect to things specifically different are certainly compatible in the same subject, as, for example, a man might have perfect knowledge of geometry and imperfect knowledge of grammar. But the vision of glory and faith are specifically different. Therefore, the vision of glory does not remove faith.

Thus the argument; the response is as follows:

> We must say that perfection and imperfection of cognition are certainly compatible with respect to diverse things, but not with respect to the same thing; thus one can simultaneously have perfect knowledge of what pertains to one thing and imperfect knowledge of what pertains to another. But the present case is not like this, because faith and the vision of glory are of the same thing.

Thus SAINT THOMAS. Again, in *ST* I–II, q.67, a.3, he says:

> Opposition is the per se and proper cause why one thing is excluded by another, etc.

—as was quoted in the first conclusion. From these texts it is clear that the act of faith and the vision of the state of glory are opposed to one another by way of privation or contrariety, and not merely according to the more and less evident.

The opponent says that faith possesses some evidence, since it is a vision, according to THE APOSTLE, who says, "Now we see, etc."

SAINT THOMAS responds, in *In 3 Sent.*, d.24, q.1, a.2, qla.1, ad 1, that "sight" is taken by THE APOSTLE in the wide sense, according to which every instance of cognition is, in a wide sense and improperly, called "sight." This has been discussed at length above, in d.25, where it was seen which kind of intellective cognition is properly called "sight" and which is not. Again, in *ST*

II–II, q.1, a.4, ad 2, SAINT THOMAS responds to what THE APOSTLE says as follows:

> We must say that the things of faith can be considered in two ways. In one way in particular, and thus these things cannot be simultaneously seen and believed. In another way in general, that is, under the general aspect of object of belief, and thus these things are seen by one who believes, for he would not believe them if he did not see that they were to be believed, whether because of the evidence of signs or because of something similar.

Thus SAINT THOMAS. And understand that {387} the believer "sees" that these things are to be believed inasmuch as "sight" is taken in the wide and improper sense. In *Questions on Truth,* q.14, a.9, SAINT THOMAS speaks concerning the foregoing points as follows:

> Whenever the nature of the proper object of an act ceases to be, the act itself must cease to be. Hence, as soon as something begins to be present or evident, it cannot fall under the act of faith as an object, etc.

—as was quoted in d.25.

In response to the opponent's *fourth statement,* where he says that the vision of the state of glory is in no way opposed to the act of faith nor the act of scientific knowledge, etc., we say *first,* that there is formal opposition not only between forms contained under the same proximate genus, but also between forms belonging to different proximate genera. This is made clear as follows. A genus is divided by differences formally opposed to one another. Therefore, any two species or specific forms that come under two distinct differences of a remote genus include in their natures differences formally opposed to one another. Hence, although spiritual qualities and corporeal qualities are not contained under the same proximate genus, but under different ones, still they have a formal opposition between them. For instance, whiteness and scientific knowledge have such opposition, because extension and divisibility belong to the nature of whiteness, but indivisibility and unextendedness belong to the nature of scientific knowledge.

The falsity of what the opponent says is also made clear as follows. Not only is one species opposed to another, but also one genus to another. Vice, for instance, is opposed to virtue, and consequently everything contained under the genus of vice is, by the nature of its genus, opposed to anything contained under the genus of virtue. Concerning this point, SAINT THOMAS, in *ST* I–II, q.35, a.4, speaks as follows:

> As is said in *Metaphysics* 10, contrariety is difference with respect to form. But form is both particular and common. Hence it happens that some things are contraries with respect to the form of the genus, as are virtue and vice; and some with respect to the form of the species, as are justice and injustice, etc.

See the whole of this article.

Second, we say that, if the opponent's manner of arguing were valid, it would prove that a theological virtue, since it is essentially a supernatural form, would have no vice formally opposed to it. The falsity of this is self-evident. For to faith is opposed unbelief, to hope, presumption and despair, and to charity, hatred of God and neighbor and many other things, all of which SAINT THOMAS shows in *ST* II–II, qq.10 to 13, 20 and 21, and 34 to 43.

Third, we say that there is a difficulty as to whether the vision proper to the state of glory belongs to a proximate genus that is different from that to which other acts of understanding, which are created and are not causative of blessedness, belong. For SAINT THOMAS, in *Questions on Truth,* q.8, a.14, speaks as follows:

> It must be known that all intelligible forms belong to one genus, however much the things that they represent belong to different genera. For they are all related to the same intellective power, etc.

But whatever may be the case concerning this point, it is evident from our first two remarks that the opponent's argument is not valid.

To the opponent's *fifth statement* we respond by denying the minor premise. For what is of the nature of the act of believing is not merely and precisely that assent is made to a proposition on account of the authority of one who speaks, but rather that the proposition is not evident to or seen by the one assenting. But this is not compatible with the act of vision or the act of scientific knowledge.

Thus the response to the arguments against the first and second conclusions is clear.

II. To the Other Arguments of Durandus It remains now to say something in response to the arguments introduced at the end by DURANDUS [p. 225], by which he attempts to prove that imperfection, understood as privation or negation, is in no way of the essence or nature of the act of believing.

In response to the *first* argument we say that no privation or negation is of the essence of any act or any positive being as an integral or an essential part.

For just as a substance is not made out of non-substances, so a being is not made out of non-beings, and a being is not constituted out of a being and a non-being. Nevertheless, a privation or negation can pertain to the essence or nature of something positive as that which designates the essence in the manner of an extrinsic difference, and as that without which the essence could neither be nor be conceived. ARISTOTLE shows this clearly in *Metaphysics* 10, in the chapter beginning "But the first contrariety . . . ," as does SAINT THOMAS, in his *Scriptum* on this passage, where he says:

> First ARISTOTLE posits that the principle of contrariety is privation and possession, saying that "the first contrariety is privation and possession," because privation and possession are included in every contrariety. But not every privation is a contrary, because "privation" has many senses. For sometimes something that does not have what it should by nature have is said to be something with a privation. But such a privation is not a contrary, because it posits no nature opposed to the possession, although it does presuppose a determinate subject. Rather, a privation is said to be a contrary whenever there is a perfect privation. But since a privation as such does not admit of more and less, it cannot be called "perfect" except by reason of a nature whose distance from the corresponding possession is perfect. For instance, it is not every privation of white that is contrary to white, but only the privation most distant from white, which must be founded on some nature that is of the same genus as white, but is most distant from white, and thus it is black that we call contrary to white.
>
> Then ARISTOTLE shows how a second contrariety is derived from the first, saying that different things are said to be "contraries with respect to possession and privation" in different ways. For some things are said to be contraries by the fact that they include privation and possession within themselves, as do "black" and "white" or "hot" and "cold." Others are said to be contraries by the fact that they cause privation and possession in actuality, as do "what heats" and "what cools." Others are said to be contraries by the fact {388} that they are virtual active principles of privation and possession, as are "the able to heat" and "the able to cool." Others are said to be contraries by the fact that they are receptions of the above-mentioned, such as "being heated" and "being cooled," or by the fact that they are rejections of them, such as "removal of heat" and "removal of cold." And some things are called contraries not merely by the fact that they have the foregoing relationships to the first contrary mentioned, but also by the fact that they have the same relationships to the subsequent contraries, as when I say that fire

> and water are contraries because they possess hot and cold, which are said to be contraries by the fact that they involve privation and possession.

Thus SAINT THOMAS. Again, somewhat later, he speaks as follows:

> Although one thing may be opposed to another in four ways—in one way as a contradiction, as one not-sitting is opposed to one sitting; in another way as a privation, as one who is blind is opposed to one who sees; in another way as a contrariety, as black is opposed to white; and in a fourth way as something related to another, as son is opposed to father—the first among the genera of opposition is contradiction. The reason for this is that contradiction is included in all of the others as what is prior and more simple. For it is impossible for opposites in any genus of opposition to exist simultaneously. This is so because one of two opposites involves of its nature the negation of the other. For instance, it is of the nature of one blind that he does not see; it is of the nature of black that it is not white; and it is of the nature of a son that he is not the father of the one whose son he is.

Thus SAINT THOMAS. And in what follows in the same chapter he frequently says that privation and possession are included in every contrariety.

From these texts it is clear that, since either extreme of a contrariety is a positive entity, it is not inconsistent for a privation or a negation to be of the nature of a positive form—not as an essential or integral part of it, but as a "part of reason," one that designates and characterizes the essence as an extrinsic difference.

Since ARISTOTLE, in *Metaphysics* 10, also argues at length that every genus is divided by contrary differences, and that privation and possession, as has been said, are included in every contrariety; and since the differences that define a genus are the same as those which constitute species; it follows that differences that constitute positive species sometimes include privation in their nature.

In response to the *second* argument we say that the comparison is completely invalid in the present case. For the imperfection that accompanies the scientific knowledge of someone in the present life, namely that it is "in part," is not at all included in the definition of scientific knowledge. But "mystery" is included in the definition of faith, and hence is of the nature of faith. Thus it is clear that this novel fancy of DURANDUS, which he discovered with such hard work, hardly tells against the ancient truth of SAINT THOMAS.

Response to the affirmative argument for the question [p. 213] has been made in the proof of the first conclusion, where it was said that perfect cognition from the point of view of the subject and imperfect cognition from the point of view of the subject are, with respect to the same object of cognition, incompatible in the same subject. For this is how faith and vision are related to one another, as has often been said.

This suffices for the question.

Blessed be God.

Amen.

Whether by Human Acts Habits of Virtue Are Acquired Which Exist in the Sensitive Appetite, That Is, in the Concupiscible or Irascible Powers, as in Their Subject

In relation to the thirty-third distinction of the third book of *The Sentences,* the question is raised: Whether by human acts habits of virtue are acquired which exist in the sensitive appetite, that is, in the concupiscible or irascible powers, as in their subject.

It is argued that they may not, as follows. Contraries naturally come into being with respect to the same thing. But the contrary of virtue is mortal sin, which cannot be present in the sensitive appetite, that is, the sensuality. Therefore, the sensitive appetite cannot be a subject of virtue, and for this reason a habit of virtue cannot be generated in it by human acts.

Argument is made for the opposite conclusion as follows. THE PHILOSOPHER (*Ethics* 3.10) says concerning temperance and fortitude that "they belong to the irrational parts." But the irrational parts are the irascible and the concupiscible parts, which belong to the sensitive appetite. Therefore, some virtues are present in them as in their subject. THE PHILOSOPHER also says, in *Ethics* 2, that such habits of virtue are caused by human acts; therefore, the conclusion is true.

In this question there will be three articles: in the first the conclusions will be presented, in the second the objections, and in the third the responses.

Article I. Conclusions

First Conclusion: Certain Moral Virtues Are Present in the Sensitive Appetite—Which Is Divided into the Concupiscible and the Irasible Powers—as in Their Subject

{389} SAINT THOMAS proves this conclusion in *ST* I–II, q.56, a.4, where he speaks as follows:

> The irascible and the concupiscible powers can be considered in two ways: in one way in themselves, inasmuch as they are the parts of the sensitive appetite; in another way inasmuch as they participate in reason by the fact that they naturally obey reason. Considered in the first way, it does not pertain to them to be subjects of virtue. But considered in the second way, both the irascible power and the concupiscible power can be a subject of human virtue. For each is a principle of human acts inasmuch as it participates in reason. But it is necessary to posit virtues in these powers. For an act that proceeds from one power according as it is moved by another cannot be perfect unless both powers are well disposed to the act, just as the act of an artisan cannot be suitable unless both the artisan and his tool are well disposed for the action. Therefore, in matters concerning which the irascible and the concupiscible powers operate according as they are moved by reason, it is necessary that some habit that perfects for the purpose of acting well be present not only in the reason, but also in the irascible and concupiscible powers. And because the good disposition of a power that is moved is taken with respect to that power's conformity to the moving power, the virtue that is present in the irascible and concupiscible powers is nothing but the habitual conformity of these powers to reason.

Thus SAINT THOMAS. Again, in *In 3 Sent.*, d.33, q.2, a.4, qla.2, he speaks as follows:

> Human virtues are those by which the operation of a man is rendered good. Hence, in every power that can be the principle of human operation, there must be a habit of virtue by which the operation of the man is rendered good; otherwise, the man would not be sufficiently perfected by virtue. But every power in which something of reason—by which a man is a man—is found is a principle of human operation. Hence, since, in the irascible and concupiscible powers, which are the parts of the sensitive appetite, something of reason is present by way of participation, inasmuch as they are able to obey reason (which is not true of the powers of the nutritive part), certain virtues must be present in the irascible and concupiscible powers as in their

> subject, virtues by which it is brought about that the powers in which they are present obey reason easily.
>
> This occurs inasmuch as the passions are repressed so as not to disturb reason. Hence, in one who undergoes strong passions but is not carried away by them, a habit is indeed present in reason, one that holds reason back so that it is not carried away, but no habit is present in the powers in which the passions are present. Accordingly, the perfectly virtuous man is not the continent or abstinent man, but the temperate or moderate man, in whom not only is the higher part perfected, so that it cannot be carried away, but also the lower part moderated, so that strong passions do not arise. Thus, whatever may be the power in which the passion with which a virtue is concerned is present, that power is the subject of that virtue, as the concupiscible power is the subject of temperance and the irascible power is the subject of fortitude and gentleness.

Thus SAINT THOMAS. Again, in *Questions on the Virtues,* "On the Virtues in General", a.4, he speaks as follows:

> Concerning this question, in part everyone agrees, and in part opinions are contradictory. For it is agreed by everyone that certain virtues are present in the irascible and concupiscible powers, namely temperance in the concupiscible power and fortitude in the irascible power. But there is a difference of opinion concerning the following point. Some distinguish a twofold irascible power and a twofold concupiscible power, for they posit both an irascible and a concupiscible power both in the higher part of the soul and in the lower part; and they say that since the irascible and concupiscible powers present in the higher part of the soul belong to the rational nature, they are able to be subjects of virtue, but that those present in the lower part, which belong to the sensual or brute nature, cannot.
>
> Now this point—namely whether, properly speaking, two powers can be distinguished in the higher part of the soul, one of which is "irascible" and the other "concupiscible"—has been treated in another question. But whatever may be said concerning this point, one must in any case hold, according to THE PHILOSOPHER, that certain virtues are present in the irascible and concupiscible powers that are in the lower appetite, as others also say.
>
> This is made clear as follows. Since "virtue" names a certain completion of a power, and since a power is directed to an act, one must posit a human virtue in any power that is a principle of a human act. But an act that is said to be "human" is not one that is present in or performed by man in any way whatsoever, since plants and brute animals also perform some such acts, but

rather one that is proper to man. Now man has something proper in his act by, among other things, the fact that he is master of his act. Accordingly, any act of which man is master is a properly human act, while those acts of which he is not master even though they take place in him, such as digestion, growth, etc., are not properly human. Accordingly, human virtue can be posited in whatever is the principle of the kind of act of which man is master.

It should be known, however, that there happens to be a threefold principle of this kind of act. One is the first mover and commander, by which man is master of his act, and this is reason or will. Another is a moved mover, namely the sensitive appetite, which both is moved by the higher appetite, inasmuch as it obeys reason, and itself moves the external members by its own command. The third is what is merely moved, namely the external member. {390} Now both of the last two, namely the external member and the lower appetite, are moved by the higher part of the soul, although in different ways. For unless there is some impediment, the external member obeys the command of the higher commanding power without any opposition, according to an order of nature, as is clear in the case of the hand and the foot. The lower appetite, however, has, from its nature, its own inclination, and hence it does not obey the higher appetite on command, but sometimes opposes it. Hence ARISTOTLE says in his *Politics* that the soul rules the body by a despotic government, that is, as a master rules a slave, but that reason rules the lower parts of the soul by a royal and political government, that is, as kings and princes rule freemen in cities, who have the right and means of opposing an order of the king or prince in some matters.

Accordingly, nothing need be present in the external member for the perfection of a human act except its natural disposition, by which it is naturally moved by reason. But in the lower appetite, which is able to oppose reason, there needs to be present something by which the operation that reason commands may be carried out without opposition. For if the immediate principle of the operation is imperfect, the operation itself must be imperfect, however much perfection may be present in the higher principle. Therefore, if the lower appetite were not perfectly disposed for carrying out the command of reason, the operation, which pertains to the lower appetite as to its proximate principle, would not be in a state of perfect goodness, for it would be accompanied by opposition of the sensitive appetite, from which a sadness would accrue to the lower appetite moved by the higher one through force, as happens in the case of one who has strong desires but who, because reason forbids, does not pursue them. Therefore, when there is required an operation of man dealing with things that are the objects of the

> sensitive appetite, there is required for the goodness of the operation that there be present in the sensitive appetite a disposition or perfection by which this appetite obeys reason with ease, and this we call a "virtue."
>
> Accordingly, when there is a virtue concerning the things that properly pertain to the irascible power—as fortitude concerns feelings of fear and boldness, magnanimity concerns difficult things hoped for, and gentleness concerns feelings of anger—such a virtue is said to be present in the irascible power as in its subject. But when a virtue concerns the things that properly pertain to the concupiscible power—as chastity concerns the venereal pleasures and sobriety and abstinence concern the pleasures of food and drink—it is said to be present in the concupiscible power as in its subject.

Thus SAINT THOMAS.

From all of these texts the following argument can be formulated. Every power that is able to be a principle of a human act, and is not of its nature determined to the perfection of that act or to obeying reason, can be the subject of a virtue. But the sensitive appetite is such. Therefore, it can be the subject of a virtue.

Second Conclusion: Certain Virtues Can Be Acquired in Us by the Habituation of Operations and Caused by Our Acts

SAINT THOMAS presents this conclusion in *Questions on the Virtues*, "On the Virtues in General", a.9, where he speaks as follows:

> Since a virtue is the terminus of a power, and the terminus to which any power tends is to perform a perfect operation, that is, one that is good, it is clear that the virtue of any thing is that by which it produces a good operation. But because every thing is for the sake of its operation, and because each thing is good according as it is well disposed in relation to its end, it must be through its proper virtue that each thing is good and operates well.
>
> Now the proper good of each thing is different from the proper good of any other thing, for there are diverse perfections of diverse things, so that the good of a man is different from the good of a horse and the good of a stone. Moreover, the good of man himself is taken in different ways according to different considerations of him. For the good of man as man and the good of man as citizen are not the same. The good of man as man is that reason be perfect in knowledge of truth and that the lower appetites be ruled according to the rule of reason, for man is man by the fact that he is rational. But the good of man as a citizen is that he be directed, in relation to the city, to everyone else, and for this reason THE PHILOSOPHER says in *Politics* 3

that the virtue of man as man is not the same inasmuch as he is a good man and inasmuch as he is a good citizen.

Now man is not only a citizen of the earthly city, but also a participant in the heavenly city of Jerusalem, whose governor is the Lord, and whose citizens are the angels and all the saints, whether they reign in the state of glory and rest in heaven or are still in pilgrimage on earth, as THE APOSTLE says in *Ephesians* 2: "You are citizens among the saints and members of the household of God." But man's nature does not suffice for him to be a participant in this city; rather, he is raised up to this through divine grace. Therefore, it is clear that the virtues that belong to man inasmuch as he is a participant in this city cannot be acquired by him through his natural abilities. Hence they are not {391} caused by our acts, but are infused into us by a divine gift. But the virtues that belong to man by the fact that he is man, or by the fact that he is a participant in the earthly city, do not exceed the ability of human nature, and hence man can acquire them by his natural abilities and by his own acts.

This is made clear as follows. When someone has a natural aptitude for a perfection, if this aptitude is according to a merely passive principle, then he can acquire it—not, however, through his own act, but rather through the action of an external natural agent, in the way that air receives light from the sun. But if he has a natural aptitude for some perfection according to a principle that is at once both active and passive, then he can attain that perfection through his own act. For example, the body of a sick man has a natural aptitude for health, and because the subject is naturally receptive of health because of the natural active power of healing present in it, a sick man is sometimes healed without the action of an external agent. Now it has been shown in the preceding question that the natural aptitude for virtue that man possesses is according to principles which are active and passive. This is clear from the ordering of powers: for in the intellective part there is a principle that is, as it were, passive, namely the possible intellect, which is brought to its perfection by the agent intellect; and the possible intellect, brought to actuality, moves the will, for the good thing understood is the end that moves the appetite; and the will, moved by reason, by nature moves the sensitive appetite, that is, the irascible and concupiscible appetites, which naturally obey reason. Hence it is clear that any virtue that effects a good operation of man has an active principle in man, who, by his own act, is able to bring himself to act, whether the virtue is present in the intellect, or in the will, or in the irascible and concupiscible powers. However, a virtue present in the intellective part and one present in the appetitive part are brought to an act of virtue in different ways. For the action of the intellect, and of any cognitive power, is according as the power is somehow likened to the object of knowledge. Hence an intellectual virtue is brought into being in the intellective part according as, by the agent intellect, intelligible species are made to be present, whether in actuality or habitually, in that part. But an action of an appetitive power consists in an inclination toward the appetible object, and hence, in order for a virtue to be brought into being in the appetitive part, an inclination to something determinate must be given to it.

Now it must be known that the inclination of natural things follows from a natural form, which is why, in keeping with the requirement of the form, the inclination is toward one thing; and while the form remains, the inclination cannot be removed and its contrary cannot be introduced. For this reason, natural things do not become accustomed or unaccustomed to anything, for however much a stone is lifted upwards, it never becomes accustomed to this, but remains always inclined to downward movement. Things, however, that have an inclination in both directions do not have any form by which they are determinately inclined to one thing, but rather they are determined to one thing by their own movement. And by the very fact that they are so determined to one and the same thing, they are in a way disposed to it. And when they are many times determinately inclined to the same thing by their own movement, a determinate inclination to it is established in them, such that this introduced disposition is, as it were, a form that tends to one thing in the way that a nature does. For this reason it is said that custom is like a second nature.

Accordingly, because an appetitive power is related to two things, it does not tend to one of them except inasmuch as it is so determined by reason. When, therefore, reason frequently inclines the appetitive power to one thing, there is brought into being in the appetitive power an established disposition by which the power is inclined to the one thing to which it is accustomed. Such a disposition, established in this way, is a habit of virtue. Hence, if the virtue of the appetitive part be rightly considered, it is nothing other than a disposition or form engraved and imprinted on the appetitive power by reason. For this reason, however strong may be a disposition in an appetitive power to anything, it cannot have the essence of virtue unless it be present in something pertaining to reason. Hence, reason is also included in the definition of virtue. For THE PHILOSOPHER says, in *Ethics* 2, that "virtue is a habit resulting from choice, consisting in an intermediary, determined by reason, as the wise man would determine."

Thus SAINT THOMAS.

From this text the following argument can be formulated. Whoever has within himself a sufficient active and passive principle of a virtue, or of some other habit, can, by his own acts, cause such a virtue or habit within himself. But man is someone of this kind. Therefore, etc.

Third Conclusion: In Addition to the Moral Virtues Acquired by Human Acts, Certain Other Moral Virtues, Divinely Infused, Are Also Necessary to Man

SAINT THOMAS presents this conclusion in *ST* I–II, q.63, a.3, where he speaks as follows:

> Effects must be proportioned to their causes and principles. Now all virtues, both intellectual and moral, that are acquired by our acts result from certain natural principles already existing in us. In place of these natural principles, the theological virtues by which we are ordered to a supernatural end are conferred upon us by God. Hence, to these theological virtues there must proportionally correspond other habits, caused in us by God, that are related to the theological virtues as the moral and intellectual virtues are related **{392}** to the natural principles of the virtues.

Thus SAINT THOMAS. Again, in *In 3 Sent.*, d.33, q.1, a.2, qla.3, he speaks as follows:

> The seedplots in us of the virtues are the ordering of the will and of the reason to the good which is connatural with us. But since man has, by divine generosity, been ordered to a supernatural good, namely eternal glory, the virtues proportioned to this end cannot be caused by these seedplots of virtue. Hence, the virtues that order our life to that end must be caused by that through which there is present in us an inclination to that end, that is, by the grace of God. Hence, we must possess certain moral virtues that are infused.

Thus SAINT THOMAS.

From these texts the following argument can be formulated. Whoever is directed to a supernatural end is necessarily perfected—not merely with respect to the end, but also with respect to the means that lead to that end—by a divinely infused habit. But man, who is perfected by theological virtues with respect to the end and by moral virtues with respect to the means to that end, is someone of this kind. Therefore, certain moral virtues must be infused into him by God.

Fourth Conclusion: In Heaven, after the Resurrection, the Moral and Cardinal Virtues Will Remain

SAINT THOMAS presents this conclusion in *ST* I–II, q.67, a.1, where he speaks as follows:

> As SAINT AUGUSTINE says, in *De trinitate* 14, CICERO, in the *Hortensius,* held that after the present life the four cardinal virtues do not exist, but that in the next life men are made happy "merely by the knowledge of a nature than which nothing is better or more loveable," as AUGUSTINE says in the same place, and "this is the nature that created all natures." AUGUSTINE himself, however, subsequently determines that these four virtues do exist in the future life, but in a different way.
>
> For evidence of this, it must be known that in these virtues there is something formal and something that is, as it were, material. What is material in these virtues is an inclination of the appetitive part to passions or operations according to a certain measure. But because this measure is determined by reason, what is formal in all virtues is the very order of reason. Accordingly, it must be said that these moral virtues will not remain in the future life with respect to what is material in them. For neither culinary and venereal desires and pleasures, nor feelings of fear and boldness concerning dangers of death, nor again the distributions and sharings of things that are appropriate in the practice of the present life, will have any place in the future life. But with respect to what is formal in these virtues, they will remain most perfectly in the blessed after the present life, inasmuch as the reason of each of the blessed will be most rightly disposed concerning the things that pertain to him according to that state, and the appetitive power will be entirely moved according to the direction of reason in those matters that pertain to that state. Hence AUGUSTINE, in the same place, says that "there, prudence will be without any danger of error, fortitude without the vexation of evils to be tolerated, temperance without the opposition of pleasures; so that it will be characteristic of prudence neither to prefer any good to God nor to make it equal to him; of fortitude to adhere to God most firmly; and of temperance to take pleasure in no unwholesome weakness." And concerning justice, it is clear what act it will have there, namely to be subject to God, because even in this life it pertains to justice to be subject to a superior.

Thus SAINT THOMAS. Again, in *In 3 Sent.*, d.33, q.1, a.4, he speaks as follows:

> Each of the aforementioned virtues has two acts: one that it exercises in relation to its proper matter, and another that it has when it attains the end. For example, the brave man, while he is in the danger of battle, performs an act

> concerning the proper matter of the virtue, namely the feelings of fear and boldness; but when he has returned home as victor, he has another act to perform, namely that of rejoicing over the victory won through the preceding battle. However, as has been said, some moral virtues are infused and some acquired, and the acquired ones give direction in civic life, and so have the civic good as their end. And because this citizenship will not remain in heaven, no act—whether concerning the end or concerning the proper matter according to which they are directed to the end—will be left to these virtues, and therefore the habits mentioned will be removed. But the infused moral virtues perfect man in the spiritual life, according to which he is a citizen of the city of God, and a member of the body of Christ, which is the Church. And this citizenship will not depart, but rather be perfected, in the future life. Hence there will remain for these virtues the acts that concern the proximate end of each virtue. And therefore the habits of the infused moral virtues will remain.

Thus SAINT THOMAS.

From these texts the following argument can be formulated. There will remain in heaven any habits that perfect the powers of the soul, since they do not include any imperfection in their essence, and are not opposed to—but rather contribute to—ultimate perfection. But the habits of the infused moral virtues are of this kind. Therefore, etc.

Here the first article ends. **{393}**

Article II: Objections

§1. Against the First Conclusion

I. Arguments of Scotus In the second article, argument is made against the conclusions.

SCOTUS (*In 3 Sent.*, d.33, q.1) argues against the first conclusion by arguing that it is not only in the sensitive part that moral virtues are present. *First,* he argues as follows:

> THE PHILOSOPHER says, in *Politics* 1, that it is necessary for a prince to have virtue in order to govern rightly, and he applies this remark to the higher part of the soul.

Second, he argues as follows:

> You say that justice is present in the will. Therefore, the general arguments concerning the presence of moral virtue in the will do not prove anything.

> Again, the authority of THE PHILOSOPHER concerning what is capable of obeying reason should not be understood as referring to the sensitive appetite alone. For if by "what is capable of obeying reason" he understands only that, he does not sufficiently divide the soul inasmuch as it is capable of moral virtue. And inasmuch as he intends to treat of the soul, he divides it insufficiently, for he treats of it inasmuch as it is receptive of moral virtue and justice; and with respect to justice, at least, the will is receptive of moral virtue. But the will is neither in the reason nor in the part capable of obeying reason, at least as you understand these two parts.

Third, he argues as follows:

> Before the definition of virtue, around the middle of Book I, THE PHILOSOPHER, wishing to investigate the essence of happiness, speaks as follows: "Accordingly, the life of nutrition and growth must be set aside. Next is the sensitive life, but this seems to be shared by horse and cow and every animal. There remains the life capable of operating belonging to one who possesses reason; of this, one part is such as to be well able to be persuaded by reason, and another part is such as to possess it and to understand."
>
> From this text it is clear that THE PHILOSOPHER excludes the sensitive part because it is not capable of operating according to the moral virtues. Consequently, the latter should not be posited as present principally in that part. Therefore, what "remains," namely what is "capable of operating" in such a one, that is, in "one who possesses reason," is the part of the soul that rises above the whole sensitive part; and ARISTOTLE divides it into what "understands" and what is "well able to be persuaded." Therefore, he understands the will to be present in what is "able to be persuaded by reason," because it is clear that by what "understands" he means the intellect. Thus, it seems possible to hold, from his explicit words, that he sometimes calls the will "that which is able to obey reason." Sometimes, however, he calls the sensitive appetite "that which is able to obey reason," as he does at the end of Book I. And just as "that which is able to obey reason" is taken in two ways, so too "rational" is taken in two ways: in one way strictly and primarily, and thus it pertains to the intellect alone; in another way neither strictly nor primarily—although the will is simply speaking "rational"—and thus it pertains to the will; but in a third way, improperly and by a transfer of meaning, "that which is able to obey reason" pertains to the sensitive appetite. Accordingly, the intermediary term, which is the will, is at one time, on the basis of one of the extremes, called "rational," and at another time, on the basis of the other extreme, called "able to obey reason." For, taking

> "reason" in the strict sense, the will is "that which is able to be persuaded by reason"; but taking "reason" in an improper sense, although still for what pertains to "mind," the will is "rational," and the appetite is not merely "able to be persuaded," but also "able to obey." These words should be weighed carefully. For the free choice is "well able to be persuaded," but is not so properly "able to obey"; but the sensitive appetite, which is not free, is not properly said to be "able to be persuaded," but is "able to obey," because it is subject to the command of the will.

Fourth, he argues as follows:

> There are many authoritative texts for the above-mentioned conclusion. One is that of AUGUSTINE, who, in *De moribus ecclesiae* 15, proposes that the four moral virtues are nothing other than ordered loves. Therefore, etc.

Fifth, he argues as follows:

> The will is undetermined with respect to opposites, not merely opposite objects, but also opposite ways of being related to them, namely rightly and not-rightly. Therefore, in order that it be related to them, or act, determinately and well, it needs something that determinatively inclines it to act well, and this is virtue. Therefore, etc.
>
> The inference is clear. For the only necessity of positing virtues in powers is so that powers that of themselves are able to act rightly and not-rightly might be ruled by them.
>
> The antecedent is proved as follows. The will is able to choose anything presented to it in which the essence of its primary object is presented. But in choosing such things it can act rightly and not-rightly.
>
> If you say that it is enough for reason to present rightly, and that therefore virtue is not required in the will, but only in the reason, this is false.
>
> First, because the reason would have to err in presenting before the will errs in choosing badly, and thus there would have been error in the intellect prior to the sin of the will, which is unreasonable, because then the punishment would precede the fault.
>
> Again, because, even granting that the will could be sufficiently determined by the intellect in choosing rightly, it does not follow that a habit is not {394} generated in the will. For the intellect is even more determined to judge rightly, since, inasmuch as it has an operation that precedes the act of the will, it acts purely naturally, and nevertheless it is not denied that in the intellect, from the frequency of its acts, there is generated a habit of judging rightly, namely prudence. Since, therefore, the will is not a power of itself more determined to one thing than is the intellect, from acts frequently cho-

> sen by the will there can be generated in it a certain facility that rightly inclines it to similar acts, and that I call "virtue."

Sixth, he argues as follows:

> Habits are posited in order that the powers may through them act not only rightly, but also well, with pleasure, and readily. But even if the will could be determined by the reason to choose rightly, it could not be determined to do so with pleasure and readily without a habit of its own.
>
> This is proved as follows. If one who has previously been vicious begins to be recalled to the contrary state, the reason dictates to the will that an object contrary to the vice ought to be chosen; and although the will chooses it, it does not do so with pleasure, for the previous vicious habit is, in the first act, not immediately destroyed as a whole, but rather is not destroyed at all, or is barely diminished. This is evident from experience: for it would be pleasurable for the one who possesses the vicious habit to choose according to his previous evil custom. Therefore, in order that the will do what is dictated by reason, there is required in it a habit for choosing an act in conformity with that habit.

II. Arguments of Aureolus AUREOLUS (*In 3 Sent.*, d.33, q.1, a.3) argues against the same conclusion by arguing that the moral virtues are equally present in both appetites, that is, the sensitive and the rational appetites, as in their subjects. *First,* he argues as follows:

> There is not greater simplicity in moral virtue than in bodily health, because both are placed in the first species of quality, and again because natural things have greater unity than do moral ones. But bodily health is not a simple quality, but rather binds together many qualities. For there is health only if the humors are proportioned not merely to one another, but also in their being ordered to a nature; so that the humors themselves constitute health by befitting the nature, that is, inasmuch as they are the foundation of this relation of befittingness. Something similar is clear in the case of beauty. For the beauty of a face is not a simple quality of nose or mouth alone, but is a shaping and coloring of all parts of the face according to fittingness; and nevertheless all these, inasmuch as they are befitting, are called the one beauty of the face. In these cases no form or quality is superadded; rather, all these things, inasmuch as they are befitting, are one health or one beauty resulting from the humors or qualities, which is why, when an alteration is made in any of the humors, health is lost at once. Accordingly, this will also be true in the case of moral virtue, which binds together many qualities that all together, inasmuch as they are the foundation of a fittingness in relation to

> man, are one moral virtue, which, consequently, can be present in many subjects, just as those qualities are.

Second, he argues as follows:

> Whenever several things concur as one whole and sufficient principle in relation to an act, a habit must be posited in each of the things that concur for that act. But the sensitive and the intellective appetites do concur in a virtuous act in the nature of a single principle, as is clear from the circumstances required for the virtuous act: for there must be present choice and firmness, which pertain to the will; and also readiness and obedience of the appetite in carrying out the choice of the will, which pertains to the sensitive appetite; and many similar circumstances, so that the appetite and the will are related to one another in the nature of a single principle. Therefore a virtuous habit, while existing as a unity, must perfect both powers.

Third, he argues as follows:

> By an argument from definition, whatever the nature of a virtue belongs to, the virtue itself also belongs to. But the definition of virtue belongs to a habit that perfects both the sensitive and the intellective appetites, and not to a habit that perfects only one of them. For "virtue is something that perfects the one who possesses it and renders his operation good." But "the one who possesses it" is, precisely, man, who is not, morally speaking, perfect, unless he is perfected with respect to both appetites, because it is with respect to both that he is a principle of a certain kind of act. Hence, if the correct choice were present in the will and the sensitive appetite were rebellious, he would act with difficulty and would not be a perfect man, nor would his operation be good simply speaking, but only in a certain respect. For it is proper to the virtuous man to act with pleasure.

Fourth, he argues as follows:

> Whenever a name and its definition are assigned to something inasmuch as it is the foundation of a relation, they should be assigned to it only to stand for all of the things, taken together, upon which the relation is founded or which constitute the foundation of the relation. This is clear from the following. The term "beauty of face" is assigned only to all of the qualities and shapes that are required for the relation of befittingness belonging to beauty. But the nature of moral virtue is assigned to qualities inasmuch as they constitute the foundation of a relation of appropriateness and befittingness. But a man is not, and is not said to be, in a fitting and appropriate state unless he is well disposed with respect to both appetites, that is, unless by the will

> he chooses and adheres to the good of reason and unless the appetite is mastered. Hence, if there is a falling short in either of these, it will be said that the man is not {395} as he should be, or as it is appropriate for him to be, in the matter of virtue.

Thus AUREOLUS argues in form.

§2. Against the Second Conclusion

Argument of Durandus DURANDUS (*In 3 Sent.*, d.33, q.2) argues against the second conclusion that the acquired intellectual and moral virtues are not generated by or through acts as through an active principle. He does so as follows:

> Either habits are caused by acts immediately or they are so caused mediately. They are not caused by acts immediately, because then a certain action would immediately terminate in a habit; and since that action would be an alteration, it would follow that alteration would immediately follow upon acts and dispositions, and THE PHILOSOPHER proves the contrary of this by his meaning in *Physics* 7. Nor are habits caused by acts mediately. For if I ask you to tell me that by whose mediation acts cause a habit, you will not be able to do so, for it is difficult to imagine such a thing. Therefore, acts are not related to habits as active principle of the latter.
>
> It remains, then, that acts are related to the generation of habits as passive principles. Again, concerning this point, a distinction must be made. For, properly speaking, what receives is called a passive principle, as wax is a passive principle in relation to the figure that it receives. Sometimes, however, it is the disposition according to which what receives does receive that is called a passive principle, as softness in the wax is a passive principle of the reception of the imprint. In the first sense, it is not the acts, but the power, that is a passive principle capable of receiving habits, for otherwise, when the acts are no longer present, the habit would not remain. But in the second sense, acts constitute a passive principle in relation to habits as a preceding disposition of the latter: not as a disposition necessary for existence in the way that quantity is necessary in the wax for the reception of the imprint, because then it would follow that the habits could not exist in potency unless the acts were present; but rather as a necessarily preceding disposition for the coming to be of the habits in the way that softness in the wax is a disposition for the reception of the figure. But there is a difference: what causes the softness of the wax need not cause the imprint; but the same thing that causes the act causes the habit, in a certain order, just as what causes heat

> in water also causes evaporation in it, in a certain order. For inasmuch as a power is more frequently brought to act, it is rendered more disposed and more ready to receive a similar act. But this disposition, or readiness, or ease, is the habit. For this reason, the same thing that causes acts, also causes their frequency, and consequently causes the habit.

Thus DURANDUS.

§3. *Against the Third Conclusion*

Arguments of Durandus DURANDUS (d.33, q.6) argues against the third conclusion that the moral virtues are not always infused together with grace and charity, and are not necessarily connected with the latter. *First,* he argues as follows:

> In baptized children, it is enough that there be infused into them in baptism what is enough for their salvation. But charity and grace are enough for salvation. Therefore, it is enough that grace and charity be infused into children in baptism. However, because charity necessarily presupposes faith and hope, it is necessary that faith and hope be infused together with charity.

Second, he argues as follows:

> If certain moral virtues were infused together with charity, they would, it seems, be as perfect as or more perfect than the acquired moral virtues, just as the wine made out of water by Christ at the wedding mentioned in *John* 2 was wine as good as or better than the wine produced by nature, and just as the health given by Christ to the sick was as perfect as or more perfect than health acquired by the beneficence of nature or through the operation of the medical art. Since, therefore, more perfect virtue more perfectly inclines to virtuous operation, if the moral virtues were infused into children in baptism, it would follow that, when they reached the state of adulthood, they would be inclined to virtuous moral acts as perfectly as or more perfectly than those who have the acquired moral virtues without the infused ones, as does the pagan who, through acquired moral virtues, lives well and decently.
>
> But this is false. For when baptized children reach the state of adulthood, they need persuasions and instructions in order to become accustomed to living virtuously just as if they had never been baptized. Therefore it does not seem that any moral virtues are infused into them in baptism. Hence the remark of CLEMENT that grace and habitual virtues are infused into children in baptism must be understood with reference to the theological virtues, and not with respect to any moral virtues whatsoever.

Third, he argues as follows:

> When sinners who are accustomed to carrying out vicious acts are converted and obtain remission of their sins through grace, the moral virtues are not infused into them. For if they were infused, by means of them such men would at once be able to readily and easily perform virtuous works, like those who have the acquired moral virtues. But this is not true. Rather, those who are newly contrite perform virtuous works with great difficulty and with the resistance of the sensitive appetite.

Fourth, he argues as follows:

> In those who are newly contrite and converted, vicious moral habits remain. But {396} it seems that neither acquired nor infused virtuous moral habits can co-exist with such habits. Therefore, etc.

Fifth, he argues as follows:

> The infused moral virtues are not infused together with grace into those who possess the acquired moral virtues prior to the infusion of grace if, for instance, a pagan practiced in the moral virtues converts to the faith, or if a virtuous believer sins mortally and afterwards converts.
>
> This is easily made clear. For such infused moral virtues would be either specifically the same as or different from the acquired virtues. They would not be the same, because different individuals of the same species cannot be simultaneously present in the same subject, as is clear from *Metaphysics* 5. And they would not be different, because then the infused virtues would be called "moral virtues" equivocally, just as the name "dog" is equivocally said of the barking animal and of the heavenly constellation. This is not right, because we neither say nor know anything of the infused moral virtues except inasmuch as we are guided by the acquired virtues, and this would not be the case if both the infused and the acquired virtues were called "moral virtues" by a pure equivocation, because thus it would be easy for a man to call "moral virtues" anything he wanted to, for by equivocation I can call what is white "black."

Sixth, he argues as follows:

> Such infused moral virtues would not be at all necessary or useful. Certainly not for choosing the substance of a good moral act, since the power alone, without any acquired or infused moral virtue, suffices for this purpose: for good acts can and do precede any such virtue, since moral virtues are generated by them. Nor are such virtues necessary for the sake of a ready and easy manner of acting, because the acquired virtues accomplish all this with-

out the infused virtues, and the infused virtues do not accomplish it without the acquired virtues. Nor again are such virtues necessary to direct acts to an end beyond that to which the acquired moral virtues direct them, because that is sufficiently brought about by faith, which presents the final end, and by charity, which causes an inclination to it; hence it is not necessary to posit any infused moral virtues for this purpose.

It might be said that such virtues are necessary in order that by means of them men live the spiritual life well, just as by means of the acquired moral virtues he lives the civic life well.

But this argument is invalid. For just as man lives the civic life well by means of the acquired moral virtues, so he lives the spiritual life well by means of the theological virtues infused into us, and it is not necessary to posit infused moral virtues for this purpose.

It might be said that infused moral virtues determine a midpoint with respect to the passions in a different way than do the acquired ones. For the unbeliever who has the acquired moral virtues judges that one should not consume more food than suffices for a good bodily regime, and does this with ease by means of acquired temperance. But the believer denies the body what would provide for a good bodily regime in order to subject the body to the spirit and repress the rebellion of the flesh against the spirit.

But this argument is invalid, because both the believer and the virtuous unbeliever determine a midpoint with respect to the passions in the same way. For each of them judges by means of temperance that as much food should be consumed as provides for a good bodily regime, not merely in order to preserve the health of the body, but also so that the lasciviousness of the body not cause an impulse to an act contrary to virtue or cause difficulty in the operation of virtue. And if the virtue of the believer in some cases does more, it does not do so by means of any moral virtue, but by means of the theological virtues, or by a special movement of the Holy Spirit.

Thus DURANDUS.

§4. *Against the Fourth Conclusion*

Arguments of Durandus The same DURANDUS (d.33, q.4) argues against the fourth conclusion. *First,* he argues that the moral virtues do not remain in heaven with respect to their acts. The argument for this, he says, is as follows:

> No power, however perfected by a habit, can issue in an act unless it has a present object. But the objects of the moral virtues will not be present in heaven. Therefore, the acts of the virtues will not be present there.
>
> The major premise is made clear as follows. Whether the object is a

> cause per se or a cause sine qua non of the act, the object is in any case always required for the act.
>
> The minor premise is made clear as follows. The objects of the moral virtues are, in the case of temperance, what is desirable and pleasurable in food and sex; in the case of courage, what is frightening and saddening in dangers; and in the case of justice, things that can be shared and distributed. But these will not be present in heaven. Therefore etc.

Second, he argues that no moral virtue which perfects the sensitive appetite will remain in heaven with respect to habit.
The argument for this, he says, is as follows:

> When a subject is destroyed, its accident is destroyed. But the subject of such virtues, namely the sensitive appetite, since it is a bodily power, is destroyed in death. Therefore, so is the habit itself.
>
> And if the sensitive appetite is restored at the resurrection, either it will not be numerically the same, and consequently neither will the habits, if they are miraculously restored, be numerically the same; or, if both the appetite and such habits were numerically the same, this would not be by our action, and for this reason it could not be said that the earlier habits will remain.

Thus DURANDUS argues in form.

Here the second article terminates. {397}

Article III: Responses

§1. To the Arguments against the First Conclusion

I. To the Arguments of Scotus [*p. 255*] In the third article it remains to respond to the objections stated above.

SAINT THOMAS responds to the form, as it were, of the *first* argument of SCOTUS against the first conclusion, in *Questions on the Virtues,* "On the Virtues in General", a.5, where he presents the following argument in the first objection:

> Greater perfection is required in one who commands in order for him to command rightly, than in one who carries out the command in order for him to carry it out rightly, because the ordering of the one who carries it out proceeds from the one who commands. But the will is related to an act of virtue as the one who commands it, while the irascible or concupiscible power is related to it as the one who obeys and carries it out. Since, therefore, virtue

> is present in the irascible or concupiscible power as in its subject, it seems that it should to a greater degree be present in the will.

Thus the argument; the response is as follows:

> It must be said that a judgment of reason suffices for the will to command. For the will naturally desires what is good according to reason, just as the concupiscible power desires what is pleasurable according to sense.

Thus SAINT THOMAS. From this text it is clear that that which is the ruler or commander among the parts of the soul need not have virtue in relation to all matters, but only in relation to those for which its nature alone, unqualified by any superadded habit, does not suffice.

It can also be said that the higher part of the soul has virtue in itself. However, this part is not the will, but the reason, which is the subject of prudence, and this prudence suffices for rectifying the intellect and the will. Hence, for the sake of greater clarification of the foregoing solution, SAINT THOMAS, in the same place, speaks as follows in the principal response:

> Through a habit of virtue the power that is the subject of the habit acquires a completion in relation to its act. Hence, a habit of virtue is not necessary for that to which a power extends by the very nature of its power. Now virtue orders powers to a good, for it is that which makes the one who possesses it good and renders his operation good. But the will, by the very essence of its power, has, of itself, what virtue accomplishes in other powers, for good is its object. Thus tending toward good is related to the will as tending toward the pleasurable is related to the concupiscible power, and as being directed to sound is related to the sense of hearing. Hence the will does not require any habit of virtue to incline it toward the good that is proportioned to it, because it tends toward this by the very essence of its power. But it does require a habit of virtue in order to tend toward the good that goes beyond proportion to its power.
>
> Now since the appetite of each thing tends toward the proper good of the one desiring, a good can exceed proportion to the will in two ways: in one way by reason of the species, and in another way by reason of the individual. It does so by reason of the species when the will is raised to a good that exceeds the limits of the human good. I mean by the "human" good that of which man is capable by his natural powers, and above the human good, there is the divine good, to which charity, and similarly hope, raise the will of man. A good exceeds proportion to the will by reason of the individual, in that one may seek what is the good of another, although here the will is not

> carried beyond the limits of the human good. In this way justice perfects the will, as do all of the virtues directed to another, such as generosity, magnificence, etc., as THE PHILOSOPHER says in *Ethics* 5. Accordingly, two virtues are present in the will as in their subject, namely charity and justice. A sign of this is that, although these virtues pertain to the appetitive part, nevertheless they do not concern the passions, as do temperance and fortitude, and thus it is clear that they are not present in the sensitive appetite, where the passions are, but in the rational appetite, that is, the will, where the passions are not, for every passion is present in the sensitive part of the soul, as is proved in *Physics* 7. But those virtues that concern the passions, namely courage with respect to feelings of fear and boldness and temperance with respect to pleasures, must, by the same argument, be present in the sensitive appetite. Nor is it necessary that there be some virtue in the will by reason of these passions, because the good in the latter is what is according to reason, and the will is naturally related to this by the essence of its power, since such is the proper good of the will.

Thus SAINT THOMAS. In the following article, the sixth one, he shows how prudence is present in the practical intellect as in its subject; and in article seven he shows how certain virtues are present in the speculative intellect.

From these texts it is clear that the opponent's inference is not valid, when, from the fact that ARISTOTLE says that the virtues are present in the higher part of the soul, he wishes to infer that they are present in the will. However, we concede that some—not all, as the opponent thinks—moral virtues are present in the will as in their subject. Furthermore, perhaps the opponent was mistaken, thinking that the will is the highest power of the soul, above all others. SAINT THOMAS proves the contrary of this in *ST* I, q.82, a.3, in *Questions on Truth*, q.22, a.11, and in many other places.

In response to the *second* argument we say *first*, that the case of justice and that of fortitude or temperance are not alike, as has been said. For justice is directed to the good of another, but temperance and fortitude to one's own good. Hence, justice is present in the will, but the other virtues are not, as has been said. Concerning this point SAINT THOMAS, in *ST* I–II, q.56, a.6, speaks as follows:

> Since a power is perfected for acting by a habit, {398} a power needs a habit to perfect it for acting well, that is, a habit of virtue, whenever its own nature as a power does not suffice for this purpose. Now the nature of every power is taken in relation to its object. Hence, since the object of the will is the good of man which is proportionate to the one willing, the will does not need

> a power to perfect it for this purpose. But if there is a good to be willed which is available to man but exceeds what is proportionate to his will, whether with respect to the whole species of man, as does the divine good, which transcends the limits of human nature, or with respect to the individual, as does the good of one's neighbor, in that case the will needs a virtue. Therefore, such virtues, namely charity, justice, etc., which order the feelings of man to God or to one's neighbor, are present in the will as in their subject.

Thus SAINT THOMAS. Again, in *In 3 Sent.*, d.33, q.2, a.4, qla.3, he speaks as follows:

> Justice cannot be present in the irascible or concupiscible power as in its subject, since it is not concerned with passions. For it is proper to justice to moderate not passions, but external actions directed toward another. Hence it must be present, as in its subject, in the power to which pertains the application of external things in their being ordered to another. Now to apply, according to AUGUSTINE, is the act of the will—not the will taken absolutely, inasmuch as it is of the end, but rather the will inasmuch as it presupposes the concurrence of reason, which orders something to another. Hence justice is present in the will, taken in the latter sense, as in its subject. For, inasmuch as the will concerns the end, no moral virtue can be present in it, because it has a natural inclination, as to its proper object, to the good that is civic and connatural to man. But inasmuch as the will concerns what is ordered to the end, a moral virtue, namely justice, can be present in the will, just as prudence is present in cogitative reason. And the argument is similar concerning all of the virtues, such as generosity, magnificence, etc., which are concerned not with the passions, but with operations.

Thus SAINT THOMAS. Again, in the same text, in the solution to the third objection, he speaks as follows:

> Although the will has command over all matters and acts of the virtues, certain virtues have a matter, namely passions, that more immediately pertain to other powers. Hence the virtues that principally concern passions are present in those powers as in their subjects. But the matter of certain virtues does not pertain to any power but the will. Hence the virtues that concern that matter are present in the will as in their subject.

Thus SAINT THOMAS. He presents something similar in *ST* II–II, q.58, a.4, where he gives an argument for why justice is present in the will as in its subject.

Second, we say that SAINT THOMAS never posited that all of the moral virtues are present in that which is capable of obeying reason—taking "that which is capable of obeying" in the precise sense as "the sensitive appetite"—as in their subject. Speaking generally, however, he does call any human appetite "that which is capable of obeying reason" or "that which is rational by participation." Concerning this point, in *In 3 Sent.*, d.33, q.2, a.4, qla.3, he speaks as follows:

> It is not only the irascible and concupiscible powers, but appetite in general, that is said to be "rational by participation," as THE PHILOSOPHER says in *Ethics* 1. Hence although the will by its essence is present in the intellective part, with respect to its act it in a way participates in reason, especially according as it concerns what is for the sake of the end to which it is directed inasmuch as it has been ordered by reason. Hence it can be the subject of moral virtue.

Thus SAINT THOMAS. He says something similar in *ST* I–II, q.56, a.6, ad 2:

> It must be said that "that which is rational by participation" is not only the irascible and concupiscible powers, but "the appetitive part" "altogether," that is, in general, as is said in *Ethics* 1. But the will is included within the appetitive part. Therefore, if any virtue is present in the will, it is a moral virtue, unless it is a theological one.

Thus SAINT THOMAS. He says something similar in *ST* II–II, q.58, a.4, ad 3, where he speaks as follows:

> That which is rational by participation is not only the irascible and concupiscible powers, but "the appetitive part altogether," as is said in *Ethics* 1, for every appetite obeys reason. But the will is included in the appetitive part. Therefore, the will can be a subject of moral virtue.

Thus SAINT THOMAS.

In response to the *third* objection we say *first,* that ARISTOTLE, in the text mentioned, does not mean that no power in the sensitive part can be a subject of moral virtue, but only that the apprehensive sensitive powers cannot be. For he expressly concedes that the appetitive sensitive powers can be. Concerning this point, SAINT THOMAS, in *ST* I–II, q.56, a.5, speaks as follows:

> Certain habits are posited in the internal apprehensive sensitive powers. This is clear from what THE PHILOSOPHER says in the book *On memory,* that in the remembering of one thing after another, custom, which is, as it were, a kind of nature, is operative. But a customary habit is nothing but a condition acquired by custom that has the manner of a nature. Hence CICE-

> RO, in the *Rhetoric*, says that "virtue is a habit that has the manner of a nature and is in keeping with reason." In man, however, what is acquired in the memory and in the other apprehensive sensitive powers is not a habit per se, but something annexed to the habits of the intellective part. Still, even if there are habits in these powers, they cannot be called virtues. For a virtue is a perfecting habit by which only what is good can be performed. Hence a virtue must be present in the power that is able to complete a good act. But cognition of the true is not completed in the apprehensive sensitive powers, {399} which are rather powers preparatory, as it were, to intellective cognition. Hence the virtues by which the true is known are present not in these powers, but rather in the intellect or reason.

Thus SAINT THOMAS. And immediately after, in the solution to the first objection, he speaks as follows:

> The sensitive appetite is related to the will or rational appetite as what is moved by the latter. Hence the operation of the appetitive power is completed in the sensitive appetite, and this is why the sensitive appetite is a subject of virtue. But the apprehensive sensitive powers are related to the intellect rather as movers, since the phantasms are related to the intellect as colors are to the power of sight, as is said in *De anima* 3. Hence the operation of knowledge terminates in the intellect, and this is why the cognitive virtues are present in the intellect or reason itself.

Thus SAINT THOMAS. From this text it is clear that no virtue is posited in the apprehensive sensitive powers, because in none of them is the operation of the power completed. The case of the appetitive sensitive powers is different, because operation of the appetitive power—especially operation concerning the passions—is completed in them, and not in the will. This is a further argument why neither fortitude, nor temperance, nor any other virtue that moderates passions, is present in the will, although it may be granted that the will can have certain habits concerning such passions, habits that do not have the essence of virtue, as will be said later.

Second, we say that both appetites, sensitive and intellectual, are said to be "rational by participation" and are called "that which is capable of obeying reason" and "that which is capable of being persuaded by reason"; and moral virtue is present in both of them, in the way that has often been mentioned.

And what the opponent says—that free choice is not properly called "that which is capable of obeying"—is not valid. For however free the will may be, it can never act against every dictate of reason, since it can no more be directed to anything other than an intellected good than the power of sight can be directed to something that is not colored. The will can, however, act against this or that particular judgment inasmuch as such action can itself proceed from the intellect, as has been shown at length in Distinction 25 of Book II.

In response to the *fourth* objection we say *first,* that the authoritative text of AUGUSTINE requires a good gloss. For it is clear that neither prudence nor any other intellectual virtue is love, and similarly that neither faith nor hope is love. SAINT THOMAS shows how the authoritative text mentioned ought to be understood in *ST* I–II, q.56, a.3, where he presents the following argument:

> AUGUSTINE says in the book *De moribus ecclesiae* that every virtue is love. But the subject of love is not the intellect, but the appetitive power alone. Therefore, no virtue is present in the intellect.

Thus the argument; the response is as follows:

> It must be said that the remark of AUGUSTINE must be understood of virtue simply speaking. It is not that every such virtue is love simply speaking, but rather that it depends on love, inasmuch as it depends on the will, whose first affection is love.

Thus SAINT THOMAS. Again, in q.62, a.2, he presents the following argument:

> AUGUSTINE, in the book *De moribus ecclesiae,* says that it is clear that the four cardinal virtues are "an ordering by love." But love is charity, which is held to be a theological virtue. Therefore, the moral virtues are not distinguished from the theological ones.

Thus the argument; the response is as follows:

> It must be said that, although charity is love, not every love is charity. Accordingly, when it is said that all virtue is an ordering of love, this can be understood either with respect to love generally speaking or with respect to the love of charity. If it is understood with respect to love generally speaking, then all virtue is said to be an ordering of love inasmuch as ordered affection is required for any of the cardinal virtues, and the root and principle of every affection is love. But if it is understood with respect to the love of charity, one is not given to understand by this that every other virtue is essentially charity, but that all of the other virtues in some way depend upon charity.

Thus SAINT THOMAS.

From these texts it is clear that authoritative texts of this kind need glosses. Otherwise AUGUSTINE would be contradicting both himself and the truth in many places. For again, in *The City of God,* in a passage quoted by SAINT THOMAS in *ST* I–II, q.58, a.2, he says that virtue is "the art of living rightly." But art is an intellectual virtue. Therefore, moral virtue does not differ from intellectual virtue; rather it follows that every virtue is present in the intellect as in its subject. But SAINT THOMAS, in the same place, shows how this remark should be understood:

> AUGUSTINE takes "art" generally for any right reason. Thus he also includes prudence, which is right reason concerning things to be done, just as art is right reason concerning things to be made, in "art." And according to his remark that virtue is "the art of living rightly," the term "virtue" belongs to prudence essentially, and to other virtues by way of participation, that is, inasmuch as they are directed by prudence.

Thus SAINT THOMAS.

Second, we say that, if it were held that every virtue is love, one could not conclude from this that every virtue is present in the will as in its subject. For love is present not merely in the intellective appetite, but also in the sensitive and the natural appetites. Therefore, the authoritative text mentioned concludes nothing whatsoever concerning the question.

In response to the *fifth* objection, we deny the first consequent. For, as was said in the solution of the first objection, the will has, by the very essence of its power, what virtue accomplishes in the other powers. Hence, the will does not need a habit, of which it itself would be the subject, in order to determine it concerning the matter of the passions, whether with respect to the object or with respect to the manner of acting. Rather, {400} a habit of virtue in the practical intellect suffices, as has often been said. The case of the matter of external actions directed to another is different.

In response to the *first* argument against this point we say that reason need not err in presenting before the will errs in choosing. Nevertheless, we do say that the will never chooses perversely unless some defect in reason precedes, for instance, because reason shows what is in itself evil under the aspect of good; or because, although it does show a good, it does not do so according to the full required consideration, or does not attend to everything that should be considered; or because it is deficient in the act of advising, of judging, or of prescribing. Concerning this point, SAINT THOMAS, in *ST* I, q.63, a.1, speaks as follows:

> Mortal sin can be present in an act of free choice in two ways. In one way by the fact that it chooses some evil, as man sins in choosing adultery, or something else that is of itself evil. This kind of sin always proceeds from some ignorance or error, for otherwise, what is evil would not be chosen as a good. The adulterer errs concerning a particular—choosing, because of an inclination of passion or habit, *this* pleasure in a disorderly act as something good to be accomplished at the present moment—even if he does not err concerning the universal, but rather holds the true opinion concerning it.
>
> In another way one can sin through free choice by choosing something that is of itself good, but without the order of the required measure or rule, so that the defect that introduces sin is only on the side of the choice, which is without the required order, and not on the side of the thing chosen, for instance, if someone were to choose to pray without attending to the order instituted by the church. This kind of sin does not require prior ignorance, but merely lack of consideration of what ought to be considered. This is the way in which the angel sinned, turning himself, by a free decision, to his own good, without being ordered to the rule of the divine will.

Thus SAINT THOMAS. And he presents something similar in *In 2 Sent.*, d.5, q.1, a.1, and in many other places.

It might be said that, according to this argument, every sin of the will proceeds from ignorance, or error, or a non-consideration by the intellect, and so the penalty seems to precede the fault.

In response to this we say that the inference is invalid. For the non-consideration that precedes the first evil choice and the first fault has the nature neither of a fault nor of a penalty, as SAINT THOMAS shows in many places, especially in *Questions on Evil,* q.1, a.3, where he speaks as follows:

> A non-application of the rule of reason and divine law is understood to be present in the will prior to a disorderly choice. But one should not look for a cause of this non-application of the rule mentioned, because the very freedom of the will, through which it is able to act or not act, suffices for this. And the actual non-attending to such a rule is, considered in itself, neither an evil nor a fault nor a penalty, because the soul is not bound, and is not able, to be always attending to this rule in actuality. Rather, it gets the essence of a fault from the fact that it proceeds to such a choice without an actual consideration of the rule. Just as an artisan errs not by the fact that he is not always keeping to the measure, but rather by the fact that he proceeds to operation without keeping to the measure, similarly the fault of the will consists not in the fact that it does not actually attend to the rule of reason

> or divine law, but in the fact that it proceeds to choice without having this rule or measure at hand. Hence it is that AUGUSTINE says in *The City of God* that the will is the cause of sin inasmuch as it is deficient, but compares that defect to silence or shadows, because it is a mere negation.

Thus SAINT THOMAS. And we have discussed this point at length in Book II. However, we do concede that error or ignorance never precedes any fault of the one who sins, but rather follows upon some sin, whether actual or original. The case of non-consideration, which is a pure negation, and not ignorance, error or privation, is different, because non-consideration precedes every fault, both in the first angel and in man.

In response to the *second* argument against the above-mentioned response, we say *first,* that a habit can be generated in the will by a repetition of its acts on the passions as matter, but that any such habit has, properly speaking, the nature not of a virtue, but rather of continence or incontinence. The argument for this was touched upon above, in the solution of the third objection: the operation of the appetitive power on the passions as matter is completed not in the will, but in the sensitive appetite. Concerning this point SAINT THOMAS, in *ST* II–II, q.155, a.1, speaks as follows:

> The word "continence" is understood, by different persons, in two ways. Some call continence that by which one abstains from all venereal pleasure, and hence THE APOSTLE, in *Galatians* 5, joins continence to chastity. Thus the perfect and principal continence is virginity, and the secondary one is widowhood. Hence, according to this way of speaking, virginity, which we called a virtue above, and continence have the same nature.
>
> Others, however, say that continence is that on account of which one resists depraved desires that are strong in him. This is the way in which THE PHILOSOPHER takes "continence" in *Ethics* 7, and this is the way in which it is taken in *The Sayings of the Fathers.* In this sense, however, continence does have something of the nature of virtue, namely inasmuch as the reason is made firm against the passions so as not to be led away by them. Nevertheless, it does not attain the perfect essence of moral virtue, by which even the sensitive appetite is subjected to reason in such a way that strong passions contrary to reason do not arise in it. **{401}** Hence THE PHILOSOPHER says in *Ethics* 4 that "continence is not a virtue, but is in a way mixed," that is, inasmuch as it has something of virtue but in a sense falls short of virtue. However, taking the name "virtue" in a larger sense, to stand for any principle of praiseworthy actions, we can say that continence is a virtue.

Thus SAINT THOMAS. And in a.3 he shows how continence is present in the will as in its subject:

> Every virtue existing in a subject keeps away from that subject the disposition it has when it is subject to the contrary vice. But the concupiscible power is in the same state in one who is continent and in one who is incontinent, because in both it breaks forth in strong depraved desires. Hence it is clear that concupiscence is not in the concupiscible power as in its subject. Similarly, reason is in the same state in both, because both the continent and the incontinent man have right reason, and both, when they are without passion, hold the proposition that illicit desires should not be pursued. The primary difference between them is in the act of choice: for the continent man, although he undergoes strong desires, chooses, because of reason, not to pursue them, but the incontinent man chooses, in spite of the opposition of reason, to pursue them. Therefore, continence must be present, as in its subject, in the power of soul whose act is choice, and this is the will.

Thus SAINT THOMAS.

From these texts it is clear that habits concerning the passions are caused in the will, but that they do not perfectly or properly have the essence of virtue, because they do not completely perfect the appetite that is moved by the passions. Moreover, in the following article, SAINT THOMAS shows how continence, which is in the will, is related to temperance, which is in the <sensitive> appetite, as the imperfect is related to the perfect. For the good of reason thrives more fully in the temperate than in the continent man.

Second, we say that the intellect has greater need of a habit of virtue in order to determine its act, both with respect to the object and with respect to the manner of acting, than does the will. Thus SAINT THOMAS, in *Questions on the Virtues,* "On the Virtues in General", a.5, obj.3, presents the following argument:

> In the cognitive part of the soul there is a natural cognition of first principles, and nevertheless there is in us an intellectual virtue in relation to this cognition, namely understanding, which is the habit concerning first principles. Therefore, too, there ought to be a virtue in the will in relation to that to which the will is naturally inclined.

Thus the argument; the response is as follows:

> It must be said that cognition occurs by means of a species, and the intellective power does not suffice by itself for cognition unless it receives species from sensible things. Hence, even with respect to what we naturally know,

> there must be a certain habit that in a way begins from the senses, as is said at the end of the *Posterior Analytics*. But the will does not need any species, and thus is unlike the intellect.

Thus SAINT THOMAS. Again, in obj.2, he presents the following argument:

> The will is not only of the ultimate end, but also of the other ends. But the will can be rightly or not rightly disposed with respect to desire for the other ends. For good men propose good ends for themselves, and evil men evil ends, as is said in *Ethics* 3: "As each one is, so does the end appear to him." Therefore, some habit of virtue that perfects the will is required for its rightness.

Thus the argument; the response is as follows:

> It must be said that the natural inclination of the will is not merely toward the ultimate end, but to the end shown to it by reason. For the object of the will is a good that is understood, to which the will is directed by nature, just as any power is directed to its object provided that this is its proper good. And nevertheless, one may sin concerning this point, inasmuch as the judgment of reason is cut off by passion.

Thus SAINT THOMAS. And he speaks as follows concerning these points in *Questions on Truth*, q.24, a.2:

> Although three things, namely cognition, appetite, and operation itself, concur in our operation, the whole nature of freedom depends on the mode of cognition. For appetite follows cognition, since appetite is only for a good proposed to it by the cognitive power. The reason why appetite sometimes seems not to follow cognition is that appetite and the judgment of cognition are not taken with respect to the same thing. For appetite concerns a particular possible operation, while the judgment of reason sometimes concerns a universal that is sometimes contrary to appetite. But judgment concerning a particular possible operation as something present can never be contrary to appetite. For although one who wishes to fornicate knows as a universal that fornication is an evil, nevertheless he makes the judgment to himself that this act of fornication is, as something present, a good, and he chooses it under the aspect of a good; for no-one, as DIONYSIUS says, intends evil in acting. But if nothing hinders it, movement or operation follows on appetite. Hence, if the judgment of the cognitive power is not in someone's power, but is determined for him by something else, then neither will appetite be in his power, and consequently neither, absolutely speaking, will movement or operation etc.

Thus SAINT THOMAS.

In response to the *sixth* objection we deny the minor premise. For, as was said above, the will has, by the nature of its power and without any superadded habit, in relation to its proper good what other powers have by means of superadded habits, namely the ability to act firmly, readily, and with pleasure.

In response to the argument for the minor premise, we say that in a case in which someone who was previously vicious begins to be recalled to the opposite state, he does not at once choose with pleasure, {402} but only with difficulty. But this difficulty comes entirely from the side of the sensitive appetite, that is, because the passions of the latter oppose such a choice, and not from the side of the will, which of itself readily and with pleasure chooses its own good presented to it by reason. Concerning this point SAINT THOMAS, in *Questions on the Virtues,* "On the Virtues in General", a.4, ad 2, speaks as follows:

> There cannot be an act of reason belonging to the irascible or concupiscible power alone, apart from reason. What is most primary in an act of virtue, namely choice, belongs to reason, just as in any operation the act of the agent is more primary than the being affected of the patient. For reason commands the irascible and concupiscible powers. Therefore, virtue is not said to be present in the irascible and concupiscible powers, as if the whole act of virtue, or the main part of it, were accomplished by these powers, but rather inasmuch as, by the habit of virtue, they give the ultimate completeness of goodness to the act of virtue by the fact that they follow the order of reason without difficulty.

Thus SAINT THOMAS. Again, in *ST* I–II, q.56, a.4, ad 4, he speaks as follows:

> Two things are present in choice: intending of the end, which pertains to moral virtue, and prior acceptance of what is for the sake of the end, which pertains to prudence, as is said in *Ethics* 6. But posession of right intending of the end with respect to the passions of the soul comes about from a good disposition of the irascible and concupiscible powers. Hence the moral virtues, which concern the passions, are in the irascible and concupiscible powers, but prudence is in reason.

Thus SAINT THOMAS.

From these texts it is clear that when a vicious man begins to move away from vice and attend to virtue, it is because of the opposition of the sensitive appetite that he experiences difficulty.

It can also be said that he experiences difficulty because of habits formed in the will, namely incontinence or something similar. But, as has been said above, such habits do not, properly speaking, have the essence of vice, nor do the opposite habits, such as continence, properly speaking, have the essence of virtue. Hence, it is highly likely that, prior—whether temporally or in the order of nature—to habits of temperance, fortitude, or gentleness being formed in the irascible or concupiscible powers, habits of continence concerning desires, feelings of anger, or other passions, are formed in the will; and that conversely, prior to a habit of intemperance being formed in the concupiscible power, a habit of incontinence is formed in the will: for continence causes a disposition to temperance, and incontinence a disposition to intemperance. And it is consistent with this that no such habit is simply speaking necessarily present in the will for the sake of the will, although it may be necessary for the sake of the sensitive appetite, so that it not be led away from reason. SAINT THOMAS seems to address the question with respect to these points in *ST* II–II, q.155, a.4, ad 3, where he speaks as follows:

> The will is closer to reason than is the concupiscible power. Hence the good of reason, for which virtue is praised, is seen to be greater in reaching not merely the will, but also the concupiscible power, which occurs in one who is temperate, than if it reaches only the will, as occurs in one who is continent.

Thus SAINT THOMAS. From this text it seems that reason imprints a habit of continence in the will before it imprints a habit of temperance in the concupiscible power, just as the imperfect is prior to the perfect in the order of generation. Something has been said concerning this point in the proof of the first conclusion, namely that the temperate man is habituated in both appetites, that is, both the higher and the lower.

II. To the Arguments of Aureolus [*p. 258*] In response to the *first* argument of AUREOLUS against the same conclusion we say that it, and all of the following arguments, show that the moral virtues are in a way present in both appetites. Concerning this point SAINT THOMAS, in *ST* I–II, q.56, a.2, speaks as follows:

> There are two ways in which something can be present in two things. In one way such that it is equally present in both, and thus it is impossible for one virtue to be present in two powers. For diversity of powers is taken according to the generic features of their objects, but diversity of habits according to specific features. Hence, wherever there is a diversity of powers there is a di-

> versity of habits, but not the reverse. In another way something can be present in two or more things not equally, but according to a certain order: thus a virtue can belong to several powers in such a way that it is principally present in one but extends to others by way of diffusion; or, by way of disposition, according as one power is moved by another or receives from another.

Thus SAINT THOMAS. And in the same text he gives examples. Walking, although it is one act, "proceeds from reason as what directs, from the will as what moves, and from the locomotive power as what carries out the command." "Prudence is present in the reason as in its subject but presupposes rightness of will as its principle." And "knowledge is a prerequisite of moral virtue inasmuch as moral virtue operates according to right reason, but moral virtue is present essentially in the appetite." Thus, with respect to the present question, one can say that the moral virtues concerning the passions are in a way present in both appetites, being present essentially in the sensitive appetite, but present dispositively, causatively, or inchoatively in the will, inasmuch as they are preceded by habits in the will through which the sensitive appetite more easily submits to reason and receives the habit of virtue, as was said of continence and temperance in the reponse to the fifth objection of SCOTUS. {403}

Second, we say that the conclusion principally intended by the opponent is false. For moral virtue does not intrinsically and essentially involve two habits, one present in the will and the other in the sense-power. Concerning this point, SAINT THOMAS, in *ST* I–II, q.54, a.4, speaks as follows:

> A habit directed to operation is the perfection of a power. But every perfection is proportioned to its perfectible. Hence, just as a power, although one, extends to many things inasmuch as they agree in one thing, namely the general nature of the power's object, so too a habit extends to many things inasmuch as they are directed to one thing, such as the one special nature of the object, or one nature, or one principle. If, therefore, we were to consider a habit according to the things to which it extends, we would find multiplicity in it. But because that multiplicity is directed to some one thing to which the habit is primarily related, a habit is a simple quality, not one constituted out of many habits even if it extends to many things. For one habit extends to many things only in their being directed to the one thing from which it gets its unity.

Thus SAINT THOMAS. Again, in the same text, he argues as follows:

> A habit, since it is a quality, is a simple form. But nothing that is simple is constituted out of many things. Therefore, etc.

In response to the *first* argument we deny the major premise. For the habit of moral virtue is simpler than health or bodily beauty, just as the subject perfectible by moral virtue is simpler than the subject perfectible by health or beauty.

The *first* argument <for the major premise> is invalid, because although both are in the first species of quality as in their remote genus, they differ in proximate genus as a bodily quality differs from a spiritual one; again, because health is said to be a habit that perfects a thing in the ordering of it to its nature, but moral virtue perfects a power in the ordering of it to its operation, and operation is simpler than bodily nature; and again, because health and moral virtue are both called habits or virtues by equivocation. Concerning these points SAINT THOMAS, in *ST* I–II, q.50, a.1, speaks as follows:

> A habit is a disposition of a subject existing in potency either to form or to operation.
>
> According, then, as "habit" implies a disposition to operation, no habit is primarily present in the body as in its subject. For every operation of the body proceeds either from a natural quality of the body or from the soul moving the body. With respect to operations that proceed from nature, the body is not disposed by any habit, because the natural powers are determined to one thing, and, as has been said, a habitual disposition is required where a subject is in potency to many things. Operations that proceed from the soul through the body belong primarily to the soul itself and secondarily to its body. But habits are proportioned to operations, and hence like habits are caused by like acts, as is said in *Ethics* 2. Therefore, dispositions to such operations are present primarily in the soul, and secondarily in the body, inasmuch as the body is disposed and habituated to subserve the operations of the soul with readiness.
>
> But if we speak of the disposition of a subject to form, then an habitual disposition can be present in the body, which is related to the soul as subject to form. And in this sense health, beauty, and such things are called habitual dispositions. However, they do not perfectly have the nature of habits, because their causes are by their very nature transient.

Thus SAINT THOMAS. From this text it is clear that health and beauty on the one hand and moral virtue on the other are not univocally called "virtues" or "habits." However, SAINT THOMAS shows that a bodily habit can, without being many habits, be present in diverse partial subjects and involve several subjects, in *ST* I–II, q.54, a.1, where he speaks as follows:

> Habits are dispositions of something existing in potency to something, whether to a nature or to an operation or end of nature. With respect to habits that are dispositions to a nature, it is clear that several of them can be present in one subject from the fact that the parts of a single subject can be considered separately, and habits are named according to the dispositions of these parts. For instance, if we take the parts of the human body, the humors, inasmuch as they are disposed in keeping with human nature, constitute a habit or disposition of health; and if we take the homogenous parts, such as the nerves, bones, and flesh, their disposition in being ordered to human nature is strength or leanness; and if we take the members, such as the hand and foot, etc., their disposition appropriate to human nature is beauty. And thus several habits or dispositions are present in the same thing.

Thus SAINT THOMAS. From this text it is clear that bodily habits are equally present in diverse subjects, as the habit of health implies several humors, together with their commensuration with one another, and as beauty implies several members commensurate with one another and appropriately ordered. Consequently, such habits are not simple qualities. The case of the habits of the virtues is different. But although bodily habits are constituted out of diverse heterogeneous parts, they are not constituted out of diverse habits. Thus it is clear that the first argument for the major premise, and similarly the second one, are invalid, because certain moral things are simpler than certain natural, and especially bodily, things.

In response to the *second* argument we say that, although the will and sensitive appetite concur to make up the nature of a single active principle with respect to the act of virtue concerning the passions, nevertheless the will of itself does not {404} need to be perfected by a habit of virtue as does the sensitive appetite, even though it is perfected by certain habits that do not have the essence of virtue, as has often been said in response to the fifth and sixth arguments of SCOTUS. Nevertheless, the present argument and the preceding one presuppose one thing that is false, namely that an act of the sensitive appetite concurs in making up the matter of any moral virtue. Concerning this point, SAINT THOMAS, in *ST* II–II, q.58, a.4, speaks as follows:

> The subject of a virtue is the power whose act the virtue is ordered to rectifying. But justice is not ordered to directing any cognitive act, for we are not

> called just from the fact that we know something rightly. Therefore, the subject of justice is not the intellect or reason, which is a cognitive power. Rather, because we are called just by the fact that we do something rightly, and because the proximate principle of action is the appetitive power, justice must be present in the appetitive power as in its subject. But there are two appetites, namely the will, which is present in the reason, and the sensitive appetite, which follows on the apprehension of the sense-power and which is divided into the irascible and concupiscible powers. Now to give back to each what is his cannot proceed from the sensitive appetite, because sensitive apprehension does not extend to the ability to know the relation of one thing to another, which is a property of reason. Hence justice cannot be present in the irascible or concupiscible power, but only in the will, as in its subject. Hence THE PHILOSOPHER defines justice by an act of the will.

Thus SAINT THOMAS.

In response to the *third* argument, we deny the minor premise, which implies three things that are false. The first is that a habit constituted out of several things perfects both kinds of appetite. The second is that it is necessary for the perfection of man, especially in the matter of the passions, that both appetites be perfected by some superadded habit. The third is that in the matter of actions, and especially in the matter of justice, it is necessary that both appetites be perfected by a habit of virtue. The falsity of these three points is clear from what has frequently been said above.

In response to the *fourth* argument we deny the minor premise. For the nature of moral virtue is not attributed to diverse qualities, but to one simple habitual quality that is not constituted out of several habits or qualities.

In response to the argument for the minor premise we say that man is appropriately and fittingly related to the moral matter of the passions by the habit of prudence, which is present in the practical intellect, and by the habit of the virtue in the sensitive appetite, without any habit of virtue being posited in the will. Similarly, he is appropriately and fittingly related to the matter of action by the habit of prudence and by the virtue of justice, which is in the will, without any habit of virtue being posited in the sense-appetite. Hence, if the opponent's way of arguing were valid, it would show that moral virtue is constituted out of not only two partial habits existing in diverse subjects, but rather out of three, one in the reason, another in the will, and another in the sense-appetite. This is clear if one applies the opponent's arguments to this point. For in order for man to be in a fitting and appropriate state and to be morally perfect, the three habits mentioned are required by the arguments. The result is false and ridiculous. Hence, the habits that concur in one act of virtue do not all constitute a habit of virtue that is intrinsically one. Nor do all of the things that concur in the generation of a habit of virtue belong to its essence. Otherwise prudence would be part of every moral virtue, because prudence cannot be generated or exist or grow without them, nor can they without prudence.

§2. *To the Arguments against the Second Conclusion*

To the Argument of Durandus In response to the argument of DURANDUS against the second conclusion [p. 260] we say *first* that human acts are a principle of acquired moral or intellectual virtue not merely in the manner of a passive principle, but more truly in the manner of an active principle, or perhaps in the manner of action and production.

In response to the argument against this point we say that "habit" signifies two things: the first is a quality that is not easily changed, and the second is an ordering or a relation to a nature or to an operation of a nature. In the first sense, act immediately produces habit; but in the second sense, habit is caused by act not immediately, but subsequently. We have seen something concerning this point in a general way already. And concerning this point SAINT THOMAS, in *ST,* I–II, q.50, a.1, obj.3, presents the following argument:

> All bodily dispositions are subject to alteration. But alteration is only in the third kind of quality, which is contradistinguished from habit. Therefore, no habit is present in the body.

Thus the argument; the response is as follows:

> It must be said that the balancing of passible qualities in keeping with what is appropriate to a nature has the essence of a disposition or habit. Therefore, when alteration in the passible qualities—hot, cold, moist and dry—occurs, there occurs as a result alteration with respect to sickness and health. Primarily and per se, however, there is no alteration with respect to such habits and dispositions.

Thus SAINT THOMAS. Again, in q.52, a.1, ad 3, he speaks as follows:

> Alteration is primarily in qualities of the third kind. But there can in a secondary way be alteration in qualities of the first kind. For when alteration with respect to hot and cold occurs, the result is that the animal is altered

> with respect to {405} healthy and sick. And similarly, when there is alteration with respect to the passions of the sensitive appetite, or with respect to the apprehensive sensitive powers, there follows alteration with respect to knowledge and virtue, as is said in *Physics* 7.

Thus SAINT THOMAS. Again, in *Questions on the Virtues,* "On the Virtues in General", a.9, ad 20, he speaks as follows:

> Properly speaking, a thing is not said to be "altered" inasmuch as it achieves its proper perfection. Hence, since virtue is the proper perfection of man, man is not said to be "altered" inasmuch as he acquires virtue, except, perhaps, accidentally, inasmuch as a change in the sensitive part of the soul, in which the passions of the soul are present, pertains to virtue.

Thus SAINT THOMAS.

From these texts it is clear that alteration pertains to the habit of virtue not primarily and per se, but derivatively *(ex consequentia),* and this, with respect to three ways of speaking. The first is to say that this is because the qualities called virtues are neither acquired, nor lost, nor increased, nor diminished, unless some other alteration first occurs. The second way is to say that, although alteration can result principally in such qualities, it cannot result principally in relation, which is of the nature of habit or virtue. A third way of speaking could be to say that, although a certain change could result principally and per se in such habits, this change is not properly called an "alteration"; but this third way of speaking is less good than the others, for although it says something about good habits, it says nothing about corrupt and vicious ones, as is clear.

Second, we say that to hold that act is related to habit as having the nature of a passive principle, and not at all an active principle, is scarcely valid.

First, because a disposition, whether to form or to operation, is never more actual than that to which it disposes. But it is clear that second actuality is always more actual than is habit. Therefore, it is ridiculous to say that second actuality is related to habit not in any category of active causality, but merely in a category of passive disposition.

Again, because the position on the one hand posits that act disposes a power to receive a habit and on the other hand says that habit disposes a power to receive an act. Thus it posits a circularity in material causes and dispositions.

Again, because the position cannot maintain that acts that follow from a habit are in any way a principle of the growth of the habit. For that they are not a passive principle is clear from the fact that the habit has already been received, and no disposition temporally succeeds the form to which it disposes; nor are they an active principle, as the opponent says; and so they are in no way a principle.

Again, because the position is strange, and contrary to the common school and the sayings of the doctors.

§3. To the Arguments against the Third Conclusion

To the Arguments of Durandus [*p. 261*] In response to the *first* argument against the third conclusion, we deny the minor premise. For the three theological virtues direct man immediately to the ultimate end, namely God. But without intermediate habits, they do not suffice to direct, by way of choice, all human actions and passions to their subject, to the ultimate end, and to one's neighbor—although they may suffice to do so by way of command. Concerning this point SAINT THOMAS, in *ST* I–II, q.63, a.3, presents the following argument:

> Much less is there anything superfluous in the operations of God than in the operations of nature. But the theological virtues suffice to direct us to the supernatural good. Therefore, there are no other supernatural virtues that ought to be caused in us by God.

Thus the argument; the response is as follows:

> It must be said that the theological virtues sufficiently direct us to the supernatural end, in an incipient way, in an immediate relation to God. But the soul needs to be perfected by other virtues in relation to other things, although in an order directed to God.

Thus SAINT THOMAS. Again, in q.65, a.3, he speaks as follows:

> All of the moral virtues are infused together with charity. The reason is as follows. God operates no less perfectly in works of grace than in works of nature. But we see that in works of nature no principle of operations is present in any thing unless whatever is necessary to complete these operations is also present in it; for example, in the animals there are present organs by means of which the operations that the animal has the power to perform can be completed. But it is clear that charity, inasmuch as it orders man to the ultimate end, is a principle of all good operations that can be directed to the ultimate end. Hence, all of the moral virtues, by which man completes vari-

> ous kinds of good operations, must be infused together with charity. And thus it is clear that the infused moral virtues are interconnected not only because of prudence, but also because of charity, and that one who loses charity loses all of the infused moral virtues.

Thus SAINT THOMAS. Again, in the same place, he presents the following argument:

> It is inappropriate for several things to be directed to that for which one thing suffices. But charity alone suffices for accomplishing all operations of the virtues, as is clear from what is said in *1 Corinthians* 13: "Charity is patient, kind, etc." Therefore it seems that if one has charity, the other virtues are superfluous.

Thus the argument; the response is as follows:

> It must be said that, in order for the act of a lower power to be perfect, it is required that perfection be present not only in the higher power, but also in the lower one. For if a principal {406} agent is appropriately disposed, perfect action will not follow unless unless his instrument is also well disposed. Hence, in order that man act well in things directed to the end, it is necessary not only that he be well disposed by charity in relation to the end, but also that he have the virtues by which he is well disposed in relation to what is directed to the end. For the virtue concerning the end is principal and mover in relation to the virtues concerning what is directed to the end. Hence it is necessary to have the other virtues together with charity.

Thus SAINT THOMAS.

Nor is it valid to say that the virtues are not given to children in baptism, but only later. Hence SAINT THOMAS, in *In 4 Sent.*, d.4, q.2, a.2, qla.1, speaks as follows:

> Some say that grace and the virtues are given to children in baptism, but that the virtues are given not in themselves, but in their root, namely grace, which is the root of the virtues in the way that the essence of the soul is the root of its powers; but that later, when, once the organs are perfected, the powers are freed, the virtues flow into the powers from the essence of the soul.
>
> But this, as such, cannot be the case, because then, if children suffer madness before they reach maturity, the powers would never be set free in them, and so they would never possess the virtues explicitly. Besides, the fact that powers are tied up by some impediment impedes not habit, but act, for sleepers and drunkards possess habits, although the latter are tied up.

> Therefore, what others say is better, namely that grace and the virtues are given to children in baptism, but that the habits are tied up because of the state of childhood, just as they are in the sleeper because of his sleep; but that when childhood passes, the virtues cause an inclination to good operation if one does not resist the Holy Spirit.

Thus SAINT THOMAS.

SAINT THOMAS gives the solution to the *second* argument in *ST* III, q.69, a.4, obj.3, where he presents the following argument:

> Virtue is habit, and it pertains to the essence of habit to be a quality not easily removed by which one operates easily and with pleasure. But after baptism there remains in man a readiness for evil, by which virtue is destroyed, as well as a difficulty in doing good, which is the act of the virtues. Therefore, man does not obtain grace and the virtues by baptism.

Thus the argument; the response is as follows:

> It must be said that difficulty in doing good and readiness for evil are found in the baptized not because of a lack of the habits of the virtues, but because of concupiscence, which is not wholly removed in baptism, but is through baptism diminished so that man is not conquered by it.

Thus SAINT THOMAS. Again, in the passage of *In 4 Sent.* mentioned above, ad 4, he speaks as follows:

> Habit makes one disposed for an act by removing the indisposition that comes from the imperfection of a power, but not by removing the indisposition on the side of the body, as is clear in the case of those who are asleep.

Thus SAINT THOMAS.

From these texts it is clear that the habits of the infused virtues incline the baptized child, once he reaches adulthood, to the operations of the virtues as perfectly as, or more perfectly than, do the habits of the acquired virtues. This is so on the side of the power, but not on the side of the body, because they do not remove concupiscence or the other indispositions to good left over from original sin.

Nor is the opponent's argument valid that the baptized must be instructed in morals just as if they were not baptized. For just as they must be instructed in matters pertaining to morals, so they must be instructed in matters pertaining to faith, hope, and charity, and yet the opponent does not deny that the baptized have the theological virtues; therefore, he should not deny that they have infused moral virtues. The cause of this is given by BLESSED THOMAS in *In 3 Sent.*, d.23, q.3, a.2, where he presents the following argument:

> Habit is of itself sufficient for moving a power to an act. But a member of the faithful is incapable of the act of faith unless he is instructed. Therefore, faith is an acquired habit.

Thus the argument; the response is as follows:

> Infused habit is like innate habit. For just as natural habit is given in creation, so infused habit is given in redemption. But a natural habit, such as the habit of first principles, requires that cognition be determined by the sense-power; an acquired habit does not require this, because while it is being acquired it receives a determination from its act. Similarly, the habit of faith must receive a determination on our part. With respect to this determination, faith is said to be acquired through the science of theology, which distinguishes articles, just as the habit of first principles is said to be acquired through the sense-power with respect to the distinction of principles, but not with respect to the light in which the principles are known.

Thus SAINT THOMAS, in ad 1. Again, in ad 4 of the text quoted, he speaks as follows:

> The infused habit of faith cannot issue in act unless faith is determined either by God through revelation or by man through doctrine. And the case of the habit of first principles is similar.

Thus SAINT THOMAS. And what he says of faith he understands of every infused habit, both intellectual and moral.

But what the opponent further says about the remark of CLEMENT is false and erroneous. For CLEMENT, and all of the glossators, are speaking not only about theological virtues, but also about the others; this is true not only of CLEMENT, but also of *The Glosses of the Saints.* Hence, in commenting on the text of *Titus* 3, "He has made us saved through the cleansing of regeneration," that is, through baptism, "and of the renewing of the Holy Spirit, which He poured out on us abundantly," THE GLOSS says "for remission of sins and for abundance of virtues." But an "abundance" of virtues would not be given if only the three theological habits were infused, because they do not suffice for the spiritual life, as has been shown above in response to the first argument. {407} And many other remarks of THE SAINTS are contrary to what DURANDUS presents.

SAINT THOMAS responds to the *third* argument in *In 4 Sent.*, d.14, q.2, a.2, where he speaks as follows:

> Ease in performing the operations of the virtues can come from two things: from a preceding custom, in which case the ability or ease is not immediately, from the beginning, conferred by the infused virtue; or from a strong adherence to the object of virtue, in which case the ease is present immediately, from the beginning, in the infused virtue.

Thus SAINT THOMAS. Again, in *ST* III, q.89, a.1, he presents the following argument:

> One who possesses virtue performs the acts of the virtues without difficulty and with pleasure; hence THE PHILOSOPHER says, in *Ethics* 1, that "he is not just who does not rejoice in just action." But many who are repentant still experience difficulty in performing the acts of the virtues. Therefore, the virtues are not restored through repentance.

Thus the argument; the response is as follows:

> It must be said that sometimes after the initial act of repentance, namely contrition, there remain certain remnants of sins, namely dispositions caused by previous acts of sin, which present the penitent with difficulty in performing the acts of virtue. But inasmuch as he acts out of the inclination given by charity and the other virtues, the penitent performs the acts of the virtues with pleasure and without difficulty. It is as if a virtuous man should accidentally experience difficulty in carrying out an act of virtue on account of sleepiness, or some indisposition of the body.

Thus SAINT THOMAS. Again, in *ST* I–II, q.65, a.3, he presents the following argument:

> One who possesses a habit of virtue performs the deeds that pertain to the virtue with ease, and these in themselves please him; hence, a sign of a habit is the pleasure that occurs in the act, as is said in *Ethics* 2. But many possess charity, and are without mortal sin, who nevertheless experience difficulty in the acts of the virtues, and these acts do not please them in themselves, but only inasmuch as they are referred to charity. Therefore, many possess charity who do not possess the other virtues.

Thus the argument; the response is as follows:

> It must be said that it sometimes happens that one who possesses the habit of the virtues experiences difficulty in acting and consequently does not feel

> pleasure or complacency in the act, on account of some extrinsic supervening impediment. For example, one who possesses the habit of scientific knowledge may experience difficulty in understanding because of sleepiness or some other weakness. Similarly, the habits of the infused moral virtues sometimes experience difficulty in acting because of contrary dispositions left over from previous acts. This difficulty does not occur in the case of the acquired moral virtues, because through the exercise of the acts by which they are acquired, even the contrary dispositions are removed.

Thus SAINT THOMAS. Again, in *Questions on the Virtues*, "On the Virtues in General", a.10, ad 14, he speaks as follows:

> The passions that cause an inclination to evil are not totally removed either by acquired or by infused virtue, except, perhaps, miraculously. For there always, even after the acquisition of virtue, remains the struggle of the flesh against the spirit, of which THE APOSTLE says, in *Galatians* 5, that the flesh desires in opposition to the spirit, and the spirit in opposition to the flesh. However, through virtue, both infused and acquired, these passions are altered so that one is not uncontrollably moved by them. Acquired virtue overcomes the passions in one way, and infused virtue in another. For acquired virtue overcomes inasmuch as the struggle is less felt, which occurs through a cause belonging to the virtue itself, because through the frequent acts by which the man is made accustomed to virtue he has become unaccustomed to obeying the passions and accustomed to resisting them, from which it follows that he feels their aggravation less strongly. But infused virtue overcomes inasmuch as it brings it about that the passions, even if they agitate, do not in any way dominate. For infused virtue brings it about that the passions in no way obey the desires for sin, and it does this infallibly while it remains. But acquired virtue is deficient in this point, although in only a few cases, just as the other natural inclinations are deficient in rare cases. Hence THE APOSTLE, in *Romans* 7, says "When we were in the flesh, the passions of the sins were at work in our minds, so that etc."

Thus SAINT THOMAS. Again, in ad 15, he speaks as follows:

> Because infused virtue does not always immediately remove the feeling of the passions in the way that acquired virtue does, it does not immediately act with the same pleasure. But this is not opposed to the essence of virtue. For sometimes it is enough for virtue to act without pain; and, on account of the annoyances which it feels, it is not required that it act with pleasure, as THE PHILOSOPHER says.

Thus SAINT THOMAS.

From these texts it is clear that the antecedent of the opponent's argument is false, because not only the theological habits, but also the moral virtues, are infused.

Nor is the argument for the antecedent valid, because it is founded upon one false proposition, namely that whoever is habituated by a habit of virtue is able to perform the act of that virtue readily, with pleasure, etc. The falsity of this proposition has been shown in many places.

In response to the *fourth* objection we deny the first part of the antecedent, because no vicious habit is compatible with grace. Concerning this point SAINT THOMAS, in *Questions on the Virtues,* "On the Virtues in General", a.10, presents the following argument:

> We hold that by many evil acts, one or more vicious habits are caused in a man. But it is clear that in one act of contrition his sins are forgiven him and grace is infused into him. {408} But an acquired habit is not destroyed or generated through one act. If, therefore, the moral virtues are infused together with grace, it follows that a habit of moral virtue is present simultaneously with the habit of the vice opposed to it, which is impossible.

Thus the argument; the response is as follows:

> It must be said that, although an acquired habit is not destroyed by one simple act, an act of contrition is able to destroy a generated habit of vice by the power of grace. Hence, once a habit of intemperance is broken, it remains, along with the infused virtue of temperance, in the one who had it, but no longer with the nature of a habit, for it is on its way to being destroyed; rather, it remains as a disposition, and a disposition is not opposed to a perfected habit.

Thus SAINT THOMAS. And he says something similar in *ST* III, q.86, a.5:

> Mortal sin, from the point of view of its disorderly turning toward a changeable good, causes in the soul a disposition or habit if the act is frequently repeated. Now the fault of mortal sin is absolved inasmuch as the turning away of the mind from God is removed. But even when what is on the side of the turning-away is removed, there can still remain what is on the side of disorderly turning-toward, since the latter can exist without the former. Therefore, when the fault is absolved, nothing prevents there remaining the dispositions caused by preceding acts, dispositions called "the remnants of sin." However, they remain as weakened and diminished, so that they do not

> dominate a man, and they remain as dispositions rather than as habits, just as the "tinder" of sin also remains after baptism.

Thus SAINT THOMAS. Again, in *In 4 Sent.*, d.14, q.2, a.2, ad 4, he speaks as follows:

> Infused and acquired virtue are not of the same species. Hence, although a habit generated by frequent acts of sin is contrary to acquired virtue, it is not directly contrary to infused virtue, which is opposed to sin inasmuch as the latter is offensive to God. Hence, the habits of the vices need not be entirely removed as soon as the infused virtues have been restored, although they are impeded and diminished.

Thus SAINT THOMAS.

In response to the *fifth* argument we say that adults who possess virtues acquired before the infusion of grace are infused with other, infused moral virtues together with grace.

In response to the argument against this point we say that what is secondary has a species and specific essence different from that of what is primary, as has often been said.

In response to the opponent's remark that then the infused moral virtues would equivocally be called "virtues," etc., we say that this inference is no more valid than the following one: "The theological virtues have an essence different from that of the cardinal ones; therefore, they are only equivocally, and not univocally or analogically, called 'virtues'." Again, it is no more valid than the following one: "Fortitude and prudence have different essences; therefore, they are both called 'moral virtues' not univocally, but equivocally." It is clear that these inferences are not at all valid. The reason is as follows. "Moral virtue," like "animal," is the name not of an individual species, but of a subordinate genus that contains under itself many specific essences, or rather many subordinate genera. But it does possess one common essence for everything contained under it, namely to be a habit that perfects the appetitive power and makes its act good, whether in relation to the passions or in relation to external acts directed to another. Hence, the above-mentioned inferences are ridiculous.

In response to the *sixth* argument we say that the infused moral virtues are necessary to man for rightly directing his life and his acts to the supernatural end, and for duly proportioning his acts to the supernatural principles that are the theological virtues.

The argument against this point is invalid. For, as has been said above, in the solution of the first objection, the theological virtues are not sufficient for this purpose, since they do not perfect all of the powers of the soul that are subjects of the moral virtues, and do not have for their object the objects of the moral virtues. Hence, according to the attempted disproof, one would conclude that no-one in the present life, whether child or adult, needs any habits, whether moral or intellectual, whether infused or acquired, apart from the three theological habits, which is clearly false. Concerning the emptiness of the argument, SAINT THOMAS, in *Questions on the Virtues,* "On the Virtues in General", a.12, speaks as follows. In obj.12, he presents the following argument:

> The end is the nature of the things directed to the end. Therefore, if one possesses the theological virtues, by which man is rightly directed to God, it seems superfluous to posit other virtues.

Thus the argument; the response is as follows:

> It must be said that, just as in speculative matters there are principles and conclusions, so in matters of operation there are the end and what is directed to the end. Therefore, just as it is not enough for perfect and clear cognition that a man be, by understanding, rightly disposed with respect to principles, but he also requires scientific knowledge directed to conclusions; so, too, in matters of operation, beyond the theological virtues, by which we are rightly disposed in relation to the ultimate end, there are also necessary other virtues by which we are well ordered to what is directed to the end.

Thus SAINT THOMAS.

The response to the attack on the first response given in the argument is clear from what has been said. For the theological virtues do not, as virtues that choose or carry out acts, suffice for living the spiritual life well, granted that they do suffice to direct and prescribe everything that should be done and undergone in that life, as has often been said. Concerning this point SAINT THOMAS, in *Questions on the Virtues,* "On the Virtues in General", a.10, speaks as follows:

> Besides the virtues acquired by our acts, we must posit in man other virtues, infused by God. The reason for this can be seen from the following. "Virtue," as THE PHILOSOPHER says, "is that which makes good the one who possesses it and renders his act good." According, therefore, **{409}** as good is diversified in man, virtues, too, must be diversified. For example, it is clear

that the good of man as man and the good of man as citizen are different. And it is clear that certain operations can be appropriate to man as man that are not appropriate to him as citizen. For this reason ARISTOTLE says in *Politics* 3 that the virtue that makes a good man and the virtue that makes a good citizen are different.

But it must be considered that there is a twofold good of man: one proportioned to his nature, and another that exceeds the capacity of his nature. The reason for this is as follows. A passive principle must receive perfections from an agent in different ways, according to the diversity of the acting power. Hence we see that perfections and forms caused by the action of a natural agent do not exceed the natural capacity of the receiver: for a natural active power is proportioned to a natural passive power. But perfections and forms that come from a supernatural agent of infinite power, namely God, do exceed the capacity of the receiving nature. Hence the rational soul, which is immediately created by God, exceeds the capacity of its matter, so that the bodily matter cannot totally comprehend and enclose it; rather, there remains a power and an operation of the soul in which bodily matter does not share, something which does not happen in the case of other forms, which are caused by natural agents.

Now just as the soul, or rather man, acquired his first perfection from the action of God, so he has his ultimate perfection, which is his perfect happiness, directly from and in God. This is clear from the fact that the natural desire of man can be brought to rest in nothing other than God. For it is innate to man, through a certain desire, to be moved by effects to seek their causes, and this desire does not come to rest until it reaches the First Cause, which is God. Therefore, just as the first perfection of man, who is the rational animal, exceeds the capacity of bodily matter, so too, the ultimate perfection that man can reach, which is the blessedness of eternal life, must exceed the capacity of the whole of human nature.

Now because each thing is directed to its end through operation, and because what is directed to the end must be in some way proportioned to it, there must be certain perfections of man by which he is directed to the supernatural end that exceeds the capacity of the natural principles of man. Now this could not be the case unless, beyond those natural principles, certain supernatural principles were infused into man by God; the natural principles of man's operations are the essence of the soul and its powers, namely intellect and will, which are the principles of operation of man as man. Moreover, what was said could not be the case unless the intellect had knowledge of the principles by which it was to be directed to other things, and unless the will had a natural inclination to the good proportioned to its nature.

> Therefore, the following are divinely infused into man for performing the actions directed to the end that is eternal life: first of all grace, through which the soul has a spiritual existence; and then faith, hope, and charity, so that, by faith, the intellect might be illuminated concerning things which need to be known in a supernatural way, and so that, by hope and charity, the will might acquire an inclination to that supernatural good to which the human will is not sufficiently directed by its natural inclination. And just as the perfection of man in the mode connatural to him requires, in addition to natural principles, the habits of the virtues, so too, by divine influence, man attains, in addition to the supernatural principles mentioned above, certain infused virtues by which he is perfected for the operations which are to be ordered to the end of eternal life.

Thus SAINT THOMAS. From this text it is clear that the theological habits do not suffice for directing human operations to the end that is eternal life, or for living appropriately in the spiritual city, without the habits of the infused moral virtues; just as neither do the intellect and will, together with their natural inclinations to the good and the true, suffice, without other habits, for living appropriately in the earthly city. Again, in ad 4, he speaks as follows:

> Since there is no merit without charity, an act of acquired virtue cannot be meritorious without charity. But the other virtues are infused together with charity. Hence, an act of acquired virtue cannot be meritorious except by means of infused virtue. For a virtue directed to a lower end does not cause an act to be directed to a higher end except by means of a higher virtue. For instance, the fortitude that is a virtue of man as man directs its act to the political good only by means of the fortitude that is an act of man as citizen.

Thus SAINT THOMAS.

In response to the argument against the second response mentioned by the opponent we deny the antecedent, whose attempted proof stands upon that false and destructive foundation that we have often denied, namely that the theological virtues suffice, without the other virtues, to determine the mid-point in actions and passions in a virtuous way.

Concerning all of the foregoing, SAINT THOMAS, in *ST* I–II, q.63, a.4, speaks as follows:

> Habits are specifically distinguished in two ways. One is according to the specific and formal essences of their objects. Now the object of any virtue is a good considered in the appropriate matter. For instance, the object of temperance is the good of things pleasant to the desires of the sense of touch,

> and the formal essence of this object comes from reason, which establishes a measure in these desires, while what is material is something is on the side of the desires themselves. But it is clear that the measure imposed **{410}** on these desires by the rule of human reason and that imposed on them by divine reason are of different essences. For example, in the consumption of food, the measure established by human reason is that such consumption not harm bodily health or hinder the act of reason; but according to the rule of the divine law, it is required that man "punish his body and bring it into subjection" (*1 Corinthians* 9) by abstinence from food, drink, and other such things. Hence it is clear that acquired temperance and infused temperance differ specifically. And the argument is the same concerning the other virtues.
>
> In another way habits are specifically distinguished according to the things to which they are directed. For health of a man and that of a horse are not of the same species, because of the different natures to which they are directed. In this sense THE PHILOSOPHER says in *Politics* 3 that the virtues of citizens are different according as the latter are rightly related to different polities. And in this sense, too, the infused moral virtues, on the one hand, by which men are rightly related to being "citizens with the saints and of the household of God" (*Ephesians* 2), and the other, acquired virtues, on the other hand, by which man is rightly related to human things, are specifically diverse.

Thus SAINT THOMAS. From this text it is clear how the infused moral virtues specifically differ from the acquired ones in two ways, namely with respect to the formal essence of their object, and with respect to the ends or citizenships to which they are directed, as is said in the two last-mentioned responses, which the opponent tries to refute. Moreover, it is also clear how the theological habits do not suffice for living rightly in the polity and city of the saints.

§4. *To the Arguments against the Fourth Conclusion*

To the Arguments of Durandus [*p. 263*] In response to the *first* argument against the fourth conclusion we deny the minor premise. For, as was said in the proof of the fourth conclusion, and in a way touched on in the response to the arguments against the third conclusion, the formal object of these moral virtues is the very order of reason imposed on actions and passions; and that order will remain, in the way mentioned in the fourth conclusion. Again, SAINT THOMAS, in *Questions on the Virtues,* "On the Cardinal Virtues", a.4, presents the following argument:

> Virtues get their species from their objects. But the objects of the cardinal virtues do not remain in heaven. For prudence concerns doubtful things, about which there is counsel; and justice concerns contracts and judgments, fortitude concerns dangers of death, and temperance concerns desires for food and venereal pleasure, none of which will be present in heaven. Therefore, the cardinal virtues will not be present in heaven.

Thus the argument; the response is as follows:

> In response to the fifth objection it must be said that there are two ways in which a thing is said to be the object of a virtue: in one way as that to which the virtue is directed as to an end, as, for instance, the highest good is the object of charity, and eternal blessedness the object of hope; in another way as the matter on which the virtue operates by proceeding from that matter to something else. In this latter way the pleasures of coitus are the object of temperance: for temperance is not intent on adhering to these pleasures, but rather, by suppressing these pleasures, proceeds to the good of reason. Similarly, fortitude is not intent on adhering to dangers, but rather, by overcoming dangers, on obtaining the good of reason. And it is the same concerning prudence with respect to doubtful matters, and justice with respect to the necessary things of this life. Hence, the greater the withdrawal from these matters in the progress of the spiritual life, the more perfect will be the acts of these virtues, because the objects mentioned are related to these virtues as a *terminus a quo* from which the virtues get their species rather than as a *terminus ad quem*.

Thus SAINT THOMAS.

In response to the *second* argument we say *first* that the habits that perfect the sensitive appetite will remain in heaven in the same way their subjects do. For if a sensitive appetite which is numerically the same is restored, the habits mentioned will also be numerically the same as those that exist now; but if the sensitive appetite is not numerically, but specifically, the same as before, it will be the same concerning the habits.

Concerning this point SAINT THOMAS, in *Questions on the Virtues,* "On the Cardinal Virtues", a.4, ad 13, speaks as follows:

> Some say that the irascible and concupiscible powers, in which temperance and fortitude are present, exist in the higher part of the soul and not in the sensitive part. But this is contrary to what THE PHILOSOPHER says in *Ethics* 3, namely that there are virtues belonging to the irrational parts.
>
> Some, however, say that the powers of the sensitive part remain in the

> separated soul both in potency and in actuality. But this cannot be. For the act of a sensitive power does not exist without a body; otherwise, the sensitive souls of brute animals would be incorruptible, which is erroneous. Potency belongs to what has action. Hence it must be that such powers belong to the whole composite, and thus, after death, they will not remain in the separated soul in actuality, but only virtually, in their root, inasmuch as the powers of the soul flow from its essence. Now the virtues in question exist in the irascible and concupiscible powers by derivation; but with respect to their origin and incipience, they exist in reason or in reason's will. For the principal act of moral virtue is choice, which is an act of the rational appetite, but this choice, by an application, terminates in the passions of the irascible and concupiscible powers **{411}** as temperance and fortitude.

Thus SAINT THOMAS. Again, in *ST* I–II, q.67, a.1, ad 3, he speaks as follows:

> There are two states after the present life: one is before the resurrection, when the soul will be separated from the body; the other is after the resurrection, when souls will again be united to their bodies. Accordingly, in the state of the resurrection, the irrational powers will be present in bodily organs, just as now. Hence, fortitude will be able to exist in the irascible power and temperance in the concupiscible power inasmuch as both powers will be perfectly disposed to obey reason. But in the state before the resurrection, the irrational parts will not be present in the soul in actuality, but only in their root, namely the essence of the soul. Hence, neither will those virtues be present in actuality, but only in their root, that is, reason and will, in which seeds of these virtues exist. But justice, which exists in the will, will remain in actuality. Hence something special has been said of justice, namely that it is perpetual and immortal both by reason of its subject, for the will is incorruptible, and because its act will remain similar, as was said before.

Thus SAINT THOMAS. He presents something similar in *In 3 Sent.*, d.33, q.1, a.4, ad 4, where he speaks as follows:

> Those who say that the sensitive powers do not remain in actuality in the separated soul do nevertheless say that these powers remain in the essence of the soul as in their root. And similarly the habits of the virtues in the lower part also remain, as in their root, both in the virtues that exist in reason, and in grace itself.

Thus SAINT THOMAS.

Second, we say that, whichever way these powers are said to remain—whether as numerically or only specifically the same—the opponent does not sufficiently argue against either position. Not against the second, because our conclusion does not assert that these powers remain numerically the same, but only that infused moral virtues will exist in heaven.

Nor does he sufficiently argue against the first position. For if these virtues were miraculously, by divine action alone and without our doing anything, restored as numerically the same, it does not follow from this that one could truly say that the preceding habits will remain, in the way that the same man, miraculously resuscitated by God alone, will remain. For our action contributes nothing to whether the infused habits remain or not.

Third, we say that it is likely that all of the sensitive powers are restored as numerically the same, however much they may be destroyed or even annihilated in death. For God is able to restore as numerically the same everything positive that lasts through time and is not transient, however much it may be annihilated, as will perhaps be seen elsewhere, in Book IV. And I say the same thing of these moral virtues.

SAINT THOMAS responds to the argument on the negative side of the question [p. 246] in *In 3 Sent.,* d.33, q.2, a.4, qla.2, ad 5, where he speaks as follows:

> Mortal sin is said to exist always in reason not as if every act of mortal sin were an act of reason choosing, since mortal sin can also be present in the acts of the external members; but rather because no act takes on the essence of a mortal sin unless the consent of reason is added. Similarly, there can be no act of virtue unless it is directed by reason. And virtues can exist in the lower powers inasmuch as they participate in reason.

Thus SAINT THOMAS.

This suffices for the question.

Blessed be God.

Amen.

Whether the Gifts of the Holy Spirit Are Habits Distinct from the Virtues

In relation to the thirty-fourth and thirty-fifth distinctions, the question is raised: Whether the gifts of the Holy Spirit are habits distinct from the virtues.

It is argued that they are not, as follows. Things that have the same definition are themselves the same. But the definition of virtue fits the gifts: for each gift is "a good quality of mind by which one lives rightly etc." Similarly, the definition of a gift fits the infused virtues: for a gift is, according to THE PHILOSOPHER, "an unreturnable handing over." Therefore virtues are not distinct from gifts.

Argument is made for the opposite conclusion as follows. GREGORY in *Moralia* 1 distinguishes the seven gifts, which he says are signified by the seven sons of Job, from the three virtues, which he says are signified by the three daughters of Job. And in *Moralia* 2 he distinguishes the same seven gifts from the four cardinal virtues, which he says are signified by the four corners of a house. **{412}**

In this question there will be three articles: in the first the conclusions will be presented, in the second the objections, and in the third the solutions.

Article I: Conclusions

First Conclusion: The Gifts of the Holy Spirit Are Habits Which Are Distinct from the Infused Theological and the Cardinal Virtues

SAINT THOMAS proves this conclusion in *ST* I–II, q.68, a.1, where he speaks as follows:

If we are speaking of "gift" and "virtue" with respect to the nature signified by the names, there is no incompatibility between them. For the nature signified by "virtue" is understood according as it perfects man for acting well, while the nature signified by "gift" is understood in relation to the cause from which it comes. But nothing prevents what comes from another as a gift from perfecting someone for acting well, especially since certain virtues are infused into us by God. Hence, "gift" cannot be distinguished from "virtue" in this respect.

For this reason some have held that the gifts should not be distinguished from the virtues. But there remains no small difficulty for them, namely that of giving the reason why some virtues are called gifts, but not all, and why some things, such as fear, are counted among the gifts, but not among the virtues.

Hence others have said that the gifts should be distinguished from the virtues, but these have not given sufficient reason for the distinction, namely something common to the virtues that does not at all pertain to the gifts, and the converse.

Now others, considering that, of the seven gifts, four, namely wisdom, science, understanding, and counsel, pertain to reason, and three, namely fortitude, piety, and fear, pertain to the appetitive power, held that the gifts perfect the power of free choice according as it pertains to reason, while the virtues do so according as it pertains to will. For they found that only two virtues exist in intellect or reason, namely faith and prudence, and that the others exist in the appetitive or affective power. But if this distinction were appropriate, all of the virtues would have to exist in the appetitive power and all of the gifts in the reason.

But others, considering what GREGORY says in *Moralia* 2—namely that "the gift of the Holy Spirit, Who forms prudence, justice, fortitude, and temperance in the mind subjected to Him, fortifies that mind against particular temptations by means of the seven gifts"—have said that the virtues direct one to acting well, but the gifts to resisting temptations. But neither does this distinction suffice. For the virtues also resist the temptations leading to sins contrary to them, since each thing naturally resists its contrary; and this is especially clear in the case of charity, concerning which it is said in *Canticle* 8, that "Many waters cannot extinguish charity."

Still others, considering that these gifts are taught about in Scripture according as they were present in Christ, as is clear from *Isaiah* 11, have said that the virtues are directed to acting well simply speaking, while the gifts are directed to our becoming conformed to Christ, especially with respect to those matters in which he suffered, because these gifts shone forth above all

> in his passion. But neither does this seem to be sufficient, because the Lord Himself leads us to conformity with him above all with respect to humility and gentleness, according to the saying of *Matthew* 11, "Learn from me, because I am meek and humble of heart"; and with respect to charity, according to the remark of *John* 15, "So that you may love one another, as I have loved you"; and these virtues, too, shone forth in an eminent way in the passion of Christ.
>
> Accordingly, in order to distinguish the gifts from the virtues, we ought to follow the way of speaking of Scripture, in which they are taught to us not under the name of "gifts," but that of "spirits." For as is said in *Isaiah* 11, "There rests upon him the spirit of the Lord, the spirit of wisdom and understanding, etc." By these words we are clearly given to understand that seven things are counted there according as they are present in us by divine inspiration. Now "inspiration" signifies a certain movement from without. For it must be considered that two moving principles are present in man: one internal, namely reason, and the other external, namely God, and this is what THE PHILOSOPHER says in his chapter "On good fortune." Now it is clear that everything that is moved must be proportioned to its mover, and that the perfection of the moveable as such is the disposition by which it is well disposed to be moved by its mover. Therefore, the higher the mover, the more necessary it is that the moveable be proportioned to it by a more perfect disposition, as, for example, we see that a student must be more perfectly disposed to receive a higher doctrine from the teacher. Now it is clear that the human virtues perfect man according as he is naturally moved by reason in the interior or exterior actions he performs. Therefore, higher perfections must be present in him according to which he is disposed to be moved by God. And these perfections are called "gifts" not only because they are infused by God, but because by them man is disposed to act readily when moved by divine inspiration. As it is said in *Isaiah* 50 "The Lord shall open my ear, and I shall not oppose Him, nor draw away from Him." And THE PHILOSOPHER, {413} too, says in his chapter "On good fortune" that for those who are moved by a divine prompting it is not useful to be counseled according to human reason, but they rather follow an inner prompting, because they are moved by a principle that is better than human reason. And this is what others say, that the gifts perfect man for the acts that are above the acts of the virtues.

Thus SAINT THOMAS. And he holds the same conclusion in *In 3 Sent.*, d.34, q.1, a.1. From these texts the following argument can be formulated. In order for a moveable to be readily moved by movers that have different natures and different kinds of movement, there must be dispositions with different natures in the moveable. But the gifts and the virtues are such different kinds of dispositions. Therefore, etc.

Second Conclusion: These Gifts Will Remain in Heaven

SAINT THOMAS proves this conclusion in *ST* I–II, q.68, a.6, where he speaks as follows:

> There are two ways in which we can speak of the gifts. In one way, with respect to their essence, and thus they will be most perfectly present in heaven, as is clear from the authorititative text of AMBROSE in his book *On the Holy Spirit,* where he says: "The city of God, the heavenly Jerusalem, is not cleansed by the course of any earthly river; rather, the Holy Spirit, Who flows from the fountain of life that satisfies us with a small draught, is seen to flow in abundance in those heavenly spirits, flowing with the full torrent of the seven spiritual virtues."
>
> The reason for this is that the gifts of the Holy Spirit perfect the human mind for following the motion of the Holy Spirit, which it will do in an eminent way in heaven, when "God shall be all in all," as is said in *1 Corinthians* 15, that is, when man will be totally subject to God.
>
> In another way, the gifts can be considered with respect to the matter on which they operate. In this sense they presently operate on a certain matter on which they will not operate in the state of glory. And in this sense, as was said about the cardinal virtues above, they will not remain in heaven.

Thus SAINT THOMAS. Again, in *In 3 Sent.,* d.34, q.1, a.3, he speaks as follows:

> The mode of anything is predetermined by its proper measure; hence the mode of an action is taken from the rule and measure of the action. Therefore, since the gifts are for the sake of operating above the human mode, the operations of the gifts must be measured by a rule different from the rule of human virtue, and this rule is divinity itself, participated by man in his own mode, so that he operates no longer humanly, but as one who, as it were, has been made God by way of participation. Thus all of the gifts have a measure of operation in common.
>
> They differ, however, in the matter on which they operate. For those that perfect the active life have a matter in common with the moral virtues; while those that perfect the contemplative life have a matter in common with the theological and intellectual virtues, because the eminent object of contemplation is God, Who is the object of the theological virtues. Accordingly, the gifts that perfect the active life will not remain with respect to their actions

> on their proper matter, just as neither will the cardinal virtues remain in this sense; but they will remain with respect to their acts in relation to God, Who is the measure of operation in them, as, for example, fear will subject man to God through reverence. But the gifts that perfect the contemplative life will remain both with respect to their actions on their proper matter and with respect to their actions concerning their proper measure; but they will be perfected with respect to their measure, because, however much the gifts cause an elevation to acts above the common human mode, they can never in the present life attain the mode proper to heaven.

Thus SAINT THOMAS.

From these texts the following argument can be formulated. In any state where the human mind perfectly responds to promptings by the Holy Spirit to acts higher than human ones, man possesses dispositions or habits that make him readily moveable by the Holy Spirit to those acts. But heaven is such a state. Therefore, etc.

Here the first article terminates.

Article II: Objections

§1. Against the First Conclusion

Arguments of Scotus In the second article, argument is made against the conclusions.

SCOTUS (*In 3 Sent.*, d.34, q.1) argues against the first conclusion that the gifts, the beatitudes, and the fruits are habits that are not distinct from the virtues. *First,* he argues as follows:

> By natural reason we reason to the need for an intellectual habit that perfects the intellect concerning objects of speculation and a habit that perfects the intellect concerning what is to be done, and thus there is both a speculative and a practical intellectual habit. Similarly, by natural reason we reason to the need for a habit that perfects the appetite with respect to directing what is desirable to oneself, and also a habit that perfects the appetite with respect to directing what is desirable {414} to another; here is a first distinction between virtues of the appetitive part, which distinguishes these habits according as things are directed to oneself or to another. And if by natural reason we reason that man is not sufficiently perfected by these habits, we then reason to the need for a cognition other than acquired knowledge, but we do not sufficiently and distinctly deduce which appetitive and intellectual habits are different from those already mentioned. However, we do reason-

ably hold that those habits are necessary that the Catholic Church teaches are necessary; and thus by faith we hold that three theological virtues, which immediately perfect the soul with respect to an uncreated object, are necessary.

From these points we argue as follows. Only those habits should be posited in man in the present life by which he is perfected with respect to any objects in the present life. But such habits are the seven kinds of virtue—setting aside the acquired speculative sciences. Therefore, apart from the acquired speculative sciences, no habit should be posited in man in the present life other than the seven virtues simply speaking.

The minor premise is proved as follows. The whole object with respect to which man in the present life needs to be perfected in this life can only be God plus the creature.

Now with respect to God he is sufficiently perfected by the three theological virtues, inasmuch as he can be thus perfected to the highest degree if the habits themselves are completely perfect.

But with respect to creatures—and setting aside the speculative virtues—the intellect is fully perfected by prudence, if prudence itself is completely perfect, so that everything that is to be done and every circumstance of action is completely and perfectly known. Similarly, appetite is completely perfected by the three moral virtues, if they themselves are completely perfect, both with respect to the other and what is desirable for him, and with respect to oneself and what is desirable for oneself—whether the latter is desired primarily and directly, or secondarily and for the sake of what is primary. It is understood that none of these four cardinal virtues exists in anyone as a single habit that would be, for example, universal temperance, or universal justice, that is, justice concerning all things; rather, the individual species of justice have each their own objects.

Similarly, a man in the present life is sufficiently perfected immediately with respect to God by the three theological virtues. For faith sufficiently perfects him with respect to God to the extent that God is to be immediately understood in the present life, because no cognition can be had of God in the present life except the cognition of faith. Charity perfects man with respect to God inasmuch as God is an object of love in Himself. And hope perfects man with respect to God inasmuch as God is an object of desire appropriate to me. But it is not proper to man in the present life to have any acts directed to God other than to understand and love Him in Himself and to desire Him for myself as my good. Therefore, etc.

Similarly, man in the present life is sufficiently perfected with respect to every good other than God when he is perfected with respect to these goods,

> as objects, by the intellectual and appetitive habits. Now the habits that sufficiently perfect the intellect are the intellectual virtues. For the intellectual virtues sufficiently perfect the intellect of man in the present life, as much as is possible, for considering and syllogizing in practical matters. Moreover, the appetitive habits and appetitive virtues sufficiently perfect the appetite for desiring and loving everything that is loveable whether in itself or in being directed to something else. Therefore, a man perfected by the three theological virtues, the speculative and practical intellectual virtues, and the moral virtues that direct things both to himself and to the other, is sufficiently perfected to the extent that perfection can belong to him in the present life. Therefore, there does not seem to be any necessity to posit any habits other than the theological and the cardinal virtues.

Second, he argues as follows:

> If the virtues were habits different from the gifts, it would follow that none in one group would be the same as any in the other. But the consequent is false. For fortitude is both a virtue and a gift.
>
> If it is said that the one fortitude and the other have different natures, we respond that their objects are the same, having the same nature, and that the habits therefore have the same nature.
>
> It might perhaps be said that they are not of the same nature, because the virtues perfect in a human way, but the gifts in a superhuman way. Against this one may make several objections.
>
> *First,* charity is the most excellent gift of God according to AUGUSTINE in *De trinitate* 15. Moreover, according to THE APOSTLE in *1 Corinthians* 13, if I have fortitude "and if I give my body up to be burned"—which seems to be a superhuman manner of acting, because I would be seeking to burn for the sake of God—"but have not charity, it profits me nothing." Therefore, it seems that no gift perfects more excellently than does charity, which, however, is a virtue.
>
> *Second,* the human will can hold to the mid-point rightly with respect to the matter of courage, and therefore it can do so very rightly, and as rightly as possible for human nature. Now it is able to do this by a habit of fortitude that it intensifies to greater and greater degrees, degrees that do not alter the habit with respect to its species. Therefore it is specifically the same habit that disposes man to endure something both most perfectly and most imperfectly.
>
> But if this is impossible, and the habit rather becomes specifically different, then the habit that disposes man to enduring in the lowest degree is necessarily imperfect with respect to its act and its object. For to endure ob-

jects of fear cannot have the nature of perfection, and in order to be perfectly disposed concerning these things, one would have to have a specifically different habit.

But a multiplicity of species should not be posited without clear necessity, namely in a case where {415} one species would not suffice; but this is not the case in the question.

Third, Christ underwent sorrow in his passion, and in general, every martyr abandoned to himself—that is, every martyr for whom no miracle occurs, however much he voluntarily endures—endures with some sorrow. AUGUSTINE proves this in *De trinitate* 13, where he argues against the philosophers who say that they are blessed because they have everything they want, for if prosperity befalls them they will it, and if adversity befalls them they will it, because they endure it with patience. Against these AUGUSTINE argues that they do not have what they will in adversity: for inasmuch as it is in their power, they are unwilling that it befall them; and if it does befall them, they will to endure it patiently in order that they not be made more unhappy by loss of patience. This is a persuasive argument, because there can be no patience concerning the object of appetite as such. Therefore, martyrs who endure adversity in the present life have something that they do not altogether will, because the object of their patience is an object of will not according to the absolute nature of the latter, but only as the enduring of something that must be undergone.

Fourth, it is impossible to perform one and the same act simultaneously humanly and superhumanly. Therefore, when a gift is acquired, a virtue previously acquired or infused in baptism is removed; or, if it does remain, it will not be possible for it to issue in its act; or it will not be necessary for it to do so, because one will be able to perform the act of the virtue by means of the more perfect gift. This seems to be inconsistent, especially in the case of the theological virtues, because charity will not be removed in heaven, and faith and hope will not be removed in the present life.

Fifth, the words "humanly" and "superhumanly" are metaphorical, because every act of man is, properly speaking, human. For just as it is necessary for right action to be suited to the end, object, and circumstances, so it must also be suited to the one performing it. For it is not suitable for me to perform an act that suits a king, and even less one that suits an angel. Therefore man's right action requires that he perform it in a human manner. Accordingly, any infused habit that disposes man to act in a human manner simply speaking, disposes him to perform it absolutely speaking, whatever the action may be about.

Sixth, if someone were to pray well, and the gift of understanding were

> given to him, but he did not exercise himself with respect to the objects of belief because he did not have the acquired faith without which infused faith does not issue in action, he would still, according to you, be able to act in a superhuman manner. Therefore he would act more excellently with respect to the objects of belief than would someone else who was practiced in Sacred Scripture. This is not what we experience; rather, any such person would probably more easily err concerning the objects of belief than would another who was well practiced in Sacred Scripture.
>
> *Seventh,* there are just as many things with respect to which one should be humanly well ordered as there are with respect to which one should be superhumanly well ordered. Therefore, the mode is the same in both cases.
>
> One might say, perhaps, that the virtues dispose the will inasmuch as it is moveable by reason, but the gifts perfect it inasmuch as it is moveable by the Holy Spirit. Against this we argue as follows.
>
> *First,* it presupposes something false, namely that reason moves the will in such a way that virtue is nothing but a disposition of something in the will that can be moved by reason as a mover.
>
> *Second,* according to this position, no distinction is made between beatitudes and gifts.
>
> *Third,* by the fact that God has given a habit to the will, He is ever present to the will and its habits for the acts that suit them; just as, after He miraculously cured the blind man, He was ever present to the cured man so that the latter's power of sight could be affected. Accordingly, it is by the same thing that something is proportioned both to the First Mover and to the second. Therefore, if a power is proportioned to itself by a habit of virtue, it is by the same thing sufficiently proportioned to the Holy Spirit as the First Mover. Therefore, it is not necessary, according to this argument, to posit any other habits.

Thus SCOTUS argues in form.

§2. *Against the Second Conclusion*

Arguments of Durandus DURANDUS (*In 3 Sent.*, d.34, q.3) argues against the second conclusion that some gifts of the Holy Spirit, namely counsel, fortitude, fear, and piety, do not remain in heaven with respect to their acts.

First, he argues as follows:

> No power can be in act except in the presence of its object. But the objects of these gifts will not be present in heaven. For the gift of piety is for having compassion for one's neighbor, the gift of fear is for withdrawing from evil,

> and the gift of counsel is for deliberating in doubtful matters. But in heaven there will be no compassion for any misery, nor will there be any need for withdrawing from evil, nor will there be any doubt concerning anything to be done. Therefore, the acts of these gifts will not be present in heaven.

Second, he argues as follows:

> The aforementioned gifts perfect man in the active life. But this life will be taken away in heaven. Therefore, so will the gifts, with respect to their acts.

Thus DURANDUS.

Here the second article terminates. {**416**}

Article III: Solutions

§1. To the Arguments against the First Conclusion

To the Arguments of Scotus [*p. 303*] In the third article we must respond to the above-mentioned objections.

In response to the *first* argument of SCOTUS against the first conclusion, we deny that part of the minor premise in which he says that man is sufficiently perfected with respect to creatures, inasmuch as it is possible for him to be perfected in the present life, by the four cardinal virtues, if they are themselves completely perfect. For none of the four perfect any power of the soul inasmuch as it is capable of being moved by the Holy Spirit to a supernatural end, but only—to speak of justice, fortitude, and temperance—inasmuch as the power is capable of being moved by reason; or, such a virtue—to speak of prudence—perfects reason itself inasmuch as it is moved either by the understanding of naturally knowable principles, or in the light of faith. Concerning this point many things have been said in the proof of the first conclusion. And concerning this point SAINT THOMAS, in *ST* I–II, q.68, a.2, presents the following argument:

> It suffices for the salvation of man that he be well disposed concerning divine and human things. But he is well disposed concerning divine things by means of the theological virtues, and concerning human things by means of the moral virtues. Therefore the gifts are not necessary to man for salvation.

Thus the argument; the response is as follows:

> It must be said that man is not so perfected by the theological and moral virtues in being directed to the ultimate end that he does not always need to

> be moved by a higher prompting of the Holy Spirit, for the reason already given.

And what this reason is he shows in the same place, saying:

> The gifts are perfections of man by which he is disposed to follow the divine prompting well. Hence, in matters where the prompting of reason does not suffice and a prompting of the Holy Spirit is necessary, a gift is necessary.
>
> Now the reason of man is perfected by God in two ways: first of all, by a natural perfection, that is, according to the light of natural reason; and in another way by a supernatural perfection, through the theological virtues. And although this second perfection is greater than the first, the first is possessed by man in a more perfect manner than is the second. For the first is possessed by man with full possession, as it were, but the second is possessed imperfectly, as it were, for we love and know God imperfectly. Now it is clear that anything that perfectly possesses a nature, form, or power is able by itself to operate in accordance with what it possesses—which is not to exclude the operation of God, Who operates in an interior way in every nature and will. But what imperfectly possesses a nature, form, or power cannot operate by itself unless it is moved by another. For example, the sun, because it is perfectly lucid, can illuminate by itself; but the moon, in which the nature of light is imperfectly present, does not illuminate unless it is illuminated. Again, the doctor, who knows the art of medicine perfectly, can operate by himself; but his student, who has not yet been fully instructed, cannot operate by himself unless he is instructed by another. Accordingly, with respect to matters that come under human reason in its being directed to the end that is connatural to man, a man can operate through the judgment of reason. But if, in the same man, help is given by God through special prompting, this will pertain to a superabundance of goodness. Thus, according to the philosophers, not everyone who possesses the acquired moral virtues possesses the heroic or divine virtues.
>
> Now in directing to the supernatural ultimate end, to which reason moves inasmuch as it has been, in a way and imperfectly, informed by the theological virtues, the movement of reason does not suffice, unless there is in addition a prompting and movement by the Holy Spirit. As is said in *Romans* 8: "Those who act by the Spirit of God are sons and heirs of God"; and as is said in the *Psalm:* "Your good Spirit will lead me into a righteous land." For no-one can come into the inheritance of the land of the blessed if he is not moved and led by the Holy Spirit. Hence, in order to obtain this end, it is necessary for man to possess a gift of the Holy Spirit.

Thus SAINT THOMAS. Again, in the same place, ad 3, he presents the following argument:

> GREGORY says in *Moralia* 2 that "The Holy Spirit gives wisdom to oppose foolishness, understanding to oppose dullness, counsel to oppose impetuousness, fortitude to oppose fear, knowledge to oppose ignorance, piety to oppose hardness, and fear to oppose pride." But a sufficient remedy for removing all of these can be had through the virtues. Therefore the gifts are not necessary to man for salvation.

Thus the argument; the response is as follows:

> It must be said that not everything is knowable or possible to human reason, whether the latter be taken as perfected by a natural perfection or as perfected by the theological virtues. Thus it cannot in all cases repel foolishness and the other things mentioned in the text quoted. But God, under Whose knowledge and power all things do fall, can, by a movement of His, protect us from all foolishness, ignorance, dullness, hardness, etc. Hence the gifts of the Holy Spirit, which cause us to follow his prompting well, are said to be given to oppose these defects.

Thus SAINT THOMAS.

{417} From these texts it is clear that, besides the habits of the virtues, other habits, which we call "gifts," are necessary, because, besides the inclination given by the virtues, which are, as it were, in an active state, we need a movement that is passive on our part and active on the part of the Holy Spirit, in order to be directed to the supernatural end. And the habits of the gifts, as has been said, cause a disposition to what is passive in this movement.

In response to the *second* argument we say that the response mentioned in the course of the argument is a good one, because the fortitude that is a virtue and the fortitude that is a gift do differ specifically. In proof of this we say that the gift of fortitude perfects in a superhuman manner, as is said in the same place. In clarification of this point SAINT THOMAS, in *ST* II–II, q.139, a.1, speaks as follows:

> Fortitude implies a firmness of soul. This firmness of soul is required both in doing what is good and in enduring what is evil, especially in the case of arduous goods and evils. But man can, in a proper and connatural manner, possess this firmness in both ways, so that he does not fall away from the good because of the difficulty either of an arduous good to be performed or of a heavy evil to be endured; and in this respect fortitude is held to be either a special or a general virtue respectively. But in addition, the soul of

> man may be moved by the Holy Spirit to attain the end of any incipient operation whatsoever and to escape any imminent dangers whatsoever. This is something that exceeds the capacity of human nature: for sometimes it is not within the power of man to attain the end of his operation; or again it is not within his power to escape evils or dangers, since sometimes he is driven to death by them. Rather, it is the Holy Spirit Who does this in man, when He leads man to eternal life, which is the end of all good works and escape from all dangers. The Holy Spirit infuses into the mind a confidence in this matter and removes the opposing fear. It is in this sense that fortitude is held to be a gift of the Holy Spirit; for the gifts of the Holy Spirit concern the movement of the soul by the Holy Spirit.

Thus SAINT THOMAS. Again, in ad 1, he speaks as follows:

> The fortitude that is a virtue perfects the soul in enduring certain dangers, but is not enough to give confidence of escaping certain dangers. Rather, this pertains to the fortitude which is a gift of the Holy Spirit.

Thus SAINT THOMAS.

From these texts it is clear that, although the fortitude that is a virtue and the fortitude that is a gift of the Holy Spirit have the same material object, namely things dangerous and arduous, their formal object is not the same, because man is made firm, with respect to the same matter, by the virtue in one way and by the gift in another.

Similarly, the habits mentioned are directed to different proximate ends and therefore are specifically distinct. SAINT THOMAS discusses this point by means of a comparison in *ST* I–II, q.63, a.4—which was quoted in the preceding question, article three, in response to the sixth argument of DURANDUS against the third conclusion—where he shows how the acquired and infused moral virtues are specifically distinct.

In response to the *first* argument against the response mentioned we say that SAINT THOMAS does not hold that the gifts perfect in a higher way than do the theological virtues, especially charity. Rather, he says the complete opposite, as is clear in *ST* I–II, q.68, a.8, where he speaks as follows:

> Three kinds of virtue are distinguished, for some are theological, some intellectual, and some moral. Theological virtues are those by which the human mind is united to God; intellectual virtues are those by which reason itself is perfected; and moral virtues are those by which the appetitive powers are perfected for obeying reason. But by the gifts of the Holy Spirit all the powers of the soul are disposed to submit to the divine movement. Accordingly,

> the relation of the gifts to the theological virtues, by which man is united to the Holy Spirit Who moves him, seems to be the same as that of the moral virtues to the intellectual virtues, by which reason itself, which is capable of moving the virtues, is perfected. Hence, just as the intellectual virtues stand above the moral virtues and govern them, so the theological virtues stand above the gifts of the Holy Spirit and govern them. Hence GREGORY says in *Moralia* 1 that "the seven sons," that is, the seven gifts, "do not achieve mint condition unless everything they do is done in faith, hope, and charity." But if we compare the gifts to the other virtues, namely the intellectual and moral ones, the gifts stand above the virtues, because the gifts perfect the powers of the soul in relation to the Holy Spirit Who moves them, but the virtues perfect either reason itself or the other powers in their being directed to reason. But it is clear that what is moveable must be disposed in relation to a higher mover by a greater perfection. Hence the gifts are more perfect than the virtues.

Thus SAINT THOMAS. Again, in a.4, ad 3, he speaks as follows:

> The mind of man is not moved by the Holy Spirit unless it is united to Him in some way, just as a tool is not moved by an artisan except through contact or some other union. But the primary union of man to God is through faith, hope, and charity. Hence, these virtues are presupposed by the gifts as their roots. Hence, too, all the gifts pertain to these three virtues as derivations from them.

Thus SAINT THOMAS.

In response to the *second* argument against the response mentioned we say that the habit of the virtue of courage, however much it is intensified, cannot reach the point of making the human soul righteous and firm in {418} doing good and enduring evil in the same way that the fortitude that is a gift makes it righteous. Hence these righteousnesses differ not merely with respect to intension and remission, but also specifically, as is clear from what has been said.

Again, SAINT THOMAS, in *ST* I–II, q.68, a.2, presents the following argument:

> The gifts are directed to a perfection beyond the common perfection of virtue. But it is not necessary to man for his salvation that he achieve this perfection beyond the common condition of virtue, because such perfection comes not under precept, but counsel. Therefore, the gifts are not necessary for salvation.

Thus the argument; the response is as follows:

> It must be said that the gifts go beyond the common perfection of the virtues not with respect to kinds of deeds, which is the way that counsels go beyond precepts, but with respect to the manner of operating, inasmuch as man is moved by a higher principle.

Thus SAINT THOMAS.

In response to the *third* argument against the response mentioned we say that the gift of fortitude in Christ and in the other martyrs did not cause them to feel no bodily pain and not to suffer in a bodily way. Its effect was rather that the bodily pain did not absorb or dominate reason in any way, but was rather entirely subject to reason's command, and in addition that pleasure of soul was greater than pain of soul. BLESSED THOMAS speaks of this matter in *ST* II–II, q.123, a.8, where he asks, "Whether the courageous man takes pleasure in his act?" and responds as follows:

> There are two kinds of pleasure: one is bodily pleasure, which follows from bodily touch; the other is pleasure of soul, which follows from an apprehension of the soul. It is the latter, properly speaking, that follows from the acts of the virtues, because it is in such acts that the good of reason is recognized.
>
> Now the principal act of fortitude is either to endure certain pains that follow from an apprehension by the soul, for instance, the apprehension that a man will lose his bodily life, which the virtuous man loves not merely inasmuch as it is a natural good, but also inasmuch as it is necessary for the works of the virtues and the things which pertain to them; or again, to endure things that are painful to bodily contact, such as wounds and flagellations.
>
> Accordingly, the courageous man on the one hand has something in which he takes pleasure, that is, pleasure of soul, namely the very act of virtue and its end. But on the other hand he has something by which he is pained, with respect to both pain of soul, when he considers the loss of his own life, and bodily pain. Hence one reads in *2 Maccabees* 6 that Eleazarus says: "I endure dire pains of the body, but in my soul I gladly undergo them because of your fear." Now sensible bodily pain causes one not to feel the pleasure of soul that follows from virtue, unless, perhaps, one feels such pleasure because of the superabundant grace of God, Who may raise the soul to divine things, in which the soul feels pleasure more than it feels the pain of bodily punishments. For example, when Blessed Tiburtius fell on burning coals in his bare feet, he said that it seemed to him that he was walking on roses.

> Now the virtue of fortitude causes reason not to be absorbed by bodily pains. And pleasure in virtue overcomes pain of soul inasmuch as man places the good of virtue above bodily life and what pertains to it. Hence THE PHILOSOPHER says in *Ethics* 3 that it is not required of the courageous man that he take pleasure, that is, that he feel pleasure; rather, it is enough that he not feel pain.

Thus SAINT THOMAS. From this text it may be gathered how the virtue of fortitude does not remove all bodily pain or pain of soul, but sustains reason so that it is not absorbed by any sorrow, and so that man does not fall away from the good because of the difficulty either of some arduous deed to be accomplished or of some heavy evil to be endured. But beyond this, the gift of fortitude confers a confidence in reaching the end of any incipient deed and in escaping any evils, as was said before, at the beginning of this solution of the second principal argument. Again, in *ST* I–II, q.69, a.3, SAINT THOMAS speaks as follows:

> Virtue causes withdrawal from the consequences of the passions of the irascible power in order that man, following the rule of reason, not be excessive in these passions; but the gift does so in a more excellent way, namely such that man, following the divine will, is made to rest entirely from these passions. And virtue causes withdrawal from the consequences of the passions of the concupiscible power by using these passions in a moderate way; but the gift does so by, if necessary, driving them out entirely, or, if necessary, by taking up a voluntary sorrow.

Thus SAINT THOMAS. This point will more fully be discussed below.

In response to the *fourth* argument against the response mentioned we say that it is impossible for the same man to perform the same act both in a manner that is precisively and merely human and, simultaneously, in a superhuman manner. But there is no contradiction or impossibility in performing a single act in a superhuman manner and, simultaneously, doing so with every manner of human perfection, that is, with all the perfection in the human manner of acting as such, if one excludes negation and every imperfection that accompanies human action as such, but adds perfection; similarly, "man" adds something to "animal" and to all of the kinds that precede "animal."

Second, we say that positing—but not conceding—that these two manners of acting, namely the human and the superhuman, are incompatible, it does not follow from this that the gift would remove every habit or act of virtue. For one who has both habits can use them individually, one without the other, especially since the habit of a gift causes a greater disposition to the passive movement caused by the Holy Spirit than to an active movement caused by oneself. Hence SAINT THOMAS, in *ST* II–II, {419} q.52, a.9, ad 1, speaks as follows:

> In the case of the gifts of the Holy Spirit, the human mind stands not as mover, but rather as moved.

Thus SAINT THOMAS. Thus it is clear that one can act in a human manner while applying the virtue and in a superhuman manner while being moved by the Holy Spirit, by Whom a power of soul is moved in such a way that the power itself also does something. Thus SAINT THOMAS, in *ST* I–II, q.68, a.3, presents the following argument:

> The gifts of the Holy Spirit perfect man according as he is acted upon by the Holy Spirit. But inasmuch as man is acted upon by the Holy Spirit, he stands as, in a way, the instrument of, or something related to, the latter. But it is not fitting for an instrument, but only for the principal agent, to be perfected by a habit. Therefore, the gifts of the Holy Spirit are not habits.

Thus the argument; the response is as follows:

> It must be said that that argument concerns an instrument to which it does not belong to act, but only to be acted upon. But a man is not this kind of instrument; rather, he is acted upon by the Holy Spirit in such a way that he himself also acts, inasmuch as he possesses free judgment. Hence, he has need of a habit.

Thus SAINT THOMAS.

In response to the *fifth* argument against the response mentioned we say that the terms to operate "in a human manner" and "in a superhuman manner" are used in the discussion in their proper senses, and are not merely metaphorical.

In response to the argument against this point we say that, as has often been said above, not every act of man is, properly speaking, a human act, because no act of the vegetative or sensitive part, which do not participate in reason, is a human act.

Again, an act of man that proceeds both from the habits which make man God-like and from a movement of the Holy Spirit, is not, properly speaking, a human act. This point has been discussed in the proof of the second conclusion.

Again, SAINT THOMAS, in *In 3 Sent.*, d.34, q.1, a.1, speaks as follows:

> The gifts are given for the sake of acts that are higher than acts of the virtues. In order to understand this point, it must be known that, since virtue can be found in all things according as they each have certain proper operations, in which they are perfected by their proper virtue for performing well, when we speak of the moral matter of virtue, we understand this of human virtue, which perfects one for carrying out human operation well. Now the operation of man can be spoken of in three ways.
>
> First of all, from the point of view of the power that chooses or commands the operation, that is, the operation of reason or of some power that obeys reason, because it is by reason that man is man. But to be nourished, to see, etc., are not operations of man as man, but of man as a living thing or as an animal. In this respect, all the habits that perfect man for operations that he does not share or have in common with the brute animals can be called human virtues.
>
> In a second way an operation is called human from its matter or object, as are, for instance, operations that have as their matter human passions or operations. For thus the moral virtues are, properly speaking, called human virtues, as THE PHILOSOPHER says in *Ethics* 10, because the work of the speculative power is more divine than human, since it has necessary and eternal things, not human things, for its matter.
>
> In a third way an operation is called human from its manner, namely because in "human" operations so-called in the first and second way, a human manner is also observed. But if someone does things that pertain to man, but does them in a more than human manner, there will be an operation that is not simply speaking "human," but in a way "divine." Hence THE PHILOSOPHER, in *Ethics* 7, distinguishes virtue simply speaking from heroic virtue, which he says is divine because by excess of virtue man is made like God. And in this respect, I say that the gifts are distinguished from the virtues by the fact that the virtues perfect man for acts according to the human manner, but the gifts perfect him for acts according to a more than human manner.

Thus SAINT THOMAS. From this text it is clear that man is able to act in a superhuman manner, if not by reason of his power of choosing, at least by reason of the matter on which he acts and by reason of his manner of acting.

The argument against this response is invalid. For a superhuman operation befits a human agent inasmuch as he is made a participant in the divine nature through grace, so as to be God by way of participation, although it does not befit him by reason of human nature, which, considered in its pure natural capacities, is naked and unclothed by participation in divinity.

Again, divine and superhuman operation can befit a man inasmuch as he is an instrument moved by the Holy Spirit, although it does not befit him as a principal agent.

And the falsity and emptiness of the argument is clear in many other ways.

In response to the *sixth* argument against the response mentioned we say that it does not touch us at all, because, as has been seen already, we do not hold that some gift of the Holy Spirit is more excellent than faith, hope, or charity, or that the gift of understanding operates in a more excellent manner than does faith. Rather, we hold that the gifts presuppose the theological habits as sources and principles that direct the gifts. Nevertheless, the gift of understanding does have an act that is different from and, as it were, of a different species than the act of faith. Thus SAINT THOMAS, in *ST* II–II, q.8, a.5, ad 3, speaks as follows:

> Faith implies merely assent to what is proposed, but understanding implies a certain perception of the truth, etc.

Again, in a.6, he speaks as follows:

> Wisdom, knowledge, and counsel are directed to supernatural cognition, which is established in us by faith. "But faith comes from hearing," as is said in *Romans* 10. Hence certain things must be proposed to man for his belief not as things seen, but as things heard, to which he gives assent through faith. Now faith is primarily and principally related to the First Truth, secondarily to certain matters to be considered concerning creatures, and beyond that it extends even to the direction of human deeds, inasmuch as faith **{420}** operates through love. Accordingly, two things are required on our part concerning the things proposed for our belief through faith. The first is that these things penetrate or seize the intellect, and this pertains to the gift of understanding. But secondly, man must have right judgment concerning these things, or judge that one must adhere to them and avoid their contraries. With respect to divine things, this judgment pertains to the gift of wisdom; with respect to created things, it pertains to the gift of knowledge; and with respect to the application to individual operations, it pertains to the gift of counsel.

Thus SAINT THOMAS. From this text it is clear that the habits of the gifts presuppose the habit of faith, and that the acts of the gifts of understanding, wisdom, knowledge, and counsel presuppose the act of faith. Hence the situation that the opponent presents is impossible.

In response to the *seventh* argument against the response mentioned we deny the first consequent drawn, because, although a virtue and a gift may operate with respect to the same object or objects, they do not do so in the same way, but rather in ways that are specifically distinct, as has frequently been said. That they may operate with respect to the same matters SAINT THOMAS shows in *ST* I–II, q.68, a.4, where he speaks as follows:

> The gifts are habits that perfect man for readily following the prompting of the Holy Spirit, just as the moral virtues perfect the appetitive powers for obeying reason. But just as the appetitive powers are naturally moved by the command of reason, so all of the human virtues are naturally moved by the prompting of God as by a higher power. Hence, just as virtues are necessary in all powers of man that can be principles of human acts, namely reason and the appetitive power, so too the gifts of the Holy Spirit are necessary in them.
>
> Now reason is both speculative and practical, and in both respects there must be considered both apprehension of truth, which pertains to discovery, and judgment concerning truth. Accordingly, speculative reason is perfected for apprehension of truth by *understanding*, and practical reason by *counsel;* speculative reason is perfected for judging rightly by *wisdom*, and practical reason by *knowledge*.
>
> The appetitive power is perfected with respect to what is directed to another, by *piety*, and with respect to what is directed to oneself, by *courage*, which is opposed to the fear of dangers, and *fear*, which is contrary to inordinate desire for pleasures; as is said in *Proverbs* 14, "By fear of the Lord everyone turns away from evil," and in the *Psalm*, "Strike my flesh with fear of You, for I have feared Your judgments."
>
> Thus it is clear that these gifts concern all matters which the virtues, both moral and intellectual, concern.

Thus SAINT THOMAS. That the gifts operate concerning these matters in a different way has partly been shown above—in the response to the third argument against the response mentioned—where, at the end, it was seen how the gifts and the virtues rectify the passions of the concupiscible and irascible powers in different ways. And SAINT THOMAS shows how they rectify human actions in different ways in the text quoted there, namely *ST* I–II, q.69, a.3, where he says:

> The active life is primarily constituted by what we give our neighbors, whether under the aspect of a debt or under the aspect of a voluntary favor. For the first of these there is a virtue that disposes us not to refuse to give what we owe to our neighbors, which pertains to justice; but there is a gift that induces us to do the same thing with greater feeling, so that we fulfill the works of justice with fervent desire in the way that a hungry and thirsty man seeks food and drink with fervent desire. And there is a virtue that perfects us with respect to voluntary favors or gifts so that we give to those to whom reason dictates a gift should be made, for instance our friends or others united to us, which pertains to the virtue of liberality; but there is a gift that, because of reverence for God, considers only need in those to whom it offers gratuitous benefits, and hence it is said in *Luke* 14: "When you hold a dinner or a supper, do not invite your friends or brothers etc., but invite the poor and the weak, etc."

Thus SAINT THOMAS. Again, in *In 3 Sent.*, d.34, q.1, a.2, he elaborately and very beautifully attributes a superhuman act to each gift. The act of the gift of *understanding,* for example, is "to grasp spiritual things in their naked truth, so to speak, and not in a glass, darkly." The act of the gift of *wisdom* is as follows: "a man is united to the highest causes and transformed, so to speak, into a likeness of them, so that from within, so to speak, he may judge of others and direct not merely objects of knowledge, but also human actions and passions." By the gift of *counsel* man is made "to grasp with certitude, so to speak, what should be done, having been taught by the Holy Spirit." By the gift of *knowledge* man is made "to know with certitude what should be done as occasion arises, and knows how to live rightly in the midst of a depraved and perverse people." By the gift of *piety* it is brought about that "in sharing with another, the nature of the sharing is not understood in terms of the good of the one who shares or the one who is shared with, so that the sharing is enclosed in the limits that a man gives to another only what he owes, or as much as is useful to the one to whom it is given; rather, the nature of the sharing is understood as a divine good received by God and reflected upon oneself or another." By the gift of *fortitude* man is made "to take the divine power as a measure" in his irascible passions of hope, fear, boldness, anger, etc., "so that he tends to arduous deeds of virtue **{421}** of which he knows he is incapable by his own powers, and relying on divine aid, he does not fear dangers that exceed his powers; and not only does he not seek revenge for injuries borne, but, thinking of the reward, he even glories in them." And by the gift of *fear* man is made "to judge, out of reverence for the divine majesty, that" temporal goods, pleasures of touch, passions of concupiscence, and passions connected with concupiscence "are as dung." This is how the gifts operate in a more than human way in all matters of virtue.

For the way in which the virtues operate in a human way in these matters, and have a way of operating below that of the gifts, see what is explained at length in the same text.

It must be known, however, that in the same text, and in the preceding article, ad 5, SAINT THOMAS seems to mean that the gifts operate in a more excellent way than does faith or hope, and that only charity, among the virtues, is more excellent than the gifts. But the other virtues are, with respect to their manner of operating, inferior to the gifts, although they are not inferior simply speaking, because they have the most excellent object. Thus the remarks of the *Commentary on the Sentences* do not contradict the remarks of the *Summa,* except accidentally.

Furthermore, we say that the response the opponent quotes is good, and SAINT THOMAS maintains it in the *Summa.*

In response to the *first* argument against the response we say *first* that it is not false, but rather in all cases true that reason moves the will with respect to specification of the object, as was shown at length in Book Two.

Second, we say that reason, existing in the power of the will, moves the will to the act of choosing even with respect to the exercise of the act; and in addition moves the sensitive appetite and the external members, and all the powers that are subject to the command of the will and obedient to reason. SAINT THOMAS treats this point at length in *ST* I–II, q.17, a.1, and the eight following articles.

Third, we say that not every virtue is present in the will as in its subject, and consequently not every virtue is a disposition of the will as able to be moved by obeying reason as its mover. Nevertheless, every acquired moral virtue is an imprint of reason on the sensitive or intellectual appetite for the purpose of making the latter easily able to be moved by reason, as has often been said in the preceding Distinction. Nor does the opponent argue the contrary. Therefore, we say no more in response to the first argument against the response.

In response to the *second* argument against the response we say that the beatitudes are not distinguished from the gifts as one habit is distinguished from another, but rather as acts are distinguished from the habits that elicit them. Concerning this point SAINT THOMAS, in *ST* I–II, q.69, a.1, speaks as follows:

> Beatitude is the ultimate end of human life. But one can be said already to possess the end because of one's hope of obtaining it. Thus THE PHILOSOPHER says in *Ethics* 1 that children are called blessed because of hope. And THE APOSTLE, in *Romans* 8, says, "We have been saved in hope." Now hope concerning an end to be pursued arises from the fact that one moves toward and approaches the end appropriately, which one does by some action. But one moves toward and approaches the end that is beatitude through operations of the virtues, and above all—if we are speaking of eternal beatitude, for which reason does not suffice, but to which we are led rather by the Holy Spirit, being perfected by the gifts for obeying and following the Holy Spirit—through operations of the gifts. Accordingly, the beatitudes are distinguished from the gifts and the virtues not as habits distinguished from the latter, but as acts are distinguished from habits.

Thus SAINT THOMAS.

In response to the *third* argument against the response we say that, although the Holy Spirit assists the will and the habits of the virtues in choosing acts suitable to the will, to virtue, and to the Holy Spirit; and although, by the habit of virtue, these acts are proportioned to the Holy Spirit as the first mover of human acts, whose proximate mover is human reason but whose first and remote mover is the Holy Spirit; nevertheless, however perfect the cardinal virtues may be, the acts are not proportioned to the Holy Spirit as the mover of acts that are superhuman and exceed the capacity of reason, and to which the powers of the soul are immediately moved by the Holy Spirit, being rather acted upon than acting. Therefore, beyond the habits of the cardinal virtues, the habits of the gifts are necessary, as has often been said. Accordingly, the example of sight miraculously restored is irrelevant to the question. Concerning this point SAINT THOMAS, in *ST* I–II, q.63, a.4, ad 3, speaks as follows:

> God made the eye of the man born blind for the same act for which other eyes are formed by nature; therefore, the act was specifically the same. The argument would be the same if God willed miraculously **{422}** to cause in man the kinds of virtues that are acquired by acts. But this is not the case in question.

Thus SAINT THOMAS.

§2. *To the Arguments against the Second Conclusion*

To the Arguments of Durandus [*p. 307*] In response to the *first* argument of DURANDUS against the second conclusion we say what has already been said in the foregoing conclusion. For, as SAINT THOMAS says, in *Questions on the Virtues,* "On the Virtues in General", a.4, ad 5:

> A thing is said to be the object of a virtue in two ways: in one way as that to which the virtue is ordered as its end, as the highest good is the object of charity and eternal blessedness is the object of hope; in another way as the matter on which the virtue operates while tending away from this matter to something else. It is in the latter sense that the pleasures of coitus are matter of temperance. For the inclination of temperance is not to dwell on these pleasures, but rather, by restraining them, to tend toward the good of reason. Similarly, the inclination of fortitude is not to dwell on dangers, but rather, by overcoming them, to attain the good of reason. And it is the same with prudence concerning doubtful matters, and with justice concerning the necessary things of this life. Hence, the farther one withdraws from these objects in the progress of the spiritual life, the more perfect will be the acts of these virtues, because the objects are related to the virtues as a *terminus a quo* rather than as the *terminus ad quem* that gives the virtues their species.

Thus SAINT THOMAS. Similarly, in the question at hand, I say that the habits of the gifts, especially those of which the opponent is speaking, have a twofold object: one is material and, so to speak, a *terminus a quo;* the other is formal and, so to speak, a *terminus ad quem.* The latter is a second difference <of each of the gifts>, consisting of measurement by or conformity to this difference. The second object will remain in heaven, although the first will not. Again, SAINT THOMAS, in *In 3 Sent.,* d.34, q.1, a.3, ad 6, speaks as follows:

> The gifts that share with certain virtues an object that will remain in heaven will not themselves remain in heaven as distinct from those virtues, from which they are distinguished only with respect to imperfection and perfection in manner of operation. This is clear in the case of understanding and faith. For vision, to which faith will give way, pertains to the perfected gift of understanding, as is clear from the *Gloss* on *Matthew* 5. The same is true of wisdom, by which we are called children of God, in relation to hope, which aspires to this loftiness.
>
> But the gifts that share with certain moral virtues a matter that will not remain in heaven will themselves remain not with respect to their acts concerning the matter that they share with the virtues, but rather with respect to their acts concerning the measure, which is something they do not share

> with the virtues. Hence the acts of these gifts will remain distinct from the acts of the virtues that will be present in heaven. And the acts of these gifts will be intermediary between the acts of the theological virtues and the acts of the moral virtues that remain in heaven. For the acts of the theological virtues will concern God in Himself, for example the act of charity in loving Him. The acts of the gifts will concern God as the rule that directs in all other matters, as, for example, fear will have the reverence toward God by which in the present life one had contempt for all worldly prosperity. But the acts of the cardinal virtues will concern the end that is achieved by meritorious acts of virtue, as, for example, the act of temperance is to take pleasure in no harmful shortcoming.

Thus SAINT THOMAS. From this text it is clear that the gifts will have an object in heaven, namely God Himself, inasmuch as He is the rule that directs other things. SAINT THOMAS shows at length what acts the virtues will have in heaven in *ST* I–II, q.68, a.6, ad 2, where he speaks as follows:

> With respect to each of the gifts GREGORY presents something that will pass away along with the present life and something that will remain in the future life. For he says that "wisdom restores the mind with respect to hope and certitude concerning eternal things," and of these two, hope will pass away, but certitude will remain. Concerning understanding, he says that "by penetrating what is heard, it restores the heart and illuminates its darkness"; and of these two, the hearing will pass away—for "a man will not teach his brother," as is said in *Jeremiah* 31—but the illumination of the mind will remain. Concerning counsel, he says that "it prevents one from being impulsive," which is necessary in the present life, and again that "it fills the soul with reason," which will also be necessary in the future life. Concerning fortitude, he says that "it does not fear adversities," which is necessary in the present life, and again that "it serves the food of confidence," something that will also continue in the future life. Concerning knowledge, he presents only one feature, namely that "it conquers the hunger of ignorance," which pertains to the present state, but by what he adds, namely "in the belly of the mind," fullness of knowledge may be figuratively understood, and this also pertains to the future state. Concerning piety, he says that "it fills the innards of the heart with works of mercy," which, as far as the words go, pertain only to the present state; but that inner feeling for one's neighbors indicated by the term "innards" also pertains to the future state, in which piety will offer not works of mercy, but rather a feeling of shared joy. Concerning fear, he says that "it restrains the mind so that it takes no pride in present things," which pertains to the present state, and that "it gives comfort concerning fu-

> ture things with the food of hope," which likewise pertains to the present state {423} with respect to hope, but can also pertain to the future state with respect to the comfort concerning what is here hoped for and there obtained.

Thus SAINT THOMAS. From this text it is clear that all the gifts of the Holy Spirit will have some object in heaven, whether it be God, one's neighbor, or oneself, although it will be oneself and one's neighbor as they are directed to God, and God primarily, although not God in Himself—for in this sense He is object of the theological virtues—but rather God as the rule and measure of the acts pertaining to blessedness.

SAINT THOMAS responds to the *second* argument in *ST* I–II, q.68, a.6, where he presents the following argument:

> Some of the gifts, such as knowledge, counsel, piety, fortitude, and fear, perfect man in the active life. But the active life comes to an end with the present life, as GREGORY says in *Moralia* 6. Therefore, not all the gifts will be present in the state of glory.

Thus the argument; the response follows:

> It must be said that that argument deals with the gifts with respect to their matter. But the matter of the gifts will not be deeds of the active life; rather, all the gifts will have their own acts concerning matters that pertain to the contemplative life that is the blessed life.

Thus SAINT THOMAS.

SAINT THOMAS responds to the opposing argument [p. 299] in *ST* I–II, q.68, a.1, ad 3, where he speaks as follows:

> That definition of virtue is given according to the common mode of virtue. Hence, if we wish to restrict the definition to the virtues inasmuch as they are distinguished from the gifts, let us say that the remark that they are "that by which one lives rightly" must be taken with respect to rightness of life understood according to the rule of reason. Similarly, a gift, inasmuch as it is distinguished from an infused virtue, can be said to be that which is given by God to direct man to the movement of God Himself, and which causes a man to follow his own instincts well.

Thus SAINT THOMAS.

This suffices for the question.

Blessed be God.

Amen.

Whether the Cardinal Virtues Are Interconnected in Such a Way That He Who Possesses One Possesses All

In relation to the thirty-sixth distinction of the third book of *The Sentences,* and the four further following distinctions, up to the end of the third book, the question is raised: Whether the cardinal virtues are interconnected in such a way that he who possesses one possesses all.

It is argued that they are not, as follows. BEDE says, commenting on *Luke* 17, that the saints are more humiliated by the virtues they do not possess than exalted by the ones they do. Therefore, they possess some and not others. Therefore, the virtues are not interconnected.

Argument is made for the opposite conclusion as follows. AMBROSE says, commenting on *Luke:* "The virtues are interconnected and concatenated in such a way that he who has one of them would seem to have all."

In this question there will be three articles: in the first the conclusions will be presented, in the second the objections, and in the third the solutions.

Article I: Conclusions

First Conclusion: There Cannot Be Prudence without Moral Virtue

SAINT THOMAS proves this conclusion in *ST* I–II, q.58, a.5, where he speaks as follows:

> There cannot be prudence without moral virtue. The reason for this is as follows. Prudence is right reason concerning action not merely with respect to the universal, but with respect to the particular in which actions take place.

> Now right reason requires principles from which reasoning proceeds. And reasoning concerning particulars must proceed not merely from universal principles, but also from particular ones. Man is rightly disposed with respect to universal principles of action by his natural understanding of principles, through which he knows that nothing evil must be done, or again by a certain kind of practical knowledge. But this does not suffice for reasoning rightly concerning particulars. For it sometimes happens that a particular universal principle as something known by natural understanding or knowledge is destroyed in the particular case by a passion. For example, when one is overcome by desire, it seems to the one who desires that what he desires is good, although it is against the universal judgment of reason. Hence, just as man is rightly disposed with respect to universal principles by a natural understanding or by a habit of knowledge, so too, in order to be rightly disposed with respect to particular principles, that is, the ends of action, he must be perfected by certain habits according to which he, in a way connaturally, judges rightly concerning the end. This comes about through moral virtue. For the virtuous man judges rightly concerning the end of virtue, because "as each one **{424}** is, so does the end appear to him," as is said in *Ethics* 3. Hence, for the right reason concerning action that is prudence, it is required that man have moral virtue.

Thus SAINT THOMAS. From this text the following argument can be formulated. Right reason concerning particular actions cannot exist or be possessed without right judgment of the particular principles from which a practical syllogism proceeds. But for this there is required moral virtue; and prudence is the right reason that proceeds from such principles. Therefore, prudence cannot be possessed without moral virtue.

Second Conclusion: No Moral Virtue Can Be Possessed without Prudence

SAINT THOMAS proves this conclusion in the text quoted above, a.4, where he speaks as follows:

> Moral virtue can exist without some intellectual virtues, namely wisdom, science and art, but it cannot exist without understanding and prudence. It cannot exist without prudence for the following reason. Moral virtue is a choosing habit, that is, one that makes good choices. But in order for choice to be good, two things are required: first, that there be the required intending of the end, and this is brought about by moral virtue, which inclines an appetitive power to a good befitting reason, which is the required end; second, that man rightly understand what is directed to the end, and this can only be

> by reason rightly deliberating, judging, and prescribing, which pertain to prudence and associated virtues. Hence moral virtue cannot exist without prudence.
>
> Nor, consequently, can moral virtue exist without understanding. For it is through understanding that naturally known principles, both in speculative matters and in matters of operation, are recognized. Hence, just as right reason in speculative matters, inasmuch as it proceeds from naturally known principles, presupposes understanding of principles, so too does prudence, which is right reason concerning actions.

Thus SAINT THOMAS. From this text the following argument can be formulated. No habit that chooses according to right reason can exist without a right reason that deliberates, judges, and prescribes. But this is the way in which moral virtue is related to prudence. Therefore it cannot exist without prudence.

Third Conclusion: The Four Cardinal Virtues Are Connected in Such a Way That He Who Possesses One of Them Possesses All Four

SAINT THOMAS presents this conclusion in *ST* I–II, q.65, a.1, where he speaks as follows:

> Moral virtue can be taken in two ways, namely as perfect and as imperfect. Imperfect moral virtue, for example temperance or fortitude, is nothing other than an inclination existing in us to perform some deed in the genus of good actions, whether this inclination be in us by nature or by custom. And according to this way of taking the moral virtues, they are not interconnected. For we see that a man may, by natural constitution or by custom, be disposed to perform deeds of generosity, who is nevertheless not disposed to perform deeds of chastity.
>
> But perfect moral virtue is a habit that inclines us to perform a good deed well. And it must be said that the moral virtues taken in this way are interconnected, as is held by almost everyone. The reason for this is twofold, according to the different ways in which the cardinal virtues are distinguished.
>
> Some distinguish them by certain general features of virtue—thus discretion pertains to prudence, rectitude to justice, moderation to temperance, and firmness of soul to courage—whatever the matter may be in which these features are considered. According to this distinction, the argument for the interconnection is clear. For firmness does not receive the praise belonging to a virtue if it is without moderation, rectitude or discretion; and the argu-

> ment is the same concerning the other features. This is the argument that GREGORY gives in *Moralia* 22, where he says that "the virtues cannot be perfect with respect to the essence of virtue if they are disjoined from one another, because that prudence is not true which is not just and temperate and brave." And he adds the same thing concerning the other virtues. And AUGUSTINE gives a similar argument in *De trinitate* 6.
>
> Others, however, distinguish the virtues mentioned according to their different matters. In keeping with this distinction the argument for their interconnection is given by ARISTOTLE in *Ethics* 6, and is as follows. As was said above, no moral virtue can be possessed without prudence, because it belongs to moral virtue to make a right choice, since it is a choosing habit. Now for right choice there is required not merely inclination to an appropriate end, which is caused directly by a habit of moral virtue, but also that one rightly choose what is directed to the end, which can only occur through prudence, which is deliberative, judicative, and prescriptive of what is directed to the end. Similarly, prudence cannot be possessed unless the moral virtues are possessed, since prudence is right reason concerning actions that proceeds, as from its principles, from the ends of the actions, to which one is rightly related by the moral virtues. From this it clearly follows that the moral virtues are interconnected.

Thus SAINT THOMAS. And he presents the same conclusion in *In 3 Sent.*, d.36, q.1, {425} a.1, and in *Questions on the Virtues*, "On the Cardinal Virtues". From these texts the following argument can be formulated. Whenever things are so related that they cannot exist without yet another thing, nor that other thing without any of them, such things are perfectly interconnected. But the four cardinal virtues are so related that three of them, namely the moral virtues, cannot exist without prudence; nor can any one of the three exist without prudence; nor can prudence, which is an intellectual virtue, exist without the three other, moral virtues. Therefore the four virtues are perfectly interconnected.

Here the first article terminates.

Article II: Objections

§1. Against the First and Second Conclusions

Arguments of Scotus In the second article argument will be made against the conclusions.

SCOTUS (*In 3 Sent.*, d.36, q.1, a.2) argues against the first and second conclusions that not every virtue is necessarily connected with the prudence proper to it: rather, reason can be right and choice wrong, and in such a case prudence can exist without the moral virtue. *First,* he argues as follows:

> Commenting on *Psalm* 123:3, "They might, perhaps, have swallowed us alive," AUGUSTINE says: "They are swallowed up alive who know that evil exists and consent to it."
>
> Again, commenting on *Psalm* 68:23, "Let their table become a snare before them," he says: "Who are 'the living'? Those who consent and know ought not to consent to vice. Behold, they recognized the trap, and put their foot into it."
>
> Again, commenting on *Psalm* 118:20, "My soul has desired, etc.," he says: "Understanding leads the way, but either no feeling, or only sluggish feeling, follows."

Second, he argues as follows:

> The authoritative text and the argument of THE PHILOSOPHER in *Ethics* 2 seems to support the point. "Argument," he says, "is of little or no worth for virtue." But if rightness of intellect in considering is present, one necessarily has, by concomitance, right will. Since knowledge contributes much to considering rightly, it would consequently contribute much to willing rightly. But something else follows from what you say, namely that one should not attempt to persuade someone not to be vicious, but rather to consider in light of a habit of the understanding. For according to you, if one considers rightly in light of the habit of scientific knowledge, the will cannot at the same time be other than right. Thus one should not attempt to persuade anyone to will rightly, but only to consider rightly.
>
> Again, this is shown by the following argument. When the understanding dictates rightly, the will chooses nothing, as it can not choose what is dictated by the understanding, because then reason would be simultaneously moved by two different understandings. And since the will does not choose anything, no virtue is produced in it. But prudence is produced by right dictating. Therefore, prudence will be produced without moral virtue.

Third, he argues as follows:

> An evil choice cannot blind the intellect so that it errs concerning actions. The argument is as follows. The terms are the entire cause of the first principles, in practical matters as well as speculative ones, according to *Posterior Analytics* 1; and every syllogistic figure is of itself evident to every intellect, as is clear from the definition of the perfect syllogism in *Posterior Analytics* 1.

Therefore, once terms are apprehended and composed and a syllogistic deduction is constructed, the intellect necessarily assents to the discourse, knowledge of which depends, precisively, on knowledge of the terms of the first principles and knowledge of the syllogistic deduction. Therefore, it is impossible for the will, by means of a syllogistic deduction, to cause the intellect, which considers the principles, to err with respect to the conclusion, or, all the more, to err with respect to the principles. Therefore the intellect will in no way be blinded in such a way as to err.

You might grant the conclusion, but say that the will causes blindness because it turns the intellect away from the right consideration.

Against this I say that to turn away is not to blind, since the will could turn away while prudence is present. For it is possible that one who is prudent is not always considering what pertains to prudence, but sometimes wills other things.

Again, to will to turn away requires an understanding that is simultaneous in time and prior in the order of nature. Now either (1) that understanding is a dictate of right reason from which the will wishes to turn away the intellect, and then it would follow that the willing to turn away is not a sin, according to you, because it co-exists with the right dictate; or (2) the act of understanding that precedes the will to turn away is other than the right dictate. (1) And if the will to turn away is right, there follows the same thing as before, namely that the will to turn away is not a sin, and thus no blinding follows from it. (2) But if the act of understanding that precedes the will is not right, the blinding would not be something that follows upon the willing to turn away, because it preceded that willing.

Fourth, he argues as follows:

Either the will chooses badly when a right dictate is present, and then our conclusion follows. Or, if it chooses badly and chooses when a right dictate is not present, it chooses after some other act of understanding has been made, one that is not right, because if the understanding were right, then, according to you, the will in choosing would not sin. Therefore, the act of understanding that is not right will be prior to the evil willing, and will not be made not-right by another evil act, one of willing (and thus we have our conclusion), because there can be no circularity **{426}** proceeding to infinity between causes and effects. Consequently, the will does not cause the blindness that produces the evil dictate, because, according to you, the evil willing follows upon the dictate.

Fifth, he argues as follows:

> No-one in the present life is completely incorrigible. Therefore no-one can err completely concerning the first practical principles.
>
> The inference is proved as follows. One who errs concerning the first practical principles has nothing by which he could be moved to good, for however one tries to persuade him, he will deny something that is assumed, because nothing can be assumed with greater evidence than a first principle.

Sixth, he argues as follows:

> The damned do not assent to the saying "God must be obeyed" as something true, because then there would not be for them the worm of which it is said in the last chapter of *Isaiah,* "Their worm shall not die." For they simply speaking hate God with pleasure and without remorse of conscience.
>
> It is clear, therefore, from these points that the right dictate can be simply speaking present in the intellect without the right choice of that dictate being present in the will. Thus, since a single right act of dictating, or many repeated ones, produce prudence, prudence will in such a case be produced without any habit of moral virtue.

Thus SCOTUS, in outline.

§2. Against the Third Conclusion

Arguments of Scotus The same SCOTUS (d.36, q.1, a.1) argues against the third conclusion that the moral virtues are not necessarily interconnected. *First,* he argues as follows:

> A virtue is a perfection of man, but not of the whole man, because then one moral virtue would suffice. But when there are several partial perfections of a thing, that thing can be perfect with respect to one perfection, but imperfect with respect to another. This is clear in the case of man, to whom it belongs to have many organic parts, and who therefore can have one perfection in the highest degree while having no perfection at all in another respect: for instance, he can in the highest degree be well disposed with respect to sight or taste, but have no perfection at all with respect to hearing. Accordingly, one can in the highest degree have perfection in relation to the matter of temperance without having any of the perfection required in the matter of some other perfection; consequently, he can be simply speaking temperate, even to the point of having a habit of temperance, even if he is not brave. Nevertheless, he is not simply speaking moral without all of the moral virtues, just as one is not perfectly sentient without all of the sense-powers. But he is no less perfectly temperate although he is less perfectly moral, just

as one is no less perfectly able to see or hear although he may be less perfectly sentient.

Second, he argues as follows:

> "Virtue is a choosing habit, consisting in the intermediary in relation to us and determined by reason, that is, as the wise man would determine it" (*Ethics* 2.6). But there can be such a conformity, both of habit and of act, to the right reason according to which a virtue chooses, without the concurrence of the other virtues in the same agent. Therefore, etc.
>
> The point assumed is clear. For one would not rightly choose in the matter of temperance unless right reason, dictating such an object of choice, preceded. But the right dictate concerning the matter of one virtue can precede without any right dictating of reason concerning the matter of another virtue.

Third, he argues as follows:

> One can practice on the matter of one virtue and not another because the opportunity for acting with respect to the matter of the second virtue does not arise. Therefore, one can acquire the habit of one virtue without the other.
>
> This is confirmed as follows. One for whom the opportunity of acting with respect to the matter of the second virtue does not arise is not inclined to this act as he is inclined to the act of which he possesses the habit.
>
> It might be said, *first,* that if the matter of the second virtue does not arise in an external way, it does arise in the phantasms; and it will be necessary to choose rightly concerning them, or otherwise acquired virtue will not be preserved in any degree.
>
> Against this we argue as follows. It is possible for the intellect to consider not these phantasms, but only those to which the habit of virtue inclines. For the intellect, as is commonly said, cannot simultaneously consider two things distinctly.
>
> Therefore, if the other phantasms, which do pertain to the second virtue, do arise, it is possible for the will not to choose, whether well or badly, concerning them, but rather to command non-consideration of them and consideration of the phantasms pertaining to the virtue that is possessed.
>
> It may be said, *second,* that, although one habit can be acquired without another, still, no habit, however intensified, can have the essence of virtue unless it is conformed to the other virtues, because agreement between habit and habit is necessary in any act of virtue.
>
> Against this objection I argue *first* as follows. It follows from the objection that every virtue is for another virtue the reason for its being a virtue *(ratio essendi virtutem).* The consequent is false, but it does follow. For if the

habit of temperance is a virtue only because it accompanies another virtue, such as fortitude, then the virtue of fortitude, as accompanying temperance, will be the reason for being a virtue for temperance; and conversely, by the same argument, temperance, as accompanying fortitude, will be the reason for being a virtue of fortitude. Therefore, each **{427}** will be the reason of the other.

But the falsity of the consequent is evident. For it will follow that there is virtue before there is virtue, and that there will be no first virtue, and thus that there will be no virtue. The proof of these consequences is as follows. Let us take that habit in the category of quality called temperance. If it cannot be a virtue except through concomitance of another virtue called fortitude, then fortitude is a virtue before temperance is a virtue. And since fortitude cannot be a virtue except, according to the hypothesis, through concomitance of the virtue of temperance, therefore fortitude was a virtue before it was a virtue. By the same argument it is clear that there will be no first virtue. For <temperance> cannot be the first virtue without the concomitance of the other virtues, which already, according to the hypothesis, have the essence of virtue; and no other virtue is first, because no other one can be a virtue without the concomitance of temperance, inasmuch as it is a virtue.

In response to this it might be said that there can be a virtue by itself possessing all concomitant virtues; and that although one habit precedes another with respect to the essence by which it is this kind of habit, this is not the case with respect to the essence by which it is a virtue: rather, all habits, whether produced earlier or later, get the essence of virtue from both their own essences and mutual concomitance.

Against this objection I argue as follows. Then it would follow that a single act will produce all the moral virtues with respect to the being *(esse)* of moral virtue, which seems to be inappropriate.

The inference is proved as follows. Assume the habit that is temperance as produced; assume, subsequently, the habit that is fortitude as produced, and produced in the same degree. Nevertheless, neither of these habits will be a virtue to the extent that either of them will be a habit in the same degree that it is a virtue. Therefore, either habit will exist before virtue, or it will not. If it does, we have our conclusion, because one habit will be able to be a virtue without the other. If it does not, then all the habits come to be with the being *(esse)* of virtue through a single act, which seems to be inappropriate, because that act seems to be the act of a single virtue. And just as, if the virtue were already produced, the act would be an act of one virtue, so it is productive of one virtue, and therefore not of all.

> *Second,* I argue against the response as follows. It seems more reasonable that, among the moral virtues, species of the same genus should be interconnected than that two genera should be, because one is more inclined to be in an orderly state with respect to matter closely connected to oneself through a virtue one does possess than with respect to what is more remote. Now species in the same genus of virtue have matters that are more interconnected than are matters of virtues in different genera. But there are species of the same virtue that are not interconnected, for example virginity and conjugal chastity. Therefore, etc.

Thus SCOTUS.

Here the second article terminates.

Article III: Solutions

§1. To the Arguments against the First and Second Conclusions

To the Arguments of Scotus In the third article it remains to respond to the aforementioned objections [p. 328].

Thus, in response to the *first* argument of SCOTUS against the first two conclusions we say that from the authoritative texts that the opponent introduces one may conclude that practical knowledge can co-exist with perverse choice but not that prudence can co-exist with it. SAINT THOMAS treats of this point in *Questions on the Virtues,* "On the Virtues in General", a.6; for, in the first objection, he presents the following argument:

> THE PHILOSOPHER says in *Ethics* 2 that knowing contributes little or nothing to virtue. And he is speaking of practical knowledge, as is clear from what he adds, that many do not perform the things of which they have knowledge; for knowledge directed to a deed is knowledge of the practical intellect. Therefore the practical intellect cannot be a subject of virtue.

Thus the argument; the response is as follows:

> It must be said that THE PHILOSOPHER is there speaking about practical knowledge. But prudence signifies something more than practical knowledge. For universal judgment concerning things to be done, such as that fornication is evil, that theft is not to be done, etc., pertains to knowledge; and when this knowledge exists, it can happen that, in the particular act, the judgment of reason is cut off, so that reason does not judge rightly, which is why knowing is said to be of little help for virtue. But it pertains to prudence to judge rightly concerning individual actions inasmuch as they are to be

> done here and now, and this judgment is destroyed by any sin. Thus, while prudence remains, a man does not sin. Hence prudence contributes not a little, but rather much, to virtue, or rather, it causes virtue itself.

Thus SAINT THOMAS. Again, in *Questions on Evil,* q.3, a.9, he speaks as follows:

> As ARISTOTLE says in *Ethics* 7, where he considers strength and certitude of knowledge, SOCRATES held that knowledge cannot be overcome by passion, that is, that no man can through passion do anything that is contrary to his knowledge, and so he called all virtues "knowledge" and all sins "ignorance." From this it followed that no knower sins out of weakness, which is clearly opposed to what we experience daily.
>
> Accordingly, it must be known that "to have knowledge" can occur in different ways: in one way in the universal and in another in the particular; in one way habitually and in another in actuality.
>
> Now, *first,* it can happen that what is known habitually is not considered in actuality because of passion. {428} For it is clear that when the act of one power becomes intense, the act of another power is impeded or completely prevented; for example, when someone is intent on listening to someone else, he does not see a passer-by. This happens because all the powers are rooted in the one soul, whose intention applies each power to its own act, so that, when one is strongly intent upon the act of one power, his intentness concerning another act is diminished. Therefore, if there is strong desire, anger or something similar, he is hindered in the consideration of knowledge.
>
> *Second,* it should be considered that the passions of the soul, since they exist in the sensitive appetite, concern particulars: for a man desires this particular pleasure, just as he also senses this particular sweet thing. Scientific knowledge, however, is in the universal, and universal knowledge is not the principle of any act except inasmuch as it is applied to the particular, because acts concern particulars. Accordingly, when passion concerning some particular is strong, it opposes the contrary movement of knowledge concerning that same particular not merely by distracting one from the consideration of knowledge, as was said above, but also by destroying this consideration by way of contrariety. Thus, even if one who is in the grip of strong passion does consider a universal, his consideration will nevertheless be hindered with respect to the particular.
>
> *Third,* one must consider that the application of reason may be so fettered by a bodily alteration that reason either considers nothing whatsoever or is not able to freely consider, as is clear in the case of those who are

> asleep and the mad. Now a bodily alteration does occur in passion, so that sometimes one becomes insane through desire, anger or some such passion. Hence, when these passions are strong, because of this bodily alteration they in a way fetter reason so that it has no free judgment concerning particular things to be done. Thus nothing prevents one who knows by habituation and in the universal from sinning through weakness.

Thus SAINT THOMAS. He presents something similar in *ST* I–II, q.77, a.2, where he speaks as follows:

> The opinion of SOCRATES, as THE PHILOSOPHER says in *Ethics* 7, was that knowledge can never be overcome by passion, and hence he held that all the virtues are knowledge and all the sins ignorance. Now in a way his opinion on this point was correct. For since the will is directed to a good or apparent good, the will would never be moved to evil unless what is not good somehow appeared good to reason, and therefore the will would never tend to evil unless some ignorance or error of reason were present. Hence it is said in *Proverbs* 14, "Those who do evil err."
>
> But because it is clear from experience that many act against what they know—and this is also confirmed by divine authority, for according to *Luke* 12, "The servant who knows the will of his master and does not do it will be beaten with many blows," and as is said in *James* 4, "For him who knows the good and does not do it there is sin"—SOCRATES did not simply speaking speak the truth. Rather, one must make a distinction, as THE PHILOSOPHER teaches in *Ethics* 7. For since man uses two kinds of knowledge for acting rightly, namely universal and particular, deficiency in either suffices to hinder rightness of the deed and of the will. Accordingly, it can happen that one has knowledge in the universal, for instance that no fornication ought to be done, but nevertheless does not know in the particular that this particular act, which is fornication, ought not to be done. And this is enough to make the will not follow the universal judgment or knowledge of reason.
>
> Again, it should be considered that nothing prevents someone from habitually knowing something that he does not consider in actuality. Therefore, it can happen that one even has right knowledge concerning the individual case and not merely in the universal, but nevertheless does not consider this knowledge in actuality; and then, it does not seem unlikely that a man might act against what he does not consider in actuality.
>
> Now that a man does not consider in the particular what he knows habitually sometimes results merely from lack of intention, as, for instance, when a man who knows geometry does not intend to consider the conclusions of geometry that he has ready to hand to consider. Sometimes, howev-

> er, a man does not consider what he knows habitually because of some supervening impediment, for instance some external preoccupation or bodily infirmity. In this way, one who is in the grip of a passion does not consider in the particular what he knows in the universal inasmuch as the passion hinders such consideration.
>
> Now a passion can hinder in three ways: first, by distraction; second, by contrariety, because passion for the most part inclines to the contrary of what universal knowledge holds; third, by bodily alteration through which the reason is in a way fettered so that it cannot freely issue in act, just as sleep or drunkenness, in causing bodily alteration, fetter the use of reason. That this fettering does occur in the case of the passions is clear from the fact that when the passions are very intense man sometimes loses the use of reason: for many have become insane through excess of love or anger. It is in this way that passion induces reason to judge in the particular against the universal knowledge that it possesses.

Thus SAINT THOMAS. Again, in *Questions on Truth,* q.24, a.2, he speaks as follows:

> Appetite follows on knowledge, for appetite is only of a good proposed to it by a cognitive power. But that appetite sometimes seems not to follow on knowledge is due to the fact that appetite and the judgment of knowledge are not directed to the same thing. For {429} appetite concerns the particular possible deed, but the judgment of reason sometimes concerns a universal, which is sometimes contrary to appetite. But judgment concerning this particular possible deed as something in the present can never be contrary to appetite. For one who wishes to fornicate, although he knows in the universal that fornication is evil, nevertheless he judges for himself that, as something in the present, this particular act of fornication is a good; and he chooses it under the aspect of good, for no-one acts while intending evil.

Thus SAINT THOMAS. Again, in the same question, a.8, he speaks as follows:

> The will naturally tends to good as its object. That it sometimes tends to evil occurs only because an evil is set forth under the aspect of good, for evil is involuntary, as DIONYSIUS says in *The Divine Names* 4. Hence there cannot be sin in the movement of the will, that is, the will cannot desire evil, unless a shortcoming pre-exists in the apprehensive power by which evil is set forth to the will as good. This shortcoming in reason can happen in two ways: in one way because of reason itself, and in another way because of something extrinsic. It happens because of reason itself because, although knowledge of good in the universal—both the good that is the end and the

good that is directed to the end—is naturally, unchangeably, and without error present in reason, knowledge of good in the particular is not; rather, reason can err concerning the latter so as to judge that something that is not the end is the end, or that something that is not useful is useful.

By the same argument, the will also naturally desires the good that is the end, namely happiness in general, and similarly it naturally desires the good directed to the end, for everyone naturally desires what is useful to himself. But the sin of the will occurs in seeking this or that particular end, or in choosing this or that useful thing.

Reason may be made to fall short by something external when, through the lower powers being intensely moved by something, the act of reason is obstructed so that it does not clearly and firmly set forth its judgment concerning the good to the will; for example, when one who has right judgment concerning the preservation of chastity seeks, through desire for something pleasurable, what is contrary to chastity because the judgment of the reason has in a way been fettered by desire, as THE PHILOSOPHER says in *Ethics* 7.

Thus SAINT THOMAS. Again, in *Questions on Evil,* q.16, a.2, he speaks as follows:

Appetite is nothing but inclination toward what is appetible. And just as natural appetite follows from a natural form, so sensitive or intellective appetite follows on a form that has been apprehended, for their object is none but a good apprehended by the sense-power or by the intellect. Accordingly, evil cannot occur in the appetite by the appetite's disagreement with the apprehension on which it follows, but only by its disagreement with some higher rule.

Hence one must consider whether the apprehension on which the inclination of appetite follows is itself able to be directed by a higher rule. For if the apprehension does not have a higher rule by which it ought to be directed, it is impossible for evil to be present in the appetite.

This lack of a higher rule occurs in two cases. For the apprehension of a brute animal has no higher rule by which it ought to be directed, and hence evil cannot be present in its appetite. For it is good that such an animal be moved to desire or anger following from an apprehended sensible form, and hence DIONYSIUS says, in *The Divine Names* 4, that the good of a dog is to be maddened. Again, the divine intellect has no higher rule by which it could be directed, and hence evil cannot be present in the divine will.

In man, however, there are two kinds of apprehension that ought to be directed by a higher rule: for sensitive cognition ought to be directed by rea-

> son, and the cognition of reason by divine wisdom or law. Accordingly, there are two ways in which evil can be present in the appetite of man. In one way, because the sensitive apprehension is not ruled according to reason, and in this sense DIONYSIUS says in *The Divine Names* 4 that it is the evil of man to be beyond reason. In another way, because human reason ought to be directed according to divine wisdom and law, and in this sense AMBROSE says that sin is "transgression of the divine law." But in substances separated from a body there is only one kind of knowledge, namely intellectual, which ought to be directed according to the rule of divine wisdom, and hence in the will of these substances evil can be present by the fact that the will does not follow the order of the higher rule, namely that of divine wisdom.

Thus SAINT THOMAS.

From these texts—as well as from many others that would be too long to quote, and from what has been quoted at length in the second book—the following points are clear. *First,* that it is possible for someone to choose badly through the will and simultaneously to have right knowledge in the universal concerning what is to be done. *Second,* that it is possible for someone to have right judgment and knowledge, in actuality in the universal and by way of habit with respect to particulars, concerning what is to be done, and simultaneously to sin by choosing badly. *Third,* that it is impossible for someone to judge rightly in actuality, both in the universal and in the particular, concerning what is to be done, and simultaneously to choose perversely or sin. *Fourth,* that it is impossible for someone to make a perfect and complete act of prudence, and simultaneously to sin by choosing badly: for the perfect act of prudence is to deliberate rightly, judge rightly, and prescribe rightly concerning something particular to be done, according as it is to be done here and now and in keeping with all its circumstances. *Fifth,* that the will never sins in disagreeing with the ultimate judgment or act of reason or prudence, but rather because it disagrees with the higher rule. *Sixth,* that no appetite, whether animal, rational, or intellective, ever tends to the opposite of what is ultimately {430} set forth and prescribed to it by the apprehensive power as what absolutely ought to be done. From these points it is clear that the first argument of SCOTUS is invalid.

In response to the *second* argument we say *first* that the authoritative text of THE PHILOSOPHER is irrelevant to the question because its application is contrary to his meaning. Enough has been said about this in the solution of the first objection.

Second, we say that we do not maintain that right choice always and necessarily follows from right judgment or consideration by the intellect of a particular action. For, as has been maintained at length in the second book, the intellect does not necessitate or necessarily move the will with respect to its external act, but only with respect to its specification; and that it does so in relation to some, but not all, objects.

But we do maintain that perverse choice cannot co-exist with a perfect act of prudence or with complete rightness of reason.

Again, we maintain that right choice always and necessarily does follow from a right precept of the reason; and that choice follows from every precept, but not from every deliberation or judgment. The opponent's error and deception, as well as the strength of our response to both this and the following arguments, concern this point. It is in the sense just mentioned that all of the remarks of SAINT THOMAS in which he seems to say the opposite—namely that the will cannot be contrary to the intellect's ultimate judgment—are to be understood: for he is taking "judgment" to mean "precept." More will be said about this point in what follows, for it is the great key to this matter and many err by not understanding it. AUREOLUS says much that is good on this point.

Third, we say that one should attempt to persuade a man not merely to consider rightly, but also to will rightly, if right consideration, both in the universal and in the particular, concerning actions cannot be had without rightness of will. Enough has been said concerning this point in the first two conclusions. Moreover, SAINT THOMAS, in *Questions on the Virtues,* "On the Cardinal Virtues", a.2, speaks concerning this point as follows:

> Prudence cannot exist without the moral virtues. For prudence is right reason concerning actions. But right reason of any kind requires that one have right judgment concerning the principles from which the reasoning proceeds; for instance, with respect to the objects of geometry, one cannot have right judgment concerning the conclusions unless one has right reasoning concerning the principles of geometry. Now the principles of actions are ends, for it is in terms of these that the essence of actions is understood. But one has right judgment concerning the end through a habit of moral virtue, because, as THE PHILOSOPHER says in *Ethics* 3, "as each one is, so does the end appear to him"; for example, what is desirable as an end to the virtuous man is the good according to virtue, and what is desirable as an end to the vicious man pertains to vice; and it is similar in the case of healthy and dis-

> eased senses of taste. Hence, whoever possesses prudence necessarily also possesses the moral virtues.

Thus SAINT THOMAS. From this text it is clear that just as moral virtue requires prudence in order to judge rightly of what is directed to the end, so prudence requires moral virtue in order to make a right judgment concerning the end and to will rightly concerning it. Again, in *ST* I–II, q.58, a.5, SAINT THOMAS presents the following argument:

> A prior perfection does not depend upon a posterior perfection. But reason is prior to the sensitive appetite and moves it. Therefore intellectual virtue, which is the perfection of reason, does not depend on moral virtue, which is the perfection of the appetitive part. Therefore, it can exist without it.

Thus the argument; the response is as follows:

> It must be said that inasmuch as reason apprehends the end, it precedes appetite for the end. But appetite for the end precedes the reasoning that reasons in order to choose what is directed to the end, and this reasoning pertains to prudence. Similarly, in speculative matters, understanding of principles is the principle of the reason that syllogizes.

Again, in the same place, in the solution of the third objection, he speaks as follows:

> Prudence is not only able to deliberate well, but also able to judge and prescribe well. But it cannot do so unless the impediment of the passions, which destroy the judgment and prescription of prudence, is removed, and this occurs through moral virtue.

Again, in *In 3 Sent.*, d.36, q.1, a.1, he speaks as follows:

> There is in us an initial inclination to the act of prudence, and this is called "natural virtue." THE PHILOSOPHER calls it *deinotes*, which we can call "cleverness" *(industria)*. This can be directed both to what is good and to what is evil, and hence it is not a virtue, because a virtue is something that always makes the deed of the one who possesses it good. Thus, if one is to be brought to the point at which one's judgment is always right, something by which all error is prevented must be added to this inclination.
>
> Now there are two kinds of error in judgment. One concerns the end: this occurs in a person who has a habit of vice, which inclines the person to the act of vice as something in itself good. This kind of error concerning what is to be done is like an error concerning principles in speculative matters.

> The other error occurs in pursuit of the end, when one is led away by passions from the right conception that he has of the end, and thus it is said that pleasure destroys the judgment of prudence. This kind of error concerning what is to be done is like an error in speculative matters with respect to the flow of principles into conclusions. Now moral virtue, which causes inclination to the right end and represses passion, prevents both kinds of error. Hence prudence cannot exist without moral virtue, I mean without temperance, fortitude, and justice.

Thus SAINT THOMAS.

From all these texts it is clear that prudence presupposes, as a principle, right willing with respect to the end, although it does not presuppose, but rather causes, right choice of what is directed to the end. Consequently {431} it is apparent that one should attempt to persuade a man not only to consider rightly, but also to will and desire rightly.

Fourth, we say in response to the argument that although, if the intellect merely deliberates, judges, and dictates well, it is possible for the will not to choose, whether well or badly, as was said above; nevertheless, it is impossible for the intellect, by rightly, firmly, and steadfastly deliberating, judging, and prescribing, to dictate with respect to the whole matter of prudence or of actions, or indeed with respect to one part of prudence or moral matter, unless first—that is, first in the order of nature—the appetite is rightly and firmly inclined toward the end and the intellect has right judgment concerning the end. On the contrary, it is through moral virtue that choice in conformity with a precept follows from the precept, as has been said. Accordingly it is impossible for a habit of prudence to be produced in someone unless the following simultaneously concur: first, on the part of reason, manifestation of the end or proximate ends of moral matter through synderesis; second, on the part of appetite, right inclination toward that end; third, on the part of reason, right syllogizing, by deliberating, judging, and prescribing, concerning the means to the end; fourth, on the part of appetite, choice of what has been prescribed. Therefore, the habit of prudence and moral virtue are produced simultaneously.

Concerning these points SAINT THOMAS, in *In 3 Sent.*, d.33, q.2, a.3, speaks as follows:

> Three things are necessary for the perfection of moral virtue: the first is establishment of the end; the second is inclination toward the end established; the third is choice of what is directed to the end.

> Now the proximate end of human life is the object of reason in general, and thus DIONYSIUS says in *The Divine Names* 4 that the evil of man is to be opposed to reason. This is why what is intended in all the moral virtues is that passions and operations be brought to the rightness of reason. But rightness of reason is natural. In this way, then, establishment of the end pertains to natural reason and precedes prudence just as understanding of principles precedes scientific knowledge. Hence THE PHILOSOPHER says that prudence has as its principles the ends of the virtues.
>
> Now this good of reason is determined according as a midpoint is established in actions and passions through a due proportioning of circumstances, which is what prudence accomplishes. Hence the midpoint of moral virtue, as is said in *Ethics* 2, is according to right reason, which is prudence. In a way, then, prudence establishes the end for the moral virtues, and its act is mixed into their acts.
>
> But inclination toward that end pertains to moral virtue, which consents to the good of reason in a natural way. And this inclination toward the end is called "choice" inasmuch as a proximate end is ordered to the ultimate end. Hence THE PHILOSOPHER says that moral virtue causes right choice. But identification of that in our operations and passions by which we are able to attain this good is the act of prudence. Hence establishment of the end precedes the act of prudence and moral virtue. But inclination toward the end, or right choice of the proximate end, is an act of moral virtue primarily, but an act of prudence in its origin. Hence THE PHILOSOPHER says that rightness of choice comes to be present in the other virtues from prudence, just as rightness in the intention of nature comes from divine wisdom directing nature. And in this respect, even the act of prudence is mixed into the acts of the other virtues: for just as natural inclination comes from natural reason, so the inclination of moral virtue comes from prudence. But choice of what is directed to the end, inasmuch as the choice implies a precept of reason concerning pursuit of what is directed to the end, is an act of prudence that is proper to prudence as distinct from the acts of the other virtues.

Thus SAINT THOMAS. He says something similar in *ST* II–II, q.47, a.6, except that there he says that it pertains to prudence to establish for the moral virtues not the end, but what is directed to the end, while natural reason, which is called synderesis, establishes the end for the moral virtues; and that although the moral virtues tend toward an end established by natural reason and not by prudence, nevertheless they are helped in this matter by prudence, which prepares the way for them by arranging what is directed to the end. This latter account seems more probable. But whatever may be the case concerning this point, it is clear from the foregoing text that a habit of prudence cannot be produced in someone by any dictates of intellect or reason unless there concurs an act of appetite by which moral virtue is produced, as SAINT THOMAS says in the text quoted above, namely *ST* I–II, q.58, a.5, ad 1, where he speaks as follows:

> Inasmuch as reason apprehends the end, it precedes appetite for the end. But appetite for the end precedes the reasoning that reasons in order to choose what is directed to the end, and this reasoning pertains to prudence, etc.

Again, in *Questions on the Virtues,* "On the Virtues in General", a.7, he speaks as follows:

> The habits that exist in the intellect are related to the will in different ways.
>
> Some do not depend on the will at all except with respect to their use, and this is accidental, since their use depends in one way on the will and in another way on the habits mentioned themselves, namely science, wisdom, and art. For by these habits man is perfected not in willing to use them well, but only in being able to use them.
>
> There is a habit of intellect that does depend on the will as that from which it gets its principle: this is how prudence is related to the will.
>
> There is a habit that also gets determination of its object {432} from the will: this is the case of faith. For faith perfects the speculative intellect through a command being given to the intellect by the will. This is clear from the act of faith. For man assents by his intellect in matters above human reason only because he wills to do so; as AUGUSTINE says, man cannot believe unless he wills. Thus faith exists in the speculative intellect through the latter submitting to a command of will, just as temperance exists in the concupiscible power through the latter submitting to a command of reason. Hence the will commands the believing intellect not merely with respect to the act to be carried out, but with respect to determination of the object. For the intellect assents to a determinate object of belief through a command of the will, just as the concupiscible power tends through temperance to a midpoint determined by reason.
>
> Prudence, however, exists in the intellect or practical reason in such a way that not the object of prudence, but only the end, is determined by the will. Rather, prudence itself looks for the object. For, presupposing a good end given by the will, prudence seeks ways in which this good may be perfected and preserved.

Thus SAINT THOMAS.

In response to the *third* principal objection we say *first* that evil choice by the will or sensitive appetite cannot entirely blind the intellect concerning actions so that it errs concerning the first and most universal principles in practical matters. The intellect can, however, be blinded and err concerning secondary universal principles. Concerning this point SAINT THOMAS speaks in many places, but most importantly in *ST* I–II, q.94, a.6, where he speaks as follows:

> The following belong to natural law: certain perfectly universal principles that are known to all; and certain secondary, more particular precepts that are, as it were, conclusions close to the principles.
>
> Accordingly, with respect to the universal principles, the natural law in the universal can in no way be deleted from the hearts of men. Nevertheless it can be deleted in the case of a particular possible deed inasmuch as reason is hindered by desire or some other passion from applying a universal principle to the particular possible deed.
>
> But with respect to the secondary precepts, the natural law can be deleted from the hearts of men through wrong beliefs; this is also the way in which errors concerning necessary conclusions occur in speculative matters. Again, it can be deleted through depraved customs and corrupt habits; for example robbery—and even sins against nature, as THE APOSTLE says in *Romans* 1—are not thought to be sins by some.

Thus SAINT THOMAS. Again, in *ST* II–II, q.15, a.1, he shows what blindness of mind is:

> Just as bodily blindness is privation of the principle of bodily vision, so blindness of mind is privation of the principle of intellectual or mental vision.
>
> Now the principle of the latter includes three things. One is the light of natural reason. The soul is never deprived of this light, because the latter belongs to the nature of the rational animal. However, this light is sometimes hindered from performing its proper act because of impediments in the lower powers that the human intellect needs in order to understand, as is clear in the demented and crazed.
>
> Another principle of intellectual vision is a habitual light added to the natural light of reason. The soul is sometimes deprived of this light, and this privation is blindness, which is a punishment in the sense that privation of the light of grace is held to be a punishment. Hence it is said of certain men in *Wisdom* 2 that "Their evil blinded them."

> The third principle of intellectual vision is some first intelligible through which man understands other intelligibles. Now the mind of man can attend to or not attend to this intelligible principle. Its not attending to it happens in two ways: sometimes, by the fact that one has a will that spontaneously turns away from consideration of this principle, in the sense of the *Psalm*'s remark that "They were unwilling to understand in order to act well"; in another way, through the preoccupation of the mind with other things that it loves more, and by which it is turned away from the sight of this principle, in the sense of the *Psalm*'s remark that "Fire," that is, desire, "cut them off, and they did not see the sun." And in both ways blindness of mind is a sin.

Thus SAINT THOMAS. Again, in the same question, a.3, he speaks as follows:

> The perfection of intellectual operation in man consists in abstraction from the phantasms of sensibles. Hence, the more the intellect of man is free from phantasms of this sort, the more it will be able to consider intelligible things and direct sensible things; the intellect, as ANAXAGORAS says, must be unmixed in order to command, and an agent must dominate matter in order to be able to move it. Now it is clear that pleasure applies the attention to the things in which one takes pleasure. Hence THE PHILOSOPHER says in *Ethics* 10 that "each man does best what pleases him, and does the opposite either not at all or poorly."
>
> Now the bodily vices, namely gluttony and lust, concern the pleasures of touch, namely pleasure in food and venereal pleasure, and these are the most vehement bodily pleasures. Accordingly, by these vices the attention of man is most of all applied to what is bodily, so that by them the attention and operation of man concerning intelligible things are weakened. This occurs more through lust than through gluttony, inasmuch as venereal pleasure is more vehement than pleasure in food. Hence from lust there arises blindness of mind, which, as it were, wholly excludes knowledge of spiritual goods; but from gluttony there arises dullness of sense, which makes man weak with respect to these {433} intelligible matters. And the opposite virtues, namely abstinence and chastity, on the contrary dispose man most of all to perfection of intellectual operation. Hence it is said in *Daniel* 1 that "to these children," namely the abstinent and the continent, "God has given wisdom and learning concerning every book and every wisdom."

Thus SAINT THOMAS. From this text it is clear how the intellect can and cannot be blinded, and by what it is principally blinded.

Second, we say that, however much first principles in matters of operation are of themselves known from their terms, and however much a syllogistic form is likewise known of itself, nevertheless, one who is perversely impassioned, habituated, or otherwise badly disposed is hindered from rightly proceeding from the first principles of action to a particular action. Or, granted that he does rightly syllogize in deliberating and judging concerning the particular action, he still would not prescribe rightly. Concerning these points, SAINT THOMAS, in *Questions on Evil,* q.3, a.9, ad 7, presents the following argument:

> Whoever knows a universal, and knows that the singular is contained under the universal, simultaneously, by induction, knows the singular, as is said in *Posterior Analytics* 1. For instance, as soon as one who knows that every mule is sterile knows that this particular animal is a mule, he immediately knows that it is sterile. But if one who knows that no fornication must be committed does not know that this particular act is fornication, he would not be thought to sin knowingly, but rather in ignorance. Therefore, if he does not sin through ignorance, he knows not only with respect to the universal, but also with respect to the particular.

Thus the argument; the response is as follows:

> In response to the seventh objection it must be said that since acts of sin and virtue follow choice, and since choice is a seeking of something previously deliberated about, while deliberation is a kind of investigation, there must in any act of virtue or sin be a deduction that is, as it were, syllogistic. However, the temperate man syllogizes in one way and the intemperate man in another, the continent man in one way and the incontinent man in another.
>
> For the temperate man is moved by the judgment of reason only, and so he applies a syllogism of three propositions, deducing as follows: "No fornication should be committed; but this particular act is fornication; therefore, it should not be done." But the intemperate man follows desire completely, and so he, too, applies a syllogism of three propositions, deducing, as it were, as follows: "Every pleasurable thing should be enjoyed; but this act is pleasurable; therefore, it should be enjoyed."
>
> But both the continent and the incontinent man are moved in two directions, being moved by reason to avoid sin and by desire to commit it. In the continent man, however, the judgment of reason conquers, while in the incontinent man the movement of desire conquers. Hence, both apply a syllogism of four propositions, but for contrary conclusions. For the continent man syllogizes as follows: "No sin should be committed" is his proposition following the judgment of reason; but following to the movement of desire, he considers in his heart that "everything pleasurable should be pursued";

> but because the judgment of reason conquers within him, he takes his minor premise and conclusion under the first proposition: "This is a sin; therefore, it should not be done." But the incontinent man, in whom the movement of desire conquers, takes his minor premise and concludes under the second proposition: "This is something pleasurable; therefore, it should be pursued." The incontinent man is one who sins, properly speaking, out of weakness; therefore it is clear that, although he knows with respect to the universal, he does not know with respect to the particular, because he takes his minor premise not by following reason, but by following desire.

Thus SAINT THOMAS. And he presents something similar in *ST* I–II, q.77, a.2, and in many other places.

Now someone might object that such an impassioned or habituated man is able to listen to someone else who does rightly syllogize in practical matters, with respect to both the universal and the particular action, and that he is able to assent to what the other says; and that therefore his reason is not entirely blinded or fettered, for he is able, while such a passion or habit is present, to rightly syllogize in practical matters.

In response to this we say that although such a man, in such a condition, might externally listen to someone rightly syllogizing, he does not for this reason rightly syllogize within. On the contrary, granted that he rightly syllogizes with his voice, he does not do so with his heart. Concerning this point, SAINT THOMAS, in the text of *Questions on Evil* quoted above, obj.8, presents the following argument:

> Spoken sounds are signs of things understood, as THE PHILOSOPHER says. But if one who in actuality chooses to fornicate were questioned, he would answer that it is a sin and should not be done. Therefore, it is not true that he knows with respect to the universal and is ignorant with respect to the particular.

Thus the argument; the response is as follows:

> It must be said that, just as a drunken man may speak words that he does not understand within himself, as THE PHILOSOPHER says in *Ethics* 7, so too, even if one who is conquered by passion says externally that this particular act should be avoided, in his heart he judges that it should be done. Hence, he says one thing externally, but thinks something else within himself.

Thus SAINT THOMAS.

Third, we say that when the intellect is turned away from right syllogizing and practical judgment, this does not always happen because of the will, but rather most often because of the sensitive appetite, especially when one sins out of passion. The case is different where one sins out of malice and a corrupt habit of will. Concerning this point, SAINT THOMAS, in *ST* I–II, q.77, a.1, speaks as follows:

> The judgment and apprehension of reason are hindered because of vehement and disorderly apprehension by imagination and judgment by the estimative power, as is clear in the case of the demented. But it is clear that the apprehension of imagination and the judgment of the estimative power follow passion in the sensitive appetite, just as the judgment of taste follows the disposition of the tongue. Hence we see that men in the grip of a passion do not easily turn their imagination away from what is affecting them. {434} Consequently, the judgment of reason usually follows passion in the sensitive appetite, and consequently, so does the movement of the will, which naturally follows the judgment of reason.

Thus SAINT THOMAS.

Fourth, we say that when the will turns the intellect away from right consideration, it need not do so in the way mentioned by the opponent, namely by willing to turn the intellect away from such a consideration. For this can happen in another way, namely because the will commands the intellect to the consideration of other objects, and by this consideration the intellect is drawn away from consideration of the former object. Similarly, SAINT THOMAS says with respect to a similar question that ignorance is said to be voluntary in two ways. Concerning this point, in *Questions on Evil,* q.3, a.8, he speaks as follows:

> An act of will can precede an act of intellect, as when one wills to understand in actuality. By this argument ignorance falls under the will. But this can happen in two ways.
>
> The first is when someone directly wills to be ignorant and not to know the knowledge of salvation, in order than he not be parted from a sin that he loves. Thus, in *Job* 21, it is said of certain men that they said to God, "Depart from us; we do not want the knowledge of your ways."
>
> In a second way, ignorance is said to be voluntary indirectly, and this because man applies no effort to knowing. This is the ignorance of negligence. Now because man is not said to be negligent except when he omits to

> do what he should do, it does not seem to pertain to negligence that one does not apply his soul to knowing anything whatsoever, but only that he does not apply his soul to knowing the things he ought to know, whether simply speaking and at all times (hence ignorance of the law is held to be negligence) or in a particular case: for example, when one shoots an arrow in a place where men are usually passing, it is ascribed to him as negligence if he makes no effort to know whether someone is in fact passing at that moment, and such ignorance, arising through negligence, is judged to be voluntary.
>
> In a third way, ignorance is said to be voluntary accidentally, namely by the fact that one directly or indirectly wills something from which the ignorance follows: directly, as is clear in the case of the drunkard, who wills to drink wine excessively, by which he is deprived of the use of reason; indirectly, when someone neglects to restrain initial movements of passion that, once they have grown, fetter the use of reason with respect to particular action, so that every evil man is said to be "ignorant."

Thus SAINT THOMAS. And he says something similar in *ST* I–II, q.6, a.8; q.19, a.6; q.76, a.3; and in *In 2 Sent.*, d.22, q.2, a.2. From these texts it is clear that, just as ignorance is not only called "voluntary" because it is directly willed, so something similar can be said of the turning away of the intellect from right consideration. Thus it is clear that the will can turn the intellect away from practical reason, and yet not do so through some act of willing by which it directly wills to turn the intellect away from right consideration. Consequently, the entire deduction of the third argument is thoroughly worthless.

Fifth, we say that the turning away of the intellect from right consideration by the sensitive appetite or will can be called a "blinding" for the following reasons. Through passion in the sensitive appetite, or a habit or act in the will, not only is the intellect drawn away from right practical consideration: rather, it also meets repeated or continuous hindrance to rightly deliberating; acquires an inclination to perversely deliberating, judging, or prescribing concerning actions; and has produced within itself a perverse habit contrary to prudence. Moreover, as was said above, through such passion in the sensitive appetite, or habit or act in the will, the intellect is deprived of a certain principle of intellectual vision—not, to be sure, the natural power of intellectual vision, but its habit or act.

In response to the *fourth* principal objection we say *first* that as long as a right dictate of practical reason remains, a dictate that deliberates, judges, and prescribes with respect to both the universal and the particular, the will never chooses badly, as has often been said.

Second, we say that sometimes an error of understanding precedes a perverse choice, sometimes ignorance does, and sometimes non-consideration does. It is not necessary that the error or ignorance follow from some evil willing or that it be caused by malice of will, nor does our position say that it is.

Third, we say that evil willing can be caused not only by a perverse dictate of the intellect, but also by a perverse dictate of particular reason. For the will is moved not only by universal reason, but also by particular reason, which is called "the cogitative" or "estimative," and which apprehends singulars, forms particular and individual conclusions, and subsumes minor premises concerning particulars in the practical syllogism. Concerning this point SAINT THOMAS, in *ST* I–II, q.10, a.3, ad 3, speaks as follows:

> The will is moved not only by the universal good apprehended by reason, but also by a good apprehended by the sense-power.

Thus SAINT THOMAS. Again, in *ST* II–II, q.49, a.1, ad 1, he speaks as follows:

> Prudence applies universal knowledge to individuals, which pertain to the sense-power. Therefore, many things pertaining to the sensitive part are required for prudence.

Again, in In q.47, a.3, ad 3, he speaks as follows:

> As THE PHILOSOPHER says in *Ethics* 6, prudence exists not in the external sense-power, by which we know proper sense-objects, but in the internal sense-power, which is perfected by memory and experience for quickly judging of particular things experienced. However, this does not mean that prudence exists in the internal sense-power as in its primary subject; rather, it primarily exists in reason, but through a certain application {435} belongs to the internal sense-power.

Thus SAINT THOMAS. Again, in *ST* I, q.86, a.1, ad 2, he speaks as follows:

> The choice of a particular possible deed is, as it were, the conclusion of a syllogism of the practical intellect, as is said in *Ethics* 7. But an individual thing cannot be directly concluded from a universal proposition except through the mediation of some particular proposition taken as a minor premise. Hence universal reasoning of the practical intellect does not move <to action> except through the mediation of a particular apprehension by the sensitive part, as is said in *De anima* 3.

Thus SAINT THOMAS. Again, in *Questions on Truth,* q.10, a.5, he speaks as follows:

> Movement from the soul to things begins from the mind and proceeds to the sensitive part, inasmuch as the mind rules the lower powers. Thus the mind mixes itself into individual things through the mediation of the particular reason, which is the power of the sensitive part that composes and divides individual intentions; it is also called the cogitative power, and it has a determinate organ in the body, namely the middle chamber in the head. Now the universal knowledge that the mind has concerning operations cannot be applied to a particular act except through an intermediate power that apprehends what is individual, in such a way that a syllogism may be made whose major premise, which is the thought of the mind, is universal, but whose minor premise, which is the apprehension of the particular reason, is individual, and whose conclusion is the choice of an individual deed, as is clear from *De anima* 3.

Thus SAINT THOMAS.

From these texts it is clear that the proximate mover of the will in choosing well or badly is the particular reason. Thus it is not necessary that a perverse judgment of the intellect or universal reason always precede an evil choice of the will; rather, a perverse dictate of the particular reason, which often derives from a passion of the sensitive appetite or from a corrupt habit, suffices for the latter. Hence SAINT THOMAS, in *ST* I–II, q.78, a.1, speaks as follows:

> Man, like every other thing, naturally has an appetite for good. Hence, the fact that his appetite turns aside to evil happens because of some corruption or disorder in one of the principles in man: for this is also the way in which failure occurs in the actions of natural things.
>
> Now the principles of human acts are intellect and appetite—both the rational appetite, called the will, and the sensitive appetite. Therefore, just as sin in human acts sometimes occurs because of defect in the intellect, for instance when one sins through ignorance; and sometimes because of defect in the sensitive appetite, as when one sins out of passion; so too, it sometimes occurs because of the defect in the will that is disorder of the will.
>
> Now the will is disordered when it loves what is less good. The consequence is that one chooses to suffer the loss of a good that is loved less in order to possess a good that is loved more; it is like when a man wills to suffer the amputation of a bodily member, and does so knowingly, in order to preserve the life that he loves more. In this way, when a disordered will loves a temporal good, such as wealth or pleasure, more than the order of reason or of divine law, or more than charity or something similar, it follows

> that it wills to suffer the loss of a spiritual good in order to acquire a temporal good. But evil is nothing but privation of a good, and accordingly, one knowingly wills a spiritual evil, which is evil simply speaking, by which one is deprived of a spiritual good, in order to acquire a temporal good. Hence one is said to sin with a positive malice or a purposefulness by, as it were, knowingly choosing evil.

Thus SAINT THOMAS.

It might be said that from this it follows that the will chooses perversely, and yet there is no defect in reason.

SAINT THOMAS responds to this in the same place, obj.1, where he presents the following argument:

> Ignorance is opposed to purposiveness or positive malice. But every evil man is ignorant, according to THE PHILOSOPHER, and it is said in *Proverbs* 14 that "They err who do evil." Therefore no-one sins out of a positive malice.

Thus the argument; the response is as follows:

> It must be said that ignorance sometimes precludes the knowledge by which one simply speaking knows that this particular deed is evil; and then one is said to sin out of ignorance.
>
> Sometimes, however, ignorance precludes the knowledge by which a man at the present moment knows that this particular deed is evil, as when a sin is committed out of passion.
>
> Again, sometimes ignorance precludes the knowledge by which one knows that this evil should not be endured for the sake of obtaining that good, although one still simply speaking knows that this particular deed is evil.

Thus SAINT THOMAS. <What he says is true> at least with respect to the act of prescribing, which is the most important act of practical reason, as has often been said and will be said again.

In response to the *fifth* argument we say that no-one sins by erring with respect to the first practical principles. However, one can err with respect to proximate principles, and with respect to conclusions concerning particulars that are not rightly deduced from the principles. Concerning this point, SAINT THOMAS, in *Questions on Truth*, q.16, a.3, where he asks, "Whether synderesis may be extinguished in someone?" speaks as follows:

> That "synderesis is extinguished" can be understood in two ways. One way is with respect to the habitual light itself, and thus it is impossible for synderesis to be extinguished, just as it is impossible for the soul of man to be deprived of the light of the agent intellect, through which first principles in speculative and operative matters are known: for this light belongs to the nature of man's soul, since it is by it that he is intellectual. Of this light it is said in the *Psalms*, "The light of thy countenance is signed upon us," which light shows us what is good; for this is a response to one who had said "Who will show us what is good?"
>
> For synderesis to be "extinguished" can be understood in another way with respect to act, and this again in two ways. **{436}**
>
> In one way such that the act of synderesis is said to be extinguished inasmuch as it is completely cut off. The act of synderesis is thus extinguished in those who do not have use of their free choice or any use of reason because of an impediment caused by injury to the bodily organs from which our reason needs to receive.
>
> In another way synderesis might be said to be extinguished with respect to act by the fact that the act of synderesis is turned to its contrary. It is impossible for the universal judgment of synderesis to be extinguished in this way. With respect to a particular action, however, synderesis is extinguished whenever sin is committed in choosing. For the force of desire or another passion can so absorb reason that synderesis, in choosing, does not apply the universal judgment to the particular act. However, this does not extinguish synderesis simply speaking, but only in a certain respect. Hence, simply speaking, we concede that synderesis is never extinguished.

Thus SAINT THOMAS. Again, in the same place, ad 2, he speaks as follows:

> Because of the error present in the higher reason of heretics, their conscience does not murmur against their infidelity, so that the judgment of synderesis is not applied to the particular matter. For the judgment of synderesis remains in them in the universal, since they judge that it is evil not to believe what is said by God; but they err in this particular matter in their higher reason, because they do not believe that this particular thing was said by God.

Thus SAINT THOMAS. Again, in ad 3, he speaks as follows:

> One who possesses a habit of vice is corrupt with respect to the principles of action—not concerning the universal, but concerning the particular case, inasmuch as reason is repressed by the habit of vice so that it does not, in choosing, apply the universal judgment to the particular action. It is in this sense that the impious man who reaches the depth of sin is said to be unconcerned.

Thus SAINT THOMAS. Again, in a.2, ad 6, he speaks as follows:

> Just as in speculative matters, although false reasoning originates in principles, it does not get its falsity from the first principles, but from wrong use of them; so, too, in matters of action.

Thus SAINT THOMAS.

In response to the *sixth* argument we say *first* that the damned do not make the judgment that God must be obeyed in Himself, namely as the universal and first principle of all good; rather, they make the judgment that, as such, He must be loved. Nevertheless, they do make the judgment that He must be obeyed accidentally, namely as the one who prohibits and punishes sins and whatever pleases the perverse will of the damned. Concerning this point SAINT THOMAS, in *In 4 Sent.*, d.50, q.2, a.1, qla.5, speaks as follows:

> Feeling is moved by good or evil that is apprehended. Now God is apprehended in two ways: in one way in Himself, which is how He is apprehended by the blessed, who see Him in His essence; in another way through His effects, which is how He is seen by us and by the damned. Therefore, He Himself in Himself, since He is by essence goodness, cannot be displeasing to any will, and so whoever sees Him in His essence cannot hold Him in hatred. But some of His effects may be repugnant inasmuch as they oppose something willed, and in this respect one can hate God, not in Himself, but by reason of His effects. Hence the damned, perceiving God in the effect of His justice that is punishment, hold Him in hatred, just as they do the punishments that they endure.

Thus SAINT THOMAS. Again, in a.2, qla.2, he speaks as follows:

> God can be considered in two ways. In one way, in Himself and with respect to what is proper to Him, which is to be the principle of the whole of goodness. In this way He cannot be thought of at all without pleasure, and so in this way He is not thought of at all by the damned. In another way He can be considered with respect to something, so to speak, accidental to Him in His effects, such as punishment or something similar. In this respect thought of Him can cause sorrow, and the damned do think of Him in this way.

Thus SAINT THOMAS. Again, in ad 1, he speaks as follows:

> The damned hold God in hatred only by reason of the punishment and prohibition of what accords with their evil will. Hence they will consider Him only as a punisher and prohibitor.

Thus SAINT THOMAS.

Second, we say that although the damned judge, in the way mentioned, that God is to be hated, they can nevertheless simultaneously suffer remorse of conscience and feel sorrow and repentance concerning this hatred in the way they repent of other sins that they committed in the present life. Concerning this point SAINT THOMAS, in *In 4 Sent.*, d.50, q.2, a.1, qla.2, speaks as follows:

> Repentance of sin can occur in two ways: in one way as such, and in another way accidentally. A man repents of sin who hates sin because of the fact that it is sin; a man accidentally repents of sin who hates it by reason of something connected to it, such as punishment or something similar. The evil, therefore, do not repent as such of their sins, because the willing of the evil of sin remains in them; but they do repent accidentally, inasmuch as they are afflicted with punishment that they suffer because of sin.

Thus SAINT THOMAS. Again, in the same place, ad 1, he speaks as follows:

> The damned will iniquity; but they flee punishment, and so, accidentally, repent of the iniquity committed.

Again, in ad 3, he speaks as follows:

> It can happen that the damned, without any turning away of will, repent of their sins, because what they flee from in their sins is not what they had previously willed or sought, but something else, namely punishment.

Thus SAINT THOMAS.

It can also be said, consistently with what has been said above, that the damned suffer remorse of conscience with respect to their hatred of God and other sins inasmuch as synderesis in the universal detests such things, although synderesis in the particular does not.

Third, we say that granting—but not conceding—**{437}** that a right dictate of reason can co-exist with perverse choice, or with no choice at all, still, this cannot last long without reason soon being distorted in an act of prudence because of perverse choices. Thus, a habit of prudence is never produced without a habit of moral virtue. HENRY OF GHENT, in *Quodlibet* 12, q.14, ad 1, touches on this argument.

Fourth, we say that the argument assumes something else that is false, namely that the habit of prudence is produced by a single right practical dictate. The falsity of this is clear: on the one hand because no habit is produced by a single act, especially not a habit concerning complex statements and the second operation of the intellect; on the other hand because the habit of prudence in particular is produced only after many experiences of actions and after many memories have been acquired. Concerning these points, SAINT THOMAS, in *ST* I–II, q.51, a.3, where he asks, "Whether a habit can be produced by a single act?" speaks as follows:

> Habits are produced by acts inasmuch as a passive power is moved by some active principle. But in order for a quality to be caused in something passive, something active must entirely subdue what is passive. Thus, as we see, it is because fire cannot immediately subdue something combustible that it does not immediately burn it; rather, it gradually removes opposing dispositions, so that, entirely subduing the combustible thing in this way, it imprints its likeness on it.
>
> Now it is clear that the active principle that is reason cannot entirely subdue the appetitive power in a single act, because the appetitive power is variously related to several things. But a judgment of reason that appetite should, in keeping with certain reasons and circumstances, pursue some one thing is accomplished in a single act. Hence the appetitive power is not subdued by this one act in such a way as to be, in most cases and naturally, directed to the same thing. Therefore, a habit of virtue cannot be caused by a single act, but only by many.
>
> Now it must be considered that among the apprehensive powers, there are two passive things: one is the possible intellect itself, and the other is the intellect that ARISTOTLE calls passive, which is particular reason, that is, the cogitative together with the memorative and imaginative powers. Accordingly, with respect to the first of these passive things, there can be something active that in a single act entirely subdues the power of what is passive to it, as, for instance, one proposition known per se convinces the intellect to assent firmly to a conclusion. A probable proposition does not do this, so that a habit of opinion can be caused only by many acts of reason, even on the part of the possible intellect. But it is possible for a habit of science to be caused by a single act of reason on the part of the possible intellect.
>
> But with respect to the lower apprehensive powers, it is necessary that the same acts be repeated many times in order for something to be firmly imprinted on the memory. Thus THE PHILOSOPHER says in the book *On Memory and Recollection* that "meditation strengthens the memory."
>
> But it is possible for bodily habits to be caused by a single act if what is active has great power, as sometimes strong medicine immediately induces health.

Again, in II–II, q.49, a.1, he speaks as follows:

> Prudence concerns contingent actions. Now in such matters man cannot be directed by what is simply speaking necessarily true, but only by what happens for the most part. For principles must be proportioned to conclusions, and one must conclude like from like, as is said in *Ethics* 6. But what is true for the most part must be considered through experience. Hence THE PHILOSOPHER says in *Ethics* 2 that "intellectual virtue has birth and growth from experience and time." Now experience is constituted out of many memories, as is clear from *Metaphysics* 1. Consequently, prudence requires that one have memory of many things. Hence memory is appropriately posited as a part of prudence.

Thus SAINT THOMAS.

Fifth, we say that all the arguments presuppose one thing that is false, namely that a habit of prudence is produced only by the act of reason that is right judgment, or by a dictate expressed in a proposition in the indicative mood, namely, "This is something to be done." But this is false. For a habit of prudence is produced only by the frequently repeated primary act of prudence. And that act is not right deliberation, because this pertains to *eubulia;* nor is it right judgment, because this pertains to *synesis;* rather, it is right prescription and command. But correct will precedes correct prescription; and correct choice inevitably follows correct prescription. Therefore, a habit of prudence can never be naturally produced in someone unless there is simultaneously produced a habit of moral virtue.

I. SAINT THOMAS shows that prescription is the primary act of prudence in *ST* II–II, q.47, a.8, where he speaks as follows:

> Prudence is right reason concerning actions. Hence, the primary act of prudence must be the primary act of reason concerning actions. Now there are three acts of the latter. The first is to deliberate, which pertains to discovery, for to deliberate is to investigate. The second act is to judge concerning what has been discovered, and speculative reason does this. But practical reason, which is directed to a deed, goes further, and the third act is to prescribe, an act that consists in {438} the application of the results of deliberation and judgment to what is to be done.
>
> Because this last act is closest to the end of practical reason, it is the primary act of the latter, and consequently of prudence. A sign of this is that the perfection of art consists in judging, but not in prescribing, and hence one who, having right judgment, willingly errs in art is thought to be a better artisan than one who errs unwillingly, which seems to be caused by defect of judgment. But it is the reverse with respect to prudence, as is said in *Ethics*

> 6: for one who willingly errs, being deficient in the primary act of prudence, which is prescription, is more imprudent than one who errs unwillingly.

Thus SAINT THOMAS.

2. SAINT THOMAS shows that the prescriptive command of reason presupposes an act of the will in *ST* I–II, q.17, a.1, where he speaks as follows:

> Command is an act of reason, but one in which an act of will is presupposed. For evidence of this we must consider that, because acts of will and of reason can be brought to bear on one another inasmuch as reason reasons about willing and the will wills the intellect to reason, an act of will can be preceded by an act of reason and vice-versa. And because the force of an act that is prior remains in one that follows, it sometimes happens that there is an act of will in which something of an act of reason virtually remains, for example, as was said, the will's act of application and choice; conversely, there is sometimes an act of reason in which something of an act of will virtually remains.
>
> Now command is essentially an act of reason. For one who commands orders, by intimating or declaring, the one he commands to do something; and to order by intimation belongs to reason. But reason can intimate or declare something in two ways: in one way absolutely, and such intimation is expressed by a verb in the indicative mood, as if someone should say to another, "This is what you should do"; but sometimes reason intimates something to someone by moving him to do it, and such intimation is expressed by a verb in the imperative mood, for instance, when someone says to another, "Do this." Now the first mover among powers of the soul in the performance of an act is the will. Therefore, since a second mover moves only in virtue of a first mover, it follows that for reason to move by commanding belongs to reason by virtue of the will. Hence it remains that command is an act of reason in which there is presupposed an act of will in virtue of which reason moves by command to the performance of an act.

Thus SAINT THOMAS.

3. SAINT THOMAS shows that choice of what is commanded and prescribed by reason always accompanies the command and precept of reason in I–II, q.17, a.5, where he asks, "Whether an act of will is commanded?" and answers as follows:

> Command is nothing other than the act of a reason that directs, with a certain movement, to the doing of something. But it is clear that reason can direct an act of will: for just as it can judge that it is good to will something, so

> it can direct in commanding that it be willed. From this it is clear that an act of will can be commanded.

Thus SAINT THOMAS. Again, in obj.1, he presents the following argument:

> AUGUSTINE says in *Confessions* 8, "The soul commands the soul to will and it does not do so." But to will is an act of will. Therefore an act of will is not commanded.

Thus the argument; the response is as follows:

> It must be said that, as AUGUSTINE says in the same place, when the soul perfectly commands itself to will, it is already willing. But it sometimes happens that it commands and does not will because of the fact that it does not perfectly command. But imperfect command occurs by the fact that reason is moved on different sides to command and not to command; hence it fluctuates between the two and does not perfectly command.

Thus SAINT THOMAS. Again, in q.13, a.1, obj.2, he presents the following argument:

> It belongs to the same thing to syllogize and to conclude. But to syllogize concerning actions belongs to reason. Therefore, since choice is, as it were, a conclusion concerning actions, as is said in *Ethics* 7, it seems that it is an act of reason.

Thus the argument; the response is as follows:

> It must be said that the conclusion of the syllogism formed concerning actions does pertain to reason. It is called a "sentence" or "judgment," and choice follows from it, which is why the conclusion seems to be related to choice as to a consequent.

Thus SAINT THOMAS.

From these texts the three points mentioned above are made clear.

Accordingly, SAINT THOMAS, in *ST* II–II, q.47, a.13, concludes that true and perfect prudence cannot exist in sinners. In obj.2 he presents the following argument:

> Faith is a nobler virtue than prudence; but faith can exist in sinners; therefore so can prudence.

Thus the argument; the response is as follows:

> It must be said that faith in its essence does not imply any conformity to appetite for right deeds; rather, the essence of faith consists in knowledge

> alone. But prudence does imply directedness to right appetite, on the one hand because the principles of prudence are the ends of actions, and right judgment concerning these ends is had through the habits of the moral virtues, which cause right appetite, so that prudence cannot exist without the moral virtues; on the other hand, because prudence is preceptive of right deeds, which it cannot be unless right appetite exists. Hence, although faith is nobler than prudence because of its object, nevertheless prudence, with respect to its nature, is more opposed to sin, which proceeds from perversity of appetite.

Thus SAINT THOMAS.

It is clear, therefore, that the principal act of prudence, which is rightly to command and prescribe, cannot exist without both prior and subsequent right appetite, or, consequently, without right {439} choice. Since, then, the primary act of prudence cannot exist without right appetite existing in actuality, it follows that neither can the habit of prudence, which is produced by repetition of this act, exist without the right habit of appetite that we call moral virtue. Thus it is clear that the innovation of SCOTUS does not harm the ancient truth of SAINT THOMAS, and of ARISTOTLE in the *Ethics*.

§2. To the Arguments against the Third Conclusion

To the Arguments of Scotus [*p. 331*] In response to the *first* against the third conclusion we say that the minor premise of the argument—which says that "When there are several partial perfections, etc."—is false if it is taken universally; but if it is taken in a particular way, the syllogism is composed merely of particular propositions, and is invalid.

That the minor premise taken universally is false is clear because intellect and will are partial perfections of the soul, and yet one cannot exist without the other. The reason for this is that they are connected in a single third thing, namely the essence of the soul. But the comparison made with speech and hearing is invalid, because they do not have a necessary connection in some third thing. Thus SAINT THOMAS, in *Questions on the Virtues*, "On the Cardinal Virtues", a.2, obj.17, presents the following argument:

> As there are powers of soul, so there are bodily powers. But there is no interconnection among bodily powers, because one and the same man may have sight and not hearing. Therefore, neither is there interconnection among powers of the soul.

Thus the argument; the response is as follows:

> It must be said that a power of soul is not convertible with the essence of the soul. For although no power of soul can exist without the essence of the soul, the essence of the soul can exist without certain powers, for example sight and hearing, through destruction of the organs of which these powers are properly speaking acts.

Thus SAINT THOMAS. Again, in ad 13, he says:

> Virtues are interconneced by reason of their proximate principle, namely their genus, which is prudence or charity, but not by reason of their common principle and end, which is God.

Thus SAINT THOMAS. Again, in ad 11, he speaks as follows:

> Principles and conclusions are not convertible in speculative sciences, as they are in moral matters. Therefore, someone who grasps one conclusion does not necessarily grasp another. But he would necessarily do so if someone who grasps principles necessarily grasps the conclusions, as is the case in the present question.

Thus SAINT THOMAS. Again, in obj.4, he presents the following argument:

> According to THE PHILOSOPHER in *Ethics* 6, art is right reason concerning what can be made, just as prudence is right reason concerning actions. But a man can have right reason with respect to one kind of thing that can be made, for example tools, while not having right reason concerning others. Therefore, he can also have prudence concerning one kind of action, for example just actions, and not have it concerning another kind, for example brave actions. Thus he can have one virtue without another.

Thus the argument; the response is as follows:

> It must be said that the different kinds of things that can be made have completely dissimilar principles, and therefore nothing prevents someone from possessing art with respect to one kind but not another. But the principles of moral matters are ordered to one another in such a way that from defect in one principle there follows defect in the others as well. For instance, if one is deficient with respect to the principle that "lustful desires should not be pursued," which pertains to temperance, it will sometimes follow that in pursuing lustful desire one does an injustice, and thus violates justice. Similarly, in one and the same art or science, for instance geometry, an error in one principle introduces an error into the whole science. Hence it is that one

> cannot be sufficiently prudent with respect to the matter of one virtue unless one is prudent with respect to the matter of all virtues.

Thus SAINT THOMAS. Again, in obj.8, he presents the following argument:

> THE PHILOSOPHER says in *Ethics* 6 that we call ANAXAGORAS and THALES wise but not prudent. But wisdom and prudence are intellectual virtues. Therefore, one can have one virtue without the others.

Thus the argument; the response is as follows:

> It must be said that the intellectual virtues are not interconnected, and this for three reasons. First, because things with different kinds of subjects are not co-ordinated with one another, as was said above concerning the arts. Second, because in the sciences principles and conclusions are not convertible with one another in such a way that whoever grasps the principles grasps the conclusions, as was said to be the case in moral matters. Third, because intellectual virtue has no relation to the advantage by which man is directed to the ultimate end. Accordingly, these virtues are directed to particular goods: for example, geometry concerns certain abstractions, physics concerns mobile things, and so with the others. Hence they are not interconnected for the same reason that imperfect virtues are not interconnected.

Thus SAINT THOMAS.

From all these texts it is apparent how the moral virtues—which are related to prudence as its principles, while prudence is related to them as a conclusion—are so interconnected with prudence that none of them can be possessed without prudence, nor can prudence be possessed without all of them. For in moral matters the principle and conclusions are convertible in such a way that, when the principle is grasped, all the conclusions are grasped; and a conclusion implies all of the principles; and consequently, any conclusion implies all of the conclusions, and any principle implies all of the principles.

This interconnection, however, must be understood only with respect to the perfect virtues. The case of the imperfect virtues is different. Concerning {440} this point SAINT THOMAS, in the text quoted above, speaks as follows:

> One must speak of the perfect virtues in a different way than one does of the imperfect virtues: the perfect virtues are indeed connected with one another, but the imperfect virtues are not connected by necessity.
>
> For evidence of this it must be considered that, because virtue is something that perfects man and makes his action good, that virtue is perfect which perfectly makes man's action and man himself good; but that virtue is

imperfect which makes both man and his action good not simply speaking, but in relation to something. Now good simply speaking exists in human acts in pertaining to the rule of human acts, and there are two such rules: one that is, so to speak, connatural and proper to man, namely right reason; and another that is, so to speak, the transcendant first measure, namely God. Now man reaches rightness of reason through prudence, which is right reason concerning actions, as THE PHILOSOPHER says in *Ethics* 6. But man reaches God through charity; as is said in *1 John* 4, "He who dwells in charity dwells in God, and God in him."

Accordingly, there are three grades of virtue. There are some altogether imperfect virtues that exist without prudence and do not reach rightness of reason. Such are the inclinations toward certain deeds of virtue that some men possess even from birth; as is said in *Job* 31, "Compassion grew with me from infancy, and came out of the womb with me." But these inclinations are not present together in everyone; rather, some men have an inclination to one such thing, some to another. Now these inclinations do not have the essence of virtue. For no-one uses virtue badly according to AUGUSTINE; but one can use these inclinations badly and harmfully if he uses them without discretion, just as a horse that lacks sight will run faster the more he is driven. Hence GREGORY says in *Moralia* 22 that if what one wants to do is not done with prudence, the other virtues cannot be virtues at all. Hence, too, inclinations that are without prudence do not have the perfect essence of virtue.

Virtues at the second grade are those that reach rightness of reason but do not reach God Himself through charity. These virtues are in a way perfect, that is, with respect to the human good. However, they are not perfect simply speaking, because they do not reach the first rule, which is the ultimate end, as AUGUSTINE says in his *Contra Julianum*. Hence they also fall short of the true and perfect essence of virtue simply speaking, just as moral inclinations without prudence fall short of the true essence of virtue.

The third grade is that of virtues that are simply speaking perfect, and they are accompanied by charity. For these virtues make an act of man simply speaking good, for the act, so to speak, reaches the ultimate end.

But it must be further considered that, just as the moral virtues cannot exist without prudence, so neither can prudence exist without the moral virtues. For prudence is right reason concerning actions. Now right reasoning in any genus requires that one possess right judgment concerning the principles from which the reasoning proceeds; for example in geometry one cannot possess right judgment concerning the conclusions unless one possesses right judgment, or right reasoning, concerning geometrical principles. But the principles of actions are ends, for it is from these that actions get their essence. Now one possesses right judgment concerning the end through a habit of moral virtue. For, as THE PHILOSOPHER says in *Ethics* 3, "such as each one is, so is the end": for the end of the virtuous man is the good according to virtue, and the end of the vicious man is what is related to his vice; it is similar with respect to diseased and healthy senses of taste. Hence it is necessary that whoever possesses prudence also possess the moral virtues.

Similarly, whoever possesses charity must possess all the other virtues. For charity exists in man through a divine infusing; as is said in *Romans* 5, "The charity of God is infused into our hearts by the Holy Spirit, Who has been given to us." But whenever God gives an inclination He also gives certain forms that are principles of the operations and movements to which the things are inclined by Him. For example, He gives fire lightness, by which it readily and easily tends upwards. Thus it is said in *Wisdom* 8, "He has disposed all things sweetly." Therefore, together with charity there must be infused forms that are habits which readily produce the acts to which charity causes an inclination. But charity causes an inclination to all acts of virtue, because, since it concerns the ultimate end, it commands all acts of virtue. For any art or virtue to which an end is related commands what concerns the end; for example, the military art commands the equestrian art, and the equestrian art commands that of bridle-making, as is said in *Ethics* 1. Hence, it pertains to the graciousness of divine wisdom and goodness that together with charity the habits of all the virtues are infused; hence it is said in *1 Corinthians* 13 that "Charity is patient, kind, etc."

Therefore, if we take the virtues that are simply speaking perfect, they are interconnected because of charity: for no such virtue can be possessed without charity, and if charity is possessed, all of them are. If we take the virtues that are perfect on the second level, that is, with respect to the human good, they are interconnected through prudence: for no moral virtue can be possessed without prudence, nor can prudence be possessed without the moral virtues. Even if we take the four cardinal virtues as signifying general features of the virtues, in this respect they are interconnected by the fact that one of these features does not suffice for an act of virtue **{441}** unless all of them are present. This seems to be the way in which GREGORY explains the causes of the interconnection in *Moralia* 22.

Thus SAINT THOMAS. He presents something similar in *In 3 Sent.*, d.36, q.1, a.1.

In response to the *second* argument we say that the minor premise is false and must be denied, as is clear from what was said before. For a right practical dictate that is deliberative, judicative, and prescriptive cannot be perfect with respect to one part of the matter of morality unless it extends generally to the whole matter of morality that man encounters as what is to be done. For error concerning the matter of temperance introduces error concerning the matter of justice or fortitude, as was said. Thus, from a right dictate concerning one part of the matter of morality, precisively taken, there is never acquired an intellectual or moral habit that has the perfect essence of virtue, that is, one that someone will be able to use always rightly and in no way wrongly. Hence, besides what has been quoted—and quoted in abundance—SAINT THOMAS, in *In 3 Sent.*, d.36, q.1, a.1, speaks as follows:

> Virtue can be considered in two ways. In one way, with respect to its imperfect existence, according to which the seeds of virtue are present in us by nature, and in this sense virtue is said to be a natural inclination to the act of virtue. In this respect one virtue can be possessed without another: for some, by the nature of their constitution, are naturally disposed to generosity but prone to lust, and there are other, similar cases. In another way virtue is considered with respect to the perfect existence it receives from habituation, and in this sense it gets the name "political virtue." Taken in this way, all the virtues must be present simultaneously. Three reasons for this can be gathered from the sayings of the philosophers.
>
> The first is given by THE PHILOSOPHER in *Ethics* 6, and it is based on that which perfects any political virtue. For there is in us an initial inclination to the act of prudence, and this is called "natural virtue." THE PHILOSOPHER calls it *deinotes,* which we can call "cleverness" *(industria).* This can be directed both to what is good and to what is evil, and hence it is not a virtue, because a virtue is something that always makes the deed of the one who possesses it good. Thus, if one is to be brought to the point at which one's judgment is always right, something by which all error is prevented must be added to this inclination.
>
> Now there are two kinds of error in judgment. One concerns the end: this occurs in a person who has a habit of vice, which inclines the person to the act of vice as something in itself good. This kind of error concerning what is to be done is like an error concerning principles in speculative matters. The other error occurs in pursuit of the end, when one is led away by passions from the right conception that he has of the end, and thus it is said that pleasure destroys the judgment of prudence. This kind of error concern-

ing what is to be done is like an error in speculative matters with respect to the flow of principles into conclusions. Now moral virtue, which causes inclination to the right end and represses passion, prevents both kinds of error. Hence prudence cannot exist without moral virtue, I mean without temperance, fortitude, justice, and the like.

Again, the greater the natural inclination to what pertains to moral virtue, the more harmful it is if discourse of reason is not applied; similarly, the faster a blind man runs, the more violently he collides with things. Hence, in order for moral virtue to be perfected, it must be directed by prudence. Hence prudence is placed in the definition of moral virtue, as is clear from *Ethics* 2. This is why the political virtues must be interconnected.

The second reason for the interconnection is based on the features that must be present in every virtue in general. However, each one of these features is primarily claimed by some virtue for itself: thus fortitude claims for itself "the difficult"; temperance claims for itself "the intermediary between the superfluous and the insufficient"; justice claims for itself "what is right"; and prudence claims for itself "knowledge." Hence, each of the virtues mentioned takes its name from one of these features. But because what is greatest in any genus is cause of the other things in that genus, the other virtues in a way share a feature with the virtue that primarily claims that feature for itself. For, because the brave man, for example, is persevering with respect to the greatest difficulties, he will easily also persevere in the case of other, lesser difficulties. This seems to be the reason given by SENECA, who says that everything done well is done justly, bravely, temperately, and prudently.

A third reason can be based on the end that each virtue intends. For any virtue operates for the sake of the good of virtue. Hence, if one intends the good of virtue in the way befitting a virtuous man, he will in no way turn away from that intention. Thus THE PHILOSOPHER says in *Ethics* 4 that the prodigal man, who spends without caring for the good, easily sinks to every evil whatsoever.

Thus SAINT THOMAS. Again, in the same place, in obj.2, he presents the following argument:

Things that are interconnected must be interconnected in some one thing. But no one thing can be named in which the virtues are interconnected, except prudence. But they cannot be interconnected in prudence because, since prudence is, so to speak, an art concerning actions, it is not inconsistent that one might possess prudence with respect to one matter but not another. Therefore, it is not necessary that the virtues be interconnected.

Thus the argument; the response is as follows:

> It must be said that the prudent man proceeds from the same principle {442} with respect to all matters of virtue, namely intention of the good of reason. Hence it is impossible for prudence to be acquired with respect to one part of the matter of moral virtue and not another. It is like what happens in the arts with respect to certain matters in which art operates in the same way; for example, a carpenter makes a box out of an almond tree and out of oak in the same way. Thus the solution to the third objection is clear. For the other sciences add special principles to the common principles of wisdom, which is why one science can be known and another unknown. But the moral virtues do not add other principles beyond the principles of prudence: rather, the principles of prudence follow from the moral virtues, and are the ends of the moral virtues, as THE PHILOSOPHER says in *Ethics* 10.

Thus SAINT THOMAS. Again, in *ST* I–II, q.65, a.1, ad 4, he speaks as follows:

> The things to which the moral virtues cause an inclination are related to prudence as principles; but things that can be made are related to art not as principles, but only as matter. Now it is clear that, even if reason could be right with respect to one part of its matter and not another, it still cannot at all be called "right reason" if there is shortcoming in any of its principles; similarly, if someone errs concerning the principle "every whole is greater than its part," he cannot possesss the science of geometry, because he would have to diverge greatly from the truth in subsequent points. Moreover, things to be done are ordered to one another but things to be made are not; and so a shortcoming of prudence with respect to one part of things to be done will lead to a shortcoming with respect to others also. This does not happen in the case of things to be made.

Thus SAINT THOMAS. Again, in ad 3, he shows how all actions are ordered to one another:

> Intellectual virtues concern diverse matters that are not ordered to one another, as is clear in the case of the diverse sciences and arts. Hence, among them one does not find the interconnection found among the moral virtues, which concern passions and operations. The latter clearly are ordered to one another. For all passions arise from the first passions, namely love and hatred, and terminate in others, namely joy and sorrow; similarly all operations that are matter of moral virtue are ordered both to one another and to the passions. Thus the entire matter of moral virtue comes under the one essence of prudence.

> Now all intelligibles are ordered to first principles, and in this respect all intellectual virtues depend on understanding of principles, just as prudence depends on the moral virtues. But the universal principles, which are the object of understanding, do not depend on conclusions, which are the objects of the other intellectual virtues; whereas the moral virtues do depend on prudence, since appetite in a way moves reason, and reason appetite.

Thus SAINT THOMAS.

From these texts it is clear how the opponent assumes something false, namely that one can make a perfect and correct practical or prudential dictate with respect to the matter of one moral virtue without making a perfect dictate, whether actual or habitual, with respect to the matter of another.

SAINT THOMAS responds to the *third* objection in *ST* I–II, in the text quoted above, in response to the first argument, which is as follows:

> The moral virtues are sometimes caused by practicing acts, as is proved in *Ethics* 2. But a man can practice the acts of one virtue without practicing the acts of another. Therefore, one moral virtue can be possessed without another.

Thus the argument; the response is as follows:

> It must be said that some of the moral virtues perfect man with respect to the state common to all, that is, with respect to the things to be done that come up in every human life in common. Hence a man must practice on the matters of all the moral virtues at the same time. And if he practices acting well on all of them, he will acquire the habits of all the moral virtues. But if he practices acting well on the matter of one virtue but not another—for example, if he is rightly disposed with respect to feelings of anger but not with respect to desires, he will acquire a habit that restrains his feelings of anger, but it will not have the essence of virtue because of the shortcoming of a prudence that is corrupt with respect to desires. Similarly, the natural inclinations do not have the essence of virtue if prudence is absent.
>
> But there are some moral virtues that perfect man with respect to some eminent status of his, as do magnificence and magnanimity. Because occasion for practice on the matter of these virtues does not arise for everyone, therefore—to speak only of acquired virtue—one can possess the other moral virtues without in actuality possessing the habits of these virtues. Nevertheless, once the other virtues are acquired, these virtues are possessed in proximate potentiality. For once one through practice has acquired generosity with respect to small gifts and expenditures, then, if a great

> amount of money should come to him, he will acquire the habit of magnificence with little practice, just as a geometer with little practice acquires the knowledge of a conclusion he has never considered. And we are said to possess what we are ready to possess; as THE PHILOSOPHER says in *Physics* 2, "What is lacking in only a little seems not to be lacking at all."

Thus SAINT THOMAS. He presents something similar in *In 3 Sent.*, d.36, q.1, a.1, ad 1:

> When one practices the act of a virtue, if he simultaneously practices the act of a vice, he will never acquire any virtue, because he will not acquire prudence. Hence, in order to possess one virtue, a man must be well disposed with respect to {443} everything that is part of the conduct of life. And so, once these virtues have been acquired together with prudence, other virtues, which concern what is less often part of the conduct of life, will be produced. For by the very fact that reason's presence is habitual in the higher powers, the lower powers are able to follow its command; and the whole essence of moral virtue consists in this.

Thus SAINT THOMAS. He says something similar in *Questions on the Virtues*, "On the Cardinal Virtues", a.2, ad 9:

> There are some virtues, such as temperance, justice, gentleness, and the like, that direct man with respect to what happens in human life in general. With respect to this, while a man is practicing the act of one virtue, he must simultaneously practice the acts of the other virtues, and then acquire all the habits of these virtues simultaneously, and necessarily be well disposed with respect to everything that happens in human life in general. Otherwise, he practices one virtue but not the others, and then acquires a habit that is contrary to some virtue, one that consequently destroys prudence, without which not even the disposition he has acquired through acts of the one virtue will have, properly speaking, the essence of virtue. But once the habits concerning what happens in life in general have been acquired, one already virtually possesses all other habits of virtue, such as magnificence and magnanimity, whose acts do not often occur in human life.

Thus SAINT THOMAS.

From these texts it is clear that the habit of one cardinal virtue cannot be acquired by any practice unless the four habits of the cardinal virtues are simultaneously acquired.

1. Now in response to the replies to and arguments against the responses mentioned by the opponent, we say first that the *first* response given is worth

little, and so it is not necessary to dwell on it. For, as has been said, however it may happen that one does not simultaneously practice the acts of all the cardinal virtues—whether because the matter does not arise, or because a man is willing to practice on one part of moral matter but not all of it—no habit acquired in either way has the essence of perfect virtue or virtue properly speaking.

2. Second, we say that the *second* response given is good inasmuch as it holds that no such habit has the essence of virtue without the others. However, what the response adds concerning the agreement between virtue and virtue, and between habit and habit, in any act of virtue, does not seem to have much necessity, unless it is taken with respect to the mutual requirement between one act and another in the initial production of the virtues. For, as has been said, it is necessary to practice simultaneously on the whole of moral matter: not, indeed, such that one is simultaneously, at one and the same moment, eliciting four acts, namely of prudence, justice, fortitude, and temperance; but rather, such that the act of one virtue follows the act of another without delay.

Then, in response to the *first* argument against this response, we concede that any virtue is to any other a sine qua non cause of the latter's being a virtue. Thus justice, fortitude, and temperance are to prudence causes of its being a virtue, at least with respect to its act, inasmuch as they provide right and stable judgment of the principles from which prudence proceeds in considering, judging, and prescribing. Conversely, prudence is to fortitude, justice, and temperance cause of their being virtues inasmuch as it directs them in choosing the right means to the end, establishes in advance for them the intermediary between excess and defect, and shows the required circumstances of acts. Again, justice is to fortitude and temperance the cause of their being virtues inasmuch as it contributes to the right judgment of prudence with respect to both its own matter and that of the other virtues, and also inasmuch as any act of virtue participates a measure of rightness, which is principally the concern of justice. Similarly, fortitude and temperance are to justice causes of its being a virtue, in the way just explained.

The argument against the inference from what has been conceded in the sense just explained is not valid, because none of the difficulties mentioned follows by that inference.

Certainly not the *first* difficulty, namely that "a virtue would be a virtue before it is a virtue," because the argument for this consists in that false inference, or rather, in two false inferences. The first is this: "If the habit called temperance is not a virtue unless there is also present the other habit called fortitude, then fortitude is a virtue before temperance is a virtue." The invalidity of this inference is clear from a similar case; for this does not follow: "Socrates cannot be a father unless someone is his son; therefore someone is the son of Socrates before Socrates is the father of someone." The present case is similar. However, this inference would be good: "Temperance does not have the essence of virtue unless there is also present the habit of fortitude, but fortitude does have the essence of virtue without there being present the habit of temperance; therefore fortitude is a virtue before temperance is a virtue." But then we would deny the second part of the antecedent: for just as temperance requires fortitude in order to be a virtue, similarly fortitude requires temperance in order to have the essence of virtue.

Similarly, neither is the *second* difficulty mentioned, namely that "no virtue would be the first virtue," sufficiently deduced from the inference granted. Rather, what follows from that inference is the opposite, namely that any one of the four cardinal virtues is a first virtue. For the term "first" can be explained in two ways, affirmatively and negatively: affirmatively, such that that is called "first" which precedes and is prior to all others; negatively, such that that is called "first" to which no other is prior. Accordingly, it is clear that every virtue is a first virtue, taking "first" negatively, although none is first, taking {444} "first" affirmatively. And it is the latter, not the former, sense of the term that the opponent's argument uses. Nevertheless, we do concede that one virtue is prior to the others with respect to one kind of causality, and posterior to them with respect to another; this is evident with respect to prudence in relation to the other three, moral virtues, and vice-versa. But the opponent is speaking of a priority in duration.

3. *Third,* we say that the *third* response given is good.

In response to the argument against this response we say that the inference made by the opponent, namely that "the one act that produces the final habit will produce all the moral virtues in the being of virtue," is not a difficulty, but rather is true. For that one act operates in virtue of the many preceding acts concerning diverse matters connected with and mutually ordered to one another. For as was said above, human actions and passions, which are the matter of the moral virtues, are mutually ordered to one another. Hence it is no wonder that a single act, acting in virtue of preceding acts, should bring a single habit to completion, namely the habit of prudence, on whose completion the other habits depend for their existence as virtues. And the virtues have a bond both on the side of the object and on the side of the manner of operation, because one contributes to the perfection of the act of another, and because of the other interconnections mentioned above.

In response to the argument against this we say that the final act, as elicited, is an act of one virtue only and not of all. But it is an act of all the virtues by participation. For as was said above, the act of any virtue participates in something pertaining to prudence, something pertaining to justice, something pertaining to fortitude, and something pertaining to temperance. Concerning this point SAINT THOMAS, in *Questions on the Virtues,* "On the Cardinal Virtues", a.1, obj.1, presents the following argument:

> Things that are not distinguished from one another should not be counted together, because distinction is the cause of number, as DAMASCENE says. But the virtues mentioned, namely prudence, justice, fortitude, and temperance, are not distinguished from one another. For GREGORY says in *Moralia* 22: "There is no prudence that is not just and temperate and brave; nor is there perfect temperance that is not brave and just and prudent; nor complete fortitude that is not prudent, temperate, and just; nor true justice that is not prudent, brave, and temperate." Therefore, these ought not to be called four cardinal virtues.

Thus the argument; the response is as follows:

> It must be said that some have spoken of the above-mentioned four cardinal virtues in various ways.
>
> Some use the four above-mentioned names to signify general modes of the virtues. Thus they call all directive knowledge "prudence"; they call all rightness that proportions human acts "justice"; they call all moderation that restrains the appetite of man from seeking temporal goods "temperance"; and they call all steadfastness of soul that confirms man in what is good and sets him against the offense of every evil "fortitude." This seems to be the way that AUGUSTINE uses these names of the virtues in *De moribus ecclesiae,* and it is in this sense that the remark of GREGORY can be understood. For one of these features does not suffice for the true essence of virtue unless all the features mentioned concur. In this sense, then, the four things mentioned are called four virtues not with respect to diverse species of habits taken according to diverse objects, but rather with respect to diverse formal essences.
>
> Others, however, such as ARISTOTLE in the *Ethics,* speak of the four

> virtues mentioned as specific virtues each determined to a particular matter. What GREGORY says can also be taken in this sense, by way of overflow, inasmuch as the virtues mentioned concern the most important matters entrusted to the four general features of virtue. Hence, according to this interpretation, fortitude is temperate and temperance is brave. For one who is able to rein in his appetite so that it does not follow desires for pleasure, which pertains to temperance, is all the more able to rein in the impulse of daring in the midst of dangers; similarly, one who is able to stand firm against the dangers of death is all the more able to stand firm against the snares of pleasure. And according to this interpretation, what principally belongs to temperance passes over into fortitude, and vice-versa. The argument is the same with respect to the other virtues.

Thus SAINT THOMAS. Again, in *ST* I–II, q.61, a.4, ad 1, which has the same pattern as this text, he speaks as follows:

> These four virtues are, through an overflow, called by one another's names. For what is proper to prudence overflows into the other virtues inasmuch as they are directed by prudence. All the others overflow into one another for the reason that one who is able to do what is more difficult is also able to do what is less difficult. Thus one who is able to rein in desire for the pleasures of touch so that they do not go beyond measure, a very difficult thing to do, is by this very fact made more able to rein in the feeling of daring in the midst of dangers of death so that this feeling does not go beyond the measure, which is far easier, and accordingly fortitude is said to be temperate. Temperance is also said to be brave through overflow of fortitude into temperance, inasmuch as one who through fortitude possesses a soul that is steadfast in the face of dangers of death, a very difficult thing to do, is more able to maintain firmness of soul in the face of impulses toward pleasure. As CICERO says in *De officiis* 1: "It is not reasonable that one who is not weakened by fear should be weakened by desire; nor that one who excels in being unconquered by struggle could ever be conquered by pleasure."

Thus SAINT THOMAS. Again, in *In 3 Sent.*, **{445}** d.36, q.1, a.1, he speaks as follows:

> The second reason for the interconnection is based on the features that must be present in every virtue in general. However, each one of these features is primarily claimed by some virtue for itself: thus fortitude claims for itself "the difficult"; temperance claims for itself "the intermediary between the superfluous and the insufficient"; justice claims for itself "what is right"; and

> prudence claims for itself "knowledge." Hence, each of the virtues mentioned takes its name from one of these features. But because what is greatest in any genus is cause of the other things in that genus, the other virtues in a way share a feature with the virtue that primarily claims that feature for itself, etc.

—as was quoted above. From these texts it is clear that any act of virtue participates in the influence of every cardinal virtue, as was said above.

4. Fourth, we say that SAINT THOMAS responds to the *final* reply to the responses in many places, although he does so in different ways. For, in *ST* II–II, q.152, a.3, ad 2, he speaks as follows:

> The interconnection of the virtues is taken from what is formal in the virtues, namely charity or prudence, and not from what is material in them. For nothing prevents the matter of one virtue being available to a virtuous man without the matter of another; for example, a pauper has the matter of temperance but not of magnificence. In this way one who possesses other virtues may lack the matter of virginity, namely the integrity of flesh mentioned above. Nevertheless, he can possess what is formal in virginity by keeping ready in his mind the intention to preserve this integrity if he were able to do so; similarly, the pauper keeps ready in his soul the intention to make magnificent expenditures if he were able to do so; again, one who is prosperous keeps ready in his soul the intention to bear adversities with equanimity.

Thus SAINT THOMAS. But in *Questions on the Virtues,* "On the Cardinal Virtues," a.2, ad 7, he responds as follows:

> It must be said that virginity, according to some, does not name a virtue, but rather a certain perfect state of virtue. For not everyone who possesses a virtue possesses it at a perfect level. Hence chastity and other virtues can be possessed without virginity. Or, if it is granted that virginity is a virtue, this will be inasmuch as it implies the habit of mind according to which one chooses to preserve virginity because of Christ. And this habit can exist even in those who lack integrity of flesh, just as the habit of magnificence can coexist with lack of riches.

Thus SAINT THOMAS.

From these texts the response to the innovations of SCOTUS is clear.

SAINT THOMAS responds to the argument on the negative side of the question [p. 325] in *Questions on the Virtues,* "The Cardinal Virtues", a.2, ad 1:

> It must be said that through an inclination given by nature, or a gift of grace that inclines more to the deed of one virtue than to that of another, it can happen that one is readier for the act of one virtue than of another. Accordingly, the saints are said to possess certain virtues, namely those for whose acts they are readier, and not to possess others, namely those for whose acts they are less ready.

Thus SAINT THOMAS. But in *ST* I–II, q.65, a.3, ad 3, he glosses the authoritative text of BEDE as follows:

> It must be said that some saints are said not to possess certain virtues inasmuch as they experience difficulty in the acts of these virtues, although they possess the habits of all the virtues.

Thus SAINT THOMAS. Again, in *In 3 Sent.*, d.36, q.1, a.2, ad 1, he speaks as follows:

> The remark of BEDE must be understood of the virtues with respect to application, not habit. For various saints in various ways excel one another in applications of the various virtues; as is said of every confessor, "No-one has been like him in keeping the law of the church."

Thus SAINT THOMAS.

This suffices for the question.

Blessed be God.

Amen.

Notes on Opponents

Durandus of Saint Pourçain (d. 1332?)

The facts of Durandus's early life are not well known. Although a Dominican friar by profession, he became a bishop in 1317. His status however did not preserve him from the scrutiny of the Dominican Order, whose authorities considered his *Commentary on the Sentences* to contain more than a few non-Thomist positions. He was the object of several censures by the Order, so that he was obliged to produce a corrected version of his *Commentary,* which alone survives in the printed editions, which appeared repeatedly during the sixteenth century. He was part of the commission that examined certain positions of William of Ockham, and found 51 of them wanting. Durandus's own position in epistemology is decidedly outside of the Thomist school, but it is generally agreed that it is difficult to characterize the thought of this original, and sometimes obstinate, thinker.

Work

Durandi Sancti Portiano in Sententias theologicas Petri Lombardi Commentariorum libri 4. Paris, 1508.

Study

Koch, J. *Durandus de S. Porciano, O.P.* (Beiträge zur Geschichte der Philosophie des Mittelalters 26) Münster 1927.

John Duns Scotus (1265?–1308)

Scotus was ordained by Bishop Oliver Sutton on March 17, 1291 at Northampton, England. From this fact, scholars have inferred that Scotus was born in 1265 or 1266, since the canonical age for ordination was 26 yrs. According to an ancient, but unverifiable, tradition, Scotus was born in Duns, Scotland (near the English border), the son of a member of the lower nobility. He was proposed as one of the Franciscan priests to hear confessions at Oxford in 1300 and disputed under Phillip of Bridlington there in 1301. Scotus never, however, became a master at Oxford, although his teaching from this period drew the sustained criticism of a number of Oxford theologians, including Franciscans (e.g., Richard of Conington) as well as Dominicans (e.g., Thomas Sutton).

Scotus lectured on Peter Lombard's *Sentences,* the medieval theological textbook, several times: first, perhaps, at Oxford (1297–1299); then at Cambridge (perhaps

1301–1302); and, finally, at Paris (1302–1304). After a temporary exile from Paris (spring 1303–early 1304) owing to his opposition to Phillip the Fair's anti-papal policy (during which time he probably returned to Oxford, according to the most recent research), Scotus became regent master at Paris in 1305. His teaching career at Paris was quite brief, however, for in 1307 he was sent to lecture at the Franciscan *studium* in Cologne where he died November 8, 1308.

Writings

After years of painstaking research, scholars have established that the following works properly belong to John Duns Scotus.

Philosophical Works

Quaestiones in libros Metaphysicorum Aristotelis
Quaestiones in librum 'Isagoge' Porphyrii
Quaestiones in librum Praedicamentorum Aristotelis
Quaestiones in duos libros Perihermenias Aristotelis
Octo quaestiones in librum Perihermenias Aristotelis
Quaestiones in libros Elenchorum Aristotelis
Quaestiones in libros De anima Aristotelis

These works are presently being edited under the general editorship of Dr. Girard Etzkorn and Dr. Timothy B. Noone and being published jointly by the Franciscan Institute of St. Bonaventure University and The Catholic University of America. Scotus's *Metaphysics* questions appeared as volumes 3 and 4 of the *Opera philosophica* (St. Bonaventure, N.Y., 1997); the *Isagoge* and *Praedicamenta* questions recently appeared as volume 1 of the same series (St. Bonaventure, N.Y., 1999). In the near future, the *Periheremnias* questions and the *Elenchi* will be published as vol. 2, while the questions on the *De anima* will be printed as volume 5 of the same series.

Theological Works

Lectura super libros Sententiarum (Scotus's early Oxford lectures).

Lectura Cantagibriensis (Cambridge lectures surviving in only one MS).

Reportata Parisiensia (Reportatio Parisiensis) (Parisian lectures on the *Sentences* in the main, but some from book III done at Oxford; these survive in several versions one of which, the *Reportatio Parisiensis examinata,* is believed to have been personally checked by Scotus).

Ordinatio (Version of Oxford and Paris lectures on the *Sentences* personally revised by Scotus, but the revision is incomplete).

Quodlibetal Questions (Questions dating from Scotus's Parisian teaching career).

Collations (Collationes) (Shorter disputations, some conducted at Oxford, others at Paris).

Treatise on God as First Principle (Detailed and elaborate effort to formulate a proof for the existence of God).

Theorems (Theoremata) (Of somewhat questionable authorship, but probably Scotus).

These works are presently being produced by the *Commissio Scotistica* in Rome. To date the Commission has published the *Ordinatio* up to II d. 12 and the *Lectura* in its entirety (Civitas Vaticana: Typis Polyglottis, 1950–).

Studies

Studies of Scotus's philosophical and theological teachings are quite numerous, though mainly done in languages other than English. The best place to start is with the works of Fr. Allan B. Wolter, O.F.M.

Wolter, Allan B. *The Transcendentals and their Function in the Metaphysics of John Duns Scotus.* St. Bonaventure, N.Y., 1946.

———. *Duns Scotus on the Will and Morality.* Washington, D.C.: The Catholic University of America Press, 1986.

———. *The Philosophical Theology of John Duns Scotus,* ed. Marilyn McCord Adams. Ithaca/London, 1990.

Peter Aureolus (d. 1322)

The date of Peter Aureoli's (also spelled Aureol or Oriel in the MSS) birth is uncertain, but he was in Paris studying by 1304 and certainly became acquainted during that period with the views of John Duns Scotus whose ideas he subsequently criticized severely. He was a master in Paris, but his influence was widespread; William Alnwick, an immediate disciple of Duns Scotus, feels obliged to reply to his positions when lecturing in Bologna in the 1320s and he was remembered well enough in the 16th century to have his portrait appear on the walls of St. Isidore's Convent in Rome, the Franciscan house in Rome founded to educate Irish clergymen. He died in 1322.

Works

Compendiosa expositio evangelii Ioannis, ed. F. Stegmüller *Franziskanischen Studien,* 33 (1951), pp. 207–19.

Compendium sensus litteralis Sacrae Scripturae°, ed. P. Seebaeck, Collegium S. Bonaventurae, 1896

Scriptum super librum Sententiarum, ed. E.M. Buytaert, Franciscan Institute, St. Bonaventure, N.Y., 1952–56.

Peter's *Sentences* Commentary survives in another version printed in Rome, 1596–1605. A comprehensive critical edition is underway under the direction of Dr. Lauge O. Nielsen of the University of Cophenhagen and Dr. Katherine H. Tachau of the University of Iowa.

Studies

For a recent set of studies, see *Vivarium: Special Issue: Peter Auriol* (Leiden, 2000) and the comprehensive bibliographies listed at the end of each of the articles.

Henry of Ghent (d. 1293)

Born in Ghent, probably in the first quarter of the thirteenth century, Henry studied at Tournai at the cathedral school there, where he was canon by 1267. Thereafter, he apparently studied arts at Paris and continued his studies in the faculty of theology. By 1276, Henry was a *magister regens* in the faculty of theology at Paris where he continued to teach until his death in 1293. He was appointed archdeacon of Bruges in 1277 and archdeacon of Tournai in 1279. During this time, too, he was involved in the commission instituted by Bishop Tempier to examine the orthodoxy of teaching at the University of Paris; the commission's work is the basis for the condemnation of 1277. Henry was strongly opposed to the mendicant privilege to hear confessions and voiced his concerns frequently in the 1280s. By the time he died in 1293, one may safely say that he was the most prominent theologian in Europe, attaining a fame that, at least in theology, rivaled that of St. Thomas Aquinas.

Works

His two major writings are his *Summa quaestionum ordinariarum* and his *Quodlibeta*. The former are available in their entirety in the Paris ed. of 1520, reprinted by the Franciscan Institute in 1943, although certain parts have just begun to appear in the critical edition in progress. The *Quodlibeta* and the minor writings are in the main available in the critical edition being produced under the direction of Raymond Macken (Leuven, 1979–). Since some questions of the *Quodlibeta* are still unavailable in critical edition, one must consult the Paris edition of 1518 for these questions.

Studies

Bettoni, Efrem. *Il processo astrattivo nella concezione di Enrico di Gand*. Milan: Vita e pensiero, 1954.

Paulus, J. *Henri de Gand: Essai sur les tendances de sa métaphysique*. Paris: Vrin, 1938.

Marrone, Steven P. *Truth and Scientific Knowledge in the Thought of Henry of Ghent*. Cambridge, Mass.: Medieval Academy, 1985.

Bibliographical Note

The following references are intended to guide the reader interested in further research into the historical context and themes of Capreolus's *Defensiones*, in particular the questions on the virtues.

A useful introduction to the history of medieval thought is Armand Maurer's *Medieval Philosophy*, 2d edition, with additions, corrections, and a bibliographic supplement (Toronto: PIMS, 1982). The tradition of moral thought to which Capreolus's questions on the virtues belong is authoritatively treated by Servais Pinckaers in *The Sources of Christian Ethics*, trans. Sr. Mary Thomas Noble, O.P. (Washington, D.C.: The Catholic University of America Press, 1995).

Marcia L. Colish provides an expert discussion of the twelfth-century author of the text that gave Capreolus his order of topics in her *Peter Lombard* (Leiden–New York–Cologne: E. J. Brill, 1994 [2 volumes]).

James A. Weisheipl's *Friar Thomas d'Aquino* (Washington, D.C.: The Catholic University of America Press, 1983) remains a good introduction to Aquinas's life and works. A more recent, ampler treatment of same may be found in Jean-Pierre Torrell's *St. Thomas Aquinas: The Person and His Works (Volume I)* (Washington, D.C.: The Catholic University of America Press, 1996). The English translation of the second volume of the two-volume set, *The Spiritual Doctrine (Volume II)*, is forthcoming.

For a short, convenient history of Thomism see Romanus Cessario, *Le thomisme et les thomistes* (Paris: Editions du Cerf, 1999). Of special interest for the period between Aquinas and Capreolus is the study of the *Early Thomistic School* by Frederick J. Roensch, published by The Priory Press (Dubuque, Iowa) in 1964; although out of print, this remains the standard account of Thomism prior to Capreolus. An interesting and scholarly study of one of Capreolus's notable followers is Michael Tavuzzi's *Prierias: The Life and Works of Silvestro Mazzolini Da Prierio, 1456–1527* (Durham-London: Duke University Press, 1997).

The erudite study by Martin Grabmann, "Johannes Capreolus O.P., Der 'Princeps Thomistarum'" †1444), und seine Stellung in der Geschichte der Thomistenschule" (*Mittelalterliches Geistesleben*, Band III, pp. 370–410 [Munich: Max Hüber, 1956]), first published on the 500th anniversary of Capreolus's death, remains the *point de départ* for scholars interested in Capreolus's historical context, life, work, and influence. (R. Schenk, for example, refers to it in his article on Capreolus in *Marienlexicon* [Eos Verlag Erzabtei St. Ottilien, 1988]). The 1996 volume *Jean Capreolus et son temps: Colloque de Rodez*, ed. Guy Bedouelle, Romanus Cessario, and Kevin White (Paris, Cerf), supplies, from several perspectives, information on the various topics addressed by current scholarly interest in Capreolus.

Index of Texts of Saint Thomas

Commentary on the Four Books of the Sentences

Summa Theologiae

Index of Holy Scripture

Books of the Old Testament

Books of the New Testament

Analytical Index

On the Virtues was designed and composed in Dante with Cataneo display type by Kachergis Book Design, Pittsboro, North Carolina, and printed on 60-pound Glatfelter Natural Smooth and bound by Sheridan Books, Ann Arbor, Michgan.